INTERNATIONAL
TRADE POLICY

The last decade has been witness to far-reaching and significant developments in international trade policy. At the multilateral level of trade these have included the conclusion of the Uruguay Round of trade negotiations and the creation of the World Trade Organisation. At the regional level this liberalism has been paralleled by the expansion and development of regional trading blocs.

International Trade Policy: A contemporary analysis provides extensive, in-depth coverage of the theoretical and policy considerations, both old and new, which underlie these developments. The topics covered include:

- key theoretical and policy issues, such as voluntary export restraints; anti-dumping and unfair trading practices; agricultural protectionism; regionalism; and services;
- the issues which govern many current trade disputes, for example trade-related intellectual property rights;
- the central issues involved in setting up regional trading areas;
- trade-related investment measures and the developing world;
- the future agenda of multilateral trade negotiations, which is likely to be dominated by the environment and labour standards.

With trade negotiations becoming increasingly complex, *International Trade Policy: A contemporary analysis* presents a clear and up-to-date guide to contemporary policy and the theory upon which it is based. Written in an accessible style, the book assumes a good, basic knowledge of economics and will be invaluable to both students and policy makers in the area of international trade.

Nigel Grimwade is Principal Lecturer in Economics and Head of the Economics Division at South Bank University. He is the author of *International Trade* (Routledge, 1989) and has written extensively on the subject of international trade policy. He is currently engaged in research on the trade policy of the European Union.

INTERNATIONAL TRADE POLICY

A contemporary analysis

Nigel Grimwade

London and New York

First published 1996
by Routledge
11 New Fetter Lane, London EC4P 4EE

Simultaneously published in the USA and Canada
by Routledge
29 West 35th Street, New York, NY 10001

Routledge is an International Thomson Publishing company

© 1996 Nigel Grimwade

Typeset in Garamond by LaserScript, Mitcham, Surrey
Printed and bound in Great Britain by
Clays Ltd, St Ives PLC

British Library Cataloguing in Publication Data
A catalogue record for this book is available from the British Library

Library of Congress Cataloging in Publication Data
A catalogue record for this book has been requested

ISBN 0–415–06878–9 (hbk)
ISBN 0–415–06879–7 (pbk)

To my wife, Charlotte, and two sons, Peter and Matthew

CONTENTS

FIGURES

TABLES

TABLES

1

INTRODUCTION

THE AIM OF THE BOOK

Much attention in recent years has been centred on the multilateral trade negotiations which have been taking place under the title of the 'Uruguay Round'. These negotiations commenced in 1986 with an inaugural meeting of trade ministers held at Punta del Este in Uruguay, which was why the negotiations were named after this country. In fact, none of the negotiations subsequently took place in Uruguay. The Round was completed in December 1993, three years later than the original date set for its conclusion. A document entitled the 'Final Act' containing all the various agreements concluded between the participating countries was signed with much fanfare at Marrakech in Morocco the following April. Most of the agreements, including the provisions for the creation of a new World Trade Organisation (WTO), came into effect on 1 January 1995, while being subject to an implementation period which is different for each agreement and for different groups of countries. The Round was the eighth and last round of multilateral trade negotiations held under the auspices of the GATT (the General Agreement on Tariffs and Trade). This does not mean that there will be no future rounds. Negotiations to liberalise world trade will continue and they are likely to take the form of a 'round' although this will almost certainly differ in character from previous ones. However, the role of the GATT is now taken over by the newly created WTO. Unlike GATT, which was only ever a treaty with a provisional application, the WTO is an organisation which member states join and which has a permanent basis.

This is not primarily a book on the Uruguay Round, which covered a vast range of subject matter, was highly complex and involved a record number of negotiating countries. The agreements reached are more extensive than in any previous round. Any assessment of these agreements and their likely effects would require a more rigorous and thorough study than this book contains. Rather, this is a book about international trade policy in the 1990s. It is concerned with the issues which have been most dominant in multilateral and bilateral trade negotiations between countries in recent

1

years and which are likely to be important in the future. It does specifically discuss a number of the agreements contained in the Final Act of the Uruguay Round. However, there is no intention of adding to the existing and extensive body of research published by reputable research bodies throughout the world, such as the OECD, World Bank, IMF or GATT, on the likely effects of the Uruguay Round. The book refers to and quotes from these sources; but it does not seek to add to the conclusions already reached. Rather, the aim is to provide an explanation of what these and other trading negotiations have been about and to point to some of the issues which are likely to head the agenda in the immediate future.

The book is primarily intended for students of trade policy although it may also be helpful to fellow academics and others engaged full time in policy-making. Students of trade policy need a healthy diet of theory and policy. Trade policy issues need to be discussed in a theoretical framework if they are to be analysed and not merely described. The book seeks to provide a broad introduction to the basic theory of trade policy. Thus, most chapters contain sections which set out and discuss the simple theoretical models which economists conventionally use to analyse the effects of various kinds of trade policy intervention. However, pure theory with no application is dull, so this is not a book which is just about theory. The concern is to see how the approaches of countries to trade policy matters are consistent with the theory. For example, is the policy adopted by developed countries towards dumping appropriate, given what theory has to say about the phenomenon of dumping? In this respect, there is a normative aspect to the book. However, it is less concerned with saying what governments should do than with explaining what they do and how they do it.

It is hoped that the book will appeal equally to undergraduate and postgraduate students taking specialist courses in international economics, international trade, international political economy and international relations. It is written from the standpoint of economics but in full recognition of the fact that the subject matter of international trade policy straddles the divide separating economics from other related disciplines such as law, political science and international relations. The reader may therefore find it useful to supplement the book by reading an equivalent text written from a different standpoint, such as the text written from a legal position by Professor John Jackson entitled *The World Trading System* (1992). The present book makes no attempt to offer a treatment of the subject matter based on anything more than a superficial understanding of the legal framework to international trade policy: it is unashamedly written from the standpoint of international economics. Economics undergraduates and postgraduates will therefore get the greatest possible use from it. However, it is hoped that students drawn from other disciplines who are looking for a good economics text on trade policy will find the book useful and up to date.

THE STRUCTURE OF THE BOOK

The book adopts an essentially thematic approach, each chapter looking at a different issue considered to be of central importance to trade policy in the current decade and as the world enters the next century.

Chapter 2 deals with industrial tariffs. Tariffs were the dominant issue in the earlier rounds of the GATT. However, they have become less important as the average level of industrial tariffs has fallen steadily. Nevertheless, tariffs remain a significant impediment to market access for some products in certain markets. The issue of tariff structure also remains an important one even where average tariff levels have fallen.

Chapter 3 deals with quantitative restrictions on trade, which have arguably become more important than tariffs in many sectors of trade. The so-called New Protectionism of the past thirty years has largely assumed a nontariff form. Yet, from the standpoint of economic efficiency, such interferences with trade are almost always more harmful than tariffs. However, the term 'nontariff barrier/distortion' covers a wider range of forms of policy intervention than quantitative restrictions only.

Chapter 4 turns to what has become an arguably more serious form of interference with trade, namely, measures to tackle so-called unfair trading practices. The term 'unfair trading' has a necessarily pejorative implication. On first appearances, it would seem reasonable that countries should enjoy the right to protect their economies from unfair trading practices by other countries. In practice, 'unfair' too often means any competition which producers in the importing country cannot withstand. In other words, the mere fact that a foreign supplier can sell his product at a lower price than the producer in the importing country is often taken to mean that the foreign supplier is engaging in some practice which is in some sense 'unfair'. The two specific areas with which this aspect of trade policy is primarily concerned are dumping and subsidisation. It will be seen that international trading law allows countries to take action against imports if it can be proved that either of these practices is taking place in such a way as to cause injury to domestic producers. Growing use of antidumping and countervailing measures by developed countries such as those in the European Union and the United States has been an area of much controversy in recent years.

Chapter 5 focuses on the particular problems of the developing countries, most of which have, until recently, been outsiders in matters of international trade policy. For much of the early period of the GATT, they were little more than onlookers who saw little value in taking an active part in the negotiating process. Instead, they argued through whatever channels they could that their status warranted special and more favourable treatment, and to some degree obtained what they were seeking. GATT rules were amended to allow for special treatment for developing countries. It remains, however, uncertain how much benefit such preferential treatment has brought to these countries. Significantly, in the Uruguay Round, developing countries played a more active part, for the first time making concessions in an effort to secure equivalent concessions from the developed countries which were of more interest to them than they had been in the past. This largely reflects the changed role of developing countries. Many of them have in recent decades become major exporters of manufactures. Improved market access for their products has become an important negotiating objective. In addition, many have moved over to development strategies which, unlike the somewhat discredited inward-looking, import-substitution policies of the past, emphasise export promotion. Such outward-looking, export-oriented policies treat high tariffs and nontariff barriers as less of an asset to be held on to and more of a snare to be rid of.

Chapter 6 is concerned with the subject of agricultural protectionism. This begs the question as to whether it is right to treat agriculture differently from other sectors. From a theoretical standpoint, there would seem to be no good reason why the agricultural sector should be subject to different rules from manufacturing. In reality, it has always been treated differently and this seems likely to continue in the future. The developed countries in particular have shown a marked reluctance throughout the past fifty years to submit their farming sectors to the same rules and degree of openness as the rest of their economies. The Uruguay Round saw an important change in the previous intransigence that characterised the approach of developed countries to agricultural trade liberalisation. A package of liberalisation measures was agreed which provides for a not insignificant reduction in levels of intervention and support. It is too early to say what impact the new agreement will have on farm trade. Nevertheless, it seems unlikely that the past dichotomy between agriculture and manufacturing will come to an end.

Chapter 7 addresses the issue of regionalism and the possible conflict between attempts to achieve regional trade liberalisation and the GATT objective of multilateral liberalisation. Recent years have witnessed a resurgence of regionalism to the extent that some observers have warned of the danger that the world trading system could fragment into a series of regional trading blocs. Although GATT rules permit the formation of customs unions and free trade areas subject to certain conditions, the intention was that these would be exceptions to the overriding objective of an open, multilateral trading system based on the principle of nondiscrimination. Certain kinds of regional trading arrangements were permitted on the grounds that these could be stepping stones towards global trade liberalisation. The concern is that the current fascination with regional trading blocs of even the big players such as the USA, which in the past was the major protagonist for multilateralism, could undermine rather than strengthen global trade liberalisation.

Chapter 8 discusses the so-called new issues which were added to the agenda of multilateral trade negotiations at the commencement of the

Uruguay Round. The three main new issues covered by the Round were trade in services, trade-related intellectual property rights (TRIPs) and trade-related investment issues (TRIMs). All three issues brought GATT into previously unchartered waters. No previous GATT round had sought to tackle these issues in any serious fashion. Yet they could no longer be omitted, given their crucial importance to the developed countries. The USA in particular was not prepared to embark on a new GATT round without these issues on the agenda.

Finally, Chapter 9 makes a brave concluding attempt to identify the issues of the future. Already only six months into the life of the newly established WTO, the shape of a future agenda is emerging. Four key issues are likely to be important: trade policy and the environment; trade policy and labour standards; competition policy; and global investment issues. It is clear that the agenda for multilateral trade negotiations is changing rapidly. Negotiations are no longer concerned with the relatively simple matters of tariffs, over which countries could more easily bargain. As formal barriers have been lowered and international competition increased, trade negotiators are being forced to address a much wider range of issues. Market access is no longer concerned purely and simply with controls imposed at the border. Many other forms of government intervention, including seemingly innocuous forms of government regulation, can affect the ability of one country to sell goods in the market of another. Nor will the future agenda be concerned purely with trade matters as in the past. Rather, there will be growing demands that the newly established WTO broaden its concerns to cover issues affecting international factor movements, including direct investment abroad, labour movements and the transfer of technology.

HISTORICAL BACKGROUND

The basis for international trade policy over the last four and a half decades has been the General Agreement on Tariffs and Trade (GATT) signed in 1947. It is therefore desirable to begin with a brief survey of the historical background to the establishment of GATT and a summary of the role which it has played in world trade liberalisation over the past forty-eight years. In many respects, GATT was modelled on the prewar United States Trade Agreements Programme. This in turn came into being with the passage in 1934 of the US Reciprocal Trade Agreements Act (RTAA). The significance of the RTAA was that it gave to the US President a new and specific authority to enter into trade agreements with other countries whereby the US tariff would be reduced in return for equivalent concessions from trading partners. The overt intent was to use the US tariff as a weapon to gain easier access for US manufactures to the markets of other countries. Before the war, this took the form of bilateral agreements between the US and her major trading partners in which the US offered cuts in her own tariffs as a device for securing more open markets for US exports abroad. The impact of the programme was, however, rather limited because negotiations were largely bilateral and due to the outbreak of the Second World War. After the war, however, the US was keen to resume its tariff-cutting programme but this time on a *multilateral* rather than *bilateral* basis. GATT was largely the outcome of this process. This was strengthened by the political desire to assist the recovery of Europe following the devastation of the war and to contain the spread of communism.

Before discussing the US Trade Agreements Programme and how it led to the creation of the GATT, it is necessary to examine the nature of US trade policy before 1934. Previously, US trade policy consisted of imposing mainly high tariffs to protect domestic industry and to generate revenue for the federal authorities. The tariff was regarded as largely a matter of domestic concern and, as such, non-negotiable. The significance of the tariff as a revenue-raising device was reduced with the passage of the 16th Amendment to the US Constitution in 1913 which made a federal income tax constitutional. This reduced the previous dependence on customs duties as a source of tax revenues. Nevertheless the policy of maintaining a high tariff as a device for protecting US producers continued throughout the 1920s and early 1930s. Indeed, in several respects, US trade policy became more protectionist. The 1921 Emergency Tariff Act resulted in higher duties on imported agricultural products, a response to the slump in agricultural prices which followed the end of the war. The 1922 Fordney–McCumber Tariff Act saw the protection granted to agriculture spread to manufacturing also. Then, in 1930, the Smoot–Hawley Act raised duties still higher. An important factor in this process was the phenomenon of logrolling whereby concessions granted to agriculture enabled Congressmen from urban areas to push for higher duties on industrial goods.

However, historians seem in agreement that the policy of maintaining a high tariff during the interwar period was harmful to the US. If there had been some justification for high tariffs in the prewar period, this was not true of the interwar years. Firstly, by the time the war was over, the US had become a net exporter of merchandise. Moreover, in excess of one-half of her exports now consisted of finished and semi-finished manufactures compared with 30 per cent before 1900 (Kelly, 1963). Since many of these manufactures were produced under conditions of increasing returns or decreasing average cost, a large and growing market was important. As the domestic market for some of these goods became saturated, there was a need to seek out new markets overseas. A policy of maintaining high import tariffs was unhelpful in this respect. In the absence of a lowering of the US tariff, other countries were reluctant to grant US manufactures easier access to their home markets. At the same time, import protection was of little benefit to the new, research-intensive growth industries pioneered by the US (Meyer, 1978).

Secondly, by the time the war was over, the US had become a large net exporter of capital to the rest of the world. Before the war, she had been a net importer of capital. During the interwar years, the US played an important role in enabling other countries, especially the European economies, to finance current account balance of payments deficits. In the absence of US capital exports, these other countries would have faced major adjustment problems. Indeed, this is precisely what happened when US loans and investments were curtailed in the 1930s following the Wall Street stock market crash of 1929. This played a major role in the descent of the world economy into the Great Depression. However, the key point is that the changed status of the US from debtor to creditor necessitated a policy of low tariffs. For only by exporting more merchandise to the US could the rest of the world earn the foreign currency both to continue buying US goods and to meet the interest, amortisation and dividend payments on the loans and investments received from the US. The failure of the US to recognise this until it was too late was a major factor contributing towards the financial crisis which ensued in 1929.

In economic life, policies are often slow to respond to changed circumstances. Governments often persist with policies even when changed conditions have rendered those policies obsolete. Thus, US trade policy was at odds with the changed position of the US in the world for much of the interwar period. However, there were a number of changes which did take place in US trade policy during this period which were important for what was to follow. Firstly, the principle of the 'flexible' tariff was established in both the 1922 (Fordney–McCumber) Act and the 1930 (Smoot–Hawley) Act. The President was empowered to vary the tariff within specified limits without resort to Congress. Of course, the intention was to give to the President the freedom to raise tariffs so as to equalise foreign and domestic costs of production. If, for example, foreign companies enjoyed a fall in costs of production, giving them a competitive edge when selling to the US, the President could raise tariffs to restore competitiveness to US producers. Such a policy was highly protectionist. If enforced by all countries, it could soon stop all trade. However, an important principle had been conceded, namely, that the President could change tariffs without seeking further Congressional approval. The intended upward flexibility could become a downward flexibility in the future.

Secondly, in 1923, the US adopted an unconditional most-favoured-nation (MFN) policy. This meant that the US agreed not to discriminate in her tariff policy. All her trading partners would be treated equally. If a high tariff was imposed on imports of a certain product from one country, the same tariff would be applied to imports of that product from all other countries. Similarly, if the US entered into a trade agreement with another country whereby the US agreed to cut her tariff on a particular item, the tariff cut would be extended to all imports of that item regardless of where they came from. Before 1923, the US had adopted a *conditional* MFN policy. This meant that, if the US signed a trade agreement with another country, any tariff cut made by the US would only be extended to other countries if they offered concessions equivalent to those made by the country with whom the US had signed the agreement. Not surprisingly, such a policy did result in discrimination since some countries were unable to offer such concessions whenever the US entered into a trade agreement with a larger country. In fact, before 1923 actual US trade policy adhered more closely to an *unconditional* MFN policy. The adoption of an unconditional MFN policy in 1923 merely gave a legal basis for what was already practised. Furthermore, since at that time there were no trade agreements involving cuts in the US tariff, the change was not important. From 1922 onwards, the US tariff was to all intents and purposes non-negotiable. The situation could be described as one in which the US tariff was high and non-negotiable but nondiscriminatory. However, when in 1934 the US tariff did become negotiable, the unconditional MFN policy assumed a great importance. It meant that any tariff cuts offered by the US in a trade agreement with another country were now automatically extended to all other MFN trading partners. This made for much more rapid reductions in tariffs than would otherwise have been the case. Thirdly, after the First World War, the US largely renounced quantitative restrictions on trade. Protection took the form of high tariffs rather than import quotas. These had not been important before the war but had been extensively employed during the war. After the war, they were largely abolished except in Central and Eastern European countries where adverse conditions necessitated their retention. During the 1920s, US trade policy regarded quotas as an improper form of trade control and tariffs as the form which protection should primarily take.

The 1934 Reciprocal Trade Agreements Act followed the 1933 Democrat election victory. The Roosevelt Administration viewed trade policy as one instrument for lifting the US economy out of the economic slump of the 1930s. By offering cuts in tariffs, the US could secure easier access for its exports to other countries. Not only would lower tariffs make other countries more willing to cut tariffs on US exports, but equally the enhanced ability of other countries to sell to the US would provide them with the foreign currency to buy US goods. This was to be achieved by the US President negotiating reciprocal tariff reductions with the US's major trading partners. At the time, this was more acceptable to domestic economic interests than unilateral tariff reductions. For this purpose, Congress granted the President the authority to cut US tariffs by up to 50 per cent, initially for a period of three years, after which he could seek a renewal. This delegation of tariff-cutting authority by Congress to the President was of the utmost significance. Before 1934, Congress had jealously guarded its sole right to change the tariff. The President could propose cuts in the tariff but Congress had to give its approval. This meant that any trade agreement negotiated before 1934 could only be made effective if Congress approved. It made it difficult for any President to negotiate because neither he nor the country with whom he was negotiating could be sure that any concessions offered by the President would be approved by Congress. Not surprisingly, there were few trade agreements entered into before 1922 after which even the principle of a negotiable tariff was discarded. The 1934 Act changed the situation by giving the President the power to make meaningful offers in the course of negotiations. Moreover, the unconditional MFN policy was continued so that any concessions offered by the US in negotiations with any one country were automatically extended to all other MFN countries.

The 1934 Act gave to the US for the first time in its history an effective foreign economic policy. The US tariff was to become a weapon which the US would employ to secure both easier and fairer access to overseas markets for its goods. This change in the position of the world's largest trading nation was of enormous significance. The immediate impact was not so great. Some twenty-nine agreements were signed with various countries, the most important of which were with Canada and France in 1936 and the UK in 1939. However, the outbreak of war meant that these agreements achieved little or nothing in expanding trade. Nevertheless, they were important as forerunners of the multilateral agreements reached after the war through the GATT. Following the end of the Second World War, there was a strong desire on the part of the Allied powers to ensure a rapid return to normal peacetime conditions. In particular, they were concerned lest a brief postwar boom should give way to a protracted slump and a return to the conditions of the 1930s. A free, open and stable world trade and monetary system was seen to be important in bringing this about. The Bretton Woods Conference of 1944 helped to create the necessary monetary rules and institutions in the form of the International Monetary Fund (IMF) and the World Bank or International Bank for Reconstruction and Development (IBRD). The US was anxious to shape a similar set of rules and institutions to cover the trading side, for which the model was to be the trade agreements programme of the prewar period.

In 1945, Congress renewed the tariff-cutting authority granted to the President in 1934. Where tariff rates had been already reduced by 50 per cent under the 1934 authority, the President was permitted to make further tariff cuts of between 50 and 75 per cent of the 1934 level. Apparently, under the 1934 authority, tariff cuts of 50 per cent had been made on more than 40 per cent of US dutiable imports, so this fresh authority was very substantial (Kelly, 1963). As in 1934, the authority granted to the President was for three years. The aim of the US was to bring together a number of nations and simultaneously to negotiate tariff reductions. At the same time, the US took the initiative in a proposal for setting up a new 'international trade organisation' which was intended to be a counterpart on the trade front to the IMF and IBRD. The President's 1945 tariff-cutting authority did not include an agreement to create an ITO. Therefore, any charter for the creation of an ITO would have to be separately submitted to Congress for approval.

For these reasons, the negotiations for a multilateral agreement to reduce tariffs became separated from the negotiations for setting up an ITO. The former led to the establishment of the GATT in October 1947. However, the GATT agreement was carefully drafted not to make any reference to the creation of any organisation. The GATT was a treaty not an organisation. This was to ensure that the agreement fell within the limits of the 1945 Congressional authority granted to the US President and so therefore did not require any further Congressional approval. The negotiations for the setting up of an ITO were not complete at the time when the GATT was signed. Rather than wait for these negotiations to be concluded, it was decided to proceed with the signing of the GATT. One reason was that the President's authority was due to expire in mid-1948 so there was a need to reach agreement on cutting tariffs. The drafting of the ITO charter was completed at the Havana Conference of 1948. However, because the US Congress would not approve it, the ITO never came into being.

These events leading to the signing of the GATT are important for understanding some of the features of GATT. Firstly, the GATT treaty contained no provisions for setting up any organisation or institutions. To begin with, there was not even a secretariat; eventually, one emerged. This was based in Geneva and headed by a Director-General. Secondly, the GATT signatories were known as 'contracting parties' not members, although the expression 'GATT members' was often used colloquially. Twenty-three nations signed the GATT initially. By the time of the Uruguay Round, there were 117 contracting parties. Thirdly, the agreement was only ever applied 'provisionally' by the contracting parties. Again, this goes back to the time when the GATT was first signed; it was expected that the drafting of the GATT would be followed by the setting up of an ITO, so it was decided to apply the treaty provisionally. Technically, what happened was that eight nations (Australia, Belgium, Canada, France, Luxembourg, the Netherlands, the UK and the USA) signed the Protocol of Provisional Application and applied it provisionally from 1 January 1948, while the other fifteen nations agreed to apply it soon after. Under the Protocol of Provisional Application, the contracting parties agreed to apply fully Parts I and III of the GATT and to apply Part II 'to the fullest extent not inconsistent with existing legislation'. Part II contains most of the main substantial obligations. This meant that the contracting parties were free not to apply these provisions if they conflicted with legislation in existence at the time of becoming a GATT party. These so-called 'grandfather rights' still exist and are occasionally used to justify not applying Part II provisions.

THE GATT FRAMEWORK

GATT has served two purposes. Firstly, it has provided a set of rules to govern trade between the contracting parties. Rules are important for world trade because they create a degree of certainty for traders and hence stimulate investment and growth. Secondly, it has provided a multilateral forum for negotiating reciprocal reductions in trade barriers. Before GATT, trade negotiations were essentially bilateral affairs. This necessarily limited what they could achieve and the speed with which barriers could be lowered. Let us begin with the rules. They are set out in the major articles of the Treaty (see Table 1.1). They contain many of the principles on which US trade policy was based before the war.

Most important was *Article I*, the *Most-Favoured Nation Clause*. This required contracting parties to treat goods coming from other contracting parties equally, that is, not to discriminate. It states that

> any advantage, favour, privilege or immunity granted by any contracting party to any product originating in or destined for any other country shall be accorded immediately and unconditionally to the like product originating in or destined for the territories of all other contracting parties.

> (Article I:1)

In other words, GATT contracting parties were to accord nondiscriminatory (that is, most-favoured-nation) treatment to goods coming from (or destined for) the territories of other GATT contracting parties.

Two important exceptions to the principle of nondiscrimination were the cases of customs unions and free trade areas. Customs unions involve the abolition of internal tariffs and the adoption of a common customs tariff. Free trade areas similarly involve internal free trade but the members are free to apply whatever rate of external tariff they choose. Thus, both result in preference or discrimination being granted to goods originating from inside the customs union/free trade area. *Article XXIV* states that

> the provisions of this Agreement shall not prevent, as between the territories of contracting parties, the formation of a customs union or of a free trade area or of the adoption of an interim arrangement necessary for the formation of a customs union or of a free trade area provided that:

> (a) with respect to customs unions, duties and other regulations of commerce imposed at the institution of any such union . . . in respect of trade with contracting parties not parties to such union . . . shall not on the whole be higher or more restrictive than the general incidence of the duties and regulations of commerce applicable in the constituent territories prior to the formation of such union . . .

Table 1.1 The GATT Articles of Agreement

I	Objectives
II	General most-favoured-nation treatment
III	Schedules of concessions
IV	National treatment and internal taxation and regulation
V	Freedom of transit
VI	Antidumping and countervailing duties
VII	Valuation for customs purposes
VIII	Fees and formalities connected with importation and exportation
IX	Marks of origin
X	Publication and administration of trade regulations
XI	General elimination of quantitative restrictions
XII	Restrictions to safeguard the balance of payments
XIII	Nondiscriminatory administration of quantitative restrictions
XIV	Exceptions to the rule of nondiscrimination
XV	Exchange arrangements
XVI	Subsidies
XVII	State trading enterprises
XVIII	Governmental assistance to economic development
XIX	Emergency action on imports of particular products
XX	General exceptions
XXI	Security exceptions
XXII	Consultation
XXIII	Nullification or impairment
XXIV	Customs unions and free trade areas
XXV	The organisation for trade co-operation
XXVI	Acceptance, entry into force and registration
XXVII	Withholding or withdrawal of concessions
XXVIII	Modification of schedules
XXIX	Tariff negotiations
XXX	Amendments
XXXI	Withdrawal
XXXII	Contracting parties
XXXIII	Accession
XXXIV	Annexes
XXXV	Nonapplication of the agreement between particular contracting parties
XXXVI	Trade and development: principles and objectives
XXXVII	Undertaking relating to commodities of special export interest to LDCs
XXXVIII	Outline of joint action on trade and development

(b) with respect to a free trade area . . . the duties and other regulations of commerce maintained in each of the constituent territories and applicable at the formation of such free trade area . . . to the trade of contracting parties not included in such area . . . shall not be higher or more restrictive than the corresponding duties and other regulations of commerce existing in the same constituent territories prior to the formation of the free trade area . . .

(Article XXIV:5)

Customs unions and free trade areas were permitted, provided that they did not result in a higher level of restriction on imports from other contracting parties than existed before their formation.

Article XI prohibits altogether one particular type of trade restriction, namely quantitative restrictions. Once again, this provision was a carry-over from US trade policy in the prewar period. The 1922 Tariff Act prohibited this method of restricting imports, regarding tariffs as the proper form of import protection. Article XI states that

No prohibitions or restrictions other than duties, taxes or other charges, whether made effective through quotas, import or export licences or other measures, shall be instituted or maintained by any contracting party on the importation of any product of the territory of any other contracting party or on the exportation or sale for export of any product destined for the territory of any other contracting party.

(Article XI:1)

However, there were certain exceptions. These were 'export prohibitions or restrictions to prevent or relieve critical shortages of foodstuffs' or other 'essential products', 'import or export prohibitions necessary to the application of standards or regulations for the classification, grading or marketing of commodities' and 'import restrictions on any agricultural or fisheries product . . . necessary to the enforcement of governmental measures which operate: (i) to restrict the quantities of the like domestic product to be marketed or produced . . . (ii) to remove a temporary surplus of the like domestic product . . . (iii) to restrict the quantities permitted to be produced of any animal product the production of which is directly dependent . . . on the imported commodity'. The exception granted to agricultural imports was especially important. It arose because of the existence in many countries of government policies unique to agriculture for regulating output.

Contracting parties were permitted to introduce trade restrictions additional to those already in existence in certain situations. These were specified in the Treaty. One important case was that of dumping. *Article VI* states that:

13

The contracting parties recognise that dumping, by which products of one country are introduced into the commerce of another country at less than the normal value of the products, is to be condemned if it causes or threatens material injury to an established industry in the territory of a contracting party or materially retards the establishment of a domestic industry.

(Article VI:1)

Dumping is thus defined as a situation in which goods are sold on the foreign market at a price which is below their 'normal value'. This is defined as 'the comparable price, in the ordinary course of trade, for the like product when destined for consumption in the exporting country'. If no such 'comparable price' exists, 'the highest comparable price for the like product for export to any third country in the ordinary course of trade, or . . . the cost of production of the product in any country plus a reasonable addition for selling cost and profit' can be used. Contracting parties were permitted to impose antidumping levies on such imports provided that the duty did not exceed the margin of dumping, defined as the difference between the export price and the normal value. Similarly, there was a provision for imposing so-called 'countervailing duties' to offset any subsidy granted to the exporter. As with antidumping duties, this was not to exceed the amount of the subsidy granted.

Another important exception was restrictions to safeguard a country's balance of payments. *Article XII* states that

any contracting party, in order to safeguard its external financial position and its balance of payments, may restrict the quantity or value of merchandise permitted to be imported.

(Article XII:1)

However, the restrictions imposed were not to exceed those necessary to remedy the situation and had to be progressively relaxed as conditions improved. Moreover, any country making use of this Article to introduce or intensify trade restrictions had to do so in consultation with other GATT contracting parties.

Selective trade restrictions were also allowed under *Article XIX*, if imports of a particular product caused or threatened 'serious injury' to domestic producers. Article XIX states that

If, as a result of unforeseen developments and of the effect of the obligations incurred by a contracting party under this Agreement, including tariff concessions, any product is being imported into the territory of that contracting party in such increased quantities and under such conditions as to cause or threaten serious injury to domestic producers in that territory of like or directly competitive products, the contracting party shall be free, in respect of such product, and to the extent and for such time as may be necessary to prevent or remedy such injury, to suspend the obligation in whole or in part or to withdraw or modify the concession.

(Article XIX:1(a))

This is the so-called Safeguard or Escape Clause which allowed a contracting party to withdraw any tariff concession made in the past and impose a higher tariff for such time and to the extent necessary to remedy the injury to domestic producers caused or threatened by the imports. However, there was a requirement that notice of the intention to take any such action should be given in writing so as to provide opportunity for consultation. In exceptional circumstances, where delay would cause irreparable damage to the country concerned, provisional action could be taken without consultation. The intention was that, through consultation, it should be possible to reach agreement and avoid the necessity for such measures. However, if this was not possible, the importing country could proceed with its action. In this case, the affected parties could suspend concessions or obligations on trade with the party taking the action.

A further ground on which a contracting party was permitted to impose trade restrictions was for the promotion of economic development in a developing country. *Article XVIII* states:

The contracting parties recognise . . . that it may be necessary . . . in order to implement programmes and policies of economic develop-ment designed to raise the general standard of living of their people, to take protective or other measures affecting imports, and that such measures are justified in so far as they facilitate the attainment of the objectives of this Agreement.

(Article XVIII:2)

This applied 'particularly to those contracting parties the economies of which can only support low standards of living and are in early stages of development'. These countries were permitted 'to grant the tariff protection required for the establishment of a particular industry' and to 'apply quantitative restrictions for balance of payments purposes in a manner which takes full account of the continued high level of demand for imports likely to be generated by their programmes of economic development' (Article XVIII:2).

In addition to these rules governing the conduct of trade policy, GATT sought to bring about an expansion of world trade through a reciprocal lowering of tariff and other trade barriers. Not only did the contracting parties agree to refrain from certain kinds of trade restrictions and practices, they also undertook to meet periodically to negotiate a lowering of existing tariff barriers. This is provided for in *Article XXVIII bis* which states that

The contracting parties recognise that customs duties often constitute serious obstacles to trade; thus negotiations on a reciprocal and mutually advantageous basis, directed to the substantial reduction of the general level of tariffs and other charges on imports and exports and in particular to the reduction of such high tariffs as discourage the importation even of minimum quantities . . . are of great importance to the expansion of international trade.

(Article XXVIII:1 bis)

The agreement provides for both selective product-by-product negotiations – which was the approach preferred in the US under the prewar trade agreements programme – or any other approach. A horizontal reduction of all duties by some uniform amount makes for a quicker reduction since it avoids the complications inherent in a product-by-product approach. As we shall see, the early GATT rounds followed the product-by-product approach. Negotiations could take the form of duty reductions or of binding duties at their existing levels, that is, an undertaking not to raise them.

Article XXVIII provides for the modification or withdrawal of concessions after three years if the concessions granted have caused difficulty. These were the so-called 'open seasons' when GATT parties could renegotiate concessions which subsequently caused difficulties. However, the aim of such renegotiations was 'to maintain a general level of reciprocal and mutually advantageous concessions not less favourable to trade than that provided for in this Agreement prior to such negotiations'. In other words, this should involve offering other concessions equivalent to those originally offered but now withdrawn. In the event of agreement not being reached, any country with a principal supplier interest was free to withdraw 'substantially equivalent concessions' negotiated with the other party.

In addition to the provisions for withdrawing concessions, *Article XXV* permitted a general 'waiver' of GATT rules to be granted to a contracting party. This required a two-thirds majority of votes cast by the contracting parties. In this case, a contracting party could be freed from its obligations under any particular area of the Treaty. *Article XXVII* was also important in this respect because it permitted any contracting party to withhold from any new GATT contracting party concessions granted to other contracting parties. It states that:

This Agreement . . . shall not apply as between any contracting party and any other contracting party if:

(a) the two contracting parties have not entered into tariff nego-tiations with each other, and

(b) either of the contracting parties, at the time either becomes a contracting party, does not consent to such application.

(Article XXVII:1)

This clause was used extensively when Japan joined the GATT in 1955 and has been used on a number of other occasions since.

INTRODUCTION

With effect from 27 June 1966, a new *Part IV* was added to the GATT Treaty. This dealt with the general area of trade and development and represented an attempt by the developed contracting parties to give greater recognition to the problems of developing countries. One of the most important aspects of this addition to the GATT Treaty were the provisions for nonreciprocity in trade negotiations involving developed and developing contracting parties. *Article XXXVI:8* states that:

The developed contracting parties do not expect reciprocity for commitments made by them in trade negotiations to reduce or remove tariffs and other barriers to the trade of less developed countries.

In other words, developing countries were not required to offer tariff concessions to developed countries in return for concessions received from them.

As we explained earlier, GATT was never intended to be an organisation, only a treaty. Therefore, the Treaty contained no provisions for any institutions to administer the GATT and very few concerned with procedures for rule application and dispute settlement. As far as institutions go, the GATT Secretariat emerged as the effective 'executive branch' of the GATT but it had no legal basis in the Treaty. (There was, however, provision for an Executive Secretary, who, after 1965, was known by the title 'Director-General'.) The principal body of the GATT was the contracting parties meeting collectively. *Article XXV* provided for the contracting parties to act jointly:

Representatives of the contracting parties shall meet from time to time for the purpose of giving effect to those provisions of this Agreement which involve joint action and, generally, with a view to facilitating the operation and furthering the objectives of this Agreement.

(Article XXV:1)

When the contracting parties acted jointly in this way, each had one vote. Unless otherwise specified, decisions of the contracting parties were taken on the basis of a majority of votes cast. In practice, much decision-making was settled by a process of consensus rather than by voting. For the purpose of carrying out their business, the contracting parties created a variety of sub-groups. The most important was the *Council* which was set up by a resolution of the contracting parties in 1960. It consisted of representatives of all the contracting parties and initially met on a monthly basis. Because this became increasingly difficult as the number of CPs rose, a 'Consultative Group of 18' was set up in 1975. This consisted of the leading trading nations plus representatives of the major categories of other contracting parties. For each major negotiating round, there existed also a Trade Negotiations Committee (the TNC).

With regard to procedures for rule application and dispute settlement,

17

the GATT Treaty said very little. Reference has already been made to Article XXV which provided for joint action by the contracting parties and gives to the contracting parties the authority to interpret the GATT. Some of these interpretations are given in the annexe to the main treaty; others have emerged subsequently in the form of various agreements covering particular issues (for example, the 1979 Antidumping Code which interpreted Article VI of the GATT). Other interpretations have been made from time to time by the contracting parties usually acting together by consensus.

Article XXII and *Article XXIII* are the main articles concerned with procedures for dispute settlement. Article XXII:1 establishes the duty of each contracting party to

> accord sympathetic consideration to, and shall afford adequate opportunity for consultation regarding, such representations as may be made by another contracting party with respect to any matter affecting the operation of this Agreement.

This establishes the right of each contracting party to bilateral consultation. If, however, a country feels that it has been unfairly treated in bilateral talks, Article XXII:2 establishes its right to multilateral consultation via the GATT. In the event of an inability to settle a dispute through consultation, a contracting party may invoke *Article XXIII* which states that

1 If any contracting party should consider that any benefit accruing to it directly or indirectly under this Agreement is being nullified or impaired or that the attainment of any objective of the Agreement is being impeded as the result of

   (a) the failure of another contracting party to carry out its obligations under this Agreement, or
   (b) the application by another contracting party of any measure, whether or not it conflicts with the provisions of the Agreement, or
   (c) the existence of any other situation,

   the contracting party may, with a view to satisfactory adjustment of the matter, make written representations or proposals to the other contracting parties which it considers to be concerned. Any contracting party thus approached shall give sympathetic consideration to the representations or proposals made to it.

2 If no satisfactory adjustment is effected between the contracting parties concerned within a reasonable time . . . the matter shall be referred to the CONTRACTING PARTIES. The CONTRACTING PARTIES shall promptly investigate any matter so referred to them and shall make appropriate recommendations to the contracting parties which they consider to be concerned, or give a ruling on the

matter, as appropriate. . . . If the CONTRACTING PARTIES consider the circumstances serious enough to justify such action, they may authorise a contracting party or parties to suspend the application to any other contracting party or parties of such concessions or other obligations under this Agreement as they determine to be appropriate in the circumstances . . .

Thus, the aggrieved party must have demonstrated 'nullification' or 'impairment' before Article XXIII could be invoked. It is clear that this did not just cover the failure of another contracting party to carry out one or more of its obligations under the GATT. Any action by another contracting party which harmed the trade of another was covered. The aim of the procedure was to secure an 'adjustment' of the matter by the parties involved. If, however, this failed, the contracting parties, that is the GATT, were authorised to make a ruling. The way in which this subsequently worked was that the matter was referred to a panel of experts who acted in their own capacity, not as representatives of their governments. The panel report would then be sent to the contracting parties for approval. In most cases, it would be automatically adopted although the offending party could block approval by voting against the report since the GATT worked on the basis of consensus. The provision permitting the contracting parties to authorise suspension of concessions or obligations was only used on one occasion. This happened in 1952 when the Netherlands were allowed to suspend 'appropriate' concessions to the United States after the US had imposed import restrictions on Dutch dairy products. In fact, it had no effect on the US action.

In addition to providing a set of rules to govern world trade, the GATT provided a forum within which multilateral trade negotiations could take place. This was important, since all previous trading negotiations between countries to liberalise their trade with each other were essentially bilateral affairs. Bilateral negotiations are necessarily much slower than multilateral negotiations. Countries are also less willing to make concessions where negotiations are bilateral for fear of throwing away bargaining counters in future negotiations with other trading partners. Thus, multilateral negotiations achieve a greater degree of liberalisation more rapidly. GATT negotiations took place in a series of so-called 'rounds' beginning with the First Round in Geneva and ending with the Uruguay Round (the eighth) between 1986 and 1993. In each of these rounds, countries conducted essentially bilateral negotiations but simultaneously. At the same time, any concessions which one country made to another had to be multilaterally applied, that is, extended to all other contracting parties on an MFN basis. Each of the GATT rounds tended to follow an extension of the US President's tariff-cutting authority, for without Congressional authority meaningful negotiations could not take place. At the same time, no multilateral negotiations were possible without the active participation of the United States. The results of the various rounds of tariff-cutting are discussed in the next chapter.

CONCLUSION

The remaining chapters of this book examine in greater depth some of these aspects of the GATT. Attention is focused on those issues which have topped the agenda of multilateral trade negotiations in recent years and those likely to be important in the future. On 31 December 1994 the GATT's life came to an end. Its role was taken over by the new World Trade Organisation (WTO). Henceforth, all the responsibilities previously exercised by the GATT now become the responsibility of the WTO. As the following chapters will explain, this amounts to more than a mere change of title. The WTO is an organisation with a permanent, legal existence and with a broader range of responsibilities than the GATT. The death of the GATT and the birth of the WTO represents something of a watershed in the history of international trade policy. The GATT continues to exist as an agreement. (Technically, there are two GATT agreements, GATT 1994 being different from GATT 1947.) In theory, countries could, if they so wished, remain GATT signatories but not WTO members. However, its status remains that of a treaty. Institutionally, the WTO is now the body responsible for trade policy internationally. As later chapters will demonstrate this represents a significant institutional change in trade policy.

2

INDUSTRIAL TARIFFS

INTRODUCTION

In the period since the establishment of the GATT, great progress has been made in reducing tariffs on industrial goods. Very little attempt was made to tackle the problem of nontariff barriers until the seventh (Tokyo Round) of 1973–9. Similarly, before the successful conclusion of the recent Uruguay Round, trade in agricultural goods was largely exempt from GATT rules. One result of this tariff-cutting process is that tariffs are now much less important as an impediment to trade in industrial products. Increasingly, other types of barrier have become more important.

However, it is not true that tariffs no longer matter. High tariffs still exist on particular products. Moreover, a country's tariff structure may be more protectionist than the average level of its tariff suggests. This chapter begins by examining the economic effects of tariffs and the procedure which is conventionally used for measuring the welfare loss from tariffs. It continues with a discussion of some difficulties involved with the orthodox model and considers modifications which incorporate imperfections in both product and factor markets. Next, the relevance of tariff structure and the concept of the effective rate of protection are introduced. The chapter concludes with a survey of the process of tariff liberalisation up to and including the Uruguay Round.

THE NATURE AND EFFECTS OF TARIFFS

A tariff is a tax or levy on an imported product. It may take the form of either a specific or an *ad valorem* duty. In the case of a specific duty, the tariff is a fixed amount per unit of the product imported. An *ad valorem* duty is a tariff which is a certain percentage of the unit value. Generally, *ad valorem* tariffs are more popular than specific tariffs mainly because they keep pace with inflation. (A weakness is that they may import inflation to an otherwise inflation-free country.) However, specific tariffs are still important. For example, prior to the Uruguay Round, roughly one-third of all tariff lines in the US were covered by specific duties, about 13 per cent in Japan and 10 per cent in the United States (Yeats, 1979). *Ad valorem* tariffs may relate to the FOB (free-on-board) or CIF (cost, insurance and freight) value of imports. This can be important because the FOB value of imports is less than the CIF value. Article VII of the GATT which deals with customs valuation procedures does not prescribe any right method. Most countries use the CIF basis of customs valuation although the United States has always used the FOB method.

The effects of a tariff may be analysed using partial or general equilibrium analysis. General equilibrium analysis is more satisfactory since it takes account of the effects on all sectors of the importing country, not just the protected sector, and the way in which these secondary effects may feed back to the protected sector. On the other hand, partial equilibrium analysis is acceptable where the tariff imposed protects a relatively small sector of the economy. Taking the case of a small importing nation, Figure 2.1 depicts the effects of a tariff imposed on a product imported by a small importing nation on the assumption that the market for the product is perfectly competitive. Figure 2.1(a) shows the demand for and supply of the importable product in the importing country. D_0D_0 is the demand curve for the product in the importing country and S_0S_0 is the domestic supply curve. Figure 2.1(b) shows the quantity of the product imported at different prices, given by the excess of domestic demand over domestic supply. When domestic demand equals domestic supply, imports are zero. Since the country is a small importing nation, it has no influence over the world price which is OP_0. At OP_0 demand is OQ_1 and home producers supply OQ_0. Excess demand of Q_0–Q_1, which is equal to OQ_4 in Figure 2.1(b), is satisfied by imports. If a tariff is levied at a rate of T, the post-tariff price of imports becomes $(1 + T)P_0$. This enables home producers to raise their prices to the same level. Demand falls to OQ_3 but domestic supply increases to OQ_2. Excess demand falls to Q_2–Q_3, equal to OQ_5 in Figure 2.1(b), and is satisfied by imports.

The imposition of a tariff has at least five different effects. Firstly, a reduction in consumption (from OQ_1 to OQ_3) in the importing country, the *consumption effect*. Secondly, an increase in domestic production (from OQ_0 to OQ_2), the *protective effect*. Thirdly, imports are reduced (from Q_0Q_1 to Q_2Q_3 or from Q_4 to Q_5), the *balance of trade effect*. Fourthly, the tariff generates revenue for the importing country (equal to the tariff, TP_0 multiplied by imports Q_2Q_3 which is area C in each figure), the *revenue effect*. Finally, the tariff reduces economic welfare in the importing country, the *welfare effect*. On the one hand, the tariff increases the incomes of domestic producers and the government. On the other hand, it reduces the real incomes of consumers by raising the price of the imported product. However, because the welfare loss to consumers exceeds the gain to domestic producers plus government, the importing country suffers a net

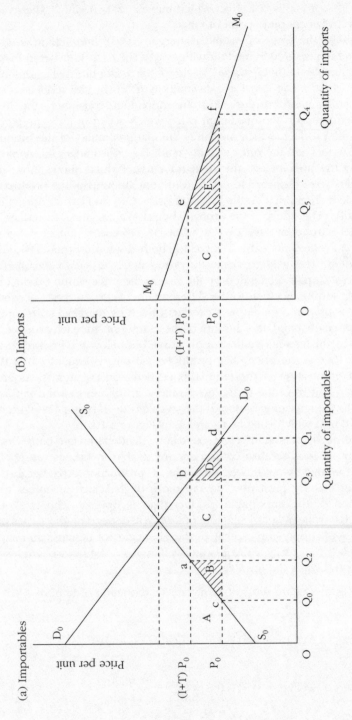

Figure 2.1 The small-country partial equilibrium model of the effects of a tariff

welfare loss. It is this last effect which makes tariffs harmful when viewed from a purely economic point of view.

Following the work of Arnold Haberger (1963), the welfare costs of a tariff can be measured in the following way. (The basic idea behind welfare triangle analysis can be traced back to Jules Dupuit, 1844, and Alfred Marshall, 1920.) The loss for consumers is given by the reduction in so-called 'consumers' surplus'. For an individual consumer, this is the difference between the maximum price which a consumer is prepared to pay for the product (which measures the marginal utility of the product to the consumer) and the price actually paid. For consumers as a whole, it is equal to the area below the demand curve (which shows how much consumers were prepared to pay for different amounts of the product) and above the market price. At the pre-tariff price, OP_0, in Figure 2.1(a), it is the area D_0dP_0. The effect of the tariff is, by raising the price, to reduce total consumer surplus by area $(A + B + C + D)$. However, part of this loss to consumers represents extra income for both domestic producers and the government. The gain to domestic producers is equal to the increased 'producers' surplus' generated by the rise in the price of the product sold. Producer surplus is equal to the difference between the price at which a supplier is prepared to supply a product (given by marginal costs) and the market price obtained. It is the sum of these amounts for each producer and is given by the area above the supply curve but below the market price. In Figure 2.1(a), at the price OP_0, producers' surplus is equal to area P_0cS_0. After the imposition of the tariff, this is increased by area A. As area C represents tariff revenue to the government, it follows that the *net loss* of welfare to the importing nation or the so-called *deadweight loss* of the tariff is areas $B + D$ which is equal to area E in Figure 2.1(b).

Conceptually, this deadweight loss can be divided into two parts: firstly, a consumption loss because consumers are unable to buy as much of the product as they would like; secondly, a production loss because the importing country must now devote more of its scarce resources to the production of the importable product than is optimal. The size of the welfare loss from any particular rate of tariff will depend on the slopes of the demand and supply curves, that is, the elasticities of demand and supply. The lower the elasticities, the less the welfare loss. The net welfare loss can be estimated using the formula:

Net loss of welfare = $0.5 \times$ tariff rate $\times$ reduction of imports

or

Net loss of welfare = $0.5TP_0\{(Q_0 - Q_1) - (Q_2 - Q_3)\}$

or

Net loss of welfare = $0.5TP_0(Q_5 - Q_4)$

Where the elasticities of demand and supply, e_d and e_s, are known, the formula for estimating the welfare gain is:

Net welfare gain = $0.5T(e_dDT) + 0.5T(e_sST)$

where T is the tariff reduction, D the original quantity demanded and S the original quantity supplied. The formula may be used to measure the cost of a particular tariff to an importing country provided that the value of elasticities is known. Equally, it may be used to estimate the potential gain to a country from lowering or eliminating a particular tariff.

In a number of respects, this analysis of the effects of a tariff is over-simplified. Firstly, it is restricted to the case of a *small* importing nation which faces a world price over which it has no influence. The analysis needs to be modified for the case of a *large* importing nation which is able to influence the world price. In this case, the imposition of a tariff is likely to force down the world price of the good. If so, the loss in economic welfare from the higher tariff will be partially or even wholly offset by the gain from improved terms of trade. Figure 2.2 illustrates this case.

D_0D_0 is the demand curve for the product in the importing country and S_0S_0 is the domestic supply curve. S_0S_t is the total supply (domestic plus foreign) curve obtained by adding to domestic supply the amount which foreigners will supply at different prices. (S_0S_t is flatter than S_0S_0 because world supply is more elastic than domestic supply but not perfectly elastic as in the case of a small importing nation.) Under free trade, demand is OQ_1, domestic supply is OQ_0 and imports are Q_0Q_1 which is equal to OQ_4. Now, suppose a tariff is imposed at the rate of T. The effect is to cause foreigners to supply less at each and every price the total supply curve shifts vertically upwards to $S_0 S_T$. The distance between the new and the old supply curve equals the amount of the tariff, that is, TP_1. The new equilibrium price is $O(1 + T)P_1$. Consumption is reduced by Q_3Q_1 to OQ_3. Domestic production is increased by Q_0Q_2 to OQ_2. Imports fall from Q_0Q_1 to Q_2Q_3 which is equal to OQ_5.

The tariff reduces consumer surplus by the amount $(A + B + C + D)$ as in the small-country model. However, the revenue effect is given by areas $(C + E)$. Part of the revenue accruing to the government of the importing nation is a redistribution of income from foreign suppliers to that government. This is area E. It thus represents the increase in the economic welfare of the importing country resulting from the imposition of a tariff. It arises because foreign suppliers cut the price at which they supply the product from OP_0 to OP_1. Assuming no change in the importing country's average export prices, the fall in its average import prices leads to an improvement in its terms of trade. The loss of welfare from the tariff is then given by the difference between triangles $(B + D)$ equal to area F and rectangle E, the gain to the importing country from the improvement in its

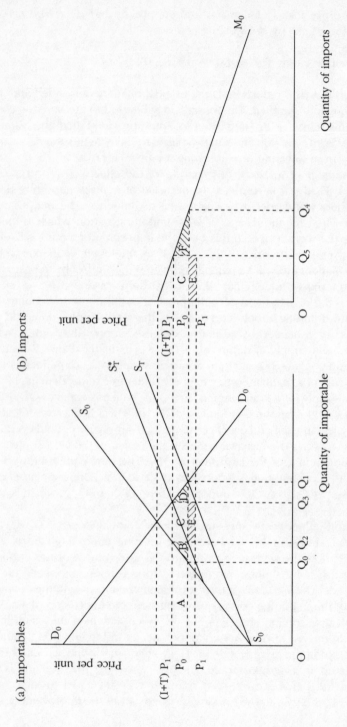

Figure 2.2 The large-country partial equilibrium model of the effects of a tariff

terms of trade. It is possible for rectangle E to be greater than triangles B and D in which case a tariff could raise the welfare of the importing country. An 'optimum tariff' which would maximise the difference between area E and areas (B + D) can be constructed. It is given by the formula $t = 1/e$ where e is the elasticity of supply of imports (given by the slope of the import function in Figure 2.2(b)). (An import function shows the relationship between the quantity of imports supplied by the rest of the world and the price per unit in the importing country.) If this is known, a large importing nation could raise economic welfare by imposing a tariff. In this case, a tariff would not harm the importing country although it would reduce the welfare of the exporting country. It thus risks the danger that other countries would retaliate. If so, the importing country could lose. This case of retaliation was analysed by Harry Johnson (1953), who showed that, although one or other country might end up better off, both could not gain from a trade war. It also has limited practical usefulness as governments mostly lack the information required to be able to construct an optimum tariff. On the other hand, it may create an economic rationale for countries coming together in regional trading blocs with a common external tariff which could be used to force favourable movements in their combined terms of trade (see Chapter 7).

A second and more important drawback with the orthodox model set out above is that it assumes perfect markets. There is an implicit assumption that both product and factor markets are perfectly competitive. One aspect of this is the assumption that imports are perfect substitutes for the domestically produced good with which they are competing. Put another way, the elasticity of substitution between imports and domestically produced goods is infinite. From this it follows that there will exist a *single price* for the product. The model can be made somewhat less restrictive by allowing for differences in quality such that goods of higher quality carry a price premium. However, the point remains that, when the price of imports rises due to the imposition of a tariff, the price of home-produced substitutes rises by the same amount. What happens if imports are not perfect substitutes for importables; that is to say, if the elasticity of substitution between imports and importables is finite? Then, if the price of imports rises on account of a tariff, the price of home-produced goods may not rise by the same amount. Equally, if the price of imports falls, the price of home-produced substitutes need not fall by the same amount. Figure 2.3 sets out a model used by Batchelor and Minford (1977) for analysing the welfare effects of a tariff under imperfect competition.

D_0D_0 and S_0S_0 are respectively the demand curves and domestic supply curves for import *substitutes* in the importing country. D_2D_2 is the demand for *imports*. Before the imposition of a tariff, the price of import substitutes is OP_0 and of imports OP_2. A tariff is imposed on imports at the rate T such that the price of imports rises to $O(1 + T)P_2$ and the demand for imports falls

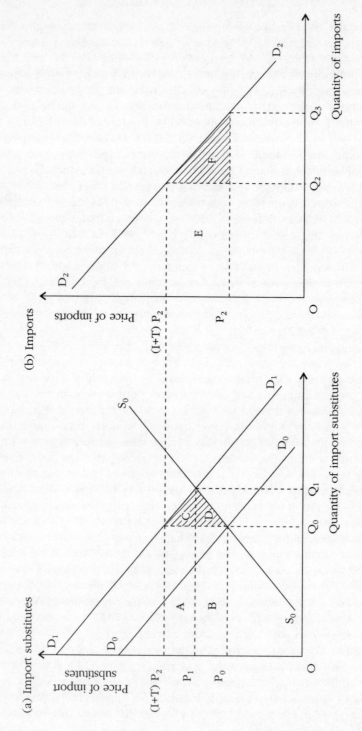

Figure 2.3 The welfare effects of a tariff on imports under imperfect competition

to OQ_2. This increases the demand for import substitutes causing D_0D_0 to shift to D_1D_1 and the price to rise to OP_1. However, since import substitutes are only imperfect substitutes (the elasticity of substitution is finite), there is only a limited switch in consumer demand from imports to import substitutes. In the case of perfect competition, the switch is total, which is why the price of import substitutes rises by the same amount as the price of imports. The vertical distance between the two demand curves in Figure 2.3(a) represents the amount of the tariff, TP_0, showing that the price of import substitutes has risen by less than the price of imports. It follows that consumers suffer a welfare loss from both a rise in the price of import substitutes (P_1P_0) and a rise in the price of imports (TP_2). This will be less than in the orthodox model. On the other hand, domestic producers enjoy less of an increase in producers' surplus. Diagrammatically, the loss to consumers is given by areas E + F of which area E represents increased government revenues. So the net loss of welfare is area F which is equal to areas C + D in 2.3(a). (In Figure 2.3(a) the total loss to consumers is areas A + B + C + D of which A and B go either to producers or to the government leaving a net loss of areas C plus D.) Mathematically, the formula for measuring the welfare loss can be written as either:

Net welfare loss = $0.5TP_2(Q_2 - Q_3)$

or

Net welfare loss = $0.5TP_0(Q_0 - Q_1)$.

On the other hand, it has been demonstrated that, in such industries, the effect of a tariff reduction is to lead to more intra-industry trade (the simultaneous export and import of products belonging to the same industry). The welfare gains from intra-industry specialisation come in the form of an increased variety of goods for consumers to choose from rather than lower prices (see Greenaway, 1982; Greenaway and Milner, 1986.) Greenaway and Milner (1986) define the 'pure' gains from intra-industry trade as resulting from 'the ability [of international trade] to permit some consumers to locate closer to their ideal variety than under autarky' (p. 151). These gains need be no less than the gains which result from increased inter-industry trade. However, they are less amenable to measurement and will not be fully estimated by the conventional approach. On the other hand, intra-industry trade may lead to price reductions if the advantages of longer production runs and the stimulus of increased competition lead to lower costs. It is now a well-attested feature of many differentiated goods industries that production typically takes place under conditions of increasing returns (decreasing unit costs). Intra-industry trade in such goods makes possible longer production runs and thereby fuller exploitation of such scale economies. If trade also increases competition, these cost savings will be passed on in lower prices.

Imperfections in factor markets may also modify some of the above analysis. Where factor markets are imperfect, short-run adjustment problems may result. If factor markets were perfect, resources released from import-competing industries as a result of tariff cuts would be immediately re-employed in newer expanding industries. Two general sources of market imperfection may be identified. Firstly, impediments to both the occupational and geographical mobility of labour segment the labour market such that workers displaced from the import-competing sector cannot immediately be re-employed in the expanding sector. This results in a bigger decline in the wages of workers employed in the import-competing sector than would have occurred otherwise. Secondly, the failure of wage-rates to fall sufficiently to ensure that those seeking work match the number of workers firms are prepared to take on at the going rate. This results in large-scale structural unemployment. In these cases, trade expansion results in short-run private and social adjustment costs which may with difficulty be estimated. These will take the form of both declining capital values and wage-rates in the import-competing industry and the costs to individuals and society of higher transitional unemployment. These short-run adjustment costs may need to be deducted from the static welfare gains accruing from tariff reductions if the true gain from reducing tariffs is to be properly estimated. On the other hand, as Banks and Tumlir (1986) have convincingly argued, many of these so-called 'costs' are not costs in the strict economic meaning of the word. A cost is only a cost if it cannot be avoided. Since many of the so-called 'adjustment costs' arise from avoidable imperfections in the market, it remains questionable whether they should be so regarded. For example, governments can facilitate speedier adjustment by reforming the labour market in such a way as to ensure that wage-rates more fully reflect the demand–supply balance at any given time. However, where adjustment costs have been taken into account in empirical studies of the costs of protection, they have not generally been found sufficient to offset the potential gain from tariff liberalisation (for example, see Cable, 1981).

Attempts at estimating the static welfare loss from tariffs have found it to be much smaller than is often thought to be the case. Equally, estimations of the welfare gain likely to result from eliminating or reducing tariffs have found this to be quite small. This is not altogether very surprising given the reduced importance of tariffs as a barrier to trade. Moreover, the static welfare gain from a lowering of tariffs captures only the immediate gain to countries resulting from an improved allocation of global resources. It takes no account of the longer-run dynamic gains which may be more important. As stated above, these are likely to be especially important where tariff reductions lead to increased intra-industry specialisation. They take the form of lower average costs resulting from both an expansion of the market facing exporters and cost savings brought about in response to increased competition. Whereas the static gains affect only the proportion of output which is traded, the dynamic gains are spread over the entire output of the firm or industry in question and are therefore potentially much greater. A particularly important aspect of the gain from lower tariffs is the guarantee which it gives to exporters that improved market access is permanent. This is especially the case where countries bind tariffs at a particular level. The assurance that tariffs will not be raised may encourage exporters to undertake costly investment in increased capacity which they might otherwise have considered too risky. Not only will such increased investment generate faster growth in the world economy as a whole, it should also bring further cost savings as efficient low-cost producers expand at the expense of less efficient high-cost competitors. Through this process of intensified competition, an important restructuring process may take place in which substantial high-cost excess capacity is eliminated, yielding significant cost savings (see Owen, 1983).

REASONS FOR COUNTRIES TO IMPOSE TARIFFS

If tariffs impose costs on countries, why do countries impose tariffs? There are several possible explanations. Firstly, governments often act irrationally because they are ill informed. In brief, they act in ignorance of the damage which tariffs are inflicting on the country. Mistakenly, they believe tariffs to be beneficial to the economy as a whole. Although not an implausible explanation, it lacks credibility. Governments employ advisers, who include professionally trained economists. It would seem improbable that governments could remain ignorant of the costs of tariff protection for very long. Some other motive must therefore exist. One possibility is the existence of some other noneconomic benefit which is considered sufficiently important to justify the economic cost. Governments pursue many objectives which are not part of the economists' calculus. This is undoubtedly a reason for many of the tariffs which governments impose. An example is the tariff protection given to an industry deemed to be of vital strategic importance to the country (such as a tariff on imported steel products). Another example is tariff protection granted so as to raise the relative incomes of a particular sector or social group (such as farmers) thought to be at special disadvantage. Economists cannot comment on whether governments should or should not pursue such objectives. However, they can point to the costs of doing so and insist that these be set against any expected benefit. Moreover, they can ask whether a tariff is the best way of achieving the objectives being sought. There might be other policy instruments (for example, a subsidy) which could achieve the intended objective more efficiently or at less cost.

31

Yet a third reason for tariffs is the possibility that they bring some *economic* gain which more than offsets the static welfare loss measured by the conventional model. Attention has already been drawn to the optimum tariff argument although it was argued that this has rather limited practical application.

There are at least two other situations in which a tariff might conceivably be beneficial. In the first, the market for a product is imperfectly competitive such that firms are able to earn supernormal profits in the long run. A tariff might then be used to 'shift' profits from foreign firms to domestic firms and therefore from the exporting to the importing country (see Brander and Spencer, 1981, 1984; Krugman, 1986). Such profit-shifting or 'rent-snatching' tariffs may enable the tariff-imposing country to raise its economic welfare at the expense of others. This is similar to the optimum tariff argument set out above. Like the optimum tariff, the argument holds only under certain fairly restrictive assumptions (see Grossman, 1986). Its application is confined to so-called 'strategic' industries dominated by a few sellers and in which entry barriers limit the potential for new firms to enter the industry and compete away excess long-run profits. There is the further problem of selecting or 'targeting' the right industries to protect. High long-run profits may be a return for greater risk rather than an indication that competition is absent. Moreover, in most cases a tariff is inferior to a subsidy as a method for supporting such an industry. This is because a subsidy does not raise the price of the imported good and therefore inflicts no consumption loss on the importing country. Finally, as with the optimum tariff, there is a danger that a profit-shifting tariff will provoke foreign retaliation, leaving both countries worse off.

The second situation is where significant 'externalities' exist which do not enter into the private cost–benefit calculation of the orthodox model. This will be the case where the growth of the protected industry has important spillover effects on other sectors of the economy, such as high-technology, knowledge-intensive industries that generate knowledge which can be shared with other branches or sectors. For example, there are strong linkages of this kind between the various branches of the electronics industry, such as consumer electronics and electronic components, which might be used to justify protection. On the other hand, as with the preceding case, a tariff is nearly always inferior to a subsidy if such protection is considered desirable. Even then, there is a problem in determining the optimal level of subsidy since the excess of social over private return is not easily quantifiable. The case of a newly established or infant industry in a developing country constitutes a further extension of this argument. Once again, the preference must be for a subsidy rather than a tariff.

A fourth reason why tariffs are imposed is that a sudden surge of imports can cause serious adjustment problems for the importing country.

Adjustment difficulties arise because of imperfections in both product and factor markets. If markets were perfect, a sudden surge of imports need not cause any problem for an importing country. Resources would instantly shift out of the declining sector and into the expanding sectors of the economy with little or no cost. To the extent that the exchange rate is free to find its own level, it will fall as a consequence of the rise in imports and this depreciation will lead to an expansion of exports. If the declining sector were more labour-intensive than the expanding sector such that the number seeking work exceeded jobs available, a relative decline in the wage-rate would ensure that the labour market cleared. In reality, market imperfections mean that full adjustment only takes place in the long run. A temporary import tariff may buy time for the importing country to enable adjustment to take place. On the other hand, a tariff could equally well forestall adjustment, if the tariff is retained beyond the time needed. Moreover, an import tariff is no substitute for the importing country adopting adjustment measures to facilitate the necessary shift of resources. These may include removing particular types of market imperfection which prevent adjustment from taking place.

Although tariffs may be imposed for economic reasons other than those listed above, most of these are much less soundly based. For example, most tariffs imposed to protect domestic producers from low-wage competitors in other countries have no rational economic justification. This is because low wage-rates are frequently offset by low labour productivity. Even if labour costs per unit of ouput are lower, tariffs merely serve to prevent specialisation taking place based on differences in comparative costs. Tariffs imposed for this reason are therefore based on ignorance. Alternatively, they are a response to pressures exerted by particular vested interest groups in the importing country which have succeeded in winning over the government of the day. The desire to placate the producers or workers employed in a particular industry faced with more intense foreign competition overrides the interests of the country as a whole. Many examples of this can be found. Much of the agricultural protection which the advanced industrialised countries grant to their farmers is the result of governments yielding to political pressures, disregarding the cost to the country as a whole. In some countries, farmers have a political influence which is disproportionate to their numerical weight in the population. Recently, economists have shown considerable interest in exploring this political dimension to making tariff policy. This has taken the form of attempts to construct politico-economic models of tariff determination. For example, Frey (1984, 1985) has explained how tariff policy is formulated in a political market place in which there exist opposing forces for and against protection. Because tariffs benefit some groups of society, albeit at the expense of the rest, there will always be some with interests who favour protection. Usually, these will be producers and workers in the import-competing industries. Opponents of tariff protection will comprise consumers and exporting firms who face higher costs from tariff protection. However, generally speaking, pro-tariff interests are better organised and therefore better able to influence the decision-making process. Furthermore, while the gain to society as a whole from free trade generally exceeds the loss to producers/workers in the import-competing industry, the societal benefit is diffuse while the loss to producers/workers in the import-competing industry is highly concentrated. When expressed per head, the benefit to consumers or buyers of the product from free trade may be quite small, while the loss to producers/workers in the import-competing industry will be quite large. It follows that pro-tariff groups may have a greater incentive to resist tariff reductions than anti-tariff groups have to strive for them. Thus, tariffs may be retained simply because political pressures make it difficult or impossible to remove them. Significantly, some empirical studies have found that conservatism is the major factor influencing the structure of tariff rates between industries (Lavergne, 1983).

THE STRUCTURE OF TARIFFS

Although the average level of industrial tariffs has fallen significantly in recent decades, the average level of a country's tariffs can be deceptive in concealing a highly protectionist tariff *structure*. Indeed, a country's tariff structure may become more protectionist at the same time as the average level of tariffs falls. This is because of the phenomenon of *tariff escalation*. Tariff escalation occurs whenever the nominal rate of tariff applied to a particular industry increases with the stage of production or degree of fabrication. The more nearly finished the product, the higher the level of tariff imposed.

Table 2.1 gives some examples of tariff escalation. It shows the average tariff calculated from the trade-weighted tariffs of ten major developed countries and twenty-one developing countries at each stage of the processing chain for a selection of commodities. Because a high proportion of the exports of developing countries are concentrated in unprocessed primary commodities, they face higher tariff barriers when exporting to the developed countries than the average rate of tariff might suggest. It follows too that reductions in nominal rates of tariff will be of little benefit to developing countries unless the degree of tariff escalation is also lowered. It should be noted that the tariff structures of developing countries also escalate.

A further consequence of tariff escalation is that it creates a disincentive for developing countries to invest in processing capacity. For example, on the figures given in Table 2.1, a major sugar exporter such as Mauritius faces a 20.0 per cent tariff if she exports refined sugar but only a 1.0 per cent tariff if she exports raw sugar. It is often argued that the effect of tariff escalation is

Table 2.1 Average tariffs applied by major developed and developing countries at different stages in the processing of various product groups

Processing chain	Developed country (%)	Developing country (%)
Meat		
Fresh and frozen meat	6.2	6.6
Prepared meat	8.4	21.9
Fish		
Fresh and frozen fish	4.3	10.9
Fish preparations	4.1	30.1
Vegetables		
Fresh vegetables	6.9	16.6
Vegetable preparations	13.2	26.9
Fruit		
Fresh fruit	7.4	17.0
Fruit preparations	17.1	11.1
Vegetable oils		
Oilseeds	0.0	18.1
Vegetable oils	4.4	26.5
Tobacco		
Unmanufactured	1.2	126.0
Manufactures	18.1	662.1
Sugar		
Sugar and honey	1.0	23.5
Sugar preparations	20.0	24.3
Cocoa		
Beans, powder & paste	1.0	11.6
Chocolate and products	3.0	29.7
Rubber		
Crude rubber	0.0	7.2
Rubber manufacture	3.9	19.4
Leather		
Hides and skins	0.1	4.8
Leather	2.9	17.5
Leather articles	7.2	33.9
Wood		
Wood, rough	0.0	8.0
Wood, shaped	0.3	13.1
Veneer and plywood	1.7	23.5
Wood manufactures	3.5	27.6
Cotton		
Raw cotton	0.0	3.2
Cotton yarn	3.0	29.7
Cotton fabrics	5.8	32.1
Iron		
Iron ore	0.0	2.6
Pig iron	2.2	7.4
Ingots and shapes	2.2	12.1
Bars and plates	3.4	19.9

Processing chain	Developed country (%)	Developing country (%)
Other metallic ores		
Ores, nonferrous	0.0	4.1
Wrought and unwrought metals	2.4	18.2
Phosphates		
Natural phosphates	0.0	12.8
Phosphatic fertiliser	3.2	9.4
Petroleum		
Crude petroleum	0.5	5.1
Refined petroleum	1.0	12.8

Source: Finger and Olechowski (1987)

to shut developing countries into an export structure that is heavily dependent on unprocessed primary commodities. Does this matter? It may do so if trade in unprocessed primary commodities grows at a slower rate than that of processed commodities.

It is also frequently argued that that the prices of primary commodities have a long-run tendency to fall relative to those of manufactured goods. This argument was first put forward by Raul Prebish (1950) and H. Singer (1950). In fact, the empirical evidence for this proposition is mixed. Moreover, even if there is such a tendency at work, it is by no means clear that it should result in a welfare loss for developing countries because not all primary producers are developing countries and not all developing countries are primary producers. Another concern arises from the high volatility of primary commodity prices. Over-dependence on a few primary commodities for export earnings could mean that developing countries face a highly unstable balance of payments. This may further jeopardise long-run economic growth. It should be noted that fluctuations in primary commodity prices will only result in unstable export earnings if the prices of different export commodities are positively correlated. If, however, they are negatively correlated, a fall in the price of one commodity might be offset by a rise in the price of another with no adverse effect on the stability of export earnings. It should be pointed out that, even if the nominal tariff were the same at each stage of processing, the tariff structure of developed countries might still create a bias against processing, because of differences in the elasticities of demand for products at different stages of processing. If the elasticity of demand for the finished product is higher than for the semi-finished product or raw material, then the same rate of nominal tariff will have a greater effect on the demand for the finished product than for the semi-finished product or raw material. There is some evidence that demand elasticities increase with fabrication, so nominal tariffs would need to be lower at the final stages of processing to avoid any distortion to trade (Yeats, 1987).

One way of measuring the importance of tariff escalation is to make use of the theory of the *effective rate of protection*, put forward by the Australian economist Max Corden (see Corden, 1971). According to this theory, where tariff structures escalate, the *nominal rate of protection* underestimates the true level of protection enjoyed by a domestic industry. The latter is best measured by estimating the effects of the *entire* tariff structure of a country on the value added by the domestic industry. Value added is basically the difference between a producer's sales and purchases of goods during the period in question. It must not be confused with profit, since, out of value added, the producer must meet all other costs and pay a profit to shareholders. The tariff structure of a country will affect the value added of a protected industry in two ways: firstly, a tariff on the producer's finished product will enable him to sell his product for a higher price; secondly, a tariff on intermediate products will raise the costs of materials used in the production process. The effective rate of protection takes account of both tariffs.

The formula for calculating the effective rate of protection is:

$$Te = (V_1 - V)/V \times 100$$

where V is the value added per unit of output without tariffs and V_1 is the value added per unit of output with tariffs. Suppose that a producer imports materials to the value of £100,000 in one quarter. The value of sales of the finished product are £150,000 so value added is £150,000 − £100,000 = £50,000. Now suppose that an import tariff is imposed on both the finished product and the materials but that the tariff on the finished good is higher than the tariff on materials. Suppose a tariff of 20 per cent is imposed on imports of the finished good but of only 10 per cent on imports of the intermediate product. The effect of the tariff on the finished good is to enable the producer to raise the price by 20 per cent, increasing the value of his sales to £180,000. However, the tariff on intermediate goods raises the cost of these goods to £110,000. His value added now becomes £180,000 − £110,000 = £70,000. Using the formula above, the effective rate of protection is:

$$Te = (7,000 - 5,000)/5,000 \times 100$$
$$= 2,000/5,000 \times 100$$
$$= 40\%$$

The nominal rate of protection, which was only 20 per cent, gives a misleading impression because it fails to take account of tariff escalation. By focusing on the effects of a country's whole tariff sructure on the value added of the protected industry, the effective rate of protection demonstrates the full extent of the protection given by tariffs to the producers.

Whenever tariffs escalate, the effective rate of protection will be positive and higher than the nominal rate of protection. If tariffs raise the cost of an industry's inputs by more than the rise in the price of its output, the effective rate of protection could be negative. Such cases do arise, such as in a developing country pursuing an import-substitution strategy which involves high tariffs on imported intermediate goods but no tariff on the finished good.

Table 2.2 gives some estimates of the effective rate of protection in certain developed countries for various processed commodities. The estimates show very high levels of effective protection for certain product groups – notably, tobacco manufactures (EC and Japan), processed meat products (EC and Japan), vegetable oils (EC and Japan), coffee extracts (EC and Japan), preserved fruits (EC and US), processed vegetables (EC), chocolate (Japan) and wool fabrics (US). In low value-added products such as vegetable oils, effective tariffs have been estimated to be some eight times nominal tariffs (Yeats, 1987).

The concept of effective protection may be widened further to take into account the effects of nontariff barriers. Where nontariff barriers exist on

Table 2.2 Estimates of the effective rate of protection for selected processed commodities in certain developed countries

Processed commodity	EC (%)	Japan (%)	United States (%)
Processed meat products	51.7	59.6	4.4
Preserved sea food	26.5	23.2	2.5
Preserved fruits	40.8	21.6	72.5
Processed vegetables	37.9	40.2	20.2
Coffee extracts	45.5	76.6	0.0
Chocolate	*	82.6	0.1
Wood manufactures	9.2	1.3	10.3
Paper and paperboard	5.5	13.7	0.7
Articles of paper	12.6	0.7	8.7
Rubber manufactures	4.5	1.1	–0.4
Cotton yarn	7.6	13.7	18.3
Wool yarn	1.1	14.0	18.1
Jute yarn	7.2	19.8	4.7
Cotton fibres	11.8	10.0	13.5
Wool fabrics	5.1	25.3	85.8
Jute fabrics	10.0	5.3	*
Leather	6.0	21.2	8.1
Leather manufactures	9.9	18.6	17.5
Vegetable oils	50.6	49.6	–1.5
Tobacco manufactures	117.4	156.0	9.4

Source: Yeats (1987)

Note: * No effective tariff rate is given since the ratio of the input to the final product tariff could not be computed.

both the final product of an industry and intermediate products used by the industry, the industry's value added is affected. For example, an import quota or voluntary export restraint (see Chapter 3) increases the price of the restricted product in the importing country in much the same way as a tariff. Similarly, a domestic subsidy may reduce costs to a domestic producer or increase the value of output sold. When all these factors are taken into account, an estimate known as the 'effective rate of assistance' (ERA) is obtained. In practice, it may be difficult to obtain the information needed to estimate the ERA for every product although plausible guesses can often be made. However, where the ERA can be measured, it constitutes a better measure of the true rate of protection enjoyed by an industry for the purposes of trade negotiation.

TARIFF-CUTTING THROUGH THE GATT

There are two ways in which a country may reduce tariffs: unilaterally or reciprocally through negotiation. It is often thought that unilateral tariff-cutting must be harmful to a country. If one country cuts its tariffs, the argument goes, it will surely experience an increase in imports and a decrease in domestic production and employment. If, on the other hand, it enters into an agreement with one or more countries through which tariffs are cut reciprocally, any increase in imports can be matched by an increase in exports. The argument is of course a false one. Unilateral tariff-cutting will always benefit a country for the reasons set out above. Of course, output and employment will fall in the import-competing sectors. However, because other countries are now exporting more goods to the tariff-cutting country, incomes in the rest of the world will rise and as a result their imports from the tariff-cutting country should also increase. To the extent that the imports of the tariff-cutting country exceed its exports, the exchange rate will fall, making its exports more competitive in world markets and its imports less competitive until equilibrium is restored. Only if the exchange rate is kept rigidly fixed will any problem arise.

Nevertheless, few countries have been willing to cut their tariffs unilaterally. One reason may be opposition from vested-interest groups who stand to lose from tariff reduction. It is likely that producers and workers in the protected import-competing sector will resist any reduction in the level of protection hitherto enjoyed. On the other hand, if tariff cuts are presented as a price paid to gain equivalent concessions in the markets of other countries, it may be possible for the government to play off pro-trade forces in the export sector against the antitrade groups in the import-competing sector. This would favour the multilateral negotiated approach. Moreover, tariffs are often seen by governments as bargaining counters which can be used to prise open foreign markets for the country's exporting industries. Governments are reluctant to throw away a valuable bargaining weapon. Instead, they seek something in return for any tariff cut which they may contemplate making. This is the basis on which the GATT has operated. Countries trade tariff cuts in return for equivalent 'concessions' granted by other countries. Under the GATT, countries agree to meet periodically for the purpose of negotiating reciprocal and mutually beneficial reductions in their tariffs. These take place in the so-called 'rounds'.

The procedure adopted is that countries provide schedules listing tariffs to be bound: that is, the country concerned agrees not to levy a tariff in excess of the rate stipulated in the tariff schedule. Concessions take the form of either adding products to the list of tariffs to be bound or binding tariffs at lower rates than before. In the early rounds of the GATT, tariff bindings were relatively more important than actual tariff cuts. However, once most tariffs had been bound, subsequent concessions took the form of tariff reductions. A tariff binding is no less important to an exporting country than a tariff cut. By assuring the exporter that a tariff will not be unilaterally raised, it enables that exporter to make investment plans based on the certainty that existing terms of access to the foreign market are guaranteed. However, a tariff binding does not mean that the listed tariff can never be increased. Two procedures do permit an increase in a bound tariff. Firstly, under Article XXVIII, every three years a contracting party can at so-called 'open seasons' renegotiate any scheduled concession although it will be required to offer compensation in the form of equivalent concessions to other countries adversely affected. Alternatively, if it cannot wait that long, it may invoke Article XIX, the so-called Escape or Safeguards Clause, which allows a tariff to be increased when a sudden surge of imports is causing or threatening serious injury to domestic producers. Once again, it must, if necessary, offer compensation in the form of equivalent concessions to any other country thereby harmed.

It is possible for countries to negotiate tariff reductions on a bilateral or multilateral basis. Before the GATT, most negotiated tariff cuts took place on a bilateral basis. When negotiations are bilateral, it is usually not possible to achieve as rapid a reduction in tariffs as when negotiations are multilateral. This is because of the 'principal supplier constraint'. The tariff reductions offered by a country in the course of a negotiation will necessarily be confined to those products for which the country with whom she is negotiating is the principal supplier. If countries apply the principle of nondiscrimination (that is, most-favoured-nation treatment), any tariff reduction offered by one country to another must automatically be extended to all other countries which enjoy MFN status. Therefore, offering tariff cuts on products for which the other country is not the principal supplier would mean throwing away a potential negotiating counter in subsequent negotiations with third countries. For example, if Country A concedes to Country B a large tariff reduction on a product for which

Country C is the principal supplier, Country A would have given up a valuable bargaining counter in any subsequent negotiation with Country C. For these reasons, progress in cutting tariffs was slow before the GATT came into being.

By contrast, tariff negotiations through the GATT are multilateral. Countries may still negotiate with each other on a bilateral basis but these negotiations will take place simultaneously and within a multilateral framework. Likewise, the results of any tariff negotiated between any pair of countries are multilaterally applied. The most-favoured-nation rule requires that any tariff cut offered by one country to another is automatically extended to all other countries. Thus, the GATT makes possible both multilateral negotiations and the multilateral application of any concessions made. Such an approach permits much more rapid progress in cutting tariffs. In particular, it overcomes the principal supplier constraint which dogged the bilateral approach. Since Country A is negotiating simultaneously with both Countries B and C, it need not hold back in offering tariff cuts to Country B on products for which Country C is the principal supplier. A tariff cut on such products will first be offered to Country C and, if accepted, then subsequently extended to Country B in such a way as to maximise bargaining power in the two sets of negotiations.

An important issue concerns the method of tariff bargaining to be employed. In the first five rounds of the GATT, the approach adopted was an item-by-item or request-and-offer one. Negotiations took the form of countries submitting requests for tariff cuts on individual products followed by offers of cuts on others. This followed the procedure adopted in most prewar bilateral trade negotiations. Such an approach has a number of disadvantages. Firstly, it creates opportunities for special-interest groups in importing countries to argue that they are being treated unfairly and thereby to apply pressure opposing tariff reductions. Secondly, where different tariff cuts are being made on different products, it is more difficult for negotiators to work out the multilateral balance of concessions offered and received. This slows down the negotiation process and may make agreement more difficult to reach. For these reasons, a new linear across-the-board approach was adopted in the sixth round. The method was simply to seek agreement on a certain rate of tariff reduction to be applied across the board to most products. Each nation was allowed to submit a list of exceptions. However, once the rate of linear reduction was agreed, further negotiations need only cover the issue of exceptions. In the Kennedy Round, the formula was a 50 per cent reduction in duties on all manufactured goods with exceptions for sensitive goods including steel, clothing, textiles and footwear.

A weakness of the linear approach used in the Kennedy Round was that it applies the same rate of cut to high-tariff as to low-tariff products. This favours countries with an uneven tariff structure. Thus, in the seventh round, the EC, which had a fairly level Common External Tariff (CET), argued against a simple linear formula which, it was argued, suited the United States with its many tariff peaks and valleys. Instead, a lengthy search took place for a formula which would ensure that high tariffs were cut by more than low tariffs. What emerged was a complex formula proposed by Switzerland which involved a compromise between the two approaches:

$$T_1 = aT_0/(a + T_0)$$

where T_0 is the initial tariff rate, T_1 is the tariff rate after the reduction and a is a coefficient which can take any value greater than zero. Suppose that the coefficient is fixed at 16. If the initial tariff is 10 per cent, the new tariff will be $(16 \times 10)/(16 + 10) = 6.15$ per cent. If, however, the initial tariff is 50 per cent, the new tariff would be $(16 \times 50)/(16 + 50) = 12.12$ per cent. The tariff reduction is greater in the latter case (76 per cent) than in the former (39 per cent). Negotiations were concerned with the size of the coefficient to apply for each country. This may be contrasted with a simple linear formula:

$$T_1 = aT_0$$

where $(1 - a)$ is the percentage reduction in tariffs. For example, using the linear formula, a 50 per cent tariff cut means that a 10 per cent tariff becomes a tariff of 5 per cent.

Table 2.3 summarises the eight trade negotiating rounds of the GATT which have taken place since 1947. Each round of the GATT has tended to follow a renewal of the tariff-cutting authority of the US President. The reason for this is that no meaningful negotiations are possible without a willingness of the United States, as the world's largest trading nation, to negotiate. This is only possible if Congress is willing to grant the President the requisite authority. The significance of this authority is that any agreement which the President enters into can only be accepted or rejected in its entirety when it comes before Congress for ratification. Congress is not empowered to amend any particular part of the agreement. Were it able to do so, any tariff cuts made by the President in the course of negotiations would lack credibility and therefore limit the concessions other countries were prepared to make to the US. This authority is only ever for a fixed period of time and so, when the old authority expires, new authority must be sought. Moreover, the extent of any authority granted, as well as any qualifications added, are important in determining how much the President can offer in any round. In all, the level of industrial tariffs was reduced from an average of 40 per cent in 1945 to 4.7 per cent after the completion of the Tokyo Round. The recently concluded Uruguay Round further reduced industrial tariffs by an average of more than one-third.

As measured by the reduction in tariffs achieved, the first and sixth rounds were the most important of the earlier rounds. The Tokyo Round achieved a similar level of tariff cut while the recent Uruguay Round has

Table 2.3 The trade negotiating rounds of the GATT, 1947–94

Round	Date	No. of countries	Value of trade covered (US$bn)	Average tariff cut (%)	Average tariffs afterwards (%)
Geneva	1947	23	10	35	n.a.
Annecy	1949	33	n.a.		n.a.
Torquay	1950	34	n.a.		n.a.
Geneva	1956	22	2.5		n.a.
Dillon	1960–1	45	4.9		n.a.
Kennedy	1962–7	48	40	35	8.7
Tokyo	1973–9	99	155	34	4.7
Uruguay	1986–93	117	464	38	2.9

Source: Updated from Jackson (1992)

gone even further in this respect. The *first round* at Geneva in 1947 took place under the US tariff-cutting authority of 1945, which empowered the President to make tariff reductions of up to 50 per cent of the rates in force on 1 January 1945. The greatest concessions were made by the United States. The US was keen to gain the accession of other countries to the GATT, and therefore prepared to make significant concessions. These affected some 78 per cent of her total imports and over two-thirds involved bindings of tariffs. Tariff reductions averaged 35 per cent of the *ad valorem* rate and affected 56 per cent of dutiable imports (Finger and Olechowski, 1987). No new tariff-cutting authority was granted by Congress to the US President until 1955, but the 1945 authority was extended both in 1948 and 1951. The 1945 authority was however sufficient to permit two further GATT rounds. The *second round* at Annecy in 1949 was largely concerned with the accession of new contracting parties, of which Italy was the largest. In this Round, the US gave away much less in concessions than she received. Instead, it was for the new contracting parties to make concessions in order to gain admission to the GATT. The US made concessions on only 39 per cent of her imports; 80 per cent took the form of tariff bindings. The average tariff reduction was 37 per cent but affected only 6 per cent of dutiable imports (Finger and Olechowski, 1987). The *third round* at Torquay in 1951 was also concerned with the accession of new contracting parties, West Germany being the largest country to join. This time, the US made concessions on a mere 7 per cent of her imports. The average tariff reduction was 26 per cent, affecting 15 per cent of her dutiable imports (ibid.).

In 1955, the US President was given a new tariff-cutting authority, although much less than in 1945. It was for tariff cuts of only 15 per cent of the rates applying on 1 January 1955, to be effected in three annual instalments of 5 per cent each. Moreover, the legislation contained a number of restrictive clauses which provided for increased protectionism. However, it was sufficient to cope with the main task of the *fourth round* held at Geneva in 1956. This was the accession of Japan. The United States was keen to gain the acceptance of other contracting parties to Japan becoming a new contracting party. A number were reluctant. To overcome their reluctance, the US made further concessions on 9 per cent of her total imports with an average tariff reduction of 15 per cent, affecting 20 per cent of her dutiable imports (Finger and Olechowski, 1987). Even then, fourteen out of thirty-five GATT members invoked Article XXXV which allowed them to withhold GATT treatment from Japan until they had negotiated with her themselves. It was some while before Japan was treated as a full GATT signatory.

The *fifth round*, the so-called 'Dillon Round' followed the new US tariff legislation of 1958. This authorised the President to cut tariffs by up to 20 per cent of the rates prevailing on 1 July 1958 with no more than a 10 per cent reduction in any one year. It was designed to cope with the problems arising from the formation of the new European Community in 1958. The EC was a customs union involving internal free trade plus a common external tariff. Article XXIV of the GATT allowed the formation of customs unions provided that the arithmetical average of pre-union external tariffs was no lower than the average post-union common external tariff. However, if this involved some members increasing the tariff on any of their trade with other GATT contracting parties, the latter were entitled to compensation. The EC offered a 20 per cent cut in the Common Customs Tariff although this had not come into full operation. In return, the United States offered an *ad valorem* tariff reduction of 20 per cent on 19 per cent of her dutiable imports.

The *sixth round*, the 'Kennedy Round', took place between 1964 and 1967 and followed the passage of the 1962 US Trade Expansion Act. The 1962 Act gave to the President greater authority than ever before and for a longer period to cut tariffs. The President was authorised to cut tariffs by up to 50 per cent of the rates applying on 1 July 1962 over five years. On products for which the EC and the US together accounted for 80 per cent or more of trade, tariffs could be reduced by more than 50 per cent or eliminated altogether. This envisaged the UK joining the EC, since it would have had very little application otherwise. The Trade Expansion Act was a response to the challenge posed by the formation of the EC and EFTA. Although she favoured European integration largely for political reasons, the US was afraid that the preferential nature of these two trading blocs would cause trade diversion from the US to Western Europe (see Chapter 7 for a definition and explanation of the concept of trade diversion). The Common Agricultural Policy was also seen as a threat to US agricultural trade while the proposed Common External Tariff was deemed likely to increase US investment in Europe, aggravating the US balance of payments. Unlike in earlier rounds, most of the concessions made by the US were in the form of tariff reductions rather than bindings since there were few tariffs left to bind. The average US tariff cut was 44 per cent on 64 per cent of dutiable imports (Finger and Olechowski, 1987). Unlike in the first round, the US insisted that other industrialised countries made equivalent concessions. Consequently, other countries also made substantial tariff cuts affecting an estimated 70 per cent of dutiable imports (excluding cereals, meat and dairy products). Two-thirds of the reductions were of 50 per cent or more, and around another one-fifth were between 25 and 50 per cent. In addition, some progress was made in tackling certain kinds of nontariff barriers.

In 1967, for the first time since 1947, the President's tariff-cutting authority was allowed to lapse, thus it was some while before a new round of trade negotiations could take place. There was a feeling in Congress that substantial concessions had already been made in the Kennedy Round and that no further concessions could therefore be afforded for the time being. At the same time, the worsening US balance of payments was seen as a constraint. Anxieties about the growing threat posed to US manufacturing by the emergence of the newly industrialising countries also dampened any enthusiasm for a further bout of tariff-cutting. Nevertheless, by 1974 opinion in Congress had changed. One reason for this was the challenge posed for the United States by the admission of the UK to the EC in 1973 and the enlargement of the EC from six to nine members. The US was anxious to draw the new enlarged EC back into fresh trade negotiations. The 1974 Trade Act empowered the President to make further tariff cuts of up to 40 per cent of the rate existing on 1 January 1975 over a five-year period. As under the 1962 Act, these were to be staged over five years (ten years in exceptional circumstances). However, in several respects the Act was much less liberal than that of 1962. Not only was the basic authority a smaller one, but there were many more qualifications permitting higher tariffs in certain circumstances. In particular, the Act reduced the control of the executive branch over trade policy and vested more power with Congress and the independent International Trade Commission. Since the latter two were more likely to be influenced by pro-tariff interests, the likelihood was that US trade policy would become less liberal.

Nevertheless, the *seventh round*, the Tokyo Round, did result in further significant tariff reductions. Tariffs on industrial products were cut by a weighted average of 33 per cent. The United States reduced her tariff on industrial products by a weighted average of 30 per cent, the EC by a weighted average of 28 per cent and Japan by a weighted average of 46 per cent (GATT, 1979a). These were to be implemented over eight years commencing on 1 January 1980. This increase in the staging of tariff cuts in comparison with previous rounds clearly weakened the impact of the final agreement. Moreover, by the time the Tokyo Round took place, tariffs had become much less important than nontariff barriers. Although some progress was made in confronting this problem, the agreements reached fell a long way short of what had been hoped for.

Table 2.4 sets out the average level of tariffs in leading trading countries following the completion of the Tokyo Round. The average applied tariff was generally lower than the average MFN (most-favoured-nation) tariff because of the various preferences countries granted to goods from other countries with whom they had special trading arrangements (for example, the preferences which developed countries granted to manufactures coming from developing countries). The divergence between MFN and applied rates measures the extent to which countries departed from the MFN (nondiscrimination) principle.

Table 2.5 sets out the average level of tariffs in the developed countries by product groups following the completion of the Tokyo Round. This shows a much lower level of tariffs for food and raw materials than for manufactures. The average tariff for manufactures disguises a still quite high tariff rate applied to clothing and textiles and to footwear.

THE URUGUAY ROUND

Although the agenda of the Uruguay Round was noteworthy for its inclusion of a wide range of new issues, tariffs remained an important item. The 1986 Ministerial Declaration launching the Round stated that:

Table 2.4 Post-Tokyo Round trade-weighted average MFN and applied tariffs in selected developed countries

Country	Average MFN tariff rate (%)	Average applied tariff rate (%)
United States	3.9	3.8
EEC[a]	4.2	2.5
Japan	3.5	3.0
Canada	6.5	4.5
Sweden	3.5	0.8
Norway	4.8	1.0
Switzerland	3.0	1.0
New Zealand	13.6	10.9
Austria	9.9	2.0
Finland	4.8	1.0
Australia	12.4	8.2

Source: Finger and Olechowski (1987)

Note: [a]The trade-weighted rates are based on the external trade of the EEC.

Negotiations shall aim, by appropriate methods, to reduce or, as appropriate, eliminate tariffs including the reduction or elimination of high tariffs and tariff escalation. Emphasis shall be given to the expansion of the scope of tariff concessions among all participants.

(GATT, 1986)

Thus, it was acknowledged that further progress could be made in the elimination of certain tariffs. There was to be a clear emphasis on dealing with the problem of high tariffs and tariff escalation. There was also agreement that, in contrast with previous rounds, tariff cutting should not be limited to the big developed market economies but should embrace a larger number of participants. At the 1988 Mid-term Review, four aspects of tariff liberalisation were highlighted as being necessary to address. These were tariff escalation, tariff peaks, low 'nuisance' tariffs and the need to increase the level of bindings (GATT, 1988). It was further agreed that the target should be an overall tariff reduction of 'at the minimum, the [tariff] reduction achieved by formula participants in the Tokyo Round', that the scope of tariff bindings should be widened and that special account should be taken of the needs of developing countries (GATT, 1988).

Table 2.5 Post-Tokyo Round average MFN and applied tariff rates by product group in developed countries[a]

Product group	Average MFN tariff rate (%)	Average applied tariff rate (%)
All food items	6.4	5.3
Food & live animals	6.5	5.3
Oilseeds & nuts	5.3	4.0
Animals & veg. oils	0.1	0.2
Agricultural raw materials	0.8	0.5
Ores & metals	2.3	1.5
Iron & steel	5.1	3.4
Nonferrous metals	2.3	1.3
Fuels	1.1	0.6
Chemicals	5.8	3.1
Manufactures (excluding chemicals)	7.0	7.9
Leather	5.1	11.9
Textile yarn & fabrics	11.7	9.0
Clothing	17.5	3.3
Footwear	13.4	3.0

Source: Finger and Olechowski (1987)

Note: [a]Developed countries comprise Australia, Austria, Canada, EC, Finland, Japan, Norway, New Zealand, Sweden, Switzerland and the United States.

A key issue was the method of tariff-cutting to be used. The majority of countries, including those in the EC, favoured a formula approach similar to that used in the Tokyo Round. This, however, was opposed by the US at an early stage. At the commencement of negotiations, the US showed reluctance to make large tariff reductions, arguing that it was now the turn of other countries to do so. At the same time, she made clear a preference for a request-and-offers approach alongside so-called reciprocal zero-for-zero deals in particular sectors. The latter entailed countries agreeing on sectors in which tariffs could be totally eliminated. However, the EC was not prepared to include many sectors in the zero-for-zero deals unless the US offered more cuts in its high tariffs, particularly on textiles and other sensitive products. The US zero-for-zero list initially included pharmaceuticals, construction machinery, medical equipment, steel (subject to reaching a multilateral agreement providing for the elimination of state subsidies), paper and wood products, nonferrous metals, electronics, fish and alcoholic drinks. Also, she proposed that tariffs on chemicals be harmonised at very low levels. The EC was strongly opposed to eliminating tariffs on electronic goods since EC chip manufacturers enjoyed a 14 per cent tariff on semiconductors (see *The Financial Times*, 18 December 1992). Disagreement between the US and the EC created a hurdle to completing the market-access negotiations as other participants were unwilling to make offers without the two major trading blocs establishing the essential framework.

A breakthrough was achieved by the so-called Quad countries (US, EU, Japan and Canada) at the Tokyo economic summit in July 1993. A market-access package emerged which found common ground in the face of the seeming deadlock which existed between US and EU positions. It was agreed that tariffs should be completely eliminated on pharmaceuticals, construction equipment, medical equipment, steel, beer, furniture (subject to certain exceptions), farm equipment and spirits. Tariffs on chemicals would be harmonised at low levels. Tariffs on 'high tariff' products (carrying tariffs of 15 per cent or more) would be cut by up to 50 per cent, including textiles. Tariff cuts averaging at least one-third would be made on all other products. The latter included wood, paper and pulp, and scientific equipment which the US had originally earmarked for zero-for-zero tariff treatment (see *The Financial Times*, 9 July 1993). Throughout the autumn immediately preceding the conclusion of the Round, disagreements between the Quad countries continued to threaten the final agreement. The average tariff cut of only 26 per cent being offered by the EU was generally considered to be inadequate and certainly below that offered by other countries. On the other hand, the US was accused of offering 50 per cent tariff cuts on only one-half the tariff peaks identified as included in the July agreement. Instead, the US offered more zero-for-zero tariff deals, including electronics. Japan was also criticised for offering 50 per cent reductions on fewer than one-half of her tariff peaks (see *The Financial Times*, 13 October 1993).

As the 15 December deadline for reaching agreement on tariff reductions approached, it became clear that a line-by-line tariff-cutting agreement could not be achieved. Instead, the plan was to finalise an agreement on tariff cuts for about fifteen to twenty countries which collectively accounted for the bulk of world trade. The main elements of the Final Agreement were reported in *The Financial Times* (16 December 1993) as:

1 *Tariff bindings.* The proportion of trade in industrial products subject to bound tariffs was to be increased from 78 per cent to 97 per cent in developed countries and from 21 per cent to 65 per cent in developing countries.

2 *Extent of tariff reductions.* Tariffs were to be reduced on an estimated US$464 billion-worth of imports of industrial products of developed countries out of a total of US$612 billion worth not already tariff free.

3 *Tariff elimination.* Tariffs were to be eliminated on a wide range of goods, bringing the proportion of tariff-free developed country imports to 43 per cent. The major trading nations agreed to eliminate tariffs on all products listed for zero-for-zero treatment at the July summit plus wood and paper products, toys and some fish products.

4 *Tariff cuts.* A trade-weighted average reduction of 38 per cent was to be made in the tariffs of developed countries from 6.3 per cent to 3.9 per cent. Table 2.6 summarises the overall tariff-cutting results of the Round. The US and EU agreed that tariffs on chemical products were to be harmonised at around 3 per cent. Above-average tariff cuts were made on high-tariff products including industrial electronics. The US also offered to cut tariffs on certain textiles and some glass and ceramic products. In general, tariff cuts on textiles and clothing were proportionately smaller than on other industrial products.

5 *Agricultural tariffs.* Tariff equivalents on agricultural imports were also to be subject to a 36 per cent overall reduction.

6 *Tariff escalation.* Some progress was made in reducing tariff escalation. Tariff escalation was to be eliminated for paper products, products made from jute and from tobacco, and reduced for products made from wood and metals.

There appears to be universal agreement that the tariff-cutting aspect of the Uruguay Round achieved more than looked probable at one stage. The overall reduction in tariffs was close to 40 per cent, which is more than was achieved in the Tokyo Round and more than the target of one-third set at the commencement of the Uruguay Round. The tariff cuts were of course to be staged, so the benefits will take a number of years to filter through. The staging period was six years for developed countries and ten years for developing countries, a little quicker than in the Tokyo Round. The increase in the proportion of tariffs which are now bound and the elimination of tariffs on certain products represent important gains. On the other hand,

Table 2.6 Average tariff reductions achieved in the Uruguay Round for industrial goods

| Country group | Imports from MFN origins (US$bn) | Trade-weighted average tariff (%) | | Average tariff cut (%) |
		Pre-Uruguay Round	Post-Uruguay Round	
Developed countries	736.9	6.3	3.9	38
Canada	28.4	9.0	4.8	47
EU	196.8	5.7	3.6	37
Japan	132.9	3.9	1.7	56
USA[a]	420.5	4.6	3.0	34
Developing countries[b]	305.1	15.3	12.3	20
Economies in transition	34.7	8.6	6.0	30

Source: Hoda (1994), quoted in Schott (1994)

Notes: [a]Based on data provided by USTR
[b]Based on bound rates, not applied rates

there remain a number of high tariffs in particular sectors, most notably agriculture, which remain to be tackled in subsequent rounds. The Round notably failed to bring about substantial reductions in tariff peaks, in particular in the textiles and apparel sector. With regard to the problem of tariff escalation, some progress was made in reducing the difference between tariffs applied to processed as compared with unprocessed products, and for some products tariff escalation was eliminated altogether. Although more remains to be done in reducing tariff barriers, the Uruguay Round has gone a long way to reduce further the importance of tariffs as an impediment to world trade.

CONCLUSION

Tariffs represent the oldest form of protectionism. They inflict welfare losses on importing countries although the measurable loss is small relative to total trade. Nevertheless, countries still impose tariffs. Since there are few sound economic arguments for tariffs, it follows that governments must either be pursuing some noneconomic objective or have chosen to promote the particular interests of those benefiting from protection at the expense of the common good. It follows that countries can increase economic welfare by reducing or eliminating tariffs. Since this may be more difficult to bring about unilaterally, the preferred means is to negotiate reciprocal trading agreements with other countries by which all participants simultaneously cut their tariffs. The main forum in which this has taken place over the past forty-nine years has been the GATT.

Successive rounds of multilateral tariff negotiations through the GATT have substantially reduced the importance of tariffs as a barrier to trade in industrial products. Nevertheless, it should not be concluded that tariffs no longer matter. Low average tariff levels may disguise high-tariff peaks on particular products. Moreover, tariffs can and often are raised. High rates of effective protection also mean that tariff structures may grant higher levels of protection to domestic producers than nominal rates of protection indicate. Moreover, up to the Uruguay Round, tariff reductions were largely confined to industrial products. Agricultural trade remained highly protected although mainly by nontariff measures. One significant result of the Uruguay Round is that these barriers must be converted into tariffs and then progressively lowered by amounts similar to other tariffs. This is discussed further in Chapter 6. In a similar fashion, so-called 'grey area' measures impeding trade in industrial products are to be subject to tariffication. This is discussed in the next chapter. Paradoxically, therefore, tariffs will become more important in future years as certain nontariff barriers are converted to tariffs. It follows that tariffs will remain an important issue in international trade policy in the immediate future.

3

QUANTITATIVE TRADE RESTRICTIONS AND SAFEGUARDS

INTRODUCTION

In the previous chapter, we saw that much of the success of the GATT rounds in liberalising world trade after 1947 was in the considerable reduction in the average level of industrial tariffs. One result of this appears to have been a growth of other forms of protectionism. These have taken a variety of different forms, often grouped together under the general heading of 'nontariff barriers' (NTBs). The next two chapters examine some of the most important forms of nontariff restraint on trade. In this chapter, the focus is on quantitative restrictions. Two of the most important forms are import quotas and voluntary export restraints (VERs). The latter, in particular, have come to play an increasingly important role in what is variously referred to as 'managed trade' or 'administered protectionism'. The following chapter will examine two other highly important forms of nontariff protectionism, namely antidumping policy and subsidies. These are both linked to the notion of so-called 'unfair trading'.

However, before examining the main forms of nontariff protectionism, it will be necessary to take a broader look at its nature and scope. It will be seen that there is a wide variety of different ways in which governments may grant protection to a domestic industry. It will also be apparent that many forms of government intervention in the economy have either secondary or incidental effects on trade flows. As government intervention in the economies of most countries increased in the 1960s and 1970s, the importance of nontariff distortions to trade has, not surprisingly, increased at the same time. It was not always the case that interference with trade was the primary or even secondary intention of such measures. However, as tariff barriers were being lowered at the same time, the effects of such measures on international competition could not be ignored. Moreover, to the extent that tariff rates were bound at lower levels than before, it was always tempting for a government wanting to grant protection to a domestic producer to use one or more of these measures for protectionist purposes. Indeed, it will be seen that attempts to measure both the extent and frequency of nontariff interventions in trade show that nontariff protection-ism has become more important in recent decades. This has come to be referred to as the 'New Protectionism' to distinguish it from the old-style tariff protectionism of the past.

Some of the forms of the New Protectionism such as import quotas and voluntary export restraints are potentially more damaging than tariffs. The original GATT agreement proved largely inadequate for coping with this new challenge. Furthermore, the forms of negotiation used to bring about a lowering of tariffs were generally inappropriate for dealing with nontariff barriers. One aspect of this is the difficulty of quantifying the impact of a nontariff barrier on trade. It therefore becomes impossible to negotiate balanced, reciprocal reductions in the level of NTBs in the same way as happens with tariffs. That is to say, where a country wishes to match concessions made with concessions received, there may be a problem of how to quantify the effects of any reduction in the level of a particular NTB. New approaches had to be explored. It was not until the Tokyo Round that any serious attempt was made to come to grips with the problem of nontariff barriers. The approach used was largely one of developing new codes dealing with particular types of NTBs which acted as extensions to the basic GATT agreement and to which countries had to agree to adhere. For example, in the next chapter the codes agreed to cover antidumping policy and subsidies will be discussed.

A close link exists between some types of nontariff protectionism and the GATT rules for so-called 'emergency protection'. When drafting the GATT Escape or Safeguards Clause, the intention of the architects of the GATT was to provide a route whereby countries could, in the event of an emergency, retreat from tariff concessions granted in previous negotiations. For example, if a domestic industry was threatened by a sudden surge of imports, a country may wish to raise a tariff which had been bound in the course of a previous round. Unless countries could be assured of an escape in an emergency from obligations entered into in the past, they would be unwilling to make meaningful concessions in tariff-cutting rounds. In practice, countries have often preferred to bypass the Safeguards Clause when faced with a demand from a domestic industry for protection. Instead, some form of quantitative restriction on trade has often been introduced. Many voluntary export restraint arrangements have often come into being for precisely this reason. Therefore, this chapter concludes with a discussion of the issue of safeguards and explores the debate which has surrounded the issue of its reform.

TYPES OF NONTARIFF BARRIERS

Olechowski (1987) has defined NTBs as 'all public regulations and government practices that introduce unequal treatment for domestic and foreign goods of the same or similar production'. This covers a wide variety of different forms of trade restriction, including those where the intent is to reduce imports and those which serve some other purpose but where a reduction of imports is a secondary effect. Sometimes, a distinction is drawn between *direct* and *indirect* forms of nontariff intervention to distinguish between those where the primary intent is to restrict imports (direct) and those where there exists some other purpose but where imports are nevertheless affected (indirect) (Greenaway, 1983). Sometimes, a distinction is made between *nontariff barriers* and so-called *nonborder measures* (Finger and Olechowski, 1987). A nonborder measure is any measure other than border measures (for example, a tariff or quantitative import restriction) which also affects trade (Messerlin, 1987). For instance, subsidies to domestic producers are a nonborder measure which may distort trade. The expression *managed trade* is sometimes used with reference to trade that is subject to forms of nontariff intervention (see, for example, Page, 1981). An expression frequently used to refer to the use of nontariff measures for restricting imports is *administered protection* (Bhagwati, 1988). This is useful because it emphasises that the intensity of nontariff forms of protection can usually be altered without the need for the enactment of any new legislation. By way of contrast, any change in the level of a tariff does require the prior consent of the legislature. (Yet another often-used expression is that of 'contingent protection'. This was first used by Grey, 1986, to refer to forms of protection which depend upon demonstrating that imports have caused injury to domestic producers. These include safeguard measures, which are discussed towards the end of this chapter, and antidumping policy, which is discussed in the next chapter.)

One of the problems involved in any examination of the nature of NTBs is how to classify the wide variety of different types which exist. An approach often used in the classification of NTBs is to list them according to whether trade-distortion is the primary intention of the authorities responsible. Using this approach, Walter (1972) distinguished between three types of NTBs: those with a trade-distorting intent; those with only a secondary trade-restriction intent; and those with no trade-restriction intent but with spillover effects on trade. The different types of NTBs in each category are given in Table 3.1.

For each type of NTB, a distinction is drawn between quantitatively operating measures and measures which operate through prices and costs. Thus, measures such as import quotas, voluntary export restraints or embargoes, which are clearly intended to restrict trade, operate by placing quantitative limits on imports/exports. Other measures such as variable import levies (common in agricultural trade), antidumping duties or subsidies to import competitors are also intended to restrict imports but work essentially by either raising the price of imports (variable import levies and antidumping duties) or lowering the price of domestically produced

Table 3.1 Types of nontariff barriers classified according to the normal intention of the measure

Type 1 measures (trade-distorting intent for imports)	*Type 2 measures* (secondary trade restrictive intent)	*Type 3 measures* (spillover effects on trade)
A Quantitatively operating	1 Communications media restrictions	1 Government manufacturing and distribution monopolies covering products such as armaments
1 Global import quotas	2 Quantitative advertising restrictions	2 Government structural and regional development policies
2 Bilateral import quotas		3 *Ad hoc* government balance of payments measures
3 Restrictive licensing		4 Variations in national tax schemes
4 Liberal licensing		5 Variations in national social insurance systems
5 Voluntary export restraints		6 Variations in allowable capital-depreciation methods
6 Embargoes		7 Spillovers from government-financed defence, aerospace & nonmilitary projects
7 Government procurement		8 Scale effects induced by government procurement
8 State trading practices		9 Variations in national standards, regulations and practices
9 Domestic content regulations		10 External transport charges & government-sanctioned international transport agreements
B Operating on prices/costs	1 Packaging & labelling regulations	11 Port transfer costs
1 Variable import levies	2 Health & sanitary regulations measures	
2 Advance deposit requirements	3 Safety & industrial standards	
3 Antidumping duties	4 Border tax adjustments	
4 Countervailing duties	5 User taxes & excises	
5 Subsidies to import competitors	6 Customs clearance procedures	
6 Credit restrictions on importers	7 Customs classification procedures	
7 Tax benefits for import competitors	8 Customs valuation procedures	
8 Discriminatory internal freight costs	9 Exchange restrictions	
9 International commodity agreements	10 Disclosure regulations	
10 Orderly marketing agreements	11 Government-provided entrepreneurship R&D financing & related aids for import-competing industries	

Source: Laird and Yeats (1990)

import substitutes. However, there exists a wide range of measures where a restriction of imports is not the primary intention behind the measure. Health and safety regulations are a good example of this. Foreign goods may be denied entry because they fail to meet the health and safety regulations of the importing country. Alternatively, foreign suppliers must incur additional costs to adapt their product to ensure that it does meet those regulations. Finally, there are other measures where not even the secondary intent is to restrict imports (or boost exports) but which nevertheless have spillover effects on trade. For example, government aids given to producers for the purposes of promoting structural or regional development may distort trade by lowering the costs of domestically produced import substitutes (or reducing the price of exports).

EXTENT OF NONTARIFF BARRIERS AND MEASURES

How important are NTBs as a barrier to or distortion of trade? Page (1981) sought to estimate what proportion of trade was *managed* or *controlled* and compared the results for 1980 with six years earlier. This measurement of managed trade included all international agreements such as international commodity agreements, agricultural policies of developed countries, market-sharing agreements, and so on, and purely national controls such as quotas, antidumping duties, origin rules, price controls, voluntary export restraints, and the rest. However, because of problems of identification and measurement, it excluded other national controls such as subsidies, technical, health and safety standards, customs procedures, which may be introduced for legitimate domestic reasons but which may nevertheless distort trade. Her results are shown in Table 3.2.

This shows that in 1974 40 per cent of world trade was covered by NTBs. By 1980, this had risen to nearly 48 per cent. For manufactures, nearly 13 per cent of total trade was covered by NTBs in 1974. By 1980 this had risen to nearly 24 per cent. Thus, NTBs are more important in nonmanufacturing than in manufacturing trade. However, the share of trade in manufactures covered by NTBs appears to have risen much faster over the period covered. Some interesting differences exist between countries. The proportion of the trade of the developed OECD countries (that is, western industrialised countries) subject to NTBs is generally lower than for other countries. However, especially for manufactures, the proportion rose faster for the OECD than for other countries. Although these results are not shown in Table 3.2, Page found that trade between industrialised and developing countries was more managed than trade among industrialised countries. For example, in 1979 62 per cent of OECD imports from developing countries was managed compared with only 24 per cent from other OECD countries. Similarly, 30 per cent of OECD manufacturing imports from developing countries was managed compared with 11 per cent from OECD countries (Page, 1981).

Table 3.2 Managed trade as a share of world trade, which is managed trade, by country, 1974–80 (%)

Country	All goods			Manufactures		
	1974	1979	1980	1974	1979	1980
Belgium/ Luxembourg	27.5	33.4	34.0	0.7	9.1	10.0
Denmark	29.5	42.8	43.2	0	21.1	21.7
France	32.8	42.6	42.7	0	16.0	16.2
Germany	37.3	47.1	47.3	0	17.9	18.3
Ireland	26.8	33.5	34.0	1.5	11.0	11.7
Italy	44.1	52.2	52.3	0	16.1	16.4
Netherlands	32.5	39.8	40.1	0	12.8	14.8
United Kingdom	38.5	47.4	47.9	0.2	17.0	17.4
EC (9)	35.8	44.5	44.8	0.1	15.7	16.1
Australia	17.9	34.8	34.8	7.8	30.0	30.0
Austria	20.8	30.3	30.3	0	13.1	13.1
Canada	22.4	18.3	18.3	11.4	5.8	5.8
Finland	32.9	33.6	33.6	3.1	3.5	3.5
Greece	100.0	100.0	100.0	100.0	100.0	100.0
Iceland	20.6	31.2	31.2	1.3	15.7	15.7
Japan	56.1	59.4	59.4	0	4.3	4.3
Norway	16.3	33.7	33.7	0	24.6	24.6
Portugal	25.5	27.5	27.5	10.5	11.7	11.7
Spain	32.2	52.3	52.3	0	37.1	37.1
Sweden	24.7	36.3	36.3	3.1	19.4	19.4
Switzerland	16.9	18.3	18.3	2.1	3.4	3.4
Turkey	100.0	100.0	100.0	100.0	100.0	100.0
United States	36.2	44.4	45.8	5.6	18.4	21.0
OECD (22)	36.3	43.8	44.3	4.0	16.8	17.4
Other developed (3)	97.5	97.9	97.9	97.7	97.8	97.8
Oil exporters (15)	54.0	65.3	65.3	45.8	59.8	59.8
Nonoil developing (81)	49.8	46.8	46.9	25.0	22.7	22.8
World (122)	40.1	47.5	47.8	12.9	23.0	23.6

Source: Page (1981)

Notes: Managed trade is defined as any trade that is subject to some nontariff control by exporter, importer or both.

Finger and Olechowski (1987) used two indices to measure the extent of NTBs in world trade:

1 *The import coverage ratio*: defined as the share of a country's total imports which is subject to NTBs within the total import value for a given product category.

2   *The frequency ratio*: defined as the number of import categories (i.e. tariff lines) subject to NTBs expressed as a percentage of the total number of categories.

The use of both these measures is desirable because, to a greater extent than tariffs, NTBs are discriminatory, that is, they are imposed on imports coming from a particular source (very often, the most competitive, lowest-cost supplier). Where this is the case, the frequency ratio will exceed the coverage ratio. Therefore, the extent to which they diverge measures the degree to which NTBs are discriminating against imports from particular countries. Their results are shown in Table 3.3. These show the proportion of imports coming from other developed and developing countries to fifteen developed-country markets (the EC (10), Finland, Japan, Norway, Switzerland and the United States) subject to NTBs. Using the coverage ratio, in 1984, 17 per cent of the value of imports coming from other developed countries and 19 per cent of the imports coming from developing countries were subject to NTBs. Using the frequency ratio, 11 per cent of the categories of imports coming from other developed countries and 21 per cent coming from developing countries were subject to NTBs.

Thus, NTBs affect imports from developing countries more than those from other developed countries. Overall, the figures are lower than those of Page (1981) because NTBs are defined more narrowly. The figures show that most NTBs are concentrated in four sectors: agriculture; vehicles; iron and steel; and textiles and clothing. The proportion of imports of

Table 3.3 The sectoral pattern of developed-country nontariff barriers, 1984

| | Percentage covered by NTBs | | | |
| | Value of imports from | | No. of categories from | |
Product category	Developed countries	Developing countries	Developed countries	Developing countries
All	17	19	11	21
Agricultural	44	33	42	35
Fuels and ores	18	10	13	11
Industrial	14	21	7	18
Textiles	25	62	20	58
Steel	50	46	21	21
Footwear	2	4	14	14
Electrical machines	10	7	5	8
Vehicles	30	3	6	10

Source: Finger and Olechowski (1987)

agricultural goods subject to NTBs is noticeably higher than for manufactures. (NTBs on agricultural imports coming from both developed and developing countries are high although the percentages are somewhat higher for imports from developed countries.) Within the manufacturing sector, NTBs are particularly common in the steel and textiles sectors. In textiles, this is highest for imports coming from developing countries. Finally, it is noticeable that, for imports coming from developing countries, a higher proportion of product categories are subject to NTBs than of the value of total imports. However, the reverse is true for imports from developed countries. This suggests, to a greater extent than for imports coming from other developed countries, that imports coming from developing countries are subject to NTBs which are source-specific (Finger and Olechowski, 1987).

Using the Walter (1972) typology of NTBs, Laird and Finger (1986) showed that the amount of imports of the developed countries affected by so-called 'hard-core' NTBs (Types 1 and 2 in Table 3.1) has increased significantly in recent decades. This is consistent with the findings of Page (1981). One effect of NTBs is to slow the growth of imports of those products subject to NTBs and thereby to reduce their share in the total of all imports. Failure to take account of this effect means that the *incidence* of NTBs on trade is underestimated. Therefore, it is necessary to use constant trade weights given by the share of a particular item in total imports in the base year. The weights used in Table 3.4 are constant 1981 trade weights. Using Walter's (1972) estimates of the frequency and coverage ratios of NTBs for 1966 and those of UNCTAD for more recent years, they examined changes in the frequency and coverage of NTBs. Their results are set out in Table 3.4.

It can be seen that the share of imports *affected* (frequency ratio) by NTBs rose from US$29.5 billion or about 25 per cent in 1966 to US$355 billion or about 48 per cent in 1986. In other words, the proportion of imports of developed countries affected by NTBs almost doubled in the twenty-year period from 1966 to 1986. The table shows that the share of imports of the EC countries affected by NTBs *more than* doubled such that, in 1986, the EC had a higher ratio than any of the other developed countries covered. The table also shows that that NTBs are generally more important when measured by the frequency ratio (trade affected) than by the coverage ratio (trade covered). This is further evidence that a high and possibly rising proportion of NTBs are country-specific, that is, discriminatory. With regard to product groups, Laird and Yeats found that the frequency of NTBs was highest in the case of foods. The share of all food product groups subject to NTBs rose from 36 per cent in 1966 to 89 per cent in 1986, reflecting the growth in agricultural protectionism in the developed countries over this period. For manufactured goods, the frequency of NTBs also rose alarmingly from 5 per cent in 1966 to to 51 per cent in 1986. The highest levels of NTB-affected trade were found in transport equipment, textiles and

Table 3.4 Changes in developed countries' imports covered and affected by nontariff barriers, 1966–86

	Imports covered by 1986 NTBs				Imports affected by 1966 and 1986			
	Type 1 NTBs[a]		Type 1+2 NTBs[a]		1966 NTBs		1986 NTBs	
	%	US$bn	%	US$bn	%	US$bn	%	US$bn
All countries	15.9	118.7	27.2	204.7	25.3	29.5	48.0	355.5
EC	18.6	60.8	29.8	97.1	20.8	14.7	54.1	169.2
Belgium-Lux.	10.4	2.3	32.6	7.2	30.5	2.2	74.5	16.5
Denmark	6.6	0.6	18.6	1.7	4.6	0.2	37.2	3.4
France	51.5	31.4	62.5	38.1	16.1	2.0	81.6	49.8
Germany, FR	12.1	10.1	21.0	17.5	24.1	4.0	40.9	34.1
Greece	11.7	0.5	15.2	0.7	n.a.	n.a.	25.8	1.1
Ireland	9.0	0.2	20.4	0.5	1.8	0.0	39.5	1.0
Italy	9.2	4.7	14.5	7.4	26.9	2.4	30.1	15.3
Netherlands	13.2	4.1	33.3	10.3	31.1	1.1	78.6	24.4
UK	11.1	6.9	22.2	13.7	15.8	2.8	38.1	23.6
Finland	32.4	4.5	43.2	6.0	15.2	0.2	51.3	7.1
Japan	14.4	19.0	36.9	48.8	31.4	3.6	43.5	57.5
Norway	12.5	1.9	12.5	1.9	31.0	0.8	23.2	3.5
Switzerland	17.4	5.3	40.7	12.3	19.2	0.8	50.1	15.2
US	11.9	27.3	16.8	38.5	36.4	9.4	45.0	103.1

Source: Laird and Yeats (1990)

Note: [a]See Table 3.1 for a listing of Type 1 and Type 2 NTBs.

clothing, and ferrous metals, with the biggest increases occurring in textiles and clothing and ferrous metals.

To summarise, it is clear that a high and probably rising proportion of trade is subject to and affected by nontariff barriers. The figure was already high by the mid-1960s but since then has increased significantly. This is true of developed-country imports from both developed and developing countries. NTBs are most common as a barrier to trade in agricultural products and their intensity has been rising in recent years, reflecting the growth of agricultural protectionism in the developed countries. However, a feature of the growth of nontariff protectionism is that it has been particularly pronounced in manufacturing trade where NTBs have in the past been lower. Much of the increase has been on developed-country imports from developing countries. The sectors most affected have been clothing and textiles, iron and steel, and vehicles. These have been among the industries experiencing particular difficulties in many of the developed countries in recent decades. Finally, it is apparent that a large and growing proportion of the NTBs which have spread in recent decades have been discriminatory in nature, being targeted at particular exporters of the products in question.

IMPORT QUOTAS

One of the most common kinds of quantitative restriction on trade is the import quota. This is most often used to control imports of primary commodities, and textile and clothing products covered by the Multi-Fibre Arrangement (MFA). It involves governments putting a physical limit on the quantity of a particular product which may be imported during a particular period of time. It may be *global*, applied to all imports of a particular product regardless of source. Alternatively, many quotas are *bilateral*, confined to imports coming from a specific source. Governments issue licences to importers permitting them to import a specified quantity of the product. Licences may be issued administratively or auctioned to the highest bidder. If the latter, a further possibility is that the quotas are tradable between importers.

Figure 3.1 illustrates the effects of a nondiscriminatory (i.e. global) import quota applied by an importing country to a particular product and allocated on a pro rata basis. DD is the domestic demand curve for the product and $S_D S_D$ the domestic supply curve. OP_0 is the world price of the product. Under free trade, domestic producers will supply the quantity OQ_0, consumers will buy the quantity OQ_3 and imports will amount to $Q_0 Q_3$ (= rt = OQ_5). Next, a quota equal to wv is imposed. Then, total (domestic plus foreign) supply is represented by the supply curve S_{F+D}. Demand equals supply at the price OP_1. Price has risen from OP_0 to OP_1. Consumption falls by $Q_2 Q_3$ to OQ_2. Domestic supply rises by $Q_0 Q_1$ to OQ_1. Imports are of course equal to the quota wv = $Q_1 Q_2$ = OQ_4. The effect of the quota is to make the import function, $M_0 M_0$, become vertical at $M_1 M_1$ because the quantity of imports is now unaffected by changes in price. Comparing the effects of a quota with those of a tariff, it is clear that the effects are much the same. In both cases, prices rise. As with a tariff, consumers suffer a welfare loss equal to areas A + B + C + D. Area A constitutes increased producers' surplus and is therefore not a loss to the importing nation. In the case of a tariff, area C represents revenue to the government of the importing nation. However, this is not the case for a quota except when quotas are auctioned. If quotas were auctioned, the government would be able to sell them for the price $P_0 P_1$, generating revenue equal to area C. If, however, quotas are allocated according to some other criteria, the main beneficiary would be importers, who would buy imports at the price OP_0 and sell them at the price OP_1. Therefore, area C constitutes economic rent for importers and, as such, is not a loss to the

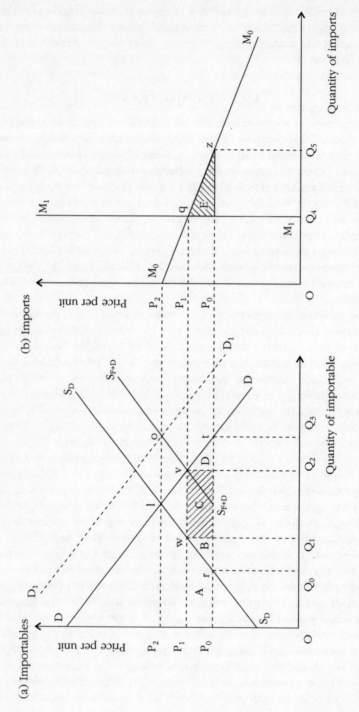

Figure 3.1 The effects of an import quota on the importing country

importing nation. This leaves areas B + D = area E as the net welfare loss or deadweight loss from the quota. This is exactly the same as for a tariff.

In view of the fact that the welfare loss from a quota is identical with that of a tariff, it may seem strange that quotas are widely regarded as being more harmful than tariffs. One reason is that quotas involve the state allocating licences to importers whereas tariffs rely on the price mechanism. If it is left to government officials to allocate licences, importers will seek to bribe them in order to get bigger quotas. Even if officials are not open to bribes, decisions must still be made about which firms are to be allocated licences and how much the licence should permit each to import. Government officials lack the information to make the right (that is, most efficient) decisions. One solution would be to auction licences to the highest bidder. This is preferable since it will ensure that licences go to the producers who can make the most efficient use of imports.

Secondly, where the quota-restrained product is a raw material or intermediate good used as an input by other industries, quotas create rigidities in the structure of production within the importing country unless licences are marketable. Efficient producers who require more of the input cannot expand production while less efficient producers who are compelled to reduce production fail fully to utilise their quotas. Similarly, where the quota-restrained input is used by two or more industries, industries whose product faces increasing demand may be unable to expand output at the expense of other industries whose products face falling demand.

Thirdly, where quotas are administratively allocated, the degree of protection and therefore the deadweight loss resulting from the quota will increase over time. Thus, in Figure 3.1, a rise in domestic demand causes the demand curve to shift from DD to D_1D_1. In the absence of any increase in the quota, all the increase in demand has to be satisfied by higher-cost domestic production rather than lower-cost imports. Consequently, price rises to OP_2. In the case of a tariff, a rise in demand is met fully by imports and the price does not rise at all.

Finally, to a greater extent than tariffs, quotas are discriminatory although they do not have to be. Too often, they are targeted at the world's lowest-cost suppliers of the product.

There would therefore seem to be merit in taking a tougher attitude towards import quotas than towards tariffs. This is indeed the position of the GATT. Article XI opposes all forms of quantitative restriction on trade except in special circumstances. However, the exceptions have been extensively used such that import quotas remain an important barrier to trade. One exception is where quotas are needed to enforce 'standards or regulations for the classification, grading or marketing of commodities in international trade' (Article XI, 2:b). Another is agricultural products where restrictions are required in order to restrict domestic supply or to remove a temporary surplus of the domestic product (Article XI, 2:c). Quotas affecting agricultural imports were also subject to the 1955 waiver granted to the United States that arose out of a statute passed by Congress in 1951 mandating quotas on certain agricultural imports. Subsequently, other countries used the US waiver to excuse similar practices. (See Chapter 6 for a fuller discussion of agricultural protectionism.) Not surprisingly, quotas are much more common in agricultural trade.

Article XII also permits the use of quotas for the purpose of safeguarding a country's balance of payments. However, any such restrictions must be progressively relaxed as the country's balance of payments improves. In other words, they are to be temporary. Interestingly, the GATT rules authorise quotas rather than tariffs where trade restrictions are needed for balance of payments conditions. In practice, countries have generally preferred tariff 'surcharges' as a device when faced with such difficulties. Developing countries, which frequently encounter balance of payments problems, have made considerable use of this provision to impose import quotas. Particularly important in this respect is Article XVIII of the GATT under which developing countries have fairly broad freedom to impose quantitative restrictions on imports for general developmental reasons (see Chapter 5 for a fuller discussion).

Finally, a major departure from the GATT rules on quotas was allowed in the case of textile and clothing products following the Long-term Cotton Textile Arrangement (LTA) of 1962. This was preceded by the Short-term Arrangement (STA) of 1961–2. The STA came into being following a GATT working party report to investigate the problem of textile protectionism. A variety of different measures, illegal under the GATT, already existed in a number of developed countries for controlling textile imports. The report found that there was a problem of 'market disruption' caused by import surges from low-wage countries. The STA permitted quotas on cotton fabrics and clothes as a temporary measure pending the completion of negotiations. The LTA, which lasted until 1973, required importing countries to drop their existing restrictions on imports of cotton textiles but allowed new ones only if and when they faced market disruption from actual or planned imports. These could take the form of import quotas, but the quotas must not be less than actual trade before the disruption and were to have a built-in growth factor of 5 per cent a year, that is, they were to allow for an expansion of trade of this amount. The Multi-Fibre Agrement (MFA) replaced the LTA of 1962. It extended the arrangements to cover noncotton textiles including man-made or synthetic fibres such as polyester and acrylic. The 1974 MFA was for three years only but was replaced by MFA2 in 1978. Each subsequent MFA similarly lasted for three years and was followed by a new agreement, each of which involved some modification of the previous one. Textiles trade is discussed more extensively in Chapter 5.

VOLUNTARY EXPORT RESTRAINTS

One of the commonest forms of quantitative restriction on trade in recent decades has been the *voluntary export restraint* (VER). Hamilon (1985b) has defined this as 'the outcome of negotiation between two governments resulting in the exporting country limiting its export supply to the importing country'. In fact, a VER need not, and frequently does not, take the form of a government-to-government agreement. It may equally take the form of an agreement between industry groups in the exporting and importing country, for example, through an industry association. (Such agreements may, however, contravene antitrust laws.) The governments of the two countries, however, are likely to be tacitly in favour of the accord and may even have been instrumental in bringing it about.

Yet another possibility is an agreement between the government of one country (usually, the importing country) and a nongovernment group in the other (for example, the exporting industry of another country). In a number of countries, government-to-government agreements are referred to as *orderly marketing arrangements* (OMAs). In the United States, OMAs are legally distinct from arrangements involving industry participation. OMAs are legally binding, meaning that the terms of the agreement cannot be modified in any way without the consent of both of the parties. Typically, the agreement will include detailed rules about export supply, rights of consultation and the monitoring of trade flows. The term *voluntary restraint arrangement* (VRA) is frequently used to cover, in addition to OMAs, arrangements with industry participation. By way of contrast, there are many kinds of more 'informal' agreements which are not legally binding. These may take the form of some sort of statement by the exporting country designed to ensure that the exports of a particular product are kept below a certain limit. In this case, the exporting country has the right at any time to abandon or modify the restriction. In some cases, the arrangement merely entails exporters making some 'forecast' or prediction about export volume with some undertaking about the monitoring of exports. In effect, these amount to restrictive arrangements also.

Usually, a VER will involve either a restraint on export volume or a minimum export price. Where there is a limitation on export volume, this may be expressed in terms of some maximum absolute level of exports or in terms of some maximum share of the market of the importing country. Kostecki (1987) distinguishes three different methods of dividing up the importing country's market between domestic and foreign producers: the home-industry-first approach; the exporters-first approach; and the market-share approach. The differences are important for determining how expansion or decline of the market is shared out between domestic and foreign producers. In the home-industry-first approach, domestic producers are given a certain minimum level of sales. It follows that, if the market declines, all the risks are born by foreign producers. In the exporters-first approach, exporters are given a certain level of sales. If the market declines, the risks fall entirely on the domestic producers. In the market-share approach, exporters are given a certain percentage share of the market. If demand falls, domestic and foreign producers lose out equally so the risks are shared evenly. Usually, the government of the exporting country will undertake to allocate export quotas to its own producers. The export quota may be given in either volume or value terms but volume quotas are more common. Quotas may be allocated to exporters on the basis of some predetermined criteria or they may be auctioned. Usually, the export limitation is for some specified period of time, rarely more than five years, although it may be, and frequently is, subsequently renewed.

It is apparent that there are many similarities between VERs and bilateral import quotas. Indeed, the economic effects of the two are similar. The obvious differences are that bilateral quotas are restrictions which are generally imposed by an importing country on the exports of another country and the task of enforcing these limitations resides entirely with the importing country. As we have seen, the GATT rules governing the use of import quotas are fairly clear even if the permitted exceptions to the rules mean that quotas are still widely used. However, the legal position with regard to VERs has always been more uncertain. In two respects, VERs would appear to involve a clear breach of GATT rules. Firstly, Article XI, which prohibits quantitative restrictions on trade covers both import *and* export restrictions. Secondly, since most VERs are discriminatory, they violate the most-favoured-nation rule set out in Article I. However, problems arise because, in many cases, the involvement of governments in bringing about the restriction is not always clear-cut. GATT rules do not cover the actions of private companies. In some cases, nongovernment bodies are the originators of the restraint. Further problems arise because VERs are negotiated agreements, not unilaterally imposed measures. It is therefore not obviously the case that the rights of another contracting party are being violated. Finally, the fact that trade is being restricted is not obvious in all cases, especially when the VER takes the form of a 'prediction' or 'forecast' of export trend. For these reasons, VERs fall into the category of what have come to be called *'grey area' measures*: measures whose legality under existing GATT rules is uncertain.

A major problem has been that few countries have sought to test the legality of a VER by making a complaint to the GATT. This is not surprising since the two parties directly affected have agreed to the arrangement, and presumably they would not have done so had there been a better alternative. Only some third party which feels it is being harmed by a VER agreed between two other countries is likely to make a complaint. Even this is improbable since other exporting countries stand to gain from the restriction by being able to export more to the importing country. On the other hand, one effect of a VER may be to cause the exporting country to divert exports to some third market. If so, producers in the latter may regard the increased competition as the direct result of the VER and, if injured, call upon the authorities to lodge a complaint against the VER. One case of a third-country complaint to the GATT was that lodged by the EC in 1987 against the US–Japan Semiconductor Agreement. The agreement contained two aspects. Firstly, an undertaking by the Japanese government to increase the share of the domestic market taken by foreign producers. Secondly, an undertaking by both countries not to sell below agreed minimum prices in the US and third markets. The second aspect was the source of the EC complaint since the effect of the agreement was to raise the cost of memory chips to European computer manufacturers. The complaints panel found in favour of the EC and the two countries were forced to modify this aspect of the agreement.

Although VERs have only been widely used in the last few decades, they date back to the 1930s and were applied to trade in *textiles*. The first example appears to have been an agreement reached in 1937 between the American and Japanese trade associations to limit Japan's textile exports to the US. Recognising the existence of a 'special' problem facing the textile industry, the US administration allowed such an agreement to be reached. The only alternative would have been discriminatory quotas; this was not legally possible and would have run counter to the trade agreements policy of the Roosevelt Administration of that time (Wolf, 1989a). At the time, the VER was regarded as being a temporary measure to deal with an 'exceptional' situation and was not intended to set any precedent for other sectors in the future. In actuality, things turned out rather differently. After the Second World War, the problems of the US textile industry remained. Beginning in 1955, further voluntary export restraints were applied by Japan to her exports of cotton textiles to the US. In January 1955, Japan gave American officials details of a five-year programme of 'voluntary' export controls. In fact, the restrictions were extracted under pressure from the US administration, which in turn might have been forced by Congress to implement import quotas had restrictions not been offered. These controls did not end the matter as exports from other textile-producing countries expanded to take the place vacated by Japan, leading to demands to extend controls to other countries.

The problems were not confined to the US. In 1959, Hong Kong, India and Pakistan reached a voluntary export agreement with the UK regulating trade in cotton fabrics. The US administration, however, was unable to persuade Hong Kong to apply similar restraints on cotton exports to the US. In the 1960s, political pressure built up on the Kennedy Administration to give support to the US textile industry. The problem was how to do this without the use of import quotas which would have violated the GATT rules and would have led to further demands for protection from other sectors similarly faced with severe import competition. The solution was, first, the Short-term Cotton Textile Arrangement (STA) of 1961 and then a year later the Long-term Cotton Textile Arrangement (LTA). In 1973, it was replaced by the Multi-fibre Arrangment (MFA). The MFA extended the LTA to trade in textiles and clothing made of synthetic fibres. Thus, trade in textiles and clothing has been subject to more or less permanent control for much of the period since just before the Second World War. Strictly speaking, the controls applied to trade in textiles and clothing under the LTA and MFA were bilateral quotas. Nevertheless, since they are agreed between exporting and importing countries after negotiation, they are in essence the same as a VER.

Gradually, VERs were extended to sectors other than textiles. The three where VERs have been most widely used are automobiles, steel and consumer electronics. One of the earliest examples of a VER in *automobiles* was the agreement which the UK entered into with Japan in 1977, which froze Japan's share of the UK automobile market at 11 per cent. This took the form of a market-sharing agreement between the industry associations of the two countries although with overt support from the two governments. At about the same time, France negotiated a similar agreement with Japan. In May 1981, the US negotiated a VER with the Japanese government which effectively reduced US imports from Japan by 140,000 units (about 7.5 per cent) from their 1980 level. As with textiles, this came into being under threat of statutory quotas. Following the US–Japan agreement, West Germany negotiated an agreement with Japan designed to limit the rate of increase of Japanese exports to the FRG to 10 per cent a year. The Netherlands and Belgium also negotiated agreements with Japan which froze the Japanese share of the market at its 1980 level. Some of these agreements subsequently expired but several others were renewed. With the decision to establish a Single Market in which goods could no longer be checked as they crossed national borders, it became impossible for the EC to operate national VERs. In the absence of any border controls, quotas in 'controlled' markets would be undermined as cars were imported from 'uncontrolled' markets. Therefore, in June 1991, the various national VERs then in place were replaced with a new Community-wide VER freshly negotiated with Japan. Although the details of this agreement have been the source of much controversy, it appears that the agreement freezes the share of the EC market at its then existent level. This means that the volume of Japanese cars sold in the EC can only increase if demand for cars increases at the same time. The agreement also includes sub-ceilings for the various member state markets where national VERs previously operated. At the same time, the EC declared its intention to abolish all controls on imports of Japanese cars by the end of the decade.

With regard to *steel*, many of the VERs which came into being were responses to alleged cases of dumping or subsidised trading and were presented as being alternatives to the imposition of antidumping or countervailing measures. The first VER was negotiated in 1968 between the US and both Japan and the EC. This lasted until 1974 when imports fell below the ceilings and the agreement was not renewed. In 1977 a so-called 'trigger-price mechanism' was introduced which provided the US industry with protection from imports sold in the US below a stated reference price based on estimates of costs of production in Japan. There also appears to have been a tacit agreement between the US and Japan since the late 1970s limiting Japanese exports to the US. In the case of the EC, a whole series of VERs were introduced as part of the EC's crisis measures (the so-called Davignon Plan) for tackling the problems of overproduction, excess capacity, falling prices and mounting losses. Unable to sell all the steel they were producing in the depressed European market, many European producers backed by heavy state subsidies began to ship more steel to the US. The response of US producers was predictable. Rather then face antidumping measures, the EC preferred to sign a VER with the US. This came into being in 1982. It was followed by a whole spate of VERs between the US and virtually every other major foreign supplier (regardless of whether they were dumping and/or causing injury to domestic producers).

The third sector which has been most affected by the spread of VERs has been the *electronics* industry, especially consumer electronics. VERs largely date back to the late 1970s and early 1980s and have involved Japan and other Far Eastern suppliers. In a manner similar to the steel industry, VERs have often been negotiated as an alternative to antidumping measures. Allegations of dumping by Far Eastern suppliers have been rife within Western Europe and the United States. In 1977, imports of television sets to the UK from Taiwan, South Korea and Singapore were also subject to a VER. In 1979, the US negotiated a VER with Japan restricting imports of television sets. Subsequently, this was widened to include Taiwan and South Korea. In 1983, the EC negotiated a VER with Japan covering imported video-cassette recorders (VCRs). The background to this was alleged dumping by Japanese producers in the European market. This particular VER was also significant in being the first-ever EC-negotiated VER, that is, a VER negotiated by the EC on behalf of all the member states with another country. In 1986, VERs spread to the industrial electronics sector with the negotiation of the US–Japan Semiconductor Agreement referred to above. As noted above, this had two aspects: (a) an agreement entered into by Japan not to sell various kinds of semiconductors (microchips) below a stipulated price both in the US and third markets; and (b) an undertaking by Japan to increase the United States' share of the Japanese domestic market.

Tables 3.5 to 3.7 show which sectors and which countries are most affected by VERs. Table 3.5 reveals that over one-half of all VERs were applied to exports of countries other than developed countries, a proportion far exceeding these countries' share of world trade. Prominent among the restrained exporting countries were newly industrialising countries such as South Korea, China and Taiwan. Nearly one-half of all VERs applied to exports of developed countries affected Japan. Table 3.6 shows that, apart from agricultural products, which accounted for 18 per cent of all VERs, the majority of VERs were to be found in five sectors – iron and steel products, textiles and clothing, automobiles and transport equipment, electronic products and footwear. It should be noted that these are the sectors within the developed countries which, in recent decades, have experienced the greatest adjustment difficulties. Table 3.7 shows that, of the importing countries protected by VERs, the EC and the USA accounted for more than two-thirds of the total number of cases.

How much of world trade is affected by VERs? One attempt to estimate the importance of VERs as a barrier/distortion to trade estimated that, by 1987, not less than 10 per cent of world trade and about 12 per cent of nonfuel trade was *covered* by VERs (Kostecki, 1987). However, this does not tell us how much trade is affected by VERs since there is clearly some unknown quantum of trade which would have taken place had these VERs not existed. It follows that the amount of trade affected is much greater. Moreover, for certain sectors, the proportion of trade covered by VERs is

Table 3.5 The prevalence of voluntary export restraints, by restrained exporting country (excluding the Multi-fibre Agreement) 1986–7

Restrained exporting country	No. of arrangements	Percentage of total number of cases
Developed countries of which:	56	40.9
Japan	27	19.7
EC	4	2.9
Australia	4	2.9
New Zealand	3	2.2
Sweden	3	2.2
Austria	3	2.2
Developing countries of which:	54	39.4
South Korea	17	12.4
China	6	4.4
Taiwan	5	3.6
Brazil	4	2.9
Pakistan	4	2.9
South Africa	4	2.9
Socialist countries of which:	27	19.7
Eastern Europe	18	13.1
China	6	4.4
Other	3	2.2
Total	137	100.0

Source: Kostecki (1987)

Table 3.6 The prevalence of voluntary export restraints, by product group
(excluding the Multi-fibre Agreement), 1986–7

Major known VERs	No. of arrangements	Percentage of total number of cases
Iron & steel products	44	32
Textiles & clothing	25	18
Machine tools	6	4
Automobiles & transport equipment	15	11
Electronic products	10	7
Footwear	8	6
Agricultural products	24	18
Other[a]	5	4
Total	137	100

Source: Kostecki (1987)

Note: [a]Products involved were kraftliner, stainless-steel flatware, leather clothing and softwood lumber.

Table 3.7 The prevalence of voluntary export restraints, by protecting importing
country (excluding the Multi-fibre Agreement), 1986–7

Protecting importing country	No. of arrangements	Percentage of total number of trade cases
Australia	1	0.7
Austria	1	0.7
Canada	10	7.3
EC	52	38.0
Finland	2	1.5
France	2	1.5
Italy	3	2.2
Japan	4	2.9
Norway	5	3.6
Portugal	1	0.7
Spain	2	1.5
UK	8	5.8
USA	45	32.8
W. Germany	1	0.7
Total	137	100.0

Source: Kostecki (1987)

much higher. Kostecki estimated that 80 per cent of world trade in textiles
and clothing is regulated by the MFA, with part of the remainder covered by
bilateral export restraints involving non-MFA countries. An estimated 20 per
cent of world trade in steel and steel products is subject to VERs (Kostecki,
1987). The 1986 US–Japan semiconductor agreement meant that 90 per cent
of world trade in semiconductors was subject to a single VER. Finally, the

proportion of trade covered by VERs is higher than average for certain countries. Kostecki puts the import-weighted coverage of VERs at 38 per cent for EC imports from Japan and not much less than 33 per cent for US imports from Japan.

The economic analysis of VERs

Hamilton (1984c, 1985b) has analysed the economic effects of VERs in partial equilibrium terms using two models: one for the case of a *nondiscriminatory VER* involving an importing country and all foreign suppliers of the product; and the other the case of a *discriminating VER* involving an importing country and one source of supply. The case of a *nondiscriminatory VER* is set out in Figure 3.2.

$D_D D_D$ is the demand curve for the product in the importing country and $S_D S_D$ the domestic supply curve. $S_W S_W$ is the combined domestic plus foreign supply curve which is more elastic than the domestic supply curve. OP_0 is the equilibrium price under free trade with domestic consumption equal to OQ_4, domestic production equal to OQ_1 and imports equal to $Q_1 Q_4$. The importing country wishes to reduce the level of imports to $Q_2 Q_3$.

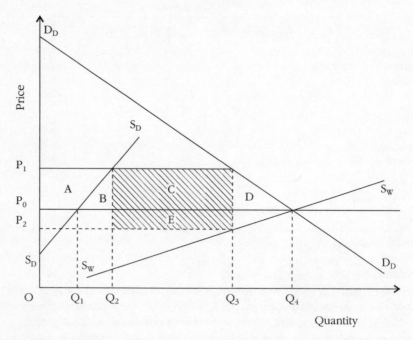

Figure 3.2 The effects of a voluntary export restraint on the importing country
Source: Hamilton (1984a)

To do this, it enters into a VER with foreign suppliers. We can imagine either that it enters into a VER with all foreign suppliers simultaneously or that the only foreign producer is the one with whom it negotiates a VER. The effect of the VER is identical to that of an import quota: the equilibrium price rises to OP_1, domestic consumption falls to OQ_3, domestic production rises to OQ_2 and imports fall to Q_2Q_3. However, although the market price in the importing country has risen to OP_1, the foreign supply price has fallen to OP_2. The logic behind this is that a nondiscriminatory VER applied to all suppliers will create excess capacity in the world industry, resulting in lower short-run marginal costs. This means that foreign suppliers can enjoy a windfall profit of P_2P_1 on every unit sold.

In Figure 3.2, the shaded area C + E is the rent income which accrues to foreign suppliers. In the case of an import quota, the equivalent of this area constitutes economic rent to importers. In both cases, this represents a loss of income for consumers but, in the case of a VER, it is also a loss to the importing country. The loss of consumer surplus is areas A + B + C + D. The net welfare loss to the importing country is B + C + D + E. This is clearly much greater than for either a tariff or an import quota. The reason for this is that a VER worsens the terms of trade of the importing country by raising the cost of imports *to the importing nation*. This does not happen with either a tariff or a quota. The fact that foreign exporters enjoy a mark-up on every unit sold is one reason why exporting countries are willing to agree to restrain their exports. What is less obvious is why the importing country should prefer a VER to a tariff or quota as a device for restricting imports. Even the hoped-for improvement in the balance of trade is only assured if the demand for imports is elastic (such that the price increase is proportionately less than the volume decrease).

The more realistic model is that of a *discriminating VER*. Most VERs are source-specific, covering some sources of supply (often the lowest-cost suppliers) but not all. They therefore have certain efffects on the pattern and not just the volume of trade and production. Figure 3.3 illustrates this case. There are three countries: the importing home country, an unrestrained partner country (or countries) and a restrained outside country (or countries). (The situation is analagous with that of a customs union made up of the importing country and the partner country. Exports from the partner country are not subject to the VER but exports from the rest of the world are.) D_DD_D is the demand curve for the product in the importing home country, S_DS_D is the supply curve in the importing home country and $S_{dn}S_{dn}$ is the combined supply curve of the importing home country and the partner country. S_WS_W is the supply curve of the outside country. (The importing home country is assumed to be sufficiently small such that the world supply price is unaffected.) OP_0 is the free-trade equilibrium price in the importing country. Domestic consumption is OQ_4, domestic production OQ_1 and imports Q_1Q_4, of which Q_1Q_2 comes from the partner country and

Q_2Q_4 from the outside country. Now, the government of the importing home country decides that it wants to increase domestic production to OQ_2. It therefore negotiates a VER with the outside country limiting its exports to DF. The partner country continues to enjoy free trade. The effect is to raise the equilibrium price to OP_1 in the importing home country. Domestic consumption falls to OQ_3, domestic production rises to the (desired) OQ_2 and imports fall to Q_2Q_3, of which BD is supplied by the partner country and DF by the outside country.

The effect of the VER is to *increase* imports from the partner country both in absolute terms (from AE to BD) and as a share of total imports (from AE/AG to BD/BF). Thus, one effect of a discriminating VER is to cause *trade diversion* away from the outside country with which the VER is negotiated and towards other countries with which no VER has been negotiated. By shifting the domestic supply curve, S_DS_D, parallel to the right so that it crosses E, it is possible to determine the amount of imports from the partner country which have been directly stimulated by the VER. Since BC = AE, CD constitutes the amount of imports from the partner country directly stimulated by the VER. Trade diversion results in a global resource allocation loss because more of world output is taking place in the partner

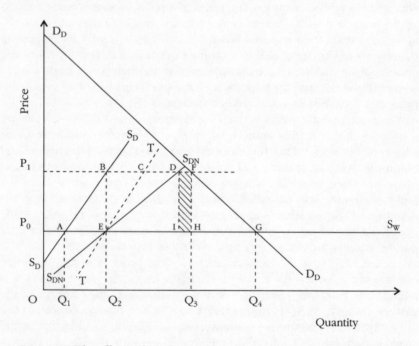

Figure 3.3 The effects of a voluntary export restraint on the pattern of trade

Source: Hamilton (1984a)

74

country where costs are higher and less in the outside country where costs are lower. Specifically, this is measured by area EDI, representing the additional resources required to produce EI. The welfare loss to the importing country is the loss in consumer surplus – area P_0P_1FG – less the gain in producer surplus – area P_0P_1BA. The partner country enjoys increased producer surplus of ABDE (of which CDE is on the increased exports of CD due to trade diversion). The outside country enjoys rent income equal to DFHI, the shaded area in the figure.

VERs may cause trade diversion not only by stimulating increased imports from 'partner countries'. A further possibility is that firms in the exporting country affected by the VER export the product via third countries to circumvent it. This may involve building plants in some 'uncontrolled' country to assemble components and parts shipped from the controlled country. To the extent that a source-specific VER simply causes imports from one foreign source to displace imports from another foreign source, the VER will fail in its objective of increasing domestic production and employment. Hamilton (1983) estimated the trade-diversion effects of VERs operated by four EC countries (France, Germany, Italy and the UK) and one EFTA country (Sweden) covering trade in textiles, clothing and footwear. Strong trade-diversion effects were found for France and Sweden, weaker effects for Italy and not much effect for the UK and Germany. Greenaway (1985) found that the UK VER on imported footwear negotiated with Taiwan in 1982 led to a dramatic increase in imports of leather and nonleather footwear from the Republic of Korea and Italy. One result of this was that the UK negotiated another VER with Korea. This illustrates the manner in which VERs often tend to spread. Eventually, the result may be that imports from all sources become subject to control. It may also be the case that, to the extent that one importing country succeeds by means of a VER in restraining imports of a particular product from a certain source, the result is to cause the latter country to transfer some of its exports to a second importing country. This may create problems for the latter, leading it also to negotiate a VER with the exporting country. Thus, VERs may spread from one importing nation to another. This will be even more the case if the exporting country derives rents from its sales to the first country which it can use to win market share in the second importing nation.

Estimating the effects of VERs

One way to compare the effects of a VER and a tariff is to calculate the ad valorem *'import tariff equivalent'* of a particular VER. This is generally obtained by comparing the domestic price after the introduction of a VER (OP_1) with the foreign price (OP_2):

$$T = (OP_1 - OP_2) / OP_2 \times 100$$

The usefulness of this measure is that it shows the equivalent *ad valorem* tariff required to achieve the same reduction in imports and increase in domestic production. Table 3.8 sets out some estimates of the tariff equivalent of various VERs (see Kostecki, 1987), some of which are very high. Kostecki estimated the trade-weighted average of the tariff equivalents to be of the order of 15 per cent. This is quite high in comparison with the average rate of tariff for manufactures. However, it is not always possible to explain the entire increase in price following the introduction of a VER as due to the restrictive nature of the VER. This is because VERs have an effect on the quality mix of imports which may itself cause a rise in the average price of the imported product. This is known as the '*upgrading*' or '*trading-up*' effect. Because a VER involves a quantity limitation on exports, the *ad valorem* tariff equivalent works out lower for high-cost, high-quality varieties. Where the price increase brought about by a VER is the same for any two varieties of different quality, since the initial price is greater for the high-quality type, the *ad valorem* tariff equivalent for that type will also be higher. In terms of the formula used above, if $(P_1 - P_2)$ is the same for all grades while P_2 is higher for high-quality grades, T will be lower. This creates an incentive for exporters to switch supplies from low-quality to high-quality varieties of the product.

Tests confirm that VERs have this effect. Feenstra (1984) found that, after the introduction in 1980 of a VER on imported Japanese cars to the US, there occurred a rise in the price of cars and that an estimated two-thirds of the rise in import prices could be attributed to quality improvements. Collyns and Dunaway (1987) also estimated that US$1,030 out of the US$1,650 estimated increase in the average price of a car sold in the US in 1984 was due to quality improvements resulting from the Japan–US VER on automobile exports. Greenaway and Hindley (1986) have produced evidence for a similar effect on Japanese exports of cars to the UK. To the extent that upgrading results, a VER may fail to protect domestic producers from foreign competition. Foreign competition may simply be shifted from one segment of the market to another.

Various attempts have been made to quantify the cost to importing countries of such measures. Generally, they involve setting the welfare cost against any benefits to the domestic industry from the VER. The main benefits claimed for VERs are threefold: they safeguard employment; they promote adjustment; and they increase the profits of domestic producers. In fact, it is by no means certain that a VER will safeguard employment in the importing country. Conceivably, in extreme circumstances, the opposite could be true. As Greenaway and Hindley (1986) show, if the domestic market is dominated by one producer, a VER *could* result in *reduced* domestic output. This will be the case where a VER is introduced covering all foreign producers, which freezes imports at the share of the market existing at the time. Then, if the domestic producer raises his price and

Table 3.8 The tariff equivalent of various voluntary export restraints

Product	Importing country/ exporting country	Measure	Tariff equivalent Year	%
Automobiles	US/Japan	VER	1984	10–20
			1983	6–8
			1982	4
			1981	2.5
	France/Japan	VER	1984	15
	Italy/Japan	VER	1984	10
	UK/Japan	VER	1984	22
Videotape recorders	UK/Japan	EF/VER	1984	3
	W. Germany/Japan	EF/VER	1984	7
	Belgium/Japan	EF/VER	1984	12
	France/Japan	EF/VER	1984	15
	Luxembourg/Japan	EF/VER	1984	25
	Greece/Japan	EF/VER	1984	35
	Denmark/Japan	EF/VER	1984	41
	Italy/Japan	EF/VER	1984	50
	Spain/Japan	EF/VER	1984	49
Steel and steel products	US/Australia, Brazil, Japan, S. Korea, Mexico, S. Africa, Spain, Sweden	VRA		
Structural steel			1985	14–16
Stainless steel			1985	16
High-temperature alloys			1985	15
Textiles and clothing	US/Hong Kong	OMA		
Cotton sweaters			1984	22
Fashion jeans			1984	10
	UK/Hong Kong	VRA	1983–4	5–10
		MFAIII	1983–4	20
Sweaters	US/Hong Kong	MFAIII	1983–5	5–50

Source: Kostecki (1987)

reduces his output, foreign suppliers must reduce their sales in order to adhere to the VER. Because buyers cannot substitute imported output for domestic output, the domestic producer's price increase need not reduce his sales. It would therefore be profitable for him to produce less than before. This is an extreme case but it serves to show that there is nothing inevitable about the presumption that a VER will safeguard employment in the protected industry: even if it increases employment, it is likely to do so only by reducing employment in some other sector of the economy. As Greenaway and Hindley (1986) explain, there are two possibilities. Firstly, the reduced quantity of imports is offset by a higher price per unit such that the value of imports is unchanged. Then, for consumers to spend more on the domestically produced good, they must spend less on some other class of good. If the latter are goods produced inside the importing country, employment must fall in the sector where spending has been reduced. Alternatively, the reduced quantity of imports is not exactly offset by the rise in price (that is, demand is inelastic), so aggregate expenditure on imports falls. This implies that the balance of payments has moved into surplus in which case the exchange rate will appreciate. This will result in either reduced exports or increased imports of other goods and lead to reduced employment in those sectors. Conceivably, the level of overall employment in the importing country may not change.

Similarly, it is not at all clear that VERs promote adjustment. In fact, as Boonekamp (1987) convincingly argues, they may just as much delay it. This will be the case if the VER is taken to mean a commitment by the government of the importing country to retain jobs in the industry. Moreover, as with all forms of protectionism, by reducing competition they make it easier for producers to continue with inefficient and out-of-date methods of production. Perhaps producers may be able to use the extra profits generated by the VER to finance costly adjustment measures but this is by no means assured. Moreover, since the profits of exporters are also enhanced, they are better able to upgrade their products and to compete more effectively in the higher-quality end of the market. This may be precisely the segment of the market in which the domestic industry was otherwise well placed to compete.

Greenaway and Hindley (1986) carried out a study of the effects of VERs which the UK negotiated on four product groups: videocassette recorders, motor cars, woven garments and nonleather footwear. The cost to the UK economy from such measures is given in Table 3.9. The figures show in the first column the net welfare loss to the British economy as a whole and were obtained by deducting any gains to producers from the costs to consumers. The costs of the VER on motor cars are given under two assumptions about the differential between British and other EC prices. (British car prices have been consistently higher than prices in continental Europe for identical models.) The cost involved is far greater than would result from the imposition of a tariff or domestic subsidy. These figures exceed most estimates of the static welfare loss from tariffs on the same products. Moreover, even on generous assumptions about employment gains, the cost per job created or maintained was extremely high and well above the average wage-rate in the protected industry at that time. In other words, it would have been cheaper to pay workers a sum equivalent to their current wage for losing their jobs.

Table 3.9 The costs to the UK economy of voluntary export restraints
covering four industries

Product group	Costs to consumers per annum (£m)	Jobs created/ maintained in industry	Cost per job per annum (£)
Videocassette recorders	80	<1,000 by end 1985	At least 80,000 in 1983 alone
Motor cars (under assumption that differential between British and other EC prices would exist in the absence of VER)	175	(a) 13,200 if Ford & Vauxhall production is assumed to increase as a result of the VER	13,250
		(b) Only BL production increases	31,500
(Under assumption that differential would not exist in the absence of VER)	>500	Nil or negative	–
Woven trousers, shirts & blouses	52	4,000	13,000
Nonleather footwear	28	3,700	7,500

Source: Greenaway and Hindley (1986)

In a study of the United States' VER with Japan covering imported
automobiles, the OECD (1987b) put the cost to the consumer at up to US$5
billion a year. It was reckoned that it may have saved between 20,000 and
35,000 US jobs in the car industry. This works out at a cost per job of
between US$90,000 and US$250,000, well above average wages. It was also
reckoned that US domestic companies benefited in extra profits between
US$18,400 and US$28,300 for each US$100,000 of lost consumer real
income. Thus, the benefits in terms of both increased employment and extra
profits to the car companies were extremely costly. Moreover, the OECD
study revealed that the VER had been of enormous benefit to Japanese
companies. Far from protecting US companies from Japanese competition,
the VER caused Japanese firms to move upmarket from compact to luxury
cars, to invest more within the United States and to build up profit reserves.
This meant that they were in a good position to cope with the appreciation
in the yen after 1985. Equally US car firms were less able to benefit from the
fall in the value of the dollar.

It is possible that a VER will freeze imports at the level prevailing before the introduction of the VER rather than reduce the volume or the share. However, as Boonekamp (1987) has explained, prices may still rise due to the effects of the VER on competition in the domestic industry. If the industry is oligopolistic, domestic producers become 'price leaders' relative to foreign producers. Any increase in the prices of domestic producers has to be followed by a similar increase in price by foreign suppliers if the VER is to be adhered to. The result is a rise in the profits of both domestic and foreign producers at the expense of the consumer. If there is a large number of firms in the domestic industry, it may be more difficult to persuade all of them to play this role, in which case the domestic price may not rise. Likewise, if not all foreign firms are covered by the VER, they may seek a larger share. In this case, it is more likely that the VER will seek to reduce the level of imports so as to bring about a rise in domestic price. Whatever the situation in the domestic market, it is clear that a VER will encourage collusion between domestic producers, resulting in less competition.

Reasons for the growth of VERs

What factors can account for the popularity of VERs in recent decades? The question needs to be addressed from the standpoint of both the importing and the exporting country. Let us begin with the *importing country*. Why do importing countries so often prefer VERs to other types of trade restriction such as an increased tariff or even an import quota which, as we have seen, are less costly? One reason is the difficulty created by using other forms of protectionism. As we shall see below, Article XIX of the GATT, the Escape Clause, does allow any contracting party to 'suspend the obligation in whole or in part or to withdraw or modify the concession' where 'as a result of unforeseen developments and of the effect of the obligations incurred by a contracting party under this Agreement, including tariff concessions, any product is being imported . . . in such increased quantities as to cause or threaten serious injury to domestic producers' (Article XIX:1). It does not state whether selective (that is, discriminatory) measures are permitted or whether any such measures have to be nondiscriminatory. However, the prevailing view appears to be that Article XIX should be interpreted in the context of the Agreement as a whole, including Article I which sets out the general requirement concerning nondiscrimination. In other words, if Article XIX is used, any increase in tariff must apply to all a country's trading partners, not just the country whose exports are creating difficulties. By way of contrast, a VER is usually negotiated only with the country whose exports are creating a problem.

Furthermore, Article XIX requires countries introducing emergency protection both to consult its trading partners affected by the measures being taken and as appropriate to negotiate compensation. If affected parties are not consulted or satisfactory agreement is not reached, the affected parties are free to suspend 'substantially equivalent concessions or other obligations'. In practice, it may be difficult to negotiate a satisfactory agreement with affected parties, in which case there is the risk of retaliation. This will affect the exports of the country taking safeguard action. In order to avoid such an outcome, the importing country may prefer to enter into a VER with the country whose exports are causing the problem. VERs are generally source-specific and so avoid upsetting third countries in the way a nondiscriminatory tariff or quota would. In fact, they contain an element of 'built-in' compensation for the exporting country in the form of the rent income which exporters enjoy. Thus, the issues of compensation and of export restraint are simultaneously dealt with in the same negotiation rather than being the subject of two or more separate negotiations.

There are also domestic political advantages for governments in using VERs in preference to other protectionist measures to deal with troublesome imports. Rising tariffs or import quotas are much more visible and thus inevitably attract public debate. In particular, they are more likely to generate opposition from consumer groups. Using a VER to appease domestic producers clamouring for protection may enable the government to pass the responsibility for the restriction on to the exporting country since the latter has the task of implementing the restraint. Tariffs or quotas may also take much longer to introduce because of the necessity for the measures to be first discussed and then approved by national legislatures. Where exports are being subsidised or dumped, a VER may again be preferred to a countervailing or antidumping duty. (A countervailing duty is a levy imposed on an imported product which has been subsidised such that the export price is lower than the domestic price, resulting in injury to producers in the importing country. An antidumping duty, which is a levy imposed on a product imported at a price below its 'normal value' (often taken to be the domestic price) and where dumping has been shown to cause material injury to domestic producers. (These practices are discussed further in Chapter 4.)) VERs avoid the lengthy and expensive procedures which an antisubsidy or antidumping action often require.

Bhagwati (1988) has argued that VERs are a porous form of protection because they can be easily circumvented. For example, exporting countries may be able to get round a VER by exporting the goods through some uncontrolled third country or by setting up an assembly plant in a third country. Upgrading the product is another method of getting round a VER. This begs the question: if they are relatively ineffective, why do governments of importing countries favour them? One explanation may be that governments do not in fact desire effective restrictions on trade but must nevertheless be seen to respond to demands for protection from legislators and their constituencies. Bhagwati has suggested that the executive branch of the government is often biased in favour of freer trade but the legislative branch is more amenable to sectional pressures for protection from interest groups. According to this view, VERs are devices used by governments to resolve conflict between the different branches of the state. If this is so, they may have certain advantages rather than constituting a hindrance to freer trade.

VERs also have certain attractions for *exporting countries*. Firstly, exporting countries are likely to prefer them to tariffs because they generate rent income for exporters whereas tariffs create revenues for the importing country. On the other hand, as Kostecki (1987) has argued, not all of the windfall gain for exporters will accrue to the exporting firm. Rather, these gains will be shared between exporters and distributors in the importing country, so they may not be as great as is often thought. Kostecki quotes one study of restraints on Japanese car exports to the US which found that 60 per cent of the windfall gains went to US dealers and only 40 per cent to Japanese car producers.

Secondly, they may have an appeal to a high-cost exporting country because they guarantee their share of the market of the importing country. They are protected from low-cost exporters from another country. This makes VERs a costly form of protection for the importing country but can explain their appeal to the exporting country. The well-established exporting firms in the exporting country will find a VER especially appealing because it makes it more difficult for newcomers to compete with them. This will be the case where the exporting country enforces the VER by allocating quotas to exporters based on some criterion such as export volume/share in the period before the VER came into being.

Thirdly, exporting countries may prefer a VER to an antidumping or antisubsidy investigation which are both costly and time-consuming. The outcome is uncertain for the duration of the investigation. Moreover, the result of such a case is often the imposition of an antidumping or a countervailing duty which may be quite punitive. As with a tariff, the revenue accrues to the importing country, whereas, with a VER, rent income is earned by the exporting country at the expense of the importing country. (However, as is explained in Chapter 4, dumping actions are sometimes settled by the exporter making price undertakings rather than by the imposition of duties. In this case, rents are transferred to the exporting country in much the same way as with a VER.)

GATT SAFEGUARD PROVISIONS AND THE GROWTH OF VERs

It is clear that there is a close connection between the growing use of VERs and the safeguard provisions of the GATT. In many respects, VERs have increasingly come into use because of deficiencies which importing countries consider to exist with the GATT Safeguard Clause (Article XIX).

Consequently, the issue of how to contain the growth of grey-area measures such as VERs has been closely linked to discussions about reform of the GATT safeguard provisions. Hence, in the remainder of this chapter, the subject of safeguards is examined. This has been a key issue on the agenda of the last two rounds of the GATT. Attempts to reform the Safeguard Clause in the course of the Tokyo Round were unsuccessful largely because of disagreement between members of the European Community and other countries over the issue of selectivity. However, agreement was finally reached in the Uruguay Round in the form of a new Agreement on Safeguards. This is intended as a clarification and reinforcement of Article XIX.

It is necessary to begin by asking why an agreement such as the GATT should need any Escape Clause. Is there any point in countries negotiating tariff reductions or tariff bindings if they are allowed, albeit in an emergency only, to withdraw such concessions? The reasons are both economic and political. At the purely economic level, the case rests on the so-called adjustment problem which can arise as a consequence of trade liberalisation. Lowering trade barriers leaves domestic industries more vulnerable to the sudden, unforeseen emergence of new sources of competition in another country. With perfectly competitive product and factor markets no problem need arise. In response to differences in prices and costs, resources would shift more or less instantaneously from declining to expanding sectors. In reality, markets are not perfect and so adjustment fails to take place sufficiently rapidly. As a result, additional costs may be created both for the owners of factors employed in the import-competing sector and for society as a whole. Temporary protection may be needed to allow time for the necessary adjustment to take place. The aim is to buy time in which factors can move out of the import-competing sector and into other expanding sectors of the economy. Furthermore, by increasing factor incomes in the protected sector, temporary protection helps to offset the private costs to factor owners that arise from adjustment. For example, higher profits may help producers to finance necessary rationalisation in the protected sector.

Closer examination shows the economic argument for such protection to be a weak one. If trade expansion creates social costs, the economically most efficient solution is to seek to remove the source of market imperfection which gave rise to the adjustment problem in the first place. For example, if the problem is imperfections in the workings of the labour market, the best solution is to reform the way in which the labour market works so as to make wage-rates more responsive to demand and supply factors. Trade restrictions serve only to impose additional costs on the rest of society. These are rarely taken into account when import barriers are imposed for adjustment reasons. On purely economic grounds, temporary restrictions can only be justified if the marginal social costs (that is, the adjustment costs to society as a whole) of allowing increased imports are found to exceed the marginal social benefits (the welfare gains from trade expansion). In most cases where temporary protection is granted, it would seem improbable that this is the case. Certainly, little or no attempt is ever made to estimate costs and benefits in this way.

If, in fact, costs are found to exceed benefits and temporary restrictions are deemed to be desirable, two further considerations need to be taken into account: firstly, how to ensure that adjustment does in fact take place during the period in which the restrictions are in place; secondly, how to ensure that import barriers are progressively lowered as adjustment takes place. The two points are related. Unless a definite timetable is established for the progressive lowering of barriers, there will be no incentive for producers in the protected sector to make the necessary adjustments. In this case, trade restrictions will delay rather than facilitate adjustment. If restrictions are retained beyond the period required, then protection will be positively harmful since the gains forfeited will exceed the costs saved. Clearly, given the tendency for temporary restrictions to remain in place for a longer period than was at first envisaged (for example, the Multi-fibre Arrangement), this is frequently the case. Indeed, the fact that temporary restrictions so often become permanent raises doubts as to whether the true motive for the restrictions in the first place is indeed the need to reduce adjustment costs.

The political case for allowing countries to introduce emergency protection is stronger. Unless domestic producers in industries where trade liberalisation is taking place are assured of a possible escape route in the event of difficulties, there will be a reluctance on their part to agree to concessions being made. In other words, the inclusion of a Safeguard Clause may help governments to secure the agreement of producers, particularly in so-called sensitive sectors, to tariff cuts and/or tariff bindings. It may serve to allay any fears among producers in sectors which have in the past enjoyed high levels of protection that they will be defenceless in the event of a sudden, unforeseen surge of imports. At the same time, by allowing temporary protection if and when an expansion of trade causes adjustment problems, it can reduce private adjustment costs to factor owners and so weaken the case in favour of high levels of permanent protection. On the other hand, it creates a risk that emergency protection will be hijacked by producer interests in declining sectors as a device for increasing economic rents at the expense of producers in expanding sectors. Almost certainly, this risk is one that has to be taken if meaningful progress is to be made in lowering trade barriers and improving market access.

The main provisions of Article XIX, as set out in the General Agreement and as it has been applied until now, can be summarised as follows:

1 It applies to 'unforeseen developments' and 'the effect of obligations incurred by a contracting party'.

2 Increased imports must cause or threaten 'serious injury' to domestic producers, but nowhere is 'serious injury' defined.

3 Action is to take the form of the suspension of obligations (in whole or in part) or the withdrawal or modification of negotiated tariff concessions.

4 Such measures may be taken for 'such time as may be necessary to prevent or remedy such an injury', that is, they should be temporary, although the duration of any such measures is not specified precisely.

5 Although selective safeguards are nowhere specifically prohibited, it must be presumed that any measures taken should be nondiscriminatory in order to conform with Article I of the GATT, especially as there is no statement to the contrary.

6 Prior notice should normally be given of any safeguard measures which a country intends to take so as to allow for consultation with countries that have a substantial interest as exporters of the product. An exception is made where delay in introducing restrictions might cause damage to a country, in which case consultation should take place 'immediately after taking such action'.

7 If, through consultation, agreement cannot be reached between the country taking the action and other interested parties, the latter are entitled to take retaliatory action against the country invoking Article XIX. This can take the form of affected parties, not later than ninety days after the action is taken, suspending 'substantially equivalent concessions or other obligations'. A period of thirty days must elapse between notice of suspension and the implementation of the retaliatory measures.

Article XIX has been widely been regarded as being inadequate as a Safeguards Clause for a variety of reasons. Firstly, the criteria for determining 'serious injury' (or the threat of it) are not specified. In many cases, any increase in imports relative to domestic production is considered to constitute serious injury. The absence of any definition of serious injury has meant that governments are more or less free to interpret it as they wish. It is left to the exporting country to prove that injury has not occurred by lodging a complaint with the GATT concerning action which has been taken. In practice, few countries have been prepared to do so.

Secondly, the types of measure which are permissible for remedying an injury are not specified. The language used in the clause, which includes a reference to 'suspension of obligations' as well as 'withdrawal or modification of concessions', seems to suggest that restrictions could take the form of quantitative restrictions and not just a tariff increase. This indeed has become normal practice, although on theoretical grounds tariffs are to be preferred to quotas. If, however, quotas are used, there is a need to ensure that they are not too restrictive.

Thirdly, there is no indication of how long such measures should be allowed, other than a vague reference to 'for such time as may be necessary to prevent or remedy such injury'. This seems to imply that such measures should be temporary but there is no guidance on when the restrictions should be eliminated. As noted earlier, if no time limit is specified, such temporary measures will fail in their objective of encouraging adjustment. A related issue is concerned with whether the need for structural adjustment measures should be stipulated as an essential requirement if temporary protection is to be permitted. It has also been suggested that, in order to encourage adjustment, there should be a requirement that restrictions are progressively lowered as the need for protection decreases.

Fourthly, the arrangements for compensating trading partners adversely affected by safeguard measures have been criticised. Because any safeguard measures must be nondiscriminatory, this may require a large number of separate negotiations with various countries whose exports have been affected. It could amount to a sizeable 'compensation bill' which may, in practice, be difficult to meet. Given that tariffs have fallen to very low levels, it may necessitate offering concessions on sensitive products still subject to high tariffs and invite opposition from domestic interests. This is one of the major reasons why countries often prefer to negotiate VERs as a way of providing safeguards to domestic producers since they avoid the need for extensive negotiations with or costly compensation being made to other trading partners. As Robertson (1992) points out, there is also an inconsistency between the fact that protection is to be temporary and agreeing compensation in the form of tariff concessions for other affected parties: once other affected parties have been compensated, there is no need to restore market access in the protected sector by eliminating the temporary restrictions. In other words, the incentive to ensure that safeguards are temporary is removed.

Finally, Article XIX has been criticised for its failure to provide any multilateral machinery for supervising the use of safeguards. Although there is a requirement that the GATT should be notified of any safeguard measures to be taken, it plays no role in examining any such measures to ensure that they conform with the requirements of Article XIX, nor does it monitor their use to ensure that the measures are temporary and are removed as and when the situation permits. The GATT only gets involved if a particular action is the source of a complaint by another contracting party, which is rare. The clear implication of Article XIX is that any disputes arising from the use of safeguards are to be settled bilaterally. Even the notification of safeguards measures is not always undertaken.

Given these weaknesses of the safeguard rules, it is not surprising that countries faced with a need to grant domestic industry temporary protection have preferred to bypass Article XIX altogether and negotiate separate safeguard measures in the form of VERs with the relevant supplier nation. Thus, by mid-1987, there had been only 134 actions under Article XIX which were notified to the GATT (Robertson, 1992), which can be contrasted with the 137 VERs identified by the GATT as being in force at about the same time (Kostecki, 1987). The majority (87) of the Article XIX actions were accounted for by the United States, Canada and Australia. The EC accounted for fourteen measures and the individual member states a further twelve. Most safeguard measures were targeted at the newly industrialising and other developing countries.

Where countries did seek safeguard remedies by invoking Article XIX, they frequently did so in ways which were questionable on a strict interpretation of the provisions of the Article. Thus, many measures appear to have been discriminatory, being targeted at particular countries. Safeguard measures have often taken the form of quotas rather than tariffs. By their very nature, quotas are discriminatory because they deny market access to new suppliers. Also, notification of safeguard measures was frequently never undertaken and trade compensation was not offered. Finally, as noted above, there are grounds for doubting whether serious injury to domestic producers was taking place in many of the cases where measures were applied. In short, Article XIX was abused as well as being bypassed. Its provisions were both too lenient, such that misuse resulted, and too severe, often resulting in countries seeking remedies by other means.

The issue of selectivity

The inadequacies of the GATT Safeguards Clause has meant that the issue of its reform has occupied a central importance in international trade policy for several decades. The growth of VERs and other grey-area measures has made it clear that Article XIX needs to be changed. Consequently, the Safeguards Clause has been a major item on the agendas of both the Tokyo and the Uruguay Rounds. One of the key issues which has plagued the attempts of the GATT countries to reach agreement has been selectivity. In the Tokyo Round, the European Community plus some Scandinavian countries argued strongly that any new set of rules should allow countries to introduce discriminatory measures. This was strongly opposed by the developing countries, which in practice were the main targets of safeguard measures. Developing countries saw the EC proposals as an attempt to legitimise the use of VERs and other grey-area measures. The failure of countries to agree on the matter of selectivity ensured that by the end of the Tokyo Round no progress had been made in negotiating a new code. Despite attempts to achieve agreement in separate negotiations after the conclusion of the Tokyo Round, the matter remained unresolved by the time of the commencement of the Uruguay Round. In the Uruguay Round the issue of selectivity once again divided the participating countries.

The case for a revision of the Safeguards Clause to allow selectivity is based on both economic and legal grounds. Firstly, there is a legal argument concerning the interpretation of Article XIX, which some see as allowing a departure from the nondiscrimination rule in the case of safeguards. Specifically, the reference to the 'suspension of obligations' could be taken to include Article I MFN obligations. But does this refer to a specific product or a particular country? Article XIX is clearly ambiguous in this respect. However, the stated position of the GATT appears to be that 'suspension of obligations' does *not* permit a departure from nondiscriminatory requirements. Secondly, advocates of selectivity argue that if GATT rules insist on nondiscrimination, countries will simply bypass Article XIX and seek remedies by other means. Indeed, as we have seen, the growth of VERs has in part resulted from what some countries see as the excessively strict requirements set out in Article XIX, including the rule that safeguard measures should be nondiscriminatory and trading partners offered compensation. Might it not be better to bring all safeguard measures under GATT discipline by allowing selectivity rather than encouraging the spread of VERs over which the GATT has little or no control? Finally, it is argued that, on economic grounds also, selective safeguards are preferable because they ensure that the exports of other countries whose trade is not contributing to the damage are not disturbed. The only country to be affected by the measures is the country whose exports have caused the market disruption.

The counterargument in favour of upholding the nondiscrimination rule is as follows. Firstly, the economic case for selectivity is a weak one. Selective safeguards are invariably aimed at the most competitive suppliers of the product in question. This, indeed, is why imports from these countries have grown faster than those of other countries. Selective safeguards not only restrict imports of a product (which in any case involves an efficiency loss), they also divert trade away from the cheapest source (adding a further distortion). There will therefore be a greater loss of economic efficiency where safeguard measures are discriminatory. Implicitly, there is an admission by an importing country which takes selective measures that its domestic industry cannot compete. If the problem is one of adjustment, why is there the need to target low-cost suppliers?

A second reason for upholding the MFN requirement is that it protects smaller countries, in particular developing countries, which might otherwise get 'picked on' by bigger, developed nations. This is because they lack the power to retaliate. Nondiscrimination is important to ensure fairness in trade policy. It is also the case that, where measures are applied equally to all suppliers, importing countries will be less inclined to resort to safeguard measures as a way of appeasing uncompetitive domestic producers. In short, it should help to ensure that the safeguard option is not abused.

Finally, selectivity makes it easier for importing countries to delay adjustment. Clearly, the incentive to adjust is less when the most competitive suppliers are excluded from the market. Moreover, suppliers who continue to enjoy access cannot be relied upon as a source of pressure on the importing country gradually to dismantle barriers after a suitable period of time.

By the time of the 1988 Mid-term Review, the Trade Negotiations Committee reported that progress had been made towards reaching agreement on many aspects of a new safeguards code. However, 'significant movement on the central issue of nondiscrimination [had] not yet materialised' (GATT, 1988), but by the end of the negotiations there had been some movement by the EC which eventually made agreement possible. Although the EC abandoned insistence on selectivity, certain aspects of the new agreement clearly do allow for discrimination in everything but name. The opposition of the developing countries appears to have been bought off by provisions which exempt the products of developing countries from safeguard measures in certain circumstances.

The new safeguards agreement

The main aspects of the new safeguards agreement are:

1 a requirement that any safeguard measure may only be applied after a proper *investigation* by the importing country in which all interested parties should be able to give evidence. This is to include views as to whether the measure is in the public interest. In critical circumstances, a measure may be taken provisionally, before a full investigation has been conducted, subject to a preliminary determination. However, in this case, the provisional measure should not last for more than 200 days and should take the form of a tariff increase refundable if the subsequent investigation determines against the measure;

2 a new *definition of serious injury* and the threat thereof. Serious injury is defined as 'a significant overall impairment of the position of a domestic industry'. With regard to the threat of serious injury, this must mean 'serious injury that is clearly imminent' and must be 'based on facts and not merely on allegation, conjecture or remote possibility'. Criteria to be used in the assessment of serious injury include 'the rate and amount of the increase in imports of the product concerned in absolute and relative terms, the share of the domestic market taken by increased imports, changes in the level of sales, production, productivity, capacity utilisation, profits and losses, and employment';

3 *restrictions on the intensity of any safeguard measure*. This should be only so much as is needed to 'prevent or remedy serious injury and to facilitate adjustment'. If quantitative restrictions are used, these should not reduce the level of imports below the average level of the previous three representative years unless it can be shown that a different level is needed;

4 a stipulation that any safeguard measure should be applied *irrespective of the source*. This would seem to rule out selective measures. In practice,

this is less certain because of the arrangements made for quota allocation, where quantitative restrictions are used. The agreement states that, where quotas are allocated among exporting nations, these should be based on the proportions supplied by the countries in question during a previous representative period. However, a country may depart from these provisions if imports from certain countries 'have increased in disproportionate percentage in relation to the total increase of imports of the product concerned in the representative period'. This sounds like discrimination under a different name;

5 *a limit on the duration of safeguard measures*: normally, safeguard measures should be applied for no longer than four years. This may be extended for another four years if necessary to prevent or remedy serious injury and provided that there is evidence that the industry is adjusting. Measures should also be progressively liberalised at regular intervals. If measures are for more than three years, they should be subject to a mid-term review to consider their withdrawal or an increased pace of liberalisation. Finally, there are provisions to ensure that no product which has been subject to safeguard measures shall again be subject to such a measure for a period of at least two years and in many cases longer;

6 provisions for consultation on *trade compensation and retaliation* where consultations have been unsuccessful. The Agreement states that the aim should be 'to maintain a substantially equivalent level of concessions and other obligations' towards other countries. To achieve this, countries taking safeguard measures should consult with their relevant trading partners and agree adequate means of trade compensation. Where agreement cannot be reached, there is provision for retaliation in the form of the suspension of 'substantially equivalent concessions or other obligations' *but not in the first three years* that a safeguard measure is in effect;

7 *special provisions for developing countries*. Safeguard measures are not to be applied against products coming from developing countries so long as the share of imports coming from a particular country does not exceed 3 per cent and that developing countries (each having a share of less than 3 per cent) collectively account for no more than 9 per cent of total imports. Developing countries may also extend the duration of safeguard measures for a period of up to two years beyond the maximum;

8 *the prohibition of all existing grey-area measures*. The Agreement provides that all grey-area measures (including VERs, OMAs, export moderation schemes, price monitoring systems, export/import surveillance, and so on) shall be phased out or brought into conformity with the Agreement within a period not exceeding four years following the establishment of the WTO. An exception can be made for one specific measure per importing country where the phase-out date is to be 31 December 1999. In the case of the EU, the exception is to be the VER governing imports of cars from Japan;

9 *provisions for notification of safeguard measures and their surveillance.*
The Agreement requires countries to notify the Committee on Safeguards
of any investigation to be initiated, finding of serious injury or decision to
impose a safeguard measure. The Committee on Safeguards is assigned a
monitoring and surveillance role to ensure that the provisions of the
Agreement are applied.

How may the new Agreement be assessed? There can be no doubt that in
several respects it represents a major improvement on the existing situation.
Perhaps the two most significant changes are the provisions for eliminating
grey-area measures over a four-year period and the introduction of a sunset
clause for safeguard measures. If implemented, the Agreement means that
all existing VERs will be scrapped or replaced with other measures which
conform with the Agreement before the end of the decade. Presumably, this
could mean their replacement with tariffs or quotas but subject to the time
limits and other requirements set out in the Agreement. Nevertheless, this
would represent a significant improvement on the existing situation, and
prohibit the future use of such measures. At the same time, the sunset clause
should ensure that temporary restrictions do not become permanent and
that adjustment takes place during the period in which the measures are in
force. In addition, the requirement that barriers should be progressively
lowered at regular intervals should further encourage the necessary
adjustment. The attempt to establish stricter conditions on the use of
safeguard measures, including a more precise definition of serious injury
and the threat thereof and the requirement that measures be preceded by an
investigation, bring the safeguard rules into line with similar rules which
apply to the use of antidumping policy. It is also to be welcomed that a limit
has been put on retaliation, if countries are to be persuaded to act legally
when dealing with problems of market disruption rather than going outside
the Agreement. Finally, the provisions to exempt developing countries from
safeguard measures in certain circumstances will give these countries some
protection against discriminatory measures.

Two areas where the Agreement might be considered less than
satisfactory both concern the nature of the safeguard measures that are
permissible. The provisions which are designed to limit the intensity of any
measure applied are to be welcomed. On the other hand, there is no
attempt to restrict such measures to tariffs even though tariffs are to be
preferred on purely economic grounds. Although provisional measures
must take the form of a tariff, this is not the case for measures imposed
following a full investigation. The undesirable characteristics of quotas were
discussed above. In particular, they freeze market shares and make it
extremely difficult for a new entrant to gain access to the market. Moreover,
they are inherently discriminatory. This means that the rejection of the
principle of selectivity is effectively undermined. Although quotas are to be

allocated on the basis of each exporter's share of the market over the previous three years, an importing country may depart from this approach in special circumstances. If it can demonstrate that imports from a particular country have increased disproportionately during this period, it could impose lower quotas. This seems to allow discrimination in special cases although the country would need the approval of the Committee on Safeguards. The concession was probably necessary to secure the agreement of those countries keen to retain some provision for selectivity. It is also true that the exemptions granted to developing countries go some way towards protecting these countries from an over-use of discriminatory measures which might be targeted at them. The crucial test will be whether or not the incentives which the Agreement provides for developed countries to make greater use of safeguards provisions to deal with adjustment problems will indeed have that effect. If they fail to do so, countries will continue to seek other less desirable methods to obtain import relief, such as antidumping. The elimination of grey-area measures will then serve merely to increase the proliferation of other forms of nontariff protection.

CONCLUSION

In this chapter, we have seen how, with the gradual lowering of tariffs, nontariff barriers in the form of quantitative restrictions have emerged to take their place. Empirical studies of NTBs clearly show that the proportion of trade covered by such measures has been increasing. An economic analysis shows that, beyond doubt, such quantitative restrictions are more harmful in terms of economic efficiency than are tariffs. It is also clear that, for a variety of reasons, these measures are more convenient and attractive as a device for controlling troublesome imports than the use of tariffs and that this accounts for their popularity. It is also apparent that the increased use of grey-area measures such as VERs is intimately bound up with the inadequacies of the GATT safeguard provisions. When faced with market disruption, countries have preferred to bypass Article XIX and seek remedies by extra-legal means. This has resulted in a proliferation of measures outside the arrangements created for this purpose and therefore not subject to any system of multilateral monitoring or surveillance. The issue of how to contain this 'New Protectionism' has therefore been linked to the reform of the safeguard rules.

After a slow start because countries were divided largely over the acceptability of selective safeguards, the negotiations to reform the safeguard rules were finally and successfully concluded. What has emerged is a new Safeguards Agreement which, although inadequate in certain respects, does represent some improvement on the previous situation. In particular, the provisions for eliminating all grey-area measures by the end of the century is important. It can only be hoped that the terms of the

Agreement will be fully implemented. For newly industrialising countries, which have so often been the target of such measures, the Agreement is most welcome. It nevertheless contains inadequacies. In particular, it does not ensure the elimination of discriminatory quantitative restrictions on trade. These will continue to be used to cope with adjustment problems even though import quotas are generally the least efficient way of doing so. The still fairly vague criteria for determining serious injury or the threat thereof are likely to mean that safeguard measures will be used to gain protection for essentially uncompetitive industries. The possibility that they could remain in place for a period as long as eight years may also undermine the attempt to ensure that measures are used only to facilitate adjustment.

4

UNFAIR TRADING PRACTICES: DUMPING AND SUBSIDIES

INTRODUCTION

One of the most contentious issues in international trade policy in recent years has been the problem of so-called 'unfair trading'. The term is a pejorative one since 'unfair' may simply mean at a price which domestic producers cannot match. Nevertheless, there have always been in international trade law some provisions designed to counter certain kinds of trading practice deemed to be unfair. Specifically, these cover two situations often closely related: the first is the case of dumping and the second the use of subsidies. Briefly, dumping refers to a situation in which an exporter is selling a good abroad at a price below that charged in its own domestic market. This can include, but is not confined to, cases where an exporter sells a good abroad at a price which is below production cost. Where dumping is taking place and where it is causing injury to domestic producers, the GATT rules permit countries to impose antidumping duties, provided only that they do not exceed the so-called 'margin of dumping'. Subsidies may have a similar effect by enabling an exporter to charge a lower price than otherwise, possibly below costs of production. Again, where subsidisation is injuring domestic producers, the GATT rules allow countries to impose countervailing duties on imports so long as this does not exceed the amount of the subsidy. But this only covers the case of an export subsidy. More recently, the GATT rules have been extended to impose discipline over domestic subsidies which may similarly distort trade.

Both issues have become important in recent years. Allegations of dumping have become rife, and in developed countries antidumping policy has become a much-used weapon to protect domestic producers against low-cost imports. Countries subject to such measures have complained that antidumping policy is being used as a form of backdoor protectionism, in many respects more insidious than old-style tariff protectionism. On the other hand, the western industrialised countries have argued for a strengthening of existing antidumping laws if their producers are to be adequately protected from countries that apply different trading rules. The issue of subsidies has assumed a similarly high profile in recent decades. The gradual lowering of tariffs has served to reveal more clearly the extent to which other forms of government intervention also create distortions to trade. Subsidies are one such example. The problem becomes particularly acute when a country with a government which is content to allow market forces to operate unimpeded trades with another country in which government intervention is the norm. The problem cannot be resolved by a simple blanket prohibition of all forms of subsidy which interfere with trade. In many cases, subsidies are justifiable as a means of tackling some particular type of market imperfection or market failure. Since these issues were less important when the GATT was first drafted, there has been a need to develop new rules and disciplines as extensions to the basic GATT framework.

The first part of the chapter discusses the subject of dumping. It is necessary to begin with the theory of dumping in order to see why it may take place and to determine what forms of it (if any) are harmful. However, much of the controversy surrounding antidumping policy centres on the legal interpretation of the rules allowing countries to take measures to combat dumping. It will therefore be necessary to examine the existing rules to see how the policy works and to determine its significance as a form of trade policy intervention. Finally, since antidumping policy was a major issue on the agenda of the Uruguay Round, the changes agreed upon during the course of the Round must be discussed.

The second part of the chapter is concerned with subsidies. Here a distinction needs to be drawn between domestic and export subsidies. Export subsidies have traditionally been regarded as an unacceptable form of government interference with trade except in special circumstances. Domestic subsidies have normally been treated differently although they may equally well result in a distortion of trade. We shall begin with a theoretical analysis of the effects of both types of subsidy. We then proceed with an examination of some reasons why governments may use subsidies as a trade policy weapon. In particular, there is a need to discuss the so-called new international economics with its attempt to demonstrate the theoretical rationale for subsidies in strategic industries. Strategic trade policy has become a key issue in recent years, particularly in respect of trade in high-technology products. Finally, the chapter concludes with a discussion of the recent attempts to introduce and extend a GATT Subsidies Code. Again, this was an important issue in the Uruguay Round and the outcome of these negotiations must be examined.

DUMPING AND ANTIDUMPING POLICY

What is dumping?

Dumping is frequently misunderstood to refer to a situation in which an exporter is selling a good below the cost of production. Although this would count as dumping, the GATT defines dumping more widely. Article VI of the GATT states that dumping occurs if 'products of one country are introduced into the commerce of another country at less than the normal value of the products' (GATT, 1969). Normal value is given by either

(a) the comparable price, in the ordinary course of trade, for the like product when destined for consumption in the exporting country, or
(b) in the absence of such domestic price . . .
  (i) the highest comparable price for the like product for export to any third country in the ordinary course of trade, or
  (ii) the cost of production of the product in the country of origin plus a reasonable addition for selling cost and profit.

(Article VI:1)

The clear implication is that normal value will usually be given by the domestic price of the 'like product' and 'in the ordinary course of trade'. However, because this may in certain circumstances be unobtainable, two other procedures are given for determining normal value. Firstly, the 'highest comparable price of the like product' when it is exported to some third country may be used. Alternatively, normal value may be constructed using costs of production in the country of origin with some reasonable mark-up for selling costs and profit.

The difference between the export price and the normal value is known as the *margin of dumping*. The GATT rules make clear that the antidumping duty cannot exceed the margin of dumping. Finally, it should be emphasised that, under the GATT rules, such dumping is only condemned 'if it causes or threatens material injury to an established industry or materially retards the establishment of a domestic industry' (Article VI:1; GATT, 1969). Thus, before antidumping duties can be imposed, the importing country must both prove that dumping has been taking place and demonstrate that material injury has been caused or threatened.

Why do firms dump?

What are the reasons why firms sell goods abroad at prices which are below the domestic price (or its equivalent)? Dumping may have many different causes. The first and best-known case is that of *price discrimination* (see Viner, 1923, and Corden, 1974, for a more extensive discussion of this case). Dumping as defined by the GATT is just one form of what economists call price discrimination, that is, charging different prices for the same product in different markets. Two conditions must be satisfied for this to take place. Firstly, the producer must be able to separate the two markets, otherwise importers in the country of origin could engage in arbitrage by importing the product from the overseas country at a lower price and selling it at a profit in the home country. Such geographical segmentation of markets may be possible due to high transport costs and/or tariff/nontariff import barriers. This is why allegations of dumping are often associated with countries which allegedly restrict imports by tariff or nontariff means. Secondly, for such a pricing strategy to be profit-maximising, the exporter must face different demand conditions in home and foreign markets. Specifically, if it faces an elastic (flat) demand curve abroad where competition is much greater and an inelastic (steep) demand curve at home, it will maximise profits by charging a higher price domestically than it charges abroad.

This is illustrated by Figure 4.1, which shows an exporter enjoying considerable market power in both the home and the foreign market. However, he faces a steeper (more inelastic) demand curve at home and hence it pays him to charge a higher price at home than abroad. With marginal costs equal to OC, the most profitable price at which to sell the product at home is OP_H which is greater than OP_F, the most profitable price to charge in the foreign market.

Figure 4.2 shows a similar case, except that the exporter enjoys market power in the domestic market only. This is more common where the product is homogeneous. The demand curve in the foreign market is horizontal (perfectly elastic), while in the home market it is downward-sloping. Marginal costs equals marginal revenue at OQ. However, with marginal costs equal to OP_F, the producer will sell only OQ_H at a price of OP_H on the domestic market. His remaining output, Q_HQ_T, is exported at the world price of OP_F. It is clear that a precondition for this kind of dumping to take place is that the exporter enjoys a high degree of market power in the exporting country. He may also enjoy some market power in the export market but this is not a requirement for price discrimination to occur.

What is less clear is why such price discrimination is harmful to the importing country. Dumping benefits consumers in the importing country who can buy the product more cheaply than otherwise. The losers are the consumers in the exporting country. Indeed, a more harmful situation would be one of 'reverse dumping' in which consumers in the importing country pay a higher price than consumers in the exporting country. It is true that, where such dumping is taking place, the domestic industry of the importing country will be smaller than it would otherwise be. However, there is no necessary reason why such dumping should threaten the survival of the domestic industry. Either domestic producers must lower their costs and prices to match those of foreign suppliers or cease producing the good.

97

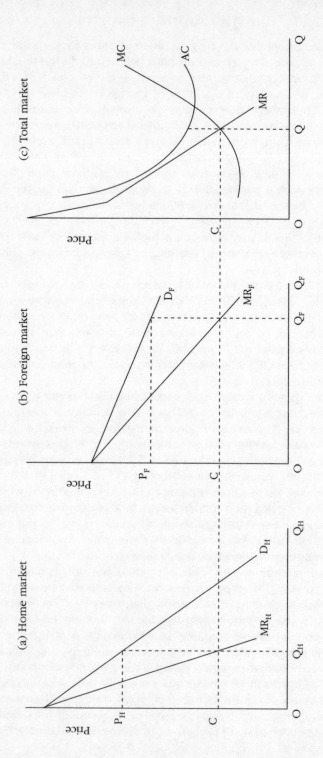

Figure 4.1 Dumping with market power at home and abroad

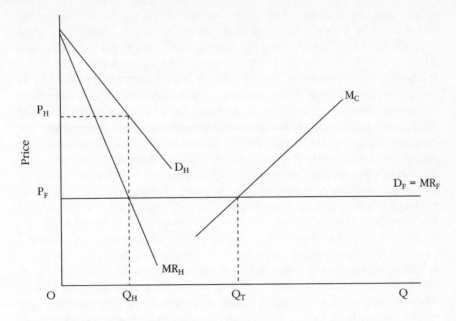

Figure 4.2 Dumping with market power in the home market only

Source: Salvatore (1989)

In the latter case, the domestic industry will decline but need not disappear. The fact that the number of domestic firms producing the product is fewer because the price of imports is lower is no justification for protection. This is true for any industry facing competition from producers in other countries willing and able to supply the goods more cheaply. Thus, the economic logic behind measures to combat dumping based on monopolistic price discrimination is not clear. The only grounds on which it makes any sense is as a measure to get the exporting country to increase market access for suppliers in other countries to the extent that tariff/nontariff barriers underlie its ability to dump. However, this begs the question whether antidumping measures are the most effective way of dealing with the problem. It is by no means clear that the threat of such measures against countries with restricted market access will have the desired effect although there are frequent claims to the contrary.

A second cause of dumping is a situation where a dominant supplier embarks on a strategy of deliberately pricing below cost in order to drive competitors out of the foreign market. Having successfully eliminated all competition, the price is raised above cost and the losses incurred during the period of price undercutting are recuperated. This is commonly referred to as *predatory pricing*. (Most of the debate about predatory pricing has taken place in a domestic rather than an international setting. Important contributions have been made by Areeda and Turner, 1975, Joskow and Klevorick, 1979; McGee, 1958, 1980; Yamey, 1972; Easterbrook, 1981, 1984.) It should be pointed out that predatory pricing entails pricing below *marginal cost*. Pricing below average cost constitutes normal behaviour whenever demand is depressed and a portion of costs is fixed. Then, so long as price is set above average variable costs, the firm is doing the best possible. There can be little doubt that predatory pricing is harmful since, if successful, it will lead to the disappearance of any element of competition in the foreign market. In the long run, consumers will suffer from having to pay prices well above marginal costs. In many countries, such practices are illegal and can result in prosecution. Cases of predatory dumping could therefore be adequately dealt with under national competition laws.

What is less clear, however, is the extent to which predatory dumping takes place in international trade. It seems improbable that, in recent years, anything more than a small fraction of antidumping cases have been concerned with such behaviour. This is because the conditions for such a strategy to be worth pursuing are highly restrictive. Firstly, the exporter must possess larger financial resources than its competitors in the foreign market or it will fail in its attempt to drive them out of the market; so it would end up with massive losses which it cannot recover. Secondly, there must exist barriers to entry in the foreign market, otherwise when prices are raised in the long run, new firms will enter the industry and excess profits will be competed away. Even where these exist, they must be sufficient to offset the prospects for higher profits which might otherwise tempt potential entrants to gain entry. Otherwise, the predator will need to hold down long-run prices to deter entry and may therefore fail to recover his short-run losses for some while to come (if at all).

These two conditions mean that cases of predatory pricing will be confined to concentrated industries characterised by significant entry barriers and in which one firm is dominant. However, not even these conditions are sufficient. Even if entry from domestic firms can be prevented, it will also be necessary to deter entry by foreign firms. This necessitates persuading the host government of the importing country to restrict access to new competitors from other countries. It is highly improbable that any government would agree to do so. Only if the exporter already enjoys global market dominance does it seem probable that he could ensure that no new competitors 'spoil the show' by entering the foreign market. These conditions suggest that cases of predatory dumping are likely to be confined to industries in which one firm accounts for a substantial share of the world market and in which the number of other firms is very small. Even then, there are cheaper ways of obtaining monopoly profits. The firms could collude to enforce a minimum price, or the more powerful firm could buy control of the others. These are likely to cost less money than a policy of holding price below cost for any length of time.

A third cause of dumping is the existence of *excess capacity* arising from a combination of demand uncertainty and short-run adjustment costs (see Ethier, 1982; Davies and McGuiness, 1982; and Bernhardt, 1984). This situation can arise in competitive industries where demand fluctuates a great deal but where in the short run firms face large adjustment costs in changing output to match demand. This is the case in many intermediate goods industries such as steel and chemicals where production occurs in continuous-run plants involving considerable changeover costs and necessitating constant use of capacity. In these industries, demand is also subject to considerable cyclical fluctuations. Because demand is uncertain, producers face the problem of choosing the right amount of capacity. If they underinvest in capacity, they will rarely overproduce but will often incur adjustment costs to increase output when demand is higher than expected. If they overinvest in capacity, they will frequently overproduce and face the necessity of making costly reductions in output when demand is lower than expected. If, however, firms can dispose of any excess output abroad, they will err on the side of overinvestment in capacity. Then, if demand is lower than expected, the surplus production can be exported abroad at a price below cost and lower than the price charged domestically. If the producer unloaded his excess output on the domestic market, the price fetched on each unit of nonexcess output would be depressed. However, by disposing of the excess output abroad, the price can be maintained on domestic sales. Some of the profits on domestic sales can then be used to offset the losses on export sales. This may still be cheaper than incurring the adjustment costs of trying to reduce output in the face of lower than expected demand.

Ethier (1982) has developed an interesting model of dumping which includes all of the ingredients referred to above. Demand is uncertain. Factors of production employed in the dumping industry are highly specific and so cannot easily be switched to some other activity if demand falls. Wages are 'sticky', which means that firms adjust to fluctuations in demand by laying off workers. One part of the workforce comprises 'essential' workers (called managers) who have to be employed whatever the state of demand. Another part comprises nonessential workers (called labourers) who can be laid off if demand falls. However, if nonessential workers are laid off, it increases the job insecurity of those who remain. To secure the employment of these workers, producers have to pay them a higher wage. Hence, faced with a fall in demand, the preferred solution of producers is to export their excess output abroad at a price below marginal costs.

The model throws up a number of possible determinants of dumping in such industries. Firstly, in countries where for legalistic/institutional reasons, the ratio of essential to nonessential workers is high, the propensity to dump may be greater. Thus, historically (although this is changing), Japanese workers have enjoyed lifetime employment guarantees such that, in Japan, adjustment can less easily be achieved by laying off workers. Similarly, most European workers have traditionally enjoyed greater employment protection rights than American workers. One effect is to make it more costly for employers in Europe to sack workers if demand falls. Secondly, the higher the rate of unemployment benefit (or other income transfer) paid to workers laid off, the easier it is for employers to lay off nonessential workers if demand falls. In such countries, the propensity to dump is accordingly lower. Thirdly, the extent to which demand fluctuations is symmetrical between countries will determine the extent of dumping. If demand fluctuates simultaneously in opposite directions in any two countries and if the fluctuations are equally pronounced, it can be shown that no dumping will take place. Where, however, fluctuations are in the same direction (for example, all countries experience a downswing at the same time) and/or fluctuations are more pronounced in one country than another, dumping will result.

Are antidumping measures justifiable in such cases? A variety of different arguments is put forward in favour of antidumping measures. Firstly, there is the argument that this is 'unfair' competition: perhaps the least convincing argument of all. Firms frequently sell a proportion of their output below cost whenever the market for the good is depressed. This is sound business practice whenever the revenues earned on such sales can be used to contribute towards the recovery of some fixed costs. It is not clear why this should be deemed 'unfair' when it takes place in the context of international trade.

A second argument is based on the existence of different cost structures in different countries, which results in some countries having a greater propensity to dump. As in Ethier's model, it may be the case that, in some countries, fixed costs account for a higher proportion of total costs than in others. In some cases, these differences may be by products of government policy, in which case offsetting measures may be considered desirable. On the other hand, it is necessary to demonstrate that imposing antidumping duties is the best way of dealing with the problem. Suppose that a particular country is more prone to being dumped on because laying-off workers is less costly. Deardorff (1990a) argues that the best policy would be either a tax on lay-offs or a subsidy to continued employment rather than antidumping measures.

Thirdly, it is argued that antidumping measures are needed to reduce employment variation. Frequent upward and downward changes in domestic ouput and employment impose considerable adjustment costs on the importing country, so the argument goes. However, the employment variations largely arise from the invariability of wage-rates. In a perfect market, wage-rates would fluctuate with little or no employment variation. A best policy would be measures to achieve greater flexibility of wage-rates. The disadvantage of less stable wage-rates should be offset against the cost to the importing country of imposing antidumping duties on imports leading to a higher price of the dumped product. Deardorff (1990) argues that, even when the problem of adjustment is considered justifiable grounds for protection, antidumping policy is not the most appropriate instrument. If an industry needs temporary protection, it would be more appropriate to do so under the GATT Safeguards or Escape Clause since the issue is an adjustment problem rather than a dumping one *per se*. Antidumping authorities are likely to be less well equipped to deal with such issues.

Fourthly, *transitional dumping* may occur when an exporter needs to price below marginal cost in order to maximise sales and expand market share. In this case, below-cost pricing is a kind of investment in the marketing of the product, deemed to be worthwhile if profits can be earned in the long run. Because this may require fixing price below marginal cost, it may be treated as predatory pricing, yet clearly it is not. One form of this occurs where a new entrant to an industry must initially set export price below those of established firms in order to attract consumers away from traditional brands. Such below-cost pricing is temporary. The intention is not to eliminate rivals but rather to gain entry to the industry. Having done so, the firm will hope to raise price and recuperate the costs incurred in the entry period. Clearly, there is nothing harmful about this kind of behaviour. On the contrary, in so far as it enables new entrants to an industry to generate more competition for established firms, the consumer should gain.

A second form of this kind of dumping may occur in high-technology industries where new products and processes are continually being developed. Very often in such industries, there will be considerable savings to be reaped in the early stages of production as a result of so-called 'learning-by-doing'. A good example of this type of product is that of DRAM – dynamic random access memory – chips where significant reductions in costs are associated with increased volume of output. Apparently, every doubling in the volume of output is associated with a 30–40 per cent reduction in costs (Tyson, 1992). Not surprisingly, the industry is one in which there have been constant allegations mainly by US and European producers of dumping by Japan and South Korea (see Yoffie, 1991; and Tyson, 1992). This may make it worthwhile for a producer initially to price the good below marginal cost in an effort to increase sales and achieve a volume of output high enough to generate such learning effects. It may result in dumping if the price is fixed lower in the foreign market than at home. For example, if sales cannot be increased any further at home, a firm might embark on an export drive based on below-cost prices designed to increase overseas sales sufficiently to achieve the required volume of output. Is this kind of dumping harmful? The main argument usually advanced for taking measures against it is to ensure that national producers get further up the experience curve than foreign firms. It is frequently argued that such industries bring special advantages to a country either because they enable domestic factors of production to earn higher returns than in other sectors of the economy or because they generate externalities or spillover benefits for the rest of the economy. Even if these arguments are accepted, it must still be demonstrated that antidumping policy is the best instrument for achieving these objectives. Clearly, it is not. Theory shows that a superior instrument would be a production subsidy granted to domestic producers sufficient to correct for the market distortion.

Finally, it is possible for dumping to appear to be taking place when in fact it is not, due to *exchange-rate variations*. Suppose that US$1 = Y100. Suppose that a Japanese product has an identical ex-factory price of Y100,000 (US$1,000) when it is sold in Japan and exported to the US. Now suppose the dollar depreciates against the yen so that $1 = Y90. Suppose also that initially Japanese exporters make no change to the price of their exports to the US. The price of the product in the US is still $1,000 which, when converted into yen at the *new* exchange rate, is Y90,000. Clearly, this is not dumping. Eventually, Japanese exporters will have to raise their prices to correct for the change in the exchange rate. However, because there may be a time lag in exporters adjusting export prices, it may show up as dumping. This position could arise where goods are sold under contract and where the currency appreciation takes place shortly before the period of investigation and before exporters have had time to raise prices. A particular problem will occur when a sudden rise in the exporter's currency takes place during the period of the investigation followed by a sudden fall. In this case, exporters leave their prices unchanged and dumping seems to be taking place. In practice, this may not be as important a cause of dumping as is sometimes thought. In the United States, allowance is often made for time lags in the response of exporters to rises in the value of the export currency as well as for so-called 'spikes' in the exchange rate. With regard to the EC, Messerlin (1989) found no evidence for a strong and positive relationship between exchange-rate variations and antidumping cases.

The economic rationale for antidumping policy is regarded by many economists as being rather weak. Most would accept that antidumping measures are justifiable in the special case where predatory pricing is found to be taking place. However, as we have seen, this is comparatively rare in practice. Therefore, one approach would be to confine antidumping to cases where export prices are below costs of production. But which costs? Clearly, not average costs, since profit-maximising firms may well sell below average costs if average costs are falling. Clearly, the relevant costs are marginal costs. Even then, as we have seen, below-cost pricing need not imply predatory intent. There would be a need to examine other criteria such as the exporter's share of the market, the existence of any entry barriers, the effects on competition, and so on. Nevertheless, if antidumping were confined to cases of below-cost pricing, this would be preferable to current practice. An alternative approach would be to tackle the problem of dumping through competition rather than trade policy. Since the major concerns are the implications of dumping for competition in the domestic market, it might be more appropriate for dumping cases to be investigated by the competition authorities. The requirement would then be simply to determine whether or not dumping is likely to result in reduced competition and higher prices to consumers in the long run. This would ensure that antidumping is not hijacked by domestic producers for protectionist purposes. If an industry needs temporary protection on grounds of adjustment, this is best dealt with under the Safeguards Clause. Antidumping policy should be restricted to the one single, theoretically valid case for intervention, namely, predatory pricing.

However, what is desirable on economic grounds is unlikely to be acceptable to policy makers or regulators in most western industrialised economies: for political reasons, no government will agree to such a restriction on the use of antidumping measures. On the contrary, the demands of these countries is for tougher measures to combat dumping. Given the fact that antidumping measures benefit producers in the protected industry and nearly always harm consumers, this is a reflection of how successfully antidumping policy has been captured by producer interests. A more promising approach may be for economists to press for measures which will curb the power of antidumping authorities and limit the misuse of antidumping. For example, any reforms which strengthen the role of consumer organisations and therefore act as a counterweight to the influence of domestic producers are to be welcomed. In the next sub-section, the actual implementation of antidumping policy is discussed and an attempt will be made to explore some of the options for reform.

Antidumping policy

The GATT's Antidumping Policy is set out in Article VI of the General Agreement and further elaborated in the Antidumping Code (GATT, 1979b). The Code was negotiated as part of the Kennedy Round and further revised in the course of the Tokyo Round. A new Code is contained in the Final Act Embodying the Results of the Uruguay Round (GATT, 1994a, 1994b) and the details of this are discussed below (pp. 120–7). The Code contains a set of rules governing antidumping policy, including the finding of dumping, the measurement of the dumping margin, the determination of injury, the imposition of duties and procedures covering the investigation of dumping by the authorities in the importing country following a complaint. It should be pointed out that it is up to any individual country to decide whether it wishes to operate an antidumping policy. The only requirement is that this should conform to the rules set out in the Article VI of the GATT and the Antidumping Code. This means that antidumping policy may and very often does differ between one country and another, which may create problems for exporters who face different rules and procedures in different countries. These may in themselves create a barrier to trade. Until recently, it was mainly the developed market economies who made use of antidumping policy.

Table 4.1 shows the number of antidumping cases initiated by countries over the years 1980–93. Since these figures say nothing about the amount of trade affected by the cases in question, it is not possible to decide whether or not the incidence of antidumping has increased. Nevertheless, for much of the period the frequency of antidumping investigations did increase. In particular, the years since 1990 show a marked increase in antidumping activity. Research by Baldwin and Steagall (1994) has shown that, over the period 1980–90, there occurred a significant increase in the number of US antidumping and countervailing duty cases. In 1980–90, the US International Trade Commission investigated 494 antidumping and 306 countervailing duty cases compared with only 172 antidumping and 10 countervailing duty cases in 1970–9. It can be seen that, for the period as a whole, most antidumping cases were initiated in four areas: Australia, Canada, the European Community and the United States. For most of the period, the United States and Australia appear to have been the leading users of antidumping policy. However, in recent years, there has been a growing number of cases originating in other developed countries and, most notably, in some developing countries. Before 1985, there had been no antidumping cases initiated by a developing country; by 1990, there were no less than forty-one cases or 23 per cent of the total number for that year. From being mainly recipients of antidumping measures imposed by developed countries, developing countries have increasingly become users of antidumping policy.

Not all cases result in antidumping measures being imposed, therefore, it may be more useful to examine which countries were the most active. Antidumping measures may take the form of either the imposition of an antidumping duty or the extraction of price undertakings from exporters. GATT figures show that, over the period from 1 July 1980 to 1 July 1990, the EU compelled 150 exporters to give price undertakings and imposed 84 definitive antidumping duties, the United States imposed 156 antidumping duties and exacted 6 price undertakings, Australia imposed duties on 174 occasions and obtained 41 price undertakings, and finally Canada imposed 156 duties and secured 11 price undertakings (GATT, 1990). On this measure, and taking duties and undertakings together, the EU emerges as the greatest user of antidumping policy. However, because the EU places much greater reliance on undertakings, it is less important in terms of duties imposed.

Table 4.1 Antidumping cases initiated, 1980–93

	Australia	Canada	EC	US	Other developed countries	Developing countries	Total
1980–1	61	48	37	24	3	0	173
	(35%)	(28%)	(21%)	(14%)	(2%)		
1981–2	54	64	39	51	2	0	210
	(26%)	(37%)	(23%)	(29%)	(1%)		
1982–3	71	34	26	19	0	0	150
	(41%)	(20%)	(15%)	(11%)			
1983–4	70	26	33	46	1	0	176
	(40%)	(15%)	(19%)	(26%)	(1%)		
1984–5	63	35	34	61	0	0	193
	(33%)	(18%)	(18%)	(32%)			
1985–6	54	27	23	63	2	3	172
	(31%)	(16%)	(13%)	(37%)	(1%)	(2%)	
1986–7	40	24	17	41	5	4	131
	(31%)	(18%)	(13%)	(31%)	(4%)	(3%)	
1987–8	20	20	30	31	9	13	123
	(16%)	(16%)	(24%)	(25%)	(7%)	(11%)	
1988–9	19	14	29	25	12	14	113
	(17%)	(12%)	(26%)	(22%)	(11%)	(12%)	
1989–90	23	15	15	24	5	14	96
	(24%)	(16%)	(16%)	(25%)	(5%)	(15%)	
1990–1	46	12	15	52	9	41	175
	(26%)	(7%)	(9%)	(30%)	(5%)	(23%)	
1991–2	76	16	23	62	21	39	237
	(32%)	(7%)	(10%)	(26%)	(9%)	(16%)	
1992–3	61	36	33	78	8	38	254
	(24%)	(14%)	(13%)	(31%)	(3%)	(15%)	

Source: GATT Secretariat; quoted in *The Financial Times*, 15 December 1992 and 25 November 1993

Table 4.2 shows which exporting countries were worst hit by antidumping duties imposed over the period 1980–9. Japan heads the list with 74, followed by the United States with 51, Korea with 40 and China and West Germany each with 32. Even these figures tell us nothing about the extent to which trade was affected by the measures imposed. However, what is clear is that antidumping policy frequently results in duties being imposed well in excess of the average level of tariff applied to the products in question. According to a study carried out by the World Bank, average tariffs in the entire US manufacturing sector would be 23 per cent today, compared with a nominal level of 6 per cent, if they were adjusted to take account of the cost of antidumping duties, in particular on steel, textiles and cars (World Bank, 1992). In other words, antidumping measures have, in effect, wiped out much of the gain achieved by tariff liberalisation. Morkre and Kelly (1994) estimated the average margin of dumping (on which the rate of duty is based) at 33.2 per cent for all US antidumping cases over the period 1980–9. Bourgeois and Messerlin (1993) similarly estimated the average dumping margin for all EC antidumping cases at 37.4 per cent for the period 1980–8. However, in the EC rates of duty were often set below margins of dumping. Messerlin and Reed (1995) estimate the average rate of antidumping duty in the EC over the period 1980–9 was 17.8 per cent (although only for cases which were terminated by *ad valorem* duties). This compares with the average MFN tariff rate for industrial products of 7.8 per cent.

Any country wishing to make use of Article VI is required to follow a carefully prescribed procedure. This requires the importing country to demonstrate by an investigation that (a) dumping, as defined by the GATT, has taken place; (b) material injury or the threat of material injury to the domestic industry exists; and (c) dumping is the cause (although not necessarily the sole cause) of the alleged injury. In the United States, the investigation into whether dumping has taken place and the investigation into whether it has resulted in injury (or the threat of it) are separated. The International Trade Commission (ITC) is charged with the responsibility for the latter and the International Trade Administration (ITA) makes an entirely separate decision about the former. By way of contrast, in the case of the EU, both aspects are considered simultaneously by the Antidumping Unit of the European Commission.

Table 4.2 Countries most frequently subject to antidumping duties, 1 July 1980–1 July 1989

Exporter	Countries imposing duties				
	Australia	*Canada*	*EC*	*US*	*Total*
EC	35	41	2[a]	29	107
Japan	21	13	12	28	74
US	16	25	10	–	51
S. Korea	14	14	2	10	40
China	12	6	3	11	32
W. Germany	11	14	–	7	32
Taiwan	11	4	–	13	28
Brazil	4	7	6	10	27
Italy	8	6	–	8	22
France	8	8	–	6	22
Canada	6	–	5	10	21
UK	6	9	–	2	17
Spain	2	4	2	6	14

Source: GATT Secretariat; quoted in *The Financial Times*, 1 July 1990

Note: [a] Spain.

During the investigation, all interested parties are allowed the opportunity to submit relevant evidence.

Provisional duties may be imposed after a preliminary finding that dumping has occurred and injury resulted. These must not be greater than the provisionally estimated margin of dumping. They should not be imposed for more than four months, or six months in exceptional cases. Provisional duties are repayable if the full investigation subsequently finds no evidence of dumping or injury or a causal link between the two. There is a provision for suspending or terminating proceedings without any duty being imposed if exporters are willing to make *price undertakings*, that is, undertakings to raise prices so as to eliminate the injurious effects of dumping (Article VII, GATT Code). In the case of the EU, price undertakings have been more common than antidumping duties. Where the investigation does result in a positive finding, *definitive duties* may be imposed provided that these do not exceed the dumping margin. The 1979 GATT Code set no limit on the duration of duties except that they should not remain in force for any longer than is necessary to counteract the dumping causing injury. An important feature of US legislation is that it imposes strict time limits on the various stages of investigation. The ITC must reach a preliminary decision within 45 days of the filing of the petition. If its decision is affirmative, the ITA has 160 days from the filing of the petition to reach its preliminary decision. Once the ITA has reached its preliminary decision, it then has 75 days to make its final determination. If its decision is affirmative, the ITC then has 45 days to make its final determination. Following an affirmative decision by the ITC, the US Customs has 7 days in which to issue an order (see Devault, 1990, for an analysis of the procedure). This strict timetable may tend to deliver the provision of evidence into the hands of the plaintiff.

The determination of dumping

The first requirement is to provide evidence that dumping has taken place. This entails a comparison of the export price with the normal value. Article VI states that the *normal value* may be determined in one of three ways:

1 'the comparable price, in the ordinary course of trade for the like product when destined for consumption in the exporting country'. Much controversy has surrounded the phrase 'in the ordinary course of trade'. In some cases, this has been taken to exclude any domestic sales made at below costs of production. Sales between associated parties, that is, when an exporter sells on the domestic market to a related company, are also not generally considered as being 'in the ordinary course of trade'. Also, when goods are not sold in sufficient quantities on the domestic market, this method is deemed to be inappropriate.

2 'the highest comparable price for the like product for export to any third
country in the ordinary course of trade' or the *export value method*. The
prices charged for the product when exported to some third market can
serve as a proxy for the domestic price. The European Commission
makes little use of this method on the grounds that there is a strong
probability that if an exporter dumps on one market he will do so on
other markets. Bellis (1990), however, believes that it has more to do with
administrative convenience. By way of contrast, the export value method
is widely used by the US Department of Commerce. (One case where this
method was used by the Commission was in 1983 and involved low-
density polyethylene (LdeP) imported from the Soviet Union, Poland,
East Germany and Hungary. It was settled by the exporters making price
undertakings. In this case, because the dumping countries were non-EC
economies, the Commission used prices in the Swedish market as a
proxy for domestic prices. However, as Messerlin (1991) has shown,
prices on the Swedish market were themselves distorted by the
cartelisation of the EC market which itself became the subject of an
antitrust decision by the EC authorities in 1988.)

3 'the cost of production of the product in the country of origin plus a
reasonable addition for selling cost and profit' or the *constructed value
method*. Costs of production are determined by adding up all costs, fixed
and variable, incurred in the course of producing the good, both the costs
of materials and of manufacture. The procedure for determining the
'reasonable addition' for selling, administrative and other general
expenses is controversial. The US provides for a minimum level of 10
per cent for general expenses but the EC bases this on actual costs
incurred. Where a product is sold through a related sales company, the
general selling expenses of the sales company are also included. These
are allocated on the basis of some criterion such as turnover. The
Antidumping Code states that 'as a general rule, the addition for profit
shall not exceed the profit normally realised on sales of products for the
same general category in the domestic market of the country of origin'.
The US practice is to add a minimum 8 per cent whereas the EC seeks to
determine a reasonable margin for profit based on the average
profitability of the exporter in his own home market. In some cases,
where no profit is realised, the EC may use the profit rate realised by
other producers of the product in their home market. The constructed
value method necessarily throws up a highly arbitrary estimate of the
normal value because of the difficulties of estimating costs and knowing
what addition to make for selling costs and profit.

Where dumping is taking place in a nonmarket economy, the practice of
using a '*surrogate domestic price*' has evolved. In nonmarket economies,
domestic prices are fixed by the state and therefore cannot be meaningfully

compared with prices in market economies; there is thus a need to find some other way of determining normal value. The procedure is to calculate a surrogate or reference price from costs of production for the like product in another country with the usual addition for selling expenses plus profit. The procedure has been much criticised. The estimate of normal value is necessarily arbitrary and makes no allowance for any cost differences between the exporting and surrogate country. Moreover, there is nothing to stop the importing country from choosing the surrogate country with the highest costs. Of course, there is a problem involved in determining normal value of a product in a nonmarket economy for the reasons given. But this raises the question as to whether it makes any sense even to try to apply antidumping laws to such countries. If there is a need on grounds of injury to domestic producers to grant protection from imports coming from such economies, Bellis (1990) has suggested that it would be better to do so through means other than antidumping policy, which necessarily results in arbitrary calculations of an intangible concept.

It is interesting to compare the frequency with which these different methods for determining normal value have been used in different countries. According to Messerlin (1989), nearly 68 per cent of all antidumping cases initiated by the EC over the period 1980–5 used either the constructed value method or the third market (surrogate country) method applicable to nonmarket economies. The export value method was not used at all. The heavy reliance on methods which seek to construct normal value from information regarding costs with an addition for selling expenses and profits is a cause for concern for the reasons given above. Even if nonmarket economies are excluded, 40 per cent of all cases initiated were based on constructed estimates. The concern is justified, given some evidence that, where constructed estimates were used, there was a greater likelihood of restrictions being imposed (Messerlin, 1989). Devault (1990) carried out a similar exercise for the United States covering the decade 1980–9. Only 45.6 per cent of all cases (measured by the combined home and US market value represented) used the domestic price method whereas 9.4 per cent used the export-value method, 15.9 per cent used the constructed-value method, 10.4 per cent used the surrogate-country method and a further 18.4 per cent used the 'best information available'. The number of cases based on best information available is disturbing. This is often used where the foreign firm is unwilling to co-operate in providing the necessary information or provides inadequate responses. Best information available can come from a number of sources including the petitioner. Not only was this was the second most frequently used method, but Devault found the average dumping margin to be much higher in these cases than in others.

Having estimated normal value, the antidumping authorities must similarly estimate the *export price* in order to determine the *margin of dumping* (if any). GATT rules state that the two prices must be compared 'at the same level of trade, normally at the ex-factory level, and in respect of sales made as nearly as possible at the same time' (Article II:6, GATT Antidumping Code, 1979). This requires that the export price be reduced by the amount of any costs of transportation or any import duties payable. Where goods are sold through a subsidiary company, the rules require countries to construct an export price 'on the basis of the price at which the imported products are first resold to an independent buyer'. Since all costs incurred between importation and resale may be deducted, the level of these costs is important. The EC was strongly criticised for making frequent use of the constructed export price method. The reason is that exporting companies which market their product through expensive resale organisations may be 'allocated' higher overhead costs than companies which sell to independent importers. This is thought to be important in the case of differentiated consumer goods. In addition, an allowance is made for the profit of the exporter's subsidiary and imputed to the exporter in the calculation of the export price. This may again be highly arbitrary.

The dumping margin is determined by taking the difference between the normal value and the export price. Usually, where possible, each export sale of the good in the importing country is compared with a weighted average normal value. This is then used to obtain a single weighted average dumping margin. However, this method gives rises to an anomaly: export sales at prices which exceed the normal value are not counted in the calculation of the dumping margin. Suppose the weighted average normal value is 100. Suppose that there are ten export sales which take place at a price of 90 and another ten sales at a price of 110. Taking all sales together no dumping has occurred. However, since the sales at 110 cannot be counted, the average dumping margin is 10 per cent. It follows that dumping may be found to exist when in fact no dumping has occurred. To understand this, suppose that the export price had been calculated as an average of the twenty export prices recorded in the same manner as the normal value. In this case, the dumping margin is zero. The argument in support of this method of calculating the dumping margin is that export sales above normal value are irrelevant to the question of whether or not dumping has been taking place. Moreover, it is argued, the actual duty is only imposed on exporters making sales below normal value. This argument surely misses the point. Take the case of a product which may as a result of changed market conditions sell at a higher price at the beginning of the period of investigation but at a lower price towards the end. This may be the case in both the domestic and the foreign markets. This is particularly true of perishable goods but may also be true of consumer durables. The above methodology will result in dumping being found when in fact none has taken place.

In comparing export prices with the normal value, a particular difficulty concerns the adjustments which should be made to ensure that the two are compared 'at the same level of trade'. As we saw above, this is normally the ex-factory level. The question is: which expenses should be deducted to make such a comparison possible? A particular anomaly arises in the case of the EU. Where goods are exported through a subsidiary and the constructed-export price method is used, the procedure is to deduct *all* selling costs plus a reasonable margin for profit. As we noted, this tends to penalise exporters who sell through related sales companies since they will be allocated higher overhead costs. However, when comparing the export price with the normal value for the purpose of determining the dumping margin, only *direct* selling expenses are deducted. For many consumer-branded products which typically incur large indirect selling expenses, this makes it inevitable that dumping will occur when none is taking place at all.

Figure 4.3 illustrates the point. A Japanese product is produced at identical cost in Japan (100) and sold at an identical arm's-length price in both the EC and Japan (150). Selling costs are also identical in both countries. So no dumping has taken place. Yet EC rules ensure that dumping will be found. To obtain the export price, all selling expenses (40) plus profit (10) are deducted from the arm's-length price (150) to give an 'export price' of 100. However, only direct selling expenses (20) may be deducted from the arm's-length domestic price to give a normal value of 130. The dumping margin is therefore 30 per cent. The US operates a similar practice except that a special adjustment is made, called the export selling price (ESP) offset adjustment, to eliminate any unfairness. Even this, however, has been criticised for failing to ensure a fair comparison. The suspicion at least exists that the practice of both the EC and US is designed to create a penalty for Far Eastern exporters of branded consumer products whose complex home distribution networks are often blamed for creating barriers to western goods. In short, the rules are intended to find dumping when in fact no dumping is occcuring and to ensure that Far Eastern producers are subject to hefty import penalties.

The determination of injury

The second stage in an antidumping investigation is the injury test. Article VI of the GATT states that dumping is condemned only if

> it causes or threatens material injury to an established industry in the territory of a contracting party or materially retards establishment of a domestic industry.

The phrase 'material injury' may be contrasted with the requirement of 'serious injury' in the GATT Safeguards Clause (see Chapter 3). Serious injury is presumably more difficult to demonstrate than material injury. This difference is frequently justified on the grounds that relief should be easier

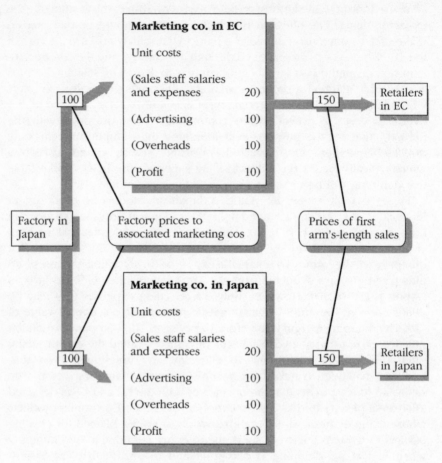

The Commission would find a dumping margin of 30% on
this export from Japan
Brackets denote items deducted by EC in constructing ex-factory cost

Figure 4.3 Illustration of EC dumping calculations

Source: Hindley (1989b)

to obtain in the case of 'unfair trading'. The Antidumping Code seeks to
define what might constitute material injury but does so in very broad
language. It states that the determination of injury is to be based on two
aspects: (a) 'the volume of dumped imports and their effect on prices in the
domestic market for like products'; and (b) 'the consequent impact of these

114

imports on domestic producers of such products'. The Code lists the following factors which should be included in an examination of the impact of dumping on the domestic industry:

actual and potential decline in output, sales, market share, profits, productivity, return on investments, or utilisation of capacity; factors affecting domestic prices; actual and potential negative effects on cash flow, inventories, employment, wages, growth, ability to raise capital or investments.

However, it states that the list is not intended to be exhaustive. In fact, the range of factors covered is so broad that almost any form of competition could have these effects. The GATT Code states:

There may be other factors which at the same time are injuring the industry, and the injuries caused by other factors must not be attributed to the dumped imports.

(Article III:4)

It might be thought that this requirement would be sufficient to prevent countries from ascribing injury to dumping when other factors are the true cause. However, with reference to the EC, Messerlin (1989) has shown that a mere correlation between an upsurge of imports and decline of domestic production is in practice considered sufficient grounds for determining material injury. The fact that two events happen at the same time says nothing about causation. Before 1982, US practice was to compare the dumping margin with the degree of price undercutting in order to determine if a relationship existed between the extent of dumping and material injury. Thus, if the extent of price undercutting caused by imports exceeded the dumping margin, it could be argued that dumping was not the cause of injury. However, after 1982, so-called 'margins analysis' was dropped. In the case of the EC, it has played no role in injury determination except in the context of the '*de minimis*' rule. The latter states that, where the dumping margin is 1.5 per cent or less, there is no material injury.

A further area of controversy concerns the practice of *cumulation*. This is the aggregation of the dumped imports of different countries when determining whether or not material injury has occurred. Suppose that four exporting countries each have a market share of 5 per cent in the importing country and are found to be dumping. Should they be treated separately or collectively? If they are treated separately, given the share of the market accounted for by imports from any one country, it might be difficult to demonstrate injury. On the other hand, if imports from all four countries are aggregated, the share of the market accounted for by dumped imports might be thought sufficient to prove material injury. One consequence of this is the way in which cumulation can penalise small exporting countries. Suppose that two large exporting countries are found to be dumping. In addition, two smaller countries are also found to be dumping but account for such a small share of the market that, if evaluated separately, it would not be considered to be a cause of material injury. By lumping the larger and smaller countries together, the importing country is able to establish material injury. As a result, the two smaller nations are subject to antidumping measures as well. As Jackson (1992) points out, this creates an effective entry barrier for small traders. The danger of a small country having to face an antidumping investigation is increased. It may well be that the costs involved in conducting a defence in such an investigation exceed the potential profits from trade. In this case, small traders may be unwilling to incur the risks of entering the foreign market. Alternatively, they may seek to align their prices with the leading prices being charged in the market so as to avoid any suspicion of dumping. Palmeter (1991) argues that 'cumulation has permitted antidumping to become a selective safeguard, with a minimal injury requirement, and with no compensation obligation'.

It is noteworthy that Article VI of the GATT states that dumping is to be condemned not only when it causes material injury to domestic producers but also where it *threatens* material injury to an established industry . . . or materially retards the establishment of a domestic industry'. In other words, the mere threat of injury can be sufficient to lead to antidumping measures being imposed. The counterargument is that an importing country must be able to act swiftly against dumping which threatens injury before injury becomes a reality. But what constitutes such a threat? In the US, there is a requirement that it be 'real and imminent' and not merely 'speculative'. In the case of the EC, relatively little use has been made of the provision. However, as Messerlin (1989) argues, the very existence of such a provision may serve to deter an exporter from increasing sales to a country with such legislation in place. For example, a decision by a producer in a newly industrialising country to increase its exporting capacity by investing in new plant could be sufficient to provoke the initiation of proceedings in one or more of the advanced industrialised countries to which it exports. Not surprisingly, several newly industrialising countries have expressed concern that the 'threat of injury' clause could in the future become a powerful weapon that effectively closes western markets to their exports.

Because of the ease with which producers can turn antidumping into a protectionist weapon, it has been argued that a 'national domestic interest' clause should be written into the GATT Code. This would require importing nations to take into account the interests of consumers and users rather than domestic producers only. The EC does require that account be taken of the interests of the EC as a whole although nowhere are these defined. In practice, no antidumping action has been dropped because of the adverse effect on consumers or users of the dumped product. There are problems in writing such a clause. For example, what should be done in a situation where demands of domestic producers conflict with those of consumers or users of the product? On the other hand, a requirement that antidumping authorities should actively solicit the views of consumers/users of the product and take these into account in their final judgement would ensure that the costs of antidumping to the importing country as a whole are considered.

The imposition of antidumping measures

In the event of a positive finding of dumping and injury, the rules permit an antidumping duty to be imposed not exceeding the margin of dumping. The Antidumping Code states that the rate of duty should be less than the margin of dumping if that is adequate for removing the injury to the domestic industry (Article VIII:1). The EU prides itself on the fact that, unlike the US, the rate of duty is set at the level required to eliminate the injury rather then being set equal to the margin of dumping. This helps to offset any bias towards finding higher dumping margins which clearly exists from the dumping methodology described above. On the other hand, as Bellis (1990) argues, if this is used as an excuse for continuing to apply methods which result in higher dumping margins, the effects of the lesser duty rule will be negative.

As explained above, the GATT Code does allow for the imposition of provisional duties during the period of the dumping investigation for up to four months (which may be extended to six months) after a preliminary affirmative finding of dumping and with sufficient evidence of injury (Article X:1). If the antidumping investigation finds no evidence of dumping or injury or both, the provisional duty must be repaid. Similarly, if the investigation finds the margin of dumping to be less than the preliminary finding and subsequent provisional rate of duty, the difference must be repaid as quickly as possible. One area of concern is the number of cases which involve the imposition of provisional duties but subsequently end with either no duty or a lower rate of duty being imposed. Tracing preliminary and final decisions made by the US International Trade Commission (ITC) and International Trade Administration (ITA) over the period 1980–9, Devault (1990) found that 66 per cent of all antidumping cases resulted in provisional measures but only 36 per cent led to definitive duties. This suggests that it was fairly easy for domestic producers to get provisional relief but that a disturbingly large number of these cases should not have resulted in any antidumping measures being introduced (mainly because of failure to pass the material injury test). This imposes an unnecessary cost both on foreign firms, which are punished unjustifiably, and on domestic firms, which waste time and money contesting their case.

Article VII of the GATT Code permits antidumping proceedings to be suspended or terminated at any time if and when exporters agree to undertakings which either revise prices or cease exports to the importing country. However, any price increase must not be higher than that required to eliminate the margin of dumping. In the case of the EC, an estimated two-thirds of all antidumping measures taken in recent years have been in the form of price undertakings (Commission of the EC, 1989). The reason for the EC's preference for price undertakings appears to be the greater ease with which price increases can be secured. In the case of a duty, exporters may raise their prices by less than the amount of the duty, although the EC now has a clause in its regulation for imposing additional duties where an exporter fails to pass on the full amount of the duty. Clearly, the settlement of an antidumping case by price undertakings is preferable for the exporter, who extracts rent at the expense of the importing nation rather than having to pay revenues to the importing authorities. The EC is proud of its greater reliance on price undertakings on the grounds that the injury caused by dumping is removed without penalising exporters (see de Clercq, 1988). A rather different view has been taken by some critics of the EC's antidumping policy. Messerlin (1989) viewed the EC bias towards price-fixing agreements as reinforcing the pro-cartel impact of antidumping policy. Stegemann (1989) argues that price undertakings are in essence legal substitutes for illegal price-fixing. He argues that, in any other situation, such price-fixing would be deemed illegal under Article 85 of the Treaty of Rome but in the antidumping context it is positively encouraged. A major weakness of the GATT provisions is that they fail to make clear the criteria which should be used in choosing between duties and undertakings. Tharakan (1993) provides some interesting evidence to show that this lack of clarity has enabled the EC to use undertakings as a trade policy weapon by, for example, refusing undertakings to exporters in countries with whom the EU runs large bilateral trade deficits.

A major issue in the Uruguay Round negotiations concerned the provisions contained in EC and US antidumping legislation for tackling *circumvention*. This is the name given to the methods which may be used by exporters to get round antidumping duties. One method is for an exporter to set up a so-called 'screwdriver' or assembly plant in the importing country and ship parts from the exporting country for assembly inside the importing country. Alternatively, the exporter may ship parts to a factory in a third country not subject to antidumping measures for re-export to the country imposing duties. Yet a third posssibility is to make physical alterations to the product so that it no longer attracts antidumping duties. It is often argued that, as production has become increasingly globalised, it is easier for exporters to circumvent antidumping duties. To deal with this problem, in July 1987 the EC introduced an important but controversial amendment to its antidumping regulations to allow the imposition of antidumping duties on imported components and parts where screwdriver plants were used to circumvent EC antidumping measures. The amendment comes into effect whenever (a) companies start up or substantially increase local assembly or production operations after the opening of antidumping investigations; and (b) imported parts or materials exceed the value of all other parts or materials by at least 50 per cent. There is a further requirement to take account, on a case-by-case basis, of the amount of research and development carried out by the assembler within the EU as well as the degree of technology applied. These provisions were strongly criticised when they were introduced. In particular, the requirement that no more than 50 per cent of the value of component and parts should come from the dumping country was seen as an attempt to compel foreign companies investing in the EC to buy parts and materials locally. It was also argued that 50 per cent was unreasonably low in the case of a company at the early stages of investment. As Bellis (1990) argues, 'what is ostensibly an anticircumvention provision is being deviated from its initial purpose to become a "buy European" instrument'.

Two of the first uses of the screwdriver plant regulation were to impose duties on Japanese manufacturers of electronic typewriters and photocopiers (see NCC, 1990, for further details). The two cases resulted in Japan lodging a complaint with the GATT. In March 1990 a GATT panel ruled that the EC's anticircumvention provisions were illegal. Firstly, the duties imposed were internal charges and not customs duties, and as such infringed Article III of the GATT. The latter requires that no internal tax be applied to imported products in such a way as to give more favourable treatment to products of national origin than like products imported from abroad. Secondly, the panel rejected the EC's argument that duties were permissible under Article XX. The latter allows deviations from GATT obligations to prevent enterprises evading obligations imposed on them which are consistent with the GATT such as the evasion of an import duty. The panel drew a distinction between action taken by a company to *evade* and action taken to *avoid* a legal obligation. The decision by a company to transfer the production of a good on which an import duty is levied to the importing country did not constitute evasion of a legal obligation and therefore was not covered by Article XX. The adoption of the panel report by the GATT Council left the EC's then-existing anticircumvention provisions in doubt. Consequently, it remained an important negotiating aim of the EC in the Uruguay Round to ammend the GATT Code so as to permit anticircumvention measures.

Finally, with regard to the *duration* of antidumping duties, the original Code merely stated that they should 'remain in force only so long as, and to the extent necessary to counteract dumping which is causing injury' (Article IX:1). In fact, the new revised Code has introduced new limits on the duration of measures, as will be explained below (p.126). The EC regulations have always had a 'sunset clause' which limits the duration of duties to five years. After five years, any duty still in existence automatically

119

expires unless an interested party can show that expiry would again lead to injury or the threat of injury. Messerlin (1989) sees merit in such a clause in weakening 'the collusive impact of antidumping actions' and allowing competition 'to surface' a few years before the duties are due to expire. On the other hand, he sees a risk that it might generate 'a race to undertakings' because the earlier an exporter can gain acceptance of undertakings, the earlier it can benefit from the sunset clause. In addition, any exporter may request a review provided that at least one year has passed since the conclusion of an investigation. In the US, an exporter who can demonstrate that no sales have taken place at less than fair value for two years and that there is no likelihood that such sales will be resumed may get an order revoked.

The GATT negotiations and the Final Act

The 1986 Ministerial Declaration launching the Uruguay Round stated that one of the objectives was 'to improve, clarify or expand, as appropriate, agreements and arrangements negotiated in the Tokyo Round of multilateral negotiations'. The Antidumping Code referred to above was one such agreement. In the negotiations which ensued, there was a clear difference between those countries which made great use of antidumping policy and others which more often than not were the victims. Countries such as the USA, those of the EU, Canada and Australia favoured changes to the Code which would make it easier for countries to catch dumpers. By way of contrast, countries such as Japan and the newly industrialising countries, which generally were on the receiving end of antidumping measures, were concerned that the rules should be made stricter. A key issue for the former group was the problem of circumvention. They were concerned with the way in which companies subject to antidumping duties could circumvent these measures either by setting up assembly plants in the importing country or by switching production to some third country and exporting to the country imposing the duties. As noted above, Japan lodged a complaint with the GATT concerning the EC's anticircumvention provisions and secured a ruling declaring these provisions to be illegal. The EC was keen to agree the inclusion in the new Code of a provision allowing countries to take measures where circumvention was found to be taking place.

In July 1990 Charles Carlisle, the Deputy Director-General of the GATT and chairman of the negotiating group dealing with antidumping, tabled a paper which proposed a compromise between the two opposing camps. On the one hand, it contained several changes which would significantly tighten the existing antidumping rules. On the other hand, in deference to the USA and the EC, it included a proposal to allow countries to act against circumvention under strict conditions. The paper met with strong resistance from Japan, which regarded the new rules as insufficiently strict and opposed the proposals for tackling circumvention. In August 1990, a second version of the Carlisle paper was prepared which was much more vague than the first. It succeeded in attracting wider support than the first version but failed in its attempt to conclude the antidumping negotiations. The antidumping code proposed in Arthur Dunkel's draft Final Act, published in December 1991, adopted a similar approach but included new concessions in an attempt to maximise agreement. In deference to Japan, it recognised that selling below cost in the launch phase of a new product was a legitimate business practice and allowable under strict conditions. Action against circumvention would be allowed but only when the cost of parts imported for assembly was more than 70 per cent of total costs. In November 1993, a matter of months before a last attempt was made to conclude the Round, the United States raised a number of further demands which temporarily threatened the conclusion of the negotiations. Some last-minute concessions were made to the US and this proved sufficient to secure agreement.

Perhaps the most significant feature of the new Code is that the provisions regarding circumvention contained in both the original Carlisle proposals and the Dunkel Draft Final Act have been omitted. Instead, the Final Act incorporates a two-sentence statement:

> The problem of circumvention of antidumping duty measures formed part of the negotiations which preceded this Agreement. Negotiators were, however, unable to agree on specific text, and, given the desirability of the applicability of uniform rules in this area as soon as possible, the matter is referred to the Committee on Antidumping Practices for resolution.

In other words, it has for the moment proved impossible to reach agreement on this issue. However, in a number of other areas, significant changes have been made to the Antidumping Code. These are incorporated in the *Agreement on the Implementation of Article VI of GATT 1994* (GATT, 1994b). The main changes are set out in the following sub-sections.

The determination of dumping

Clearer and more detailed rules are stipulated for determining if dumping has taken place. Article 2.2.1 of the new Code clarifies the conditions under which sales of a product in the domestic market of the exporting country at below cost may be treated as not being 'in the ordinary course of trade' and therefore disregarded in the determination of normal value. Three conditions must be satisfied. Firstly, such sales must be made 'within an extended period of time' which should normally be one year but in no case less than six months. Secondly, such sales must be made 'in substantial quantities' (not less than 20 per cent of the volume sold in transactions).

Thirdly, such sales must be 'at prices which do not provide for the recovery of all costs within a reasonable period of time'. It is made clear that the prices must be below weighted average costs for the investigation period as well as below costs at the time of sale for this condition to be met. These provisions will help to eliminate the practice of excluding all below-cost transactions from the estimation of normal value which can contribute towards countries obtaining an overinflated dumping margin.

Article 2.2.1.1 contains a reference to the need to make adjustments for 'start-up operations' in the determination of costs. A problem with many new products is that costs are very high in the early stages of production with the result that price is temporarily fixed below cost. The new Code states that costs must be adjusted 'for circumstances in which costs during the period of investigation are affected by start-up operations'. A footnote states that 'the adjustment made for start-up operations shall reflect the costs at the end of the start-up period or, if it extends beyond the period of investigation, the most recent costs which can reasonably be taken into account by the authorities during the investigation'.

Article 2.2.2 contains a statement that, in the calculation of normal value, where the constructed price method is used, 'the amounts for administrative selling and any other costs and for profits shall be based on actual data pertaining to production and sales in the ordinary course of trade for the like product by the exporter or producer under investigation'. As noted above, the US currently uses a fictitious 10 per cent addition for selling costs and 8 per cent for profit, which inevitably yields a highly arbitrary estimate of normal value. However, Article 2.2.2 does allow for 'any other reasonable method' where 'such amounts cannot be determined', subject to the condition that 'the amount for profit so established shall not exceed the profit normally realised by other exporters or producers on sales of products of the same general category in the domestic market of the country of origin'. This merely repeats the wording of the 1979 Code.

Article 2.4.1 contains a useful provision for ensuring that '*exchange-rate dumping*' is not subject to antidumping measures. It states that 'fluctuations in exchange rates shall be ignored and in an investigation the authorities shall allow exporters at least 60 days to have adjusted their export prices to reflect sustained movements during the period of investigation'.

Article 2.4.2 addresses the issue of how the export price should be compared with normal value in the determination of the dumping margin. It was shown above (p. 112) that where the export price is compared with a weighted average normal value, dumping can be found when in fact no dumping is taking place. Article 2.4.2 states that 'the existence of margins of dumping during the investigation phase shall *normally* [my emphasis] be established on the basis of a comparison of a weighted average normal value with a weighted average of prices for all comparable export transactions or by a comparison of normal value and export prices on a transaction to transaction basis'. It continues, 'a normal value established on a weighted average basis may be compared to prices of *individual* [my emphasis] export transactions if the authorities find a pattern of export prices which differ significantly among different purchasers, regions or time periods and if an explanation is provided why such differences cannot be taken into account appropriately by the use of a weighted average-to-weighted average or transaction-to-transaction comparison'. In other words, in exceptional circumstances, it is possible to compare the normal value 'established on a weighted average basis' with individual export prices. Hindley (1994) has argued that this comes very close to authorising the procedures referred to above which impart an upward bias to the calculation of the dumping margin. He argues that the requirement for the authorities of an importing country to provide an explanation for using this procedure is too weak and will almost certainly allow it to be used so long as a country can provide an explanation that has 'rudimentary plausibility'.

The determination of injury

One of the demands of Japan and the Asian NICs was for clearer definition of material injury or the threat of injury. Article 3 of the new Code goes some way in this direction. Article 3.3 states that *cumulation* is only permissible when (a) the margin of dumping in relation to imports from each country is more than *de minimis* (defined as less than 2 per cent of the export price) and the volume of imports from each country is not negligible; and (b) 'is appropriate in the light of the conditions of competition between imported products and the conditions of competition between the imported products and the like domestic product'. Some sort of *de minimis* cut-off had been advocated by critics of cumulation as a way of protecting smaller exporters from unfair exposure to antidumping policy.

Article 3.5 reiterates the requirement stipulated in the 1979 Code that there must exist a 'causal relationship between the dumped imports and the injury to the domestic industry'. It also goes a little further in listing factors that possibly cause injury, other than dumped imports, which might be taken into account; namely, 'the volume and prices of imports not sold at dumping prices, contraction in demand or changes in the pattern of consumption, trade restrictive practices of and competition between the foreign and domestic producers, developments in technology and the export performance and productivity of the domestic industry'.

With regard to the threat of material injury, Article 3.7 goes a little further than the original Code in listing factors which the authorities should consider in this respect. These are:

(i) a significant rate of increase of dumped imports into the domestic market indicating the likelihood of substantially increased importations;

(ii) sufficient freely disposable or an imminent, substantial increase in capacity of an exporter indicating the likelihood of substantially increased dumped exports to the importing country's market, taking into account the availability of other export markets to absorb any additional exports;

(iii) whether imports are entering at prices that will have a significant depressing or suppressing effect on domestic prices, and would likely increase demand for further imports; and

(iv) inventories of the product being investigated.

This is similar to the definition of 'threat of material injury' already given in the antidumping regulations of some users of antidumping policy. However, it is unlikely to allay the fears of the newly industrialising countries that any increase in investment in an exporting industry could trigger an antidumping investigation.

An important issue in the negotiations concerned the definition of 'domestic industry' to be used in the determination of material injury. The GATT antidumping code has always required that injury to a major proportion of the domestic industry must be established. The EC had wanted its Single Market to be divisible into regions for the purpose of determining injury. This was strongly opposed by other countries. Article 4.3 of the new Code states that where countries have achieved a degree of integration such that their combined domestic market has the characteristics of a single market, the industry of the entire area is to be taken as the domestic industry. However, Article 4.1 says that:

in exceptional circumstances the territory of a Member may, for the production in question, be divided into two or more competitive markets and the producers within each market may be regarded as a separate industry if (a) the producers within such market sell all or almost all of their production of the product in question in that market and (b) the demand in that market is not to any substantial degree supplied by producers of the product in question located elsewhere in the territory. In such circumstances, injury may be found to exist even when a major portion of the total domestic industry is not injured, provided there is a concentration of dumped imports into such an isolated market and provided further that the dumped imports are causing injury to the producers of all or almost all of the production within such market.

In this case, duties should normally only be levied on imports to the market in question. If that is not possible and only after the exporter has been given the opportunity to resolve the matter through undertakings, the importing country may impose duties without limitation. Thus, under strict conditions, the EU can presumably divide its market for the purpose of determining injury. Moreover, if undertakings cannot be secured from exporters, duties could be applied at an EU-wide level although injury may only apply to producers in one part of the EU.

Antidumping investigations

One change proposed by some countries in the negotiations was for stricter rules governing the evidence that must be provided before an antidumping investigation can be started. It was also argued that it should be made more difficult for countries to impose provisional antidumping measures without first giving the dumpers the opportunity to defend themselves and without a preliminary finding of dumping and injury. Article 5 of the new Code includes some tougher conditions which must be met before an investigation can be initiated. Article 5.4 states that an application for an investigation may only be considered if the application has the support of domestic producers collectively accounting for 50 per cent of total production 'of that part of the industry expressing either support for or opposition to the application'. . . . No investigation shall be initiated where domestic producers expressly supporting the application account for less than 25 per cent of total production of the like product produced by the domestic industry.' An important footnote to Article 5.4 states that 'members are aware that in the territory of certain Members, employees of domestic producers of the like product or representatives of those employees, may make or support an application for an investigation'. This codifies an understanding which has existed since the 1967 Antidumping Code. Article 5.8 provides for immediate termination of an investigation where the margin of dumping is *de minimis* (defined as less than 2 per cent of the export price) or the volume of dumped imports (actual or potential) or the injury is negligible (generally defined as less than 3 per cent of total imports). In the negotiations, the US unsuccessfully fought for the *de minimis* margin to be 0.5 per cent.

Article 6 of the new Code contains new procedures designed to make it easier for interested parties – defined as the exporters or foreign producers subject to investigation, the government of the exporting country and producers in the importing country – to present evidence. There is also a requirement that industrial users of a product and representative consumer organisations be given the opportunity to provide relevant information to the investigation. Article 7 states that provisional measures may only be applied if there has been a proper preliminary affirmative determination of dumping and injury.

The imposition of duties

Article 9 of the new Code contains some new and stricter procedures for reimbursing exporters who pay antidumping duties which turn out to be greater than the antidumping margin. A further important provision in the new Code concerns the case of companies in an exporting country subject to antidumping measures which were not exporting the products during the period of the investigation but which are likely to face even higher rates of antidumping duty when they commence exports to the importing country. This is because the practice of countries applying antidumping measures is often to set a higher rate of duty for imports coming from companies in the dumping country which did not provide evidence for the investigation. Article 9.5 requires the authorities in the importing nation 'to promptly carry out a review for the purpose of determining individual margins of dumping' for such exporters. The review must be carried out on an accelerated basis compared with normal proceedings, and no duties may be imposed during the review period. If, however, the review shows that such exporters have been dumping, duties may be imposed retroactively.

An important new addition to the antidumping rules is a *sunset clause* setting a five-year limit to the imposition of duties. Article 11.3 states that 'any definitive antidumping duty shall be terminated on a date not later than 5 years from its imposition . . . unless the authorities determine, in a review . . . that the expiry of the duty would be likely to lead to continuation or recurrence of dumping and injury'. The same rules apply where price undertakings are preferred to duties. This is more or less identical to the sunset clause in EC antidumping rules. Placing some limit on the duration of antidumping duties must be welcomed but, as the experience of the EC demonstrates, it is not entirely a panacea. The US was strongly opposed to the sunset clause. Apparently, over 10 per cent of US antidumping duties had been in place for more than twenty years.

A new Article 12 seeks to bring about greater transparency and openness in antidumping investigations by requiring countries to give proper public notice of investigations and of preliminary and final determinations. The same provisions apply for reviews of existing antidumping measures.

Consultation and dispute settlement

Article 17 sets in place procedures for resolving any disputes arising between members regarding antidumping. Any disputes which cannot be resolved by bilateral consultations may be referred to the Dispute Settlements Board (DSB) of the WTO for examination. However, Article 17.6 makes clear that, in its assessment of the facts, the panel should be confined to determining 'whether the authorities' establishment of the facts was proper and whether their evaluation of these facts was unbiased and objective'. In other words, the panel is not permitted to make a judgement as to whether in its evaluation the antidumping authorities came to the right conclusion. Furthermore, 'where the panel finds that a relevant provision of the Agreement admits of more than permissible interpretation, the panel shall find the authorities' measures to be in conformity with the Agreement if it rests upon one of those permissible interpretations'. These guidelines regarding the settlement of disputes arising under the new Code were included at the insistence of the US and are widely seen as leaving importing countries with considerable discretion. It seems unlikely that exporting countries will have much success in getting decisions overturned by the DSB except where measures are clearly GATT-inconsistent.

* * * *

How are we to assess the new agreement on antidumping? Before the completion of the Uruguay Round, a tightening up of the Antidumping Code was generally regarded as one of the most important tasks facing negotiators. A widely held view was that any liberalisation package would be of little value unless new rules were introduced to restrict the ease with which countries can use antidumping measures to interfere with trade. However, it became clear as negotiations proceeded that the two main users of antidumping, the United States and the EC, were not prepared to permit any reduction in the strength of their antidumping armoury. On the contrary, they pushed hard for a strengthening of the rules to permit quicker and more effective action against dumpers – for example, through the inclusion of new anticircumvention provisions within the Code. This made it almost inevitable that no agreement was likely to be very satisfactory from a free-trade point of view. The fact that no new rules were introduced to permit anticircumvention measures is surely a relief, although the present uncertainty regarding the permissibility of such an extension of antidumping is far from wholly satisfactory.

In other respects, however, the new Code is a disappointment. The main improvements are procedural. The new rules make it somewhat harder for domestic producers to bring an antidumping action. The rules also reduce slightly the degree of discretion which the antidumping authorities in the importing country currently enjoy both in the finding of dumping and the determination of injury. Although the Code fails to tackle many of the highly dubious methods which countries use to prove dumping, there are some restrictions on the methods which are acceptable for calculating the margin of dumping. There is some improved protection for smaller exporting nations and the new sunset clause ensures that, after five years, antidumping measures will automatically expire unless the importing country can demonstrate that their removal would lead to renewed dumping and injury to domestic producers.

However, these changes are unlikely to be sufficient to deter producers from seeking import relief through antidumping. The opportunities which antidumping creates for bringing relatively swift action to bear against troublesome imports will continue to make it an attractive option. Indeed, the outlawing of VERs in the new Safeguards Agreement (discussed in the previous chapter) may lead to increased resort to antidumping. The methods used to determine dumping will continue to be of questionable meaning or objectivity and are likely to continue the familiar pattern of grossly inflated dumping margins. Indeed, in several ways, the effects of the new Code are malign by actually codifying certain practices which countries have in the past used to inflate dumping margins. Although the new Code makes greater provision for other groups of producers and consumers or users of the product to be consulted and for exporters to put their case before the antidumping authorities, an opportunity has been largely missed to ensure that antidumping decisions take into account the interest of the whole of the importing country and not just the domestic producers petitioning for protection. Worse still, the Code fails to provide a satisfactory mechanism for the monitoring of antidumping decisions. Although exporting countries can appeal to the Disputes Settlement Board, the terms of reference of any panel set up to investigate such a dispute render it improbable that many cases will be reversed. In this respect, also, an opportunity has been missed to establish proper multilateral machinery for adjudicating antidumping cases which could have been used to protect exporters from the discretion of antidumping authorities taken captive by beleaguered import-competing domestic producers.

SUBSIDIES AND COUNTERVAILING DUTIES

Subsidies and their effects

A second type of unfair trade practice is the subsidy. At the outset, it is necessary to draw a distinction between an export subsidy and a domestic subsidy. In the case of an *export subsidy*, a producer receives a subsidy only on the amount which is exported. A *domestic subsidy* is paid to a producer on all that is produced regardless of whether the output is for export or the home market. In a manner similar to dumping, export subsidies allow an exporter to sell the good in a foreign market at a lower price than at home and possibly below costs of production. As with dumping, GATT rules deem such a practice to be 'unfair' if it causes or threatens material injury to producers in the importing country. Article VI allows countries to impose countervailing duties on such imports, provided that the rate of duty does not exceed the element of subsidy. As is explained later (p. 139), agricultural exports constitute an important exception to the rule.

Export subsidies may be disguised in various ways. One form of this is the use of export credit subsidies whereby governments provide subsidised credit to foreign importers who purchase goods from the exporting country using loans taken out with a bank in the exporting country. In the past, such export credit subsidies have been the subject of a special 'gentlemen's agreement' between OECD countries. The approach has been to agree limits on the amount of interest rate subsidy permissible for exports to different markets of the world. In other words, export credit subsidies have in the past not been regarded as a GATT issue.

Domestic subsidies are in some respects a more complex issue since their purpose is often not a distortion of trade. In addition to financial aid granted to a particular producer or industry, they include total or partial tax exemption, remission of tax, provision of credit on special terms, and preferential treatment in the provision of public infrastructure. Although the primary intention may not be to restrict trade, either exports or imports may be indirectly affected. If the producer or industry which is subsidised exports part of its output, the subsidy will enable it to export at a lower price than would otherwise be possible. Foreign producers may therefore regard such a subsidy as a form of 'unfair' competition. Alternatively, if the producer or industry being subsidised sells all of its output domestically but is competing with imports from abroad, the subsidy may enable it to undercut foreign exporters. In this case, the effect is similar to a tariff in discriminating against foreign-produced goods. The GATT Treaty contained no provisions to control domestic subsidies. However, in recent decades, countries have become increasingly concerned about the trade-distorting effects of these measures. The concern was greatest in countries which adopted more *laissez-faire* policies. They argued that their producers were at an increasing disadvantage when competing with imports coming from countries where governments adopted more interventionist measures. There was a sense in which, as tariffs were gradually lowered, the impact of such measures on trade was more strongly felt. It may also have been the case that growing government intervention in industry in the 1960s and 1970s meant that subsidies played a more trade-distorting role than in earlier years. More recently, however, mounting deficits have caused governments to reduce the overall level of subsidies to industry, although more careful targeting of subsidies has been an accompanying factor (Ford and Suyker, 1989).

Both export and domestic subsidies were the subject of a new Subsidies Code agreed in 1979 as part of the Tokyo Round. Its significance was that, unlike the GATT Treaty itself, it included domestic as well as export subsidies. Moreover, it went much further than the GATT Treaty in elaborating and interpreting the GATT provisions. A major deficiency of the Code was the failure to include agricultural subsidies, which have subsequently become a major source of trade-distortion (see Chapter 6 for an explanation for why agricultural subsidies were treated differently). The Leutwiler Report of 1983 listed revision, clarification and more effective rules on subsidies as one if its fifteen recommendations (GATT, 1985). Subsidies and so-called countervailing measures were included on the agenda of the Uruguay Round and a special negotiating group was set up to deal with this issue. A new Agreement on Subsidies and Countervailing

Measures (SCM) was contained within the Uruguay Round Final Act. The new Agreement is discussed below. However, before doing so, it is necessary to examine at a theoretical level the effects of the two types of subsidy on trade.

The economic effects of subsidies

Domestic subsidies

Figure 4.4 illustrates the effects of a subsidy on domestic production of a particular good of which the country is an importer. OP_W is the world price. Domestic production equals OQ_0 and domestic consumption OQ_2 and the volume of exports Q_0Q_2. The effect of the subsidy of P_WP_S (= RS) is to push the domestic supply curve S_DS_D to the right to $S_D^SS_D^S$. Domestic production increases by Q_0Q_1 and imports fall to Q_1Q_2. Domestic producers gain increased producer surplus equal to area P_WP_SRT. However, the subsidy costs the government area P_WP_SRS. So there is a net welfare loss to the importing country equal to area RTS or A. The difference between a subsidy and a tariff is that a subsidy results in no loss to consumers since the domestic price is unaffected. This means that a domestic subsidy is always to

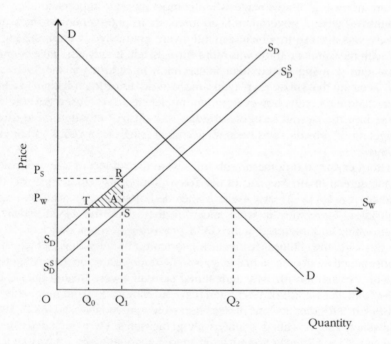

Figure 4.4 The effects of a domestic subsidy

130

be preferred to a tariff if the purpose is to increase the output of domestic producers. It is also clear that, whatever the primary intention of the subsidy, it does result in a distortion of trade. Imports are lower than before, although higher than if an equivalent tariff had been imposed.

A perfectly respectable argument for government intervention of this kind exists within economic theory. Whenever the social return on capital exceeds the private return, a subsidy is the best way of eliminating the distortion. One example is the famous infant-industry argument for protection. There are several different versions of this argument. One describes an industry in which average costs fall with output such that production is only profitable in the long run. Implicitly, this assumes some imperfection in capital markets which prevents a sufficient amount of private capital from being forthcoming. One possibility is that investors lack sufficient information about the long-run return. A second version is based on the premise that there are external economies of scale from investing in the industry, of which private investors necessarily take no account. Economists have long recognised that, where these conditions exist, a case for a subsidy can be made out. It should be pointed out that in both situations a policy measure to improve information flows and/or to reduce interest rates would be preferable to a production subsidy. Nevertheless, if these measures are not possible, a subsidy may be desirable, provided that it is no more than is necessary to correct the distortion and that it is removed when protection is no longer necessary. Moreover, a subsidy is always to be preferred to a tariff as an instrument for correcting such a distortion.

Another situation in which a domestic subsidy may be needed to overcome an externality is that of investment in the creation of knowledge as in high technology. Such investment will generate a flow of benefits for producers in other sectors who pay nothing for the knowledge obtained. This 'public goods' aspect to knowledge-creation means that innovators rarely appropriate in full the return on money invested in technological innovation. For this reason, in the absence of any subsidy, producers will underinvest in knowledge-creation. A subsidy therefore plays the role of ensuring an optimum level of investment in new knowledge by society as a whole. For these reasons, most governments subsidise both *basic* research conducted in universities and *applied* research carried out in industry. However, a problem arises because government subsidisation of such research may become a covert means whereby governments can give unfair advantage to their own producers. This will be the case whenever the degree of subsidy exceeds that required to eliminate the relevant distortion. For this reason, subsidies granted to producers in technology-intensive industries frequently give rise to friction in trade policy.

131

Export subsidies

An export subsidy is defined as a payment to an exporter of either a fixed sum of money per unit exported or a proportion of the value of the goods exported. Figure 4.5 illustrates the economic effects of an export subsidy on both the exporting and importing countries. Consider first the *exporting country*. Before the subsidy is granted, Q_1Q_2 of the product is exported to the importing country at a price of OP_0. At price OP_0, OQ_2 is produced, of which OQ_1 is consumed domestically and Q_1Q_2 is exported. An export subsidy of P_1P_2 is now paid. This has the effect of lowering the price of exports but by less than the amount of subsidy. This is because the domestic price of the good also rises. If it failed to do so, all of the output would be sold for export. It will rise by a large enough amount to ensure that producers get as much for the product domestically as they would get through exporting with the subsidy added on. Suppose the domestic price rises to OP_1 and the export price falls to OP_2 such that the difference between the two prices is the amount of the subsidy, i.e. P_1P_2. Output in the exporting country rises from OQ_2 to OQ_3 and consumption falls from OQ_1 to OQ_0. Exports now equal Q_0Q_3. Consumers lose consumer surplus given by areas (A + B), while producers gain increased producer surplus equal to area (A + B + C). The cost of the government subsidy is (B + C + D + E + F + G). Therefore, the exporting nation experiences a *net* welfare loss equal to areas (B + C + D + E + F + G) less area C which equals (B + D + E + F + G). This may be further broken down into a consumption loss (area B) (as with a tariff), a production loss (area D) (as with a tariff) and a terms-of-trade loss (represented by areas (E + F + G)) as the exporting country receives lower prices for its exports (OP_2) than before (OP_0). Next consider the *importing country*. In the importing country, price falls from OP_0 to OP_2. Demand increases from OQ_1 to OQ_2 and domestic production falls from OQ_0 to zero. Imports expand from Q_0Q_1 to OQ_2. Consumers gain extra consumer surplus equal to (W + X + Y + Z) but producers lose producer surplus equal to area W. The importing country enjoys a net welfare gain equal to (X + Y + Z).

If an export subsidy reduces the welfare of an exporting country, why do countries subsidise their exporters? Clearly, the preferable policy would be an export tax. Yet, in reality, export subsidies are more common than export taxes. Awareness of this reality has led theorists to question the assumptions implicit in much conventional analysis of trade intervention. What if the traditional assumptions of perfectly competitive markets and constant returns to scale are dropped? Then, from the point of view of the exporting nation, an export subsidy may be desirable as a strategic measure to deter foreign competition. This is what has come to be known as *strategic trade policy*. The argument is most relevant to those industries in which the market is dominated by a comparatively small number of rival sellers and in which, because of these conditions, each seller faces considerable

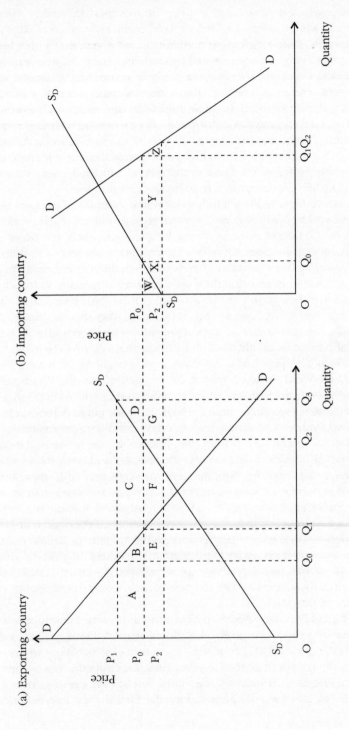

(a) Exporting country

(b) Importing country

Figure 4.5 The effects of an export subsidy on an exporting and an importing country

uncertainty when determining its price and output. Invariably, they are industries in which, because of heavy fixed costs, average costs fall sharply with output (so-called increasing returns activities) such that a high level of output is required to ensure minimal profitability. The industries which best fit this description are the high-technology or technology-intensive sectors such as civil aircraft production, the semiconductor industry, electronics, supercomputers, and so on. In these industries, the enormous fixed costs of research and development which are typically associated with the launching of a new product mean that average costs continue to fall over a substantial range of potential output. Given the limited size of the world market, it may only be possible for a few firms to achieve a sufficiently high volume of output to make investment in a new product worthwhile.

A distinctive feature of such industries is that, because of the high degree of interdependence which exists between rival producers, each producer is engaged in a constant game of trying to guess the likely reactions of his rivals to whatever he does. Of necessity, producers are forced to think and act *strategically*. The possibility therefore exists that governments may be able to play a role in assisting their own national producers to outwit rival producers in other countries. In so doing, they may succeed in raising national economic welfare at the expense of the other country. More specifically, the granting of an export subsidy to a national firm may act to deter rival producers in other countries from even entering the market for a new product. The possibility that an export subsidy might have a benign effect in a country where one of its industries has the characteristics described above was first set out by Brander and Spencer (1985) in a now celebrated article (see also Brander, 1986). They sought to demonstrate that, in so-called strategic industries, under certain conditions an export subsidy could shift economic rents from the foreign to the domestic industry. Because new firms are unable to enter the industry and compete away long-run excess profits, existing suppliers enjoy excess profits. If, therefore, by the use of subsidies a country can boost its output and market share at the expense of other countries, it can shift rent from foreign to domestic producers and improve national economic welfare. Economic rent is used here to denote both excess profits accruing to owners of capital over and above the minimum necessary to persuade them to risk their capital and that element of wages paid to labour as a payment for their specific skills. Provided that these rents exceed the cost of the subsidy, such a policy could be welfare-improving.

The original Brander–Spencer model assumed a world duopoly in which two dominant sellers competed in a global market. Firms are assumed to behave in the manner first proposed by Cournot (1838). That is to say, each firm takes the output of its rival as given and does not take into account the possibility that its own decision regarding output may cause its rival to act differently. In other words, firms ignore the fact of their interdependence and do not engage in a game of trying to guess the actions of each other. The outcome of such a situation is that the price and output of each firm ends up somewhere between that of perfect competition and that of monopoly. Each firm is able to earn excess profits in the long run, for new firms cannot enter the industry. Now, if the government in one country grants an export subsidy to its own producer, the latter will increase its production and lower its price. The best response of the rival in the foreign country is to reduce its own output. As a result, the firm in the subsidy-granting country is able to expand its market share and consequently increase its share of excess returns at the expense of its rival. An important question concerns whether or not firms behave in the manner suggested by the Cournot model.

To illustrate the argument, Krugman (1989; 1990) has suggested the following example. Suppose there are two producers, Boeing in the USA and Airbus in Europe, which are competing to sell a similar aircraft in each other's home market. (All sales are assumed to be for export and none for domestic consumption.) Suppose that the potential market for the new product is such that either firm could earn excess returns only if the other did not produce. In other words, if both produce, both lose money. The matrix below shows the outcome of various possible permutations where P denotes the choice to produce and N not to produce.

| | | Airbus | |
		P	N
Boeing	P	−5 −5	0 100
	N	100 0	0 0

Suppose that Boeing has a head start and commences production before Airbus. If Airbus now decides to produce, it will end up making losses of −5; so it will be deterred from doing so. In this case, Boeing will earn excess profits of 100. If, however, the European Union were to grant Airbus a subsidy of, say, 10 before Boeing commenced production, it would deter Boeing from doing so. For, in this case, Boeing would end up with losses of −5 while Airbus would enjoy a profit of 5. The subsidy would be enough to deter Boeing from producing, in which case Airbus would make a profit of 110. Deducting the subsidy of 10 from Airbus's profit, the welfare gain to Europe is equal to 100. Of course, Europe's gain is America's loss. Global welfare is not increased. However, the subsidy has enabled Europe to shift economic rent from American to European factor owners.

Strategic trade policy theory has attracted considerable interest in recent years as creating a rationale for an economic policy of export 'targeting', that is to say, selecting specific strategic export industries for export subsidisation. However, closer examination shows that the conclusions of the theory depend heavily on the assumptions made. If these assumptions are relaxed, it is much less apparent that such a policy would be welfare-improving. Attention has already been drawn to the assumptions made about the behaviour of firms in oligopolistic industries. As Grossman (1986) has shown, if different assumptions are made, an export subsidy may cease to be welfare-improving. The Cournot model of duopolistic behaviour employed in the Brander–Spencer model assumes that each firm first determines its optimum *output* level and then sets price accordingly. But if, instead, firms fix *price* and then adjust output accordingly, the situation changes. A position of stable equilibrium is once again achieved if each firm sets its price on the assumption that its rival's price will not be altered. However, in this case, the optimal policy for any one country ceases to be an export subsidy and becomes an export *tax*. An export tax will force the exporter to raise its price. On the same assumptions, this will compel the foreign firm to raise its price. Both countries would then enjoy higher profits than before at the expense of consumers in third countries. Of course, the same result could have been achieved by the exporter raising his price without the imposition of a tax on exports; but this suffers from a problem of credibility. From the point of view of the foreign firm, there is no assurance the exporter will maintain the higher price. Instead, he may be tempted to cheat by slightly lowering price in an effort to increase market share. For this reason, there is no certainty that the foreign firm will respond by raising its price, in which case the strategy of the exporting firm fails. Government intervention overcomes the problem by lending credibility to the action of the exporter. As Grossman (1988) argues, we simply do not know enough about how firms behave in oligopolistic industries to be certain of how they will respond to an export subsidy. Unless governments can be certain about the effects of such a policy, there is no prior assurance that the use of a subsidy will be welfare improving.

A second assumption is that entry of other producers to the industry is prevented. This is improbable except in the case of natural monopoly. The existence of large excess profits is likely eventually to induce new firms to enter the industry. Then, in the long run, excess profits will be competed away. At best, the export subsidy will yield only a temporary gain. If the effect of new firms entering the industry is to drive the price down to a competitive level, the only beneficiary of the export subsidy will be foreign consumers. Grossman (1986) argues further that the effect of the subsidy could be to induce excessive entry by producers to the industry in the subsidising country. This may have two adverse effects. Firstly, if production is subject to decreasing costs, no single firm will be able to achieve an optimum output, so resulting in higher costs. Secondly, the effect of a large number of new firms entering the industry may be to drive the long-run equilibrium price lower than before the subsidy was granted. In this case, the subsidy will permanently worsen the terms of trade of the subsidy-granting country.

A third assumption is that the product is for export only. Suppose, however, that the product is also sold domestically. In oligopolistic industries, firms tend to supply less and charge a higher price for sales to the domestic market than for export so that home consumption is sub-optimal. It follows that an increase in the amount allocated for sale domestically would raise welfare. However, an export subsidy increases the distortion by causing producers to supply *less* to domestic consumers. It follows, in this case, that an export subsidy is welfare reducing. In the absence of an effective competition policy which forces producers to price closer to marginal cost, the second-best policy for remedying the distortion would be an export *tax* not a subsidy.

Fourthly, there is a need to take into account the effect of the export subsidy on industries other than the one targeted for support. To the extent that nontargeted industries draw on the same pool of resources as the targeted one and that the supply of such resources is less than perfectly elastic, the expansion of the targeted industry will raise costs in the nontargeted industries and lower profits. At best, the losses of the nontargeted industries will merely offset some of the excess profits of the targeted one. However, there is a distinct possibility that the net effect might be unfavourable. This would be the case if the government targeted the wrong industries. It is not simply a case of selecting the industries with the highest excess profits. Account must be taken of both the amount of potential profit which can be shifted by an export subsidy and the amount of extra cost this would impose on other industries. Since this information is not available to most governments, a policy of targeting particular export industries carries the risk of being welfare-reducing rather than welfare-increasing.

Fifthly, the theory tends to ignore the problem of foreign retaliation. Since the effect of such a policy is to reap gains for domestic producers at the expense of foreign producers, it seems highly unlikely that the overseas government would not retaliate by granting a similar subsidy to its own exporter. The effects of this may be to leave both countries worse off than before. In this case, the best situation for both countries would be for neither government to intervene since the result of intervention is a subsidy war in which both countries end up worse off. On the other hand, neither country can afford not to intervene if other countries are doing so. This type of situation is known in game theory as 'prisoners' dilemma'. The solution to such a situation is for countries to reach an international agreement not to use export subsidies with a view to achieving strategic advantage. The problem with any such agreement is that each country has an incentive to cheat and grant covert illicit subsidies to its own exporters. For this reason, a country may be unwilling to co-operate in an agreement to control subsidies. This leads to the argument that countries which are seeking co-operation must resort to subsidies in a tit-for-tat manner in order to goad other countries to co-operate. In this case, the export subsidy is being used to punish other countries for engaging in practices harmful to producers in the retaliating country.

Strategic trade policy suffers from a further problem. A policy of targeting strategic export industries assumes that governments are capable of behaving in an objective manner. Even assuming they have all the necessary information at their disposal for making a rational decision, will they act dispassionately in maximising national economic welfare? The political economy of trade policy formation suggests this is unlikely. Instead, it is more likely that they will respond to whatever industrial pressure groups are most effective in lobbying for subsidies. Past experience shows that politicians will favour those groups with the greatest lobbying clout rather than act on available objective criteria. In general in the lobbying process, experience shows that producer groups tend to gain at the expense of consumer groups and the more organised industrial lobbies at the expense of the least organised. Industries located in regions containing a large number of marginal constituencies may well do better than industries in other regions. As Grossman (1986) has put it: 'the market failures in the political realm might easily outweigh those in the economic realm, leaving us with a set of strategic trade policies that would serve only the interests of those fortunate enough to gain favor'.

GATT rules on subsidies

The original GATT Treaty contained very little in the way of discipline to control the use of subsidies which might distort trade. The issue of export subsidies was dealt with as part of Article VI of the GATT. In addition to the right of a country to impose antidumping duties to counteract dumping, Article VI authorises the imposition of countervailing duties on imports which have been subsidised by the exporting country. As with antidumping duties, countervailing duties must not exceed the amount of the subsidy granted. As with dumping, the subsidy must cause or threaten material injury to an established domestic industry or retard the establishment of a domestic industry. In addition, Article XVI requires countries to notify the GATT of any trade-distorting subsidy. It further added that where a subsidy seriously prejudiced the interests of another contracting party, the subsidy-granting country should be prepared to discuss ways of limiting the subsidy. But this did not amount to very much. At the first review session in 1955, more substantive obligations were added. These are now set out in the second part of Article XVI but they relate to export subsidies only. A distinction is drawn between primary and nonprimary products. In the case of *primary* products, contracting parties are required to 'avoid the use of subsidies' on exports. However, where they are granted, they should not result in the contracting party 'having more than an equitable share of world export trade' – whatever that might mean. In the case of *nonprimary* products, it is stated that, with effect from 1 January 1958 'or the earliest practicable date thereafter', countries were to cease granting export subsidies which resulted in a price lower than the domestic price of the good. Because of the different treatment accorded to nonprimary products, developing countries saw this as a form of discrimination against their exports and therefore refused to adopt this aspect of the 1955 amendments.

The only country in the world to have made extensive use of the Article VI provisions has been the United States. Before the US Trade Act of 1974, although US importers sought to make use of countervailing law against allegedly subsidised imports, they were not very successful. Out of 191 investigations between 1934 and 1968, only 30 resulted in the imposition of countervailing duties (Destler, 1992). However, in 1974 US countervailing law was changed in a way which made relief easier to obtain. It required final action to be taken within a year of any petition for relief being received and provided for any decision that denied relief being subject to judicial review. The result was a significant increase in the number of countervailing investigations. A greater number of these resulted in affirmative decisions (35 between 1976 and 1978). However, due to a special Congressional waiver permitting the President not to impose countervailing duties for four years if the foreign government took steps to reduce its subsidy support, a significant number of these cases did not result in duties being applied. The reasons were political. The US was anxious to get the agreement of other countries on a new subsidies code as part of the Tokyo Round. In the US, subsidies were widely regarded as a means whereby other countries were able to gain an unfair advantage in trade. Existing GATT rules were considered as inadequate for coping with this situation.

On the other hand, other countries had legitimate grounds for complaint against the way in which countervailing duties could be imposed under US law. Because the countervailing laws of the US had been established before the GATT, the US was entitled to so-called 'grandfather rights' under the Protocol of Provisional Application. This meant that it was not bound to apply all the provisions contained in Article VI when these differed from US law. A specific aspect of this concerned the material injury test which makes a demonstration that imports have caused or threatened material injury to domestic producers a precondition for the imposition of countervailing duties. US countervailing law contained no such requirement, so for several decades the US was able to impose countervailing duties on imports without the need to demonstrate that imports were causing or threatening material injury to domestic producers. Other countries were insistent that, as a *quid pro quo* for any new discipline governing subsidies in trade, US countervailing laws should be brought into line with GATT law in this respect.

The 1979 Subsidies Code

The issue of subsidies was a key issue in the Tokyo Round. In particular, the US was anxious to introduce new disciplines on other countries and was prepared to bring its own countervailing laws into conformity with the GATT in order to secure an agreement. The approach adopted was to negotiate a separate stand-alone agreement or 'code' rather than seek to amend the GATT. The same device was used for tackling ten other types of nontariff barriers including antidumping (see above, p. 105). As codes are additions to the GATT rather than amendments, they only bind those countries which agree to sign the Code. The 1979 Subsidies Code had two parts or 'tracks'. The first covered *countervailing duties* and specified clearer rules, including the requirement that the subsidy be causing or threatening material injury to domestic producers. The 1979 US Trade Agreement Act revised US countervailing statutes accordingly. On the other hand, it also made clear that the full benefits of the Code would only be extended to those countries which had signed the Agreement or generally accepted its obligations. Moreover, because the Code provided for a general exception to its obligations for developing countries, the US deemed such developing countries to be ineligible to receive its full benefits. This meant that countervailing duties could be imposed on these imports without a material injury test. Alternatively, these countries could render themselves eligible to receive the full benefits of the Code by reaching separate bilateral agreement with the US. Subsequently, a number of developing countries did so. Nevertheless, a large number of countervailing duty cases which followed the 1979 Act were resolved without any injury test. A further weakness of this part of the Code was the absence of any definition of a 'subsidy' for countervailing duty purposes. There was a widely held view that this left governments with too much latitude in applying countervailing duties to imports.

The second part of the Code dealt with the obligations of countries with regard to subsidies affecting trade. The Code prohibited export subsidies on nonprimary products and went somewhat further than Article XVI. However, export subsidies affecting primary products were allowed so long as they did not result in a 'larger than equitable' share of trade (as stated in Article XVI) or depress prices unduly. The US had wanted limits imposed on both industrial and agricultural export subsidies but the EC was not prepared to accept this. The limits on primary product export subsidies were clearly much softer than those imposed on industrial products and fell a long way short of what the US had been seeking. However, for the first time, an agreement was reached on subsidies other than export subsidies. It made clear that where domestic subsidies were desirable for social or economic reasons, they should be allowed. On the other hand, it was recognised that domestic subsidies can cause or threaten injury to domestic producers and 'nullify or impair' benefits extended by one contracting party to another. Therefore, the Code required countries to avoid subsidies that have these effects. Clearly, for this to work, countries need to supply information about the various kinds of subsidy granted, but countries proved reluctant to do so. There is also the question of what kinds of assistance to industry should be classified as a subsidy. Almost every kind of government activity can be regarded as giving some assistance to domestic industry and therefore could conceivably be included. The Code failed to provide guidance. Nevertheless, the attempt to establish some discipline in relation to domestic and not just export subsidies was widely regarded as a significant step forwards. As stated above, a particular difficulty with the Code was the exception granted to developing countries. Under the Code, they were permitted to use export subsidies on industrial products. But, where these were inconsistent with their competitive and development needs, they were expected to reduce or eliminate such subsidies.

Although the Subsidies Code proved a useful first step towards bringing subsidies in trade under some form of international discipline, it left a number of issues unresolved. These were left over to the next round of GATT. Meanwhile, the incidence of US countervailing measures increased following the passage of the 1979 US Trade Agreements Act and despite the fact that a material injury test was now incorporated into US countervailing rules. In part, the reason was that the 1979 Act actually helped US firms that were petitioning for countervailing measures against allegedly subsidised foreign imports. It did so by setting strict time limits on countervailing duty cases under investigation, and this tended to favour petitioners rather than foreign suppliers, who had less time to work on and present their defence. It also provided for temporary measures to be taken against subsidised imports if there was a preliminary finding of injury, thus making possible earlier action against imports. Furthermore, responsibility for remedying unfair trade practices was passed from the Treasury to the Department of Commerce which was certain to be more sympathetic to the concerns of industry. The early 1980s witnessed a surge of countervailing cases in the US. Between 1980 and 1984 there were 249 investigations; of which 135 or 54 per cent resulted in the imposition of duties or suspension of the subsidy (Destler, 1992). The majority of these involved steel products, and were in fact resolved by the US negotiating a series of voluntary export restraint arrangements with offending countries. After 1985, the number of countervailing duty cases fell. Thus, between 1985 and 1989, there were only 96 cases. One reason for the decline was that the cases involving steel had been resolved by other countries agreeing VERs with the US. The other reason was the declining use of subsidies as interventionist policies fell out of favour and governments sought ways of reducing budget deficits.

Civil aircraft subsidies

A classic example of the problems involved in regulating the use of subsidies in trade is provided by the long-standing dispute between the US and the EC over civil aviation subsidies. Civil aircraft were the subject of a separate code negotiated as part of the Tokyo Round. This aimed to reduce tariffs and nontariff barriers affecting this trade. It also identified domestic subsidies and other special assistance given by governments to producers as a factor distorting competition between countries. The civil aircraft industry was also subject to the provisions contained in the more general Subsidies Code. However, the US expressed disappointment with the Aircraft Code in particular because it failed to establish adequate discipline over the use of subsidies by governments to gain unfair advantage in the world market. Specifically, the US was aggrieved by the extent to which Europe was subsidising the production of new aircraft as part of its Airbus programme. A particular issue, which became the subject of a US complaint to the GATT and led to the setting up of a disputes panel, concerned subsidies from the German government to Deutsche Aerospace to cover potential exchange-rate losses on the sale of Airbus aircraft as a result of a fall in the value of the dollar. The US regarded this as a blatant export subsidy, while the EC argued that it was a currency insurance scheme. The EC argued further that US companies enjoyed substantial indirect support from government subsidisation of military R&D funding and direct help from civil government budgets, such as NASA. In part, the problem arose because EC subsidies to Airbus were production and not export subsidies and therefore did not violate existing rules. Moreover, the option of using countervailing duties against the EC was hardly appropriate in this case. Although the US threatened to do so, this would only have affected Airbus sales in there and not sales in third markets. Nevertheless, the possibility of this sanction being employed did serve to persuade Europe to seek a new agreement.

On 1 April 1992, the US and the EC succeeded in reaching a bilateral agreement on civil aircraft subsidies. The US agreed to withdraw its threat to take the issue to the GATT or to take unilateral action against Airbus sales in the US. However, the parallel complaint against the German scheme for protecting Deutsche Aerospace from exchange-rate fluctuations was treated as a separate case and would not be dropped. The agreement covered all new civil aircraft with over 100 seats but did not affect subsidies granted before the agreement. Direct subsidies for aircraft production were to be banned and direct subsidies for new aircraft programmes were to be limited to 30 per cent of total development costs. This was well below the 45 per cent ceiling sought by the EC but above the 25 per cent cap demanded by the US. The US implicitly admitted that its manufacturers benefited from indirect support by agreeing, at the request of the EC, to limits on indirect subsidies also. Indirect grants were not to exceed 5 per cent of the manufacturer's civil aircraft turnover. Other aspects of the agreement included meetings twice a year for the mutual exchange of information about current and future projects and the level of government support attached to these programmes; a ban on government inducements to third countries to buy their aircraft; and provisions for the agreement to be temporarily suspended if a manufacturer were adversely affected by external factors (see *The Financial Times*, 2 April 1992). The intention was to make the bilateral agreement the centrepiece for a multilateral agreement on aircraft subsidies the following year.

However, in February 1993 the newly elected Clinton Administration indicated its intention to reopen the issue of aircraft subsidies. Faced with job losses among domestic aircraft producers, the US Trade Representative, Mickey Kantor, approached the EC for fresh consultations over Airbus subsidies. A specific issue was lack of transparency. The US claimed that loans made to members of the Airbus consortium were at significantly lower rates of interest than in the past and well below market rates. At the same time, it threatened to bring countervailing duty complaints against Airbus, an action which would entitle Airbus to terminate the agreement. Later, the US added the demand that the ceiling on direct subsidies should be lowered to 20 per cent and the agreement be multilateralised to include other countries, most notably Japan. The 1992 agreement stated that no review of the agreement or withdrawal from the agreement could happen before July 1994. On the other hand, there was pressure on both sides to reach a new multilateral agreement within the framework of the Uruguay Round before these negotiations were concluded. Not least, the EU was keen to reach a separate agreement on civil aircraft which would give it greater flexibility for aircraft subsidies than any general subsidies agreement contained in the Uruguay Round. However, in December 1993, shortly before the Uruguay Round was concluded, talks broke down. At the time of writing, agreement has still not been achieved. Interestingly, the two sides have changed their posture. The US is reported as favouring reliance on the new tighter Subsidies Code negotiated as part of the Uruguay Round (see below). It has argued that a separate agreement for aircraft is no longer necessary. By way of contrast, the EU has demanded a toughening of the Aircraft Subsidies Code, particularly with a view to placing tighter controls on indirect government support not covered by the broader general Subsidies Code. It also wants subsidy disciplines extended to aero-engines and parts, which it maintains are especially subject to such indirect support (*The Financial Times*, 19 May 1994).

The new Subsidies Code

The issue of subsidies was covered in the Uruguay Round by the same negotiating group that dealt with antidumping. Progress was initially slow because of a basic difference between those countries, in particular the United States, which were concerned about the growing use of subsidies to distort competition in trade, and other countries which were more concerned about the abuse and excessive use of countervailing duties against allegedly subsidised imports. The former wanted either the complete abolition of trade-distorting subsidies or, at least, much tougher rules to control subsidies. The latter wanted GATT rules governing the use of countervailing duties to be made stricter and in particular to avoid harassment of exporters who were trading fairly.

At the Mid-term Review, it was agreed that subsidies should be divided into three different categories: subsidies which should be prohibited; nonprohibited subsidies but against which countervailing action could be taken if they are shown to be injurious; and subsidies against which no action would be allowed. The argument was over the category into which different kinds of subsidy should be put. The US favoured putting most subsidies into the first category, whereas the EC favoured including many types of subsidy in the second and even third categories.

There was agreement that export subsidies should be prohibited. However, the US argued that many other kinds of subsidy could achieve the same effects as a straight export subsidy. She wanted this category extended to include those contingent on firms meeting domestic content or local sourcing requirements, those going to firms that are predominantly exporters, and domestic subsidies that exceed a given percentage of a company's total sales. The EC approach was to emphasise two principles: firstly, that a subsidy should only include government actions which impose a cost on the granting government; and, secondly, that a subsidy should be specific to a firm or industry. Only such subsidies would be regarded as 'actionable' and therefore subject to GATT discipline. The US argued that some kinds of subsidy might impose no cost on the government yet still confer benefits on an exporter. For example, if a government can borrow money more cheaply than a private borrower, it may be able, at no cost to itself, to lend funds to an exporter at a rate of interest below the market rate.

The specificity concept, however, was more generally acceptable to the US, being already embodied in US countervailing duty law. This would exclude all general measures used by governments which benefit all producers and therefore do not distort trade. It can reasonably be argued that, where a country makes greater use of general subsidies than other countries, any distorting effect on overall competitiveness will be eliminated through an upward appreciation of the exchange rate. Nevertheless, there is still a problem that many nonspecific subsidies might in effect bring disproportionate benefits to particular exporters or industries and thus still distort trade.

The new Subsidies Code in the Uruguay Round Final Act is entitled Agreement on Subsidies and Countervailing Measures. In Part I of the agreement, Article 1.1 defines a subsidy as 'a financial contribution by a government or any public body . . . or . . . any form of income or price support' where 'a benefit is thereby conferred'. This can include direct transfer of funds (such as grants, loans and equity infusion), tax allowances or concessions, government provision of goods and services other than general infrastructure or government assistance to a funding mechanism. This adopts the cost-to-the-granting-government approach to the definition of a subsidy favoured by the EC.

Article 2 incorporates a specificity requirement. Significantly, paragraph 2.1(c) goes most of the way to meeting possible objections to a narrow interpretation of specificity by allowing other factors to be taken into account, namely, 'use of a subsidy programme by a limited number of certain enterprises, predominant use by certain enterprises, the granting of disproportionately large amounts of subsidy to certain enterprises, and the manner in which discretion has been exercised by the granting authority in the decision to grant a subsidy'.

Part II identifies subsidies which are prohibited under the agreement and establishes a clear procedure for remedying a situation where one party considers that such a subsidy is being granted. *Prohibited subsidies* are defined as 'subsidies contingent, in law or in fact, whether solely or as one of several other conditions upon' either export performance or the use of domestic over imported goods (Article 3.1). Annex I of the agreement contains an illustrative list of export subsidies. They include governmental insurance against exchange-rate risks such as was provided by the German government to Deutsche Aerospace and which was the source of a US complaint to the GATT. They also include export credits at below-market rates of interest except where a member is party to an international agreement on official export credits (or in practice applies the provisions of such an agreement).

Part III is concerned with '*actionable subsidies*' which are defined as subsidies as defined in Article 1 which cause 'adverse effects to the interest of other Members'. This may happen in one of three ways: injury to domestic producers; nullification or impairment of concessions made by countries in the course of the Uruguay Round; or 'serious prejudice' to the interests of another member country. Except for civil aircraft, the threshold for a subsidy to be actionable is set at 5 per cent of the value of the product. (Annex IV of the agreement contains rules for calculating the *ad valorem* subsidisation.) Article 6 makes clear that 'serious prejudice' exists whenever subsidies cover losses sustained by an industry or firm, or write-off government debt *and* have a cross-border effect. The latter is defined as (a) displacing or impeding either the imports or exports of another member; (b) resulting in significant price undercutting in the market of another member; (c) resulting in an increase in the world market share of a particular primary product or commodity compared with its average share of the previous three years. Agricultural subsidies are, however, not included but are dealt with separately. As with prohibited subsidies, there is a set procedure for remedying situations arising whenever one country believes that actionable subsidies are having the above effects.

Part IV identifies a third category of *nonactionable subsidies*. These cover all nonspecific subsidies, assistance to research activities (providing that it does not cover more than 75 per cent of the costs of industrial research or 50 per cent of the costs of precompetitive development activity), regional aid (subject to certain strict conditions) and assistance to help existing facilities adapt to new environmental requirements. However, there is a requirement that members must notify the WTO of any nonactionable subsidy programmes which it intends to implement plus any subsequent changes to make sure that they conform to the conditions and criteria stipulated.

Part V deals with countervailing measures. Article 11 sets out new stricter requirements for countervailing duty investigations. There is a requirement that sufficient evidence must be provided by petitioners for both the existence of a subsidy and a causal link between subsidised imports and injury *before* an investigation is initiated. Simple assertion which is not substantiated is not sufficient. A *de minimis* requirement that the amount of the subsidy must exceed 1 per cent of the value of the product must also be satisfied. Article 12 sets out the rights of interested members and all interested parties during the investigation itself. Article 14 contains rules regarding the calculation of the amount of the subsidy. There is a general requirement that the method used must be set out in national legislation and be applied in each particular case in a way that is transparent and properly explained. In addition, further guidelines are included which make clear that government provision of equity capital, a government loan or loan guarantee, or government provision of goods or services cannot normally be treated as conferring a benefit. Article 15 sets out rules for the determination of material injury as required under Article VI. These are similar to those stipulated for antidumping. Many of the other provisions relating to countervailing duties are much the same as those provided for dumping. As with antidumping duties, there is a new sunset clause providing for duties to be terminated after five years unless it can be demonstrated through a review that subsidisation and injury would reoccur with the removal of the duty.

Finally, Parts VIII and IX contain some important provisions for developing countries and countries in transition. It is recognised that subsidies play an important role in the economic development of developing countries. The poorest of them are exempt from the general prohibition affecting all export subsidies. Other developing countries are allowed eight years in which to phase out all export subsidies, with provision for longer in exceptional cases. Where export subsidies are inconsistent with development needs, however, they must be eliminated within a shorter period of time and not increased. Any developing country which reaches 'export competitiveness' in a particular product – defined as a share of at least 3.25 per cent in world trade for two consecutive years – must phase out export subsidies within a two-year period. Developing countries are also exempt from some of the provisions relating to actionable subsidies, although not if nullification or impairment of tariff concessions or other GATT obligations occurs. Countervailing duty investigations against products from developing countries must also be terminated if the overall level of subsidy is less than 2 per cent of the value of the product (3 per cent for countries which have eliminated export subsidies within the stipulated eight-year period) or the volume of subsidised imports is less than 4 per cent of total imports. Part IX makes clear that countries in transition from a centrally planned to a market-based economy are also subject to special arrangements because of the need to use subsidies in the interim period. They have seven years in which to eliminate export subsidies. As with developing countries, actionable subsidies are not subject to the provisions for developed market economies except where there is a nullification or impairment of tariff concessions or other GATT obligations.

The new subsidies agreement clearly represents a considerable improvement on the former 1979 Code. In particular, it contains a much clearer definition of what constitutes an actionable subsidy. The prohibition of all kinds of export subsidy, with an illustrative list of what might be included, accords with US demands for the abolition of the most obvious kinds of trade-distorting subsidy. The identification of a second category of actionable subsidies with a specificity requirement and a need to demonstrate a cross-border effect provides a clearer set of rules for tackling subsidies other than export subsidy. It also meets the concerns of those countries opposed to any kind of outright ban on subsidies which are considered desirable for other reasons. The identification of a third category of nonprohibited subsidies further ensures that subsidies with no obvious trade-distorting effect are not subject to the new measures. The agreement also contains a much clearer statement of the method to be used in calculating the level of subsidy. The provisions relating to the use of countervailing duty investigations should also significantly reduce the risks to exporters who are trading fairly of being subject to harassment. Finally, there would appear to be a consensus that developing countries should be treated differently while recognising that these countries cannot forever be allowed to enjoy special treatment. An important merit of the new Subsidies Code is that it will apply to all WTO members unlike the Tokyo Round Code which applied only to those countries that chose to accept its obligations.

There remain a number of loose ends, which must be left to future rounds to knit up in the light of the experience of the new agreement. It is also the case that agricultural subsidies continue to be subject to different treatment even though the Uruguay Round has succeeded in providing for a substantial reduction in their levels. As with the antidumping provisions, the adequacy of these new arrangements will only be fully known in the light of subsequent experience.

CONCLUSION

The gradual lowering of tariff barriers by the developed market economies has brought in its wake increasing demands for a so-called 'level playing field' in international trade. Free trade, the argument goes, is not possible between countries which play by different rules. Dumping and subsidisation are seen as two ways by which some countries compete 'unfairly'. Closer scrutiny of the arguments about dumping suggest that much of this concern is ill-founded. The one case where a clear-cut argument exists for combating dumping is a situation where a dominant supplier engages in below-cost pricing with predatory intent. Such cases are certainly fairly rare. Where, however, predatory pricing is found to be taking place with harmful consequences, the matter could readily, and probably more effectively, be handled by the antitrust authorities in the importing country. Regardless, however, of whether or not an economic rationale exists for antidumping, it seems unlikely that countries will dispense with the armoury which they have created for dealing with it. If this is so, the need then becomes one of devising rules which will prevent antidumping from becoming an easy means for producers who are unable to cope with increased competition from abroad from gaining back-door protection. The frequent use of antidumping by developed market economies in recent decades suggests that it has become too easy an option for rent-seekers unable to get protection by other means. The new Antidumping Code goes some way to tackling some of the anomalies which have existed up to now. Nevertheless, in other respects, it is woefully inadequate. It is likely that countries will continue to make considerable use of the latitude which the existing rules allow. It is already the case that a growing number of investigations are originating in developing countries clearly ready to play the developed countries at their own game.

Subsidies raise somewhat more complex problems. Although the existence of an element of subsidy in the price of an imported product may be used by an importing country to justify countervailing measures equivalent to those of antidumping policy, governments may also deliberately use subsidies to distort trade. Therefore, rules are required to control the use of trade-distorting subsidies; they need to distinguish those subsidies which are clearly damaging to producers in other countries from those which are not. It is desirable that these should cover domestic as well as export subsidies. Given the absence of such rules in the past, except the provisions for countervailing measures against export subsidies, the new Subsidies Code is to be welcomed. One immediate result is certain to be an increase in the number of disputes which concern the use of subsidies. This need not matter if, as a result, WTO member states make less use of unilateral threats. Multilateral rules and procedures are to be preferred as they permit a more objective appraisal of whether a particular practice constitutes a genuine infringement of another country's trading rights. It remains to be seen how well the new Code will work. A developing belief that, in high-technology industries at least, subsidies are needed to get first-start advantages can also be expected to generate a growing number of disputes of this kind.

5

THE DEVELOPING COUNTRIES

INTRODUCTION

An important issue in international trade policy ever since the GATT came into being has been whether developing countries should be granted different and more favourable treatment on account of their special position. The GATT is based on the principle of nondiscrimination as stated in Article I, the famous Most-favoured-nation Clause. This means that contracting parties are required to treat equally products coming from other contracting parties. Thus, in the absence of any other provisions, it would preclude any country from granting more favourable treatment to poorer countries on account of them being at a lower stage of development. Another requirement is that countries should take an active part in multilateral trade negotiations. That is to say, countries should be prepared to offer concesssions to trading partners and not just receive any concessions which other countries make and which are automatically extended to all contracting parties in conformity with the nondiscrimination principle. Such reciprocity is required in order to prevent any free-riding.

The question which GATT was compelled to address was whether an exception should be made to these rules for developing countries. The arguments favouring such a policy were broadly speaking twofold. Firstly, there is the essentially normative argument that equal treatment of unequals results in unfairness because developing countries are starting from a disadvantageous situation. Therefore, trade rules should practise positive discrimination in favour of poorer countries. Secondly, there is the argument that the needs of economic development in developing countries necessitates their pursuit of different trade policies to those of developed countries. One example of this is the well-known infant-industry argument often put forward to justify developing countries' protection of newly established industries either by high tariffs or by subsidies to domestic producers. Similarly, granting special incentives to exporters is a policy which might be justified in a developing country in order to direct the economy along a virtuous path of export-led growth. It will be seen that the principle of treating developing countries differently was recognised from early on in the history of the GATT. In the 1960s, the principle of reciprocity was waived for developing countries; this meant that they were not required to offer tariff concessions in GATT negotiations but received any concessions which developed countries made towards each other. In the 1970s, in response to pressure from developing countries, a waiver was granted allowing developed countries to grant tariff preferences on products coming from developing countries.

It remains debatable whether the granting of special status to developing countries in both these respects brought much benefit to developing countries as whole. Relaxing the reciprocity requirement in the case of developing countries amounted to very little so long as the concessions made by developed countries largely affected products traded by developed countries. Moreover, as developing countries subsequently realised, the failure to play an active role in multilateral trading negotiations by offering concessions of benefit to developed countries deprived them of any bargaining counter. In the Uruguay Round, developing countries played a noticeably more prominent part, being prepared to offer more in the way of concessions to developed countries in order to extract concessions of value to themselves. In a similar manner, although the granting of tariff preferences by developed countries on manufactured products coming from developing countries may have benefited a small number of the more advanced developing countries, the gain to developing countries as a whole appears to have been quite small. The view has been expressed that developing countries would gain more from seeking larger nondiscriminatory tariff reductions by developed countries through negotiation than by seeking any extension or improvement of preferences.

The first part of this chapter explores the main issues involved in the debate about the most appropriate trade policy for developing countries which wish to achieve rapid economic growth and development. Specifically, it discusses the relative merits and demerits of outward-looking, export-oriented as opposed to inward-looking, import-substitution policies. The next section of the chapter examines how GATT rules were developed to provide special treatment for developing countries. The question is asked whether the policy of developed countries giving preferential treatment to exports coming from developing countries has been successful in assisting developing countries. A key issue in negotiations between developed and developing countries concerning special and more favourable treatment for developing countries has been the issue of graduation. This is the notion that, as developing countries grow, they should be required to assume progressively normal GATT obligations. The next section of the chapter explores this issue. Of special concern to developing countries have been the unique arrangements which were established in the early years of the GATT for exempting trade in textiles from normal GATT discipline. The chapter examines why textiles have been treated differently, and the effects of these arrangements. The Uruguay Round provides for the phasing out of the Multi-fibre Arrangement by 2005. This is discussed towards the end of the chapter along with the other effects of the Uruguay Round on developing countries.

TRADE POLICY IN DEVELOPING COUNTRIES

Much thinking in the earlier years of the postwar period regarding the most suitable trade policy for developing countries was influenced by the structuralist school with its emphasis on state planning, government intervention and trade policies which encouraged import-substitution. (Structuralism is most commonly associated with the work of the United Nations Economic Commission for Latin America in the 1950s and 1960s and its first director, Raul Prebisch.) In essence, structuralists argued that, in less developed countries, market mechanisms were unreliable due to various kinds of structural rigidities and imperfections. Where appropriate, therefore, reliance should be placed on state intervention and centralised planning. As far as trade policy was concerned, structuralists rejected open, outward-looking policies on the grounds that the nascent industries of developing countries were unable to compete with the more established industries of the developed world. Rather, the emphasis should be on promoting the development of new industries behind the shelter of high import barriers, lowering these barriers only when the industry in question had reached a size where it could stand on its own feet.

Structuralists also drew attention to what they saw as an inherent tendency for the international terms of trade to move against developing countries such that a disproportionate share of any gains from trade accrued to the already developed countries. The argument was that, over time, the world terms of trade tended to favour manufactured goods rather than primary commodities and, since developing countries exported mainly primary commodities and developed countries exported mainly manufactures, developing countries lost out to developed ones. Thus, trade with developed countries served only to widen the gap between less developed and developed countries. (This was known as the Singer–Prebisch thesis after the contributions of Singer, 1950, and Prebisch, 1950. The interested reader should see Spraos, 1980, Sapsford, 1985, and Bleaney and Greenaway, 1993, for later attempts to test the evidence for this view.) Another view was that the prices of primary commodities were inherently more unstable than prices of manufactures. Because developing countries often depended on a comparatively small number of basic commodities for export earnings, dependence on trade meant greater fluctuations in the level of economic activity and these fluctuations were assumed to be harmful to long-run growth (see MacBean and Nguyen, 1988, for a recent attempt to evaluate the evidence for this proposition).

According to this view of development, the aim of trade policy in less developed countries should be to foster import substitution in order both to conserve scarce foreign exchange and to promote the development of indigenous manufacturing industries. Agriculture was regarded as being much less important in the development process than the establishment of new manufacturing industries. Import-substitution policies should in general begin by fostering the growth of consumer goods industries through a policy of high tariffs or quotas. Once successful, the emphasis should switch to promoting the development of local intermediate and capital goods industries by the same means. In addition to tariffs and quotas, reliance should be placed on exchange controls to ration the use of scarce foreign currency, making it available at the official rate only for the purchase of essentials in a manner similar to a wartime economy. Further, to hold down the cost of imported raw materials and intermediate products needed for industrial expansion, the exchange rate for these purposes should be kept artificially high. The role of domestic policy was to ensure sufficiently buoyant demand for manufacturing goods to facilitate the growth of new manufacturing industries geared up largely to produce for the local market. Inflows of capital from abroad, including direct investment by multinational companies attracted by the need to jump high import barriers, would help to make good any deficiency in local savings.

Although such policies were pursued passionately in many less developed countries for at least the first two decades after the Second World War, there is a consensus that, in general, they were a failure. (See Greenaway and Milner, 1993, for an analysis of the demise of import-substitution prescriptions. Krueger, 1990, also provides a useful comparison of import substitution with export-promotion policies.) There were several reasons for this. Firstly, the policy failed in its aims of conserving scarce foreign exchange. The attempt to promote the development of local consumer goods industries in the first stage of the policy resulted in the import of more intermediate goods and raw materials to supply those industries. So the total volume of imports rose and the trade balance deteriorated. The second stage, which was supposed to result in the establishment of local capital goods firms and producers of intermediate products, was often never reached. At the same time, the neglect of agriculture which such policies often entailed necessitated increased food imports to feed an expanding population.

Secondly, the policy had a harmful effect on those industries in which less developed countries might hope to enjoy a comparative advantage and therefore earn these countries precious foreign exchange through exporting. By favouring the development of essentially import-competing industries producing largely for the local market, a bias was created against industries belonging to the export sector which were those in which the country was best able to compete internationally. The export sector faced a double penalty from the overvalued exchange rate: a lower price received for units sold abroad and more costly raw materials and intermediate supplies to the extent that these had to be imported from abroad.

Thirdly, the emphasis placed on increasing capital investment in manufacturing ran into the problem of inadequate domestic savings which was only partly overcome by importing capital from the developed world. Moreover, reliance on attracting large inflows of foreign capital served merely to create another kind of dependency.

Fourthly, the high levels of protection afforded to manufacturing industry raised the price of manufactures relative to agriculture and so created discrimination against the farming sector. Long-term investment in farming was thereby discouraged and because agricultural output did not increase sufficiently the need to import food was increased.

Finally, high import barriers fostered local monopolies, generally reduced competition and created a fertile ground for the bribery and corruption of state officials. Sheltered by high import barriers, local producers who often faced little or no domestic competition had no incentive to reduce costs and raise efficiency. Multinationals which were attracted to the country by a desire to jump high tariffs or quotas too often enjoyed a virtual monopoly of the local market.

In the late 1960s and early 1970s, disillusionment set in with the inward-looking, import-substitution approach to economic development. A small but significant number of developing countries switched to more outward-looking policies which placed the emphasis on export promotion. The aim of such policies was to promote the exports of developing countries by creating discrimination within the local economy in favour of the export sector. This was the exact opposite of import-substitution, which invariably discriminated against industries biased towards exporting. Since, in the initial stages of take-off, most developing countries enjoy a comparative advantage in labour-intensive manufactures, it was these branches of manufacturing which were favoured under an export-oriented policy. Governments sought to promote these sectors by a variety of policies including direct subsidies, subsidised credit, various kinds of fiscal incentive and the setting up of special export-processing zones which bestowed special privileges on foreign companies producing largely for export. In many but not all cases, tariffs were lowered and nontariff barriers such as quotas reduced or eliminated altogether. Often, exchange controls were also relaxed to make it easier for producers to obtain foreign currency at the official rate for importing raw materials and other components and parts from abroad. Fiscal and monetary policies were kept tight in order to hold down domestic costs and prices and to free resources for exporting.

Such policies were pursued with greatest effect in the newly industrialising countries of South-East Asia (particularly Hong Kong, South Korea, Taiwan and Singapore). As a result, these countries enjoyed above-average rates of economic growth. The major component of this faster growth was the rapid increase of manufacturing exports consequent upon the pursuit of export-oriented policies. The main advantages of such a strategy are as follows. Firstly, such policies give the greatest encouragement to those industries in which developing countries have the lowest relative costs. By encouraging resources to shift into those industries, they improve the use of the country's scarce resources. This contrasts with import-substitution policies which too often favoured the development of heavy, capital-intensive industry in which only the large developing countries are likely to excel. Secondly, an export-oriented strategy creates better opportunities for manufacturing industry to expand to a size and at a rate necessary to reap available static and dynamic economies of scale. In many developing countries, the home market is too small for newly established capital-intensive producers to achieve sufficient size and is unlikely to grow fast enough. On the other hand, where a developing country gets locked into a virtuous path of rapid export growth feeding through into fast domestic growth, beneficial spillover effects may be created for the entire local economy. Thirdly, a policy of lowering tariffs and reducing or eliminating other kinds of import barrier exposes local producers to increased competition and forces them to cut prices and seek out new, lower-cost methods of production. Fourthly, an export-orientated strategy creates the necessary conditions for a country to exploit the advantages obtainable from the dynamics of evolving comparative advantage. As the country develops, it can be expected to experience rising wage-rates and will eventually lose its former advantage in the simpler, highly labour-intensive goods which it used to export. The need is to invest more in physical and human capital and to develop new pockets of competitive advantage in the more sophisticated, skill-intensive and even knowledge-intensive branches of manufacturing. An outward-looking, export-oriented trade policy creates the conditions for this to happen spontaneously. By way of contrast, an inward-looking, import-substitution policy tends to shut resources into those sectors which offer developing countries the least opportunities in the future. Finally, the effect of an export-oriented policy on income distribution is benign. By favouring industries which are essentially labour intensive, export-oriented policies raise wages relative to profits in contrast with import-substitution policies which raise rents relative to wages.

In 1987, the World Bank published the results of a study carried out on trade policies pursued by some forty-one developing countries over the periods 1963–73 and 1973–85 (World Bank, 1987). Countries were classified into four groups: strongly outward-oriented; moderately outward-oriented; moderately inward-oriented; and strongly inward-oriented – according to their trade policies (see also Greenaway and Nam, 1988, for an earlier attempt to employ this type of approach to the analysis of trade policy). Table 5.1 lists the countries falling into each of the four categories in the two periods and their annual average growth rate. A strongly outward-oriented policy was defined as one in which there was little or no policy bias towards production for the domestic market. This meant that if import barriers existed, they were roughly matched by export incentives. It also meant that the exchange rate was set at an economically appropriate level. A moderately outward-oriented policy was one in which there was only a slight bias towards production for the domestic market. A low effective rate of protection with little variation between sectors and limited use of quantitative restrictions were the main criteria. (A feature of most import-substitution policies is that higher tariffs are put on imports of finished goods than on intermediate goods or raw materials.) A moderately inward-oriented policy was one in which policy was unmistakably biased towards production for the domestic market. This was the case where the effective rate of protection was quite high and variable between sectors, where quantitative restrictions were important and where the exchange rate was permanently overvalued. Finally, a strongly inward-oriented policy was one in which there existed a very pronounced discrimination in favour of production for the domestic market. This would entail very high rates of effective protection, quantitative trade barriers as the norm rather than the exception, and a grossly overvalued exchange rate. The study shows that, in both periods, the three most outwardly oriented countries enjoyed growth rates considerably in excess of other developing countries. In the period 1963–73, the moderately outward-oriented countries grew faster than the moderately inward-oriented. However, in the period 1973–85, the growth rate in the latter was slightly above that in the former, demonstrating that there was not a direct correlation between an outwardly oriented policy and fast growth. This is not surprising given that factors other than trade policy influence economic performance. Nevertheless, the World Bank (1987) concluded that, taken as a whole, the evidence supported the view that outward-looking export-oriented policies were more successful than inward-looking import-substitution policies in achieving fast growth.

Influenced by findings of this kind as well as the observation that the most successful developing countries have been those adopting such policies, a growing number of developing countries have in recent decades changed their development strategies. Many have embarked on pro-grammes of trade policy reform alongside other measures that place greater reliance on market mechanisms. Another factor in this process has been the emphasis placed by the World Bank since 1980 on trade policy reform as a

Table 5.1 The outward-looking way to faster growth: real GNP per person, annual average growth (%)

Outward-oriented				Inward-oriented			
Strongly		Moderately		Moderately		Strongly	
1963–73							
Singapore	9.0	Brazil	5.5	Yugoslavia	4.9	Turkey	3.5
S. Korea	7.1	Israel	5.4	Mexico	4.3	Dominican	
Hong Kong	6.0	Thailand	4.9	Nigeria	4.2	Republic	3.4
		Indonesia	4.6	Tunisia	4.0	Burundi	3.2
		Costa Rica	3.9	Kenya	3.9	Argentina	3.1
		Malaysia	3.8	Philippines	2.2	Pakistan	3.1
		Ivory Coast	3.5	Bolivia	2.0	Tanzania	2.7
		Colombia	3.3	Honduras	1.9	Sri Lanka	2.3
		Guatemala	2.7	El Salvador	1.4	Ethiopia	1.9
				Madagascar	1.1	Chile	1.7
				Nicaragua	1.1	Peru	1.5
						Uruguay	1.5
						Zambia	1.2
						India	1.1
						Ghana	0.4
		Cameroun	−0.1	Senegal	−0.6	Bangladesh	−1.4
						Sudan	−1.9
1973–85							
Singapore	6.5	Malaysia	4.1	Cameroun	5.6	Bangladesh	2.0
Hong Kong	6.3	Thailand	3.8	Indonesia	4.0	India	2.0
S. Korea	5.4	Tunisia	2.9	Sri Lanka	3.3	Burundi	1.2
		Brazil	1.5	Pakistan	3.1	Dominican	
		Turkey	1.4	Yugoslavia	2.7	Republic	0.5
		Israel	0.4	Colombia	1.8		
		Uruguay	0.4	Mexico	1.3		
		Chile	0.1	Philippines	1.1		
				Kenya	0.3		
				Honduras	−0.1	Ethiopia	−0.4
				Senegal	−0.8	Sudan	−0.4
				Costa Rica	−1.0	Peru	−1.1
				Guatemala	−1.0	Tanzania	−1.6
				Ivory Coast	−1.2	Argentina	−2.0
				El Salvador	−3.5	Zambia	−2.3
				Nicaragua	−3.9	Nigeria	−2.5
						Bolivia	−3.1
						Ghana	−3.2
						Madagascar	−3.4

Source: World Bank (1987)

significant element in its new programme of structural adjustment lending. Although structural adjustment loans contained many different elements, almost 80 per cent have had trade policy reform as a condition (Greenaway and Milner, 1993). Key elements were the removal of quantitative restrictions on imports, the lowering of tariffs, reductions in exchange rates which are clearly overvalued and export promotion. In 1990, a World Bank study examined some thirty-six examples of trade policy reform in nineteen countries over the entire period from 1945 to 1984 (World Bank, 1990). It found that fifteen had been successful, nine were partially reversed and twelve had collapsed. All successful programmes involved a mix of the following: reduction or elimination of import quotas, currency devaluation and tight fiscal policy. Of these measures, elimination of import quotas was found to be even more important than cutting tariffs and certain to yield positive results. An early and substantial devaluation was also found to be an important ingredient of a successful development programme but only if accompanied by tight fiscal and monetary policy. Expansionary fiscal and monetary policies were found to be the most important cause of the abandonment of trade reforms.

Two potentially adverse effects of a trade policy reform programme concern the effects of cutting tariff rates on government revenues and of lowering import barriers on unemployment. Developing countries often depend on import tariffs for revenues so that a policy of cutting tariffs can create budgetary problems. (Export taxes are also an important source of fiscal revenues in many developing countries.) However, because lower tariff *rates* lead to a higher volume of imports, tariff *revenues* need not fall, and may even rise. Moreover, if accompanied by a devaluation which causes the local currency price of imports to rise, lower tariffs may still yield more in local currency terms. It is also the case that trade reform programmes typically involve a switch from quantitative import barriers which yield no revenue to tariffs which do. Trade policy reform may also lead to a small rise in unemployment in the short run due to a decline of employment in the import-substitution sector. On the other hand, this will be offset by increased employment in other sectors (such as agriculture) which were previously subject to negative discrimination. A key factor here is whether or not trade policy reform is accompanied by a lowering of the exchange rate which boosts output and employment in the tradable goods sector.

The growing awareness among developing countries that economic growth is generally best promoted by a policy which emphasises export promotion and is mostly harmed by inward-looking policies which seek import-substitution has caused these countries to adopt a different approach towards trade negotiations with the developed countries. As noted above, for much of the postwar period, developing countries played little or no role in GATT rounds. They were largely content to reap the benefits of any tariff concessions made by the developed countries and which were auto-matically extended to developing countries on a most-favoured-nation basis but were unwilling to make concessions themselves as a bargaining counter to gain benefits of more interest to them. The GATT was widely viewed as a 'rich man's club' bringing few if any benefits to the developing world. Indeed, in the early years, a number of developing countries (such as Mexico) chose not to sign the General Agreement because they considered the rules biased towards industrial countries. Those which did sign took little or no part in any of the earlier GATT rounds.

In the recently concluded Uruguay Round, however, a significant change took place. For the first time, many developing countries took an active part and were prepared to offer concessions of value to developed countries and to accept more GATT obligations than in the past in order to achieve their particular objectives. Matters of special concern to developing countries were the need to secure improved access for products of special interest to them, such as textiles and agricultural goods, and the need to obtain a tougher and more effective disputes-settlement mechanism which would protect them against the imposition of new restrictions on their exports. This change reflected an awareness on the part of developing countries that their own interests were not served by maintaining high barriers against goods coming from the developed countries. Such barriers are more likely to impoverish the country than benefit it. Instead, the need was to secure guarantees of improved access for their exports from the developed countries in order to attract foreign investment to their economies and expand exports. To achieve this, there was a need to offer developed countries something in return. The outcome of this changed approach is discussed towards the end of the chapter, when the results of the Uruguay Round are examined. First, it is necessary to discuss how, if at all, the GATT has sought to incorporate the particular interests of developing countries.

DEVELOPING COUNTRIES AND THE GATT

The General Agreement contains only two provisions for special treatment of developing countries. Firstly, Article XVIII, entitled Governmental Assistance to Economic Development, begins by recognising that

> the attainment of the objectives of this Agreement will be facilitated by the progressive development of their economies, particularly of those contracting parties the economies of which can only support low standards of living and are in the early stages of development.
>
> (Article XVIII:1)

Further, it states that:

it may be necessary for those contracting parties, in order to implement programmes and policies of economic development designed to raise the general standard of living of their people, to take protective or other measures affecting imports . . .

(Article XVIII:2)

Section A permits a developing country to 'modify or withdraw a concession' if it 'considers it desirable, in order to promote the establishment of a particular industry with a view to raising the general standard of living of its people' (para. 7).

This is the familiar case of infant-industry protection. There are the usual provisions requiring prior consultation of other contracting parties and compensatory adjustment. Section B recognises that when a country is in the process of rapid economic development it may 'experience balance of payments difficulties arising mainly from efforts to expand their internal markets as well as from the instability in their terms of trade' (para. 8).

Therefore, a developing country is permitted, 'in order to safeguard its external financial position and to ensure a level of reserves adequate for the implementation of its programme of economic development . . . [to] . . . control the general level of its imports by restricting the quantity or value of merchandise permitted to be imported' (para. 9).

Once again, there are strict conditions, requiring consultation with other contracting parties, review of restrictions imposed by the contracting parties and, if necessary, modification of restrictions if they are found to be inconsistent with the provisions of Section B.

Sections C and D set out provisions that allow developing countries to grant infant-industry protection through quantitative restraints on imports. Again, there are the usual provisions requiring notification and consultation before measures are imposed (except where the industry requiring protection has already started production). Despite the fairly strict conditions set out in Article XVIII, developing countries have imposed quantitative restraints on imports almost at will using the existence of the Article to give legitimacy to such measures. Hindley (1987) argues that, in the past, one effect of this has been 'to deter developed countries from entering into normal GATT reciprocal bargaining with developing countries'. Since in practice a developing country can easily impose quantitative restrictions on imports under Article XVIII, the effect is to weaken any concessions made by a developing country when negotiating with a developed one.

The second set of rules within the GATT providing for special treatment of developing countries is contained in Part IV, entitled Trade and Development, which was added to the General Agreement in 1964. Perhaps the most important provision which this contains is the nonreciprocity commitment. Article XXXVI:8 states that:

the developed country parties do not expect reciprocity for commitments made by them in trade negotiations to reduce or remove tariffs
and other barriers to the trade of less-developed contracting parties.

This is generally taken to mean that there is no obligation on developing
countries to offer any tariff concessions in GATT negotiations although they
automatically receive any concessions offered by one developed country to
another and which must be extended in the usual way to all other
contracting parties. In other words, they are allowed to 'free ride'. As stated
above, this provision has proved to be of questionable value given that most
of the tariff cuts negotiated between developed countries in subsequent
GATT rounds and extended to all other countries were on products of little
or no importance to developing countries. In order to gain concessions from
the developed countries of value to developing countries, developing
countries needed to offer something else in return. As Hindley (1987) has
put it:

> It might be legislated that shopkeepers can sell their goods to
> members of some group in the community only at half price. If that is
> all that is legislated, however, it is likely to mean simply that members
> of the favoured group will have great difficulty in buying anything.

Subsequently, three additional agreements have been signed which
contain provisions for special treatment for developing countries. Firstly, the
various Tokyo Round codes dealing with nontariff barriers include special
provisions for developing countries. These cover antidumping, subsidies,
technical standards, government procurement, customs valuation, import
licensing and civil aviation. These extend GATT discipline to the particular
areas in question and/or provide greater detail about how GATT discipline
is to be applied in these areas. Secondly, in June 1971 it was decided
through the GATT to grant developed countries a waiver from Article I (the
nondiscrimination rule) to enable them to introduce a so-called Generalised
System of Preferences (GSP). The GSP scheme had originated in the 1960s
with the United Nations Conference on Trade and Development (UNCTAD).
At its first conference in 1964, a group of less developed countries known as
the Group of 77, moved a resolution calling for changes in the international
economic order, including a lowering of tariffs on goods coming from
developing countries. In 1968 at UNCTAD 2, agreement was reached on a
scheme for granting tariff preferences on imports from developing
countries. The 1971 waiver authorised the GSP programme initially for a
period of ten years, provided that any preference granted to any one
developing country was extended to all.

Thirdly, in 1979, as part of the Tokyo Round, a so-called Enabling Clause
was included in the Framework Agreements (entitled Differential and More
Favourable Treatment, Reciprocity and Fuller Participation of Developing

Countries). This provided a legal basis for extending the GSP beyond ten years without the need to secure a further waiver from Article I. In other words, it gave to the GSP scheme a permanent legal basis. Two aspects of the Enabling Clause are particularly important. Firstly, there was some reference to what has subsequently come to be known as a 'graduation' requirement. Developing countries are expected, as they grow and become able to do so, to participate more fully in the rights and obligations of the GATT, including making negotiated concessions in GATT rounds. Secondly, the Enabling Clause did not impose any legal obligation on GATT countries to extend such preferences. It merely made it legally possible for them to do so if they wished. Because such preferences were offered unilaterally and not as negotiated concessions, any developed country can at any time abandon or modify its GSP scheme without the need to provide compensation to the countries affected. The 1979 Enabling Clause also exempts developing countries from the requirements of Article XXIV, which deals with customs unions and free-trade areas. This means that developing countries may form preferential trading areas with each other which involve less than 100 per cent preferences.

TARIFF PREFERENCES

Following the GATT waiver of 1971, most of the developed countries introduced GSP schemes. Both the European Community and Japan did so in 1971 and the United States followed in 1976. The USA was the last country to do so, having been the main opponent of preferences in the 1960s. In most cases, they grant duty-free entry for all industrial products. However, this is nearly always qualified by provisions denying certain countries entitlement to preferential treatment, restricting the range of products covered and placing limits on the degree of preferential treatment permitted. For these reasons, the schemes fall a long way short of being a system of 'generalised' preferences as was originally envisaged.

Firstly, the lists of developing countries entitled to preferences are far from being all-embracing. The US excludes communist countries, countries participating in international commodity cartels such as OPEC (the Organisation of Petroleum-exporting Countries), countries expropriating US property without granting compensation, and countries refusing to co-operate in preventing narcotics entering the US. The EC scheme is formally more comprehensive in its coverage. It includes all countries which belong to the Group of 77 (some 125 countries) plus Romania and China (except textiles, where preferences were confined to countries belonging to the Multi-fibre Arrangement which had agreed bilateral voluntary export restraints with the EC). Some of these countries also enjoy special preference as members of the Lomé Convention which the EU has signed with some seventy African, Caribbean and Pacific (ACP) countries.

Secondly, the preferences do not extend to all products exported by developing countries. Most countries exclude so-called sensitive products which are often the products of most interest to developing countries. (Sensitive products are usually taken to be those which, if imported, are likely to cause a relatively high employment-displacement effect often concentrated in a particular region and therefore giving rise to a serious adjustment problem.) The US scheme excludes certain import-sensitive products; namely, textiles and apparel articles subject to textile agreements, watches, import-sensitive electronic articles, footwear articles and import-sensitive glass products. Any interested party may petition for articles to be removed or added to the list. The EC scheme includes most manufactured and semi-manufactured products but excludes many processed agricultural products.

Thirdly, all schemes are qualified by various kinds of quantitative limitation. In order to prevent exports from countries not entitled to preferences from being diverted through qualifying countries, strict rules of origin are prescribed. The US scheme requires that either the product must be imported directly from the beneficiary country or that the value of materials produced in the beneficiary country plus direct costs of processing must exceed 35 per cent. The EC requires that either the product be wholly produced within the beneficiary country or that imported materials used have been subject to 'substantial transformation'. This is defined as a transformation which brings them into a new four-digit heading of the Brussels Tariff Nomenclature (BTN). (Systems of trade classification aggregate goods at different levels. The one-digit level is the most aggregative. The degree of disaggregation increases with the number of digits such that the four-digit level represents quite a high degree of disaggregation.) The US scheme contains a 'competitive need limitation' under which a country may lose its duty-free treatment if its exports to the US exceed either 50 per cent of the total value of US imports of the product or a certain stated dollar value adjusted annually in accordance with the growth of US GNP. The EC scheme operates a system of individual tariff quotas for sensitive goods whereby any imports in excess of the quota become subject to the full MFN tariff. Processed agricultural goods are subject to a special safeguard clause which entitles the EC to reimpose tariffs if imports enter the EC in quantities or at prices which place EC producers at a serious disadvantage.

Table 5.2 shows the value of imports of OECD countries which are both eligible for and receive preferential treatment. These indicate that in 1984 US$63,899 million, or roughly 50 per cent, of the MFN dutiable imports of the OECD countries were eligible for preferential treatment. However, because of the various kinds of product exclusion and limits on preferential treatment, only US$32,341 million, or 26 per cent, received preferential treatment. Roughly two-thirds of these imports were accounted for by the United States, the EC and Japan. Considerable variations existed between

Table 5.2 Imports of preference-giving countries from beneficiaries of their schemes, 1984

| (1) Market | (2) Total | Imports (US$ million) | | | Shares (%) | | |
		(3) MFN-dutiable	(4) GSP-eligible	(5) Prefer-ential	(6) (4)/(3)	(7) (5)/(4)	(8) (5)/(3)
Australia	4,881	2,797	1,689	1,689	60.4	100.0	60.4
Austria	2,178	1,854	1,732	320	93.4	18.5	17.3
Canada	6,980	2,914	1,728	1,295	59.3	74.9	44.4
EC	80,505	30,462	23,719	8,667	77.9	36.5	28.4
Finland	1,726	680	330	285	50.8	86.3	43.8
Japan	32,553	15,268	10,042	6,037	65.8	60.1	39.5
New Zealand	1,002	297	260	260	87.7	100.0	87.7
Norway	934	293	132	68	45.0	51.3	23.2
Sweden	1,954	772	390	266	50.5	68.4	34.5
Switzerland	2,947	2,855	1,277	453	44.7	35.5	15.9
United States	89,600	65,925	22,600	13,000	34.4	57.0	19.7
Total OECD	225,259	124,087	63,899	32,341	51.5	50.6	26.1

Source: UNCTAD, quoted in Page and Davenport (1994)

Note: Australian and New Zealand data are for fiscal year 1983–4.

countries. At one extreme, 87 per cent of New Zealand's MFN-dutiable imports received preferential treatment whereas, at the other, only 15.9 per cent of Switzerland's imports were subject to preferences. In the case of some countries (notably, Australia and New Zealand), all eligible imports received preferential treatment. In other words, these last two schemes were unique in being truly generalised. In the case of other countries (notably, Austria, Switzerland and those of the EC), the ratio of GSP-eligible to GSP-preferential trade was much lower. In these cases, the true benefit was significantly reduced by exceptions, quantitative limitations, strict origin rules and safeguards. It is interesting to contrast the EC and US schemes. In the case of the EC, a large proportion of trade is eligible because few countries and few industrial products are excluded. It therefore appears more generous. However, quantitative limitations on preferences combined with stricter administrative rules and the exclusion of agricultural products mean that, in practice, it is much less generous than it appears. By way of contrast, the US scheme covers a smaller proportion of imports because more countries and products are excluded but there are no quantitative limitations on preferences.

A system of tariff preferences has economic effects equivalent to those of a regional trading bloc. At the static level, they will give rise to both trade creation and trade diversion. (See pp. 237–8 for a fuller discussion of these concepts.) The reduction of tariffs on imports from beneficiary countries will cause imports from developing countries to displace some higher-cost domestic production in preference-granting countries. At the same time, tariff discrimination against imports from nonbeneficiaries will cause some higher-cost imports from beneficiaries to displace lower-cost imports from nonbeneficiaries. From the global economic point of view, tariff preferences will only increase economic welfare if the trade-creating effect exceeds the trade-diverting effect. On the other hand, from the point of view of developing countries receiving preferential treatment, it is the total trade effect which matters regardless of whether it is due to trade creation or trade diversion. At the time when the GSP was introduced, it was argued that the net effect would be mainly trade-creating. This was because the effective rate of tariff protection in developed countries was found to be significantly and positively correlated with the comparative advantage of developing countries. As a result, a comprehensive GSP would allow developing countries to expand those industries in which they enjoyed a comparative advantage (Iqubal, 1974). But this took no account of the various exceptions and limitations which were subsequently built into the preference schemes created by the developed countries.

Various studies have been conducted to estimate these effects. Baldwin and Murray (1977) sought to estimate the impact of the GSP in the US, the EC and Japan using 1971 trade flows and theoretical preference margins. This was an *ex ante* study in which the effects of preferential tariff reductions were being estimated in advance. Their results showed that, for the United States, the expansion of trade amounted to nearly 30 per cent of 1971 trade flows, of which 80 per cent could be accounted for by trade creation. For the EC, the trade-creation effects were 20–25 per cent of 1971 trade flows. However, because the study assumed that all eligible imports would receive preferential treatment, the trade effects were overestimated. For the same reason, the study overestimated the trade-creation effect. At the same time, trade diversion was probably underestimated because it was assumed that elasticities of substitution between imports from GSP beneficiaries and nonbeneficiaries were the same as between imports from beneficiaries and domestic production (Langhammer and Sapir, 1987). Sapir and Lundberg (1984) used an econometric model to estimate the effect of tariff preferences on US trade flows for the period 1975–9 using both theoretical and actual preference margins. They found that trade-creation effects were about two and a half times larger than trade-diversion effects. Using a similar method to that of Baldwin and Murray, they estimated the trade-creation effect for all GSP-eligible products at US$2.2 billion using theoretical preference margins and US$1.3 billion using actual preference margins. The latter figure amounted to 21 per cent of GSP duty-free imports by the United States in 1979.

Langhammer (1983) sought to estimate the trade effects of the EC scheme using changes in import-consumption ratios between 1972 and 1975. Paradoxically, he found that imports from nonbeneficiary countries increased in the EC in comparison with the US and Canada, suggesting negative trade diversion. Other studies have suggested that the impact of the EC GSP was less than that of the US. This may not be surprising given that the EC, unlike the US, had already entered into a series of trading agreements with a number of other trading partners. As a consequence, the actual preferential margins enjoyed by GSP beneficiaries were significantly lower than if all EC imports from nonbeneficiaries had been subject to an MFN tariff. Furthermore, the extent of EC preferences was reduced by the quantitative limits imposed on the amount which could be imported at the preferential rate. Karsenty and Laird (1986) estimated the trade effects of the GSP schemes of all OECD countries for 1983. Because imports of textiles and clothing were subject to restrictions under the MFA, the GSP was largely inoperative for this product group and hence it may be more appropriate to exclude these products from the estimates. With textiles and clothing excluded, Laird and Sapir (1987) estimated the total trade effect of the GSP in 1983 for all OECD countries at US$4.6 billion or 3.2 per cent of MFN dutiable imports. Most of this was attributable to trade creation. However, this compares with a potential gain of US$20.6 billion if all eligible imports were included without any quantitative limitation. All studies confirm that the benefits from the GSP scheme are heavily concentrated among a few developing countries. Langhammer and Sapir (1987) estimate that three countries – Taiwan, South Korea and Hong Kong – account for about two-thirds of the trade expansion effects of the GSP. Some ten developing countries share 90 per cent of the gain. In a similar manner, most of the trade expansion resulting from the EC scheme went to a comparatively small number of developing countries. In both cases, the major beneficiaries have been newly industrialising countries. The poorest, least developed countries are found to have benefited proportionately less.

The results of these studies of the effects of the GSP may be summarised as follows. Firstly, the GSP has resulted in an expansion of developed-country imports from developing countries over and above what would otherwise have taken place. Secondly, this has largely taken the form of trade creation rather than trade diversion. However, the gain has not been very great largely because not all GSP-eligible imports are subject to preferential treatment. This is due to limited product coverage, limited country coverage and, in some cases, limitations on the extent of preferential treatment afforded. For these reasons, the trade effect is substantially below what would have resulted had the scheme been truly general. Fourthly, the gains are very unevenly distributed with the resultant trade expansion accruing to a small number of newly industrialising countries. The poorest LDCs derive very little benefit from the scheme largely because their exports consist of primary commodities rather than manufactures. These deficiencies have led to calls for a reform of the GSP. Proposals for reform have focused on (a) achieving uniformity between countries and across products to ensure simplicity, and (b) eliminating or reducing the amount of administrative discretion available to the importing country for denying GSP-eligible imports preferential treatment. With regard to (a), it is argued that inter-country differences in both the countries and the products granted preferences makes for complexity. With regard to (b), it is argued that the benefits of the scheme are reduced because exporters can never be sure that a consignment of goods eligible for preferential treatment will in fact qualify when they arrive in the importing country. The main effect of complexity and uncertainty is to discourage investment in manufacturing export industries in developing countries and thereby weaken the potentially positive effects of preferences on economic growth and development.

An alternative view is that developing countries should not expend time and energy in seeking to extract improvements to tariff preferences from developed countries for two reasons. Firstly, improved tariff preferences may be less valuable to developing countries than securing reductions in MFN tariffs. Although nondiscriminatory (MFN) tariff cuts erode margins of preference, it is argued that the loss from smaller preferences would be offset by the gain from lower tariffs. The reason is that the benefit of the GSP resides largely in its tariff-cutting rather than in its preferential element. This is born out by the evidence that preferences have resulted in significantly more trade creation than trade diversion. In some cases (for example, the EU), there is some evidence for negative trade diversion. Although a truly generalised system of preferences could yield significant trade gains for developing countries, developed countries are unlikely to make sufficient concessions in this respect to make that possible. By way of contrast, MFN tariff cuts, depending on the formula adopted, would affect a larger volume of trade because they would not be subject to the various kinds of product exceptions, country exceptions and quantitative limitations which charac- terise the GSP. Furthermore, although as a result of the 1979 Enabling Clause the GSP now has a permanent legal basis under the GATT, preferences granted do not have the same legal status as negotiated MFN tariff reductions. Whereas the latter are normally bound against future increases, this is not the case with preferences, which are regarded as gifts or favours extended by developed to developing countries. This weakens their value since they can more easily be withdrawn (and indeed frequently have been) and because there is no obligation on the importing country to offer equivalent concessions in compensation. One of the weaknesses of preferences has been that they have encouraged developing countries to hold back from seeking MFN tariff reductions because these were seen as eroding the margin of preference granted under the GSP. The World Bank

(1987) has criticised developing countries for seeking 'a Faustian exchange' in which they have 'given up a voice in reciprocal trade negotiations' in exchange for the granting of special and differential treatment. It is argued that the bargain was not worthwhile for the developing countries.

Secondly, the potential benefit from preferences is in many cases negated by the proliferation of nontariff barriers. In Table 3.3 (p. 58), an estimated 19 per cent of the value of imports of developed countries from developing countries and an estimated 21 per cent of import categories were subject to nontariff barriers, in both cases higher than the equivalent for imports from developed countries. The proportion is significantly higher in specific sectors of special interest to developing countries, such as textiles, steel products and agricultural products. It is argued that securing reductions in nontariff barriers through negotiation would bring greater benefits to developing countries than seeking improvements in preferences. Of special importance to developing countries in this context are the various bilateral quotas which have regulated much trade between developed and developing countries in textiles and clothing. As was discussed in Chapter 3, trade in textiles and clothing products was granted a special dispensation from normal GATT rules and disciplines under the Long-term Cotton Textile Arrangement (1962) and later the Multi-fibre Arrangement (MFA). The effect has been to reduce significantly the value of any tariff cuts (preferential or nonpreferential) granted by developed countries on these products. This is discussed further below. However, before doing so, it is necessary to discuss an issue which has occupied a central place in the debate about preferences; namely, the graduation issue.

GRADUATION

When, in 1979, the developed countries conceded the principle that developing countries should be afforded on a permanent basis 'differential and more favourable treatment', a *quid pro quo* was that such treatment would be gradually withdrawn as a country developed. Put differently, a developing country would be expected to participate progressively in GATT rules and obligations as it graduated towards developed-country status. It was, however, left unclear how this principle was to be applied in practice. Subsequently, both the United States and the EC incorporated the graduation principle in their GSP provisions. The United States 1984 Tariff and Trade Act, which renewed the authority first granted in 1974 enabling the President to grant preferences to developing countries, introduced fresh provisions for graduation. Under the provisions, a country is withdrawn from GSP benefits if its per capita income exceeds a specified dollar value (fixed annually). The 1984 legislation also expanded the list of conditions which may disqualify a particular country from the GSP. For example, a country which fails to provide adequate protection of US intellectual property rights may be treated as ineligible. In 1987, Chile had GSP status withdrawn because it had failed to afford its workers 'internationally recognised workers' rights'.

Similarly, products can be withdrawn from the GSP programme under various systems. The competitive-needs limitation contained in the 1974 Trade Act was referred to above, whereby a product can be withdrawn if exports exceed more than 50 per cent of the value of total US imports of the product in question or a stipulated dollar value. In addition, there is provision for discretionary product graduation whereby specific products from certain countries may be permanently excluded from the GSP as a result of petitions filed by US producers or trade unions. Decisions are based on a country's level of economic development, its competitiveness in a particular product and the overall economic interests of the US. Finally, a further provision permits the application of more stringent competitive-needs limitation for specific products of particular countries where the country in question has achieved a 'sufficient degree of competitiveness' in the exports of the product. Especially controversial are the provisions which authorise the President to waive the graduation provisions with regard either to countries or to products if it is in the interests of the United States to do so. Least developed countries have been granted a blanket waiver under this provision. However, the ostensible purpose of the waiver is to provide the President with a weapon with which to extract reciprocal obligations from advanced developing countries. In other words, countries which are prepared, for example, to grant US export concessions in the form of improved market access may be treated more favourably than others which are subject to graduation.

Not surprisingly, the principle of graduation has always been opposed by the developing countries. One argument is that it allows developed countries to practise discrimination against particular developing countries. A further criticism is that, in the absence of any multilateral agreement on how graduation is to be applied, it gives too much discretion to developed countries. It encourages unilateral and often arbitrary actions by developed countries which deny to developing countries benefits to which they are entitled under the GSP. Both arguments seem to be more concerned with how graduation is applied rather than the principle itself. It is difficult to treat seriously a claim that any country should be entitled to preferential treatment for ever, regardless of its level of economic development. At some point, a country which is successful in catching up can no longer be regarded as 'developing' and therefore entitled to be treated differently from any other already 'developed' country. Moreover, the principle of graduation is a political necessity if developing countries are to continue to enjoy preferential treatment of their imports. It is clear that producers in developed countries subject to import competition from developing countries will oppose preferences unless there are provisions which permit the withdrawal of benefits as and when a developing country achieves an agreed level of economic development. It is also the case that graduation permits the concentration of the benefit which GSPs may bring on those developing countries most in need. This is all the more desirable if the gain from GSPs is biased towards the richest developing countries.

Thus, the crucial issue seems to be the manner in which graduation is to be applied. At what point should a developing country be deemed to have graduated? What should happen when a country crosses the stipulated threshold? The simplest solution is to define a country as having graduated if its per capita income has reached a certain level. As we have seen, this approach has been adopted by the US. On the other hand, many developing countries appear opposed to such a criterion. In that case, the only alternative would be to leave each developed country to negotiate directly with those developing countries deemed to be candidates for graduation. Developed countries would have to offer something in return. They could, for example, allow a developing country some temporary continuation of preferential treatment. The alternative would be the threat to withdraw all special benefits completely. This would create the notion of what Hindley (1987) has called 'staged graduation'. As countries graduate, some but not all of the benefits of 'differential and more favourable treatment' are gradually withdrawn. GSP benefits constitute only one of the elements of such treatment. By way of example, the removal of the obligation to reciprocate constitutes another element. In this case, a requirement might be that, as a country graduates, the right not to reciprocate is removed but that it continues to enjoy GSP benefits for an agreed period. Limiting the access of developing countries to Article XVIII whereby such a country may impose quantitative restraints on imports for balance of payments reasons may be another element which could be removed as graduation takes place.

Little was achieved in the Uruguay Round with regard to this issue except in respect of the least developed countries (LDCs). This took the form of a Decision on Measures in Favour of Least Developed Countries. It was recognised that these countries constituted a special group of developing countries with specific needs and entitled to more favourable treatment than other developing countries. It was therefore stated that they,

> for as long as they remain in that category, while complying with the general rules set out in the aforesaid instruments, will only be required to undertake commitments and concessions to the extent consistent with their individual development, financial and trade needs, or their administrative and institutional capabilities.

It was also agreed that they should be given an extra year in which to submit schedules. Further provisions included regular reviews to ensure 'expeditious implementation of all special and differential measures' taken in their favour; earlier implementation of MFN concessions on tariffs and nontariff measures on products of export interest to LDCs where possible; consideration to be given to further improving GSP and other schemes for products of particular export interest to LDCs; the concerns of LDCs to be given special consideration in the implementation of the provisions of the Final Act; export interest of LDCs to be given special consideration when applying import relief measures; and increased technical assistance to be afforded to LDCs to facilitate the promotion and diversification of their exports. The application of graduation by developed countries to the imports of other advanced developing countries was left to developed countries to determine for themselves.

TEXTILES

One of the main concerns of developing countries for at least the past three decades has been the failure of the developed countries to apply normal GATT disciplines to trade in textiles and clothing products. In 1991 trade in textiles accounted for 3.3 per cent of world merchandise exports and 4.6 per cent of world exports of manufactures, while trade in clothing accounted for 3.5 per cent of world merchandise exports and 4.8 per cent of world exports of manufactures (GATT, 1993a). However, for many developing countries, textile and clothing exports account for a significant proportion of their total exports. For example, exports of texiles accounted for 48 per cent of total exports in Pakistan, 21 per cent in Egypt, 18 per cent in Bangladesh, 12 per cent in India, 11 per cent in China and Turkey and 10 per cent in South Korea. Exports of clothing accounted for 67 per cent of total exports in Macao, 52 per cent in Sri Lanka, 49 per cent in Mauritius, 35 per cent in Bangladesh, 32 per cent in Tunisia, 27 per cent in Turkey and 23 per cent in Jamaica (GATT, 1993a). Although many of the restrictions currently in place on textile imports go back much earlier, the legal basis for all trade restrictions affecting textiles and clothing products was an agreement signed in 1961 and known as the Short-term Arrangement regarding International Trade in Cotton Textiles (STA) which was replaced in the following year by the Long-term Arrangement (LTA). In 1973, this was superseded by the Multi-fibre Arrangement (MFA). Under these arrangements, trade in most textile and clothing products was 'temporarily' exempted from GATT rules and discipline.

The background to this situation was the inability of textile producers in the developed countries to cope with increased competition from producers in the developing world. Before the Second World War, both Britain and the United States introduced measures designed to protect their cotton textile industries, badly hit by the economic depression of the 1930s. In 1937, the United States consented to the signing of a so-called 'gentleman's agreement' between the US and Japanese textile trade associations limiting Japanese exports. After the war, beginning in 1955, a similar voluntary export restraint was applied by Japan to exports to the US. This was contrary to the United States' stated commitment to nondiscrimination and of questionable internal legality. As exports expanded from several other developing countries, pressure built up within the US for the President to introduce special measures to assist the textile industry. Since import quotas were illegal under the GATT, the solution was to seek an international agreement to allow exceptional treatment in the case of textiles. In 1959, discussions took place within the GATT into the problem of the so-called 'market disruption' caused by import surges from low-wage countries. The aim of the United States was not only to create a legal basis for protecting its own textile industry but also to bring under control the growing number of barriers which other developed countries had erected against imports from developing countries. Developing countries were eventually persuaded to agree to textiles being treated as an exception by assurances that protection would only be temporary.

The STA allowed countries unilaterally to impose import quotas where imports resulted in market disruption. Alternatively, quotas could be bilaterally negotiated. Market disruption was defined as a situation in which a sudden and substantial increase or potential increase in imports from a particular country caused serious damage to the domestic industry of an importing country. At the same time, quotas should not result in a lower volume of imports than that which had taken place in the previous twelve months. The LTA which was concluded in 1962 provided for a continuation of these arrangements for a further five-year period. However, in addition, it contained a provision that, where import quotas were for more than a year, the quota should be permitted to grow by at least 5 per cent a year. The LTA was endorsed by twenty-nine countries. It was renewed in 1967 and then again in 1970. Both the STA and LTA provided for a major departure from normal GATT rules in several respects. Firstly, they provided for unilateral action by countries in certain cases. Secondly, this action could take the form of import quotas which were otherwise prohibited under the GATT (except in the case of agricultural products). Thirdly, such quotas could be source-specific and therefore discriminatory. On the other hand, this was justified on the grounds that the arrangement was to be temporary. In fact, as events turned out, it lasted for much longer. In addition, there was a liberalising aspect to the Arrangement as reflected in the provision for the automatic expansion of quotas for each year they were retained. The alternative, it was argued, would have been a far more damaging proliferation of illegal restrictions which would have encouraged protectionism in other sectors and threatened the entire GATT.

In 1973, the LTA was replaced by the Multi-fibre Arrangement (MFA) which extended similar arrangements to other textile sectors including man-made or synthetic fibres such as polyester, nylon and acrylic. This was to reflect the shift in consumption away from natural fibres which had taken place in the period during which the LTA had been in force. As with the LTA, it provided for the imposition of temporary restrictions on imports where products from a particular source were causing market disruption. Alternatively, an importing country could enter into a bilateral agreement to restrict trade where there was a risk of market disruption. As with the LTA, there was a built-in growth factor of 6 per cent a year with provision for exceptions in special cases. In certain respects, the MFA was less restrictive than the previous LTA. To begin with, it required the ending of any existing restrictions that were not consistent with the GATT or MFA. Secondly, it included certain flexibility provisions which enabled an exporting country to exploit more fully the restraint levels imposed. There was a 'swing' provision which allowed an exporting country to exceed the level in any product during a year by between 5 and 7 per cent, provided that there was a corresponding decrease in other products so that exports for all products covered by the quota were not exceeded. In addition, up to 10 per cent of the unused portion of a quota could be 'carried over' in the next year. Under a similar arrangement, up to 5 per cent of a country's quota for the following year could be 'carried forward' into the present year if the country looked likely to exceed its quota for the year. The MFA was initially signed by forty-two countries.

MFA 1 lasted for four years. On 1 January 1978 it was replaced with MFA 2. This added a provision for 'reasonable departures' from MFA 1 subject to mutual agreement between importing and exporting countries. This could cover any feature of the agreement such as quota levels, the growth factor or flexibility provisions.

MFA 2 came to an end on 31 December 1981 and was replaced by MFA 3, which did away with the 'reasonable departures' clause of MFA 2 and replaced it with specific provisions for departures from particular aspects of the Arrangement under more carefully defined circumstances. In addition, MFA 3 introduced a new 'antisurge' mechanism to deal with the problem of *sudden* increases in the level of imports even when these occurred within the negotiated quota limits. This could be activated where there was a 'sharp and substantial' increase in imports, where quotas had previously been consistently underused and where imports caused or threatened serious damage to the domestic industry. It permitted the importing and exporting country mutually to agree new levels of restraint with compensation for the exporting country. Unilateral restrictions, however, could not be imposed on the exporting country. A further aspect of MFA 3 was the creation of a new mechanism for monitoring structural adjustment to ensure that temporary import restrictions did not become permanent. A standing body was established to monitor the adjustment process implying a specific obligation on importing countries to provide for the eventual removal of restrictions.

MFA 3 lasted until 31 July 1986, whereupon it was replaced with MFA 4.

Despite calls from developing countries for a phasing out of the MFA, MFA 4 merely extended the restrictions for another five years with a rather vague and qualified commitment to the eventual application of GATT rules to textiles trade. MFA 4 extended coverage to include vegetable fibres (such as linen, jute, ramie) and silk blends with a few exceptions for specified products. Least developed countries were to be excluded from controls or be given more favourable treatment. Consistently underused quotas were also to be scrapped on request. MFA 4 lasted until July 1991. The question of what, if anything, should replace it became subsumed within the Uruguay Round negotiations.

What were the effects of the LTA/MFA arrangements? Let us begin with the effects on developing-country exporters of clothing and textile products. Table 5.3 shows the effects of the MFA on imports of developed countries from developing countries for the period to 1984. The real rate of growth of imports of both clothing and textile products fell from 14.1 per cent in the period 1963–76 to 4.8 per cent in 1976–8 before growth resumed somewhat in the 1980s. The effects of MFA 1 and 2 were felt most markedly for trade in clothing products before this resumption in the 1980s. The liberalising effects of MFA 3 assisted the noticeably more rapid growth of imports after 1982, especially imports to the United States.

However, these figures do not say very much about the degree to which imports from developing countries were restricted. To begin with, not all imports of textile and clothing products were subject to quotas. Furthermore, even where quotas were imposed or negotiated, imports were only restricted if quotas had been used up. Even then, the flexibility provisions (swing, carry-forward and carry-over) referred to above could allow exporters to expand trade. Erzan *et al.* (1989) measured the extent to which the MFA restricted the trade of developing countries in the 1980s using a variety of indicators. These were: the proportion of imports subject to bilateral quotas; the proportion of imports subject to 'binding quotas' (where 90 per cent or more of a quota had been used up); the proportion of restricted imports subject to binding restrictions; and average quota utilisation rates. Their study covered three OECD countries – US, Canada and Sweden – and the EC, for the period 1981–7. Firstly, they found that the

Table 5.3 Growth of textile and clothing imports by developed countries from developing countries, 1963–84 (percentage per year in real terms)

Category	1963–76	1976–8	1978–84
Textiles	7.2	4.6	3.7
Clothing	20.9	4.8	10.9
Total	14.1	4.8	9.0

Source: Wolf (1986)

share of imports covered by restrictions was fairly stable over a range of 46–50 per cent over the period covered. However, since the number of products under quotas increased and more new suppliers were subject to the MFA, this implied that imports of restricted products grew more slowly than imports of unrestricted ones. In other words, quotas had a definite restrictive effect on the volume of imports subject to restriction. Secondly, the share of imports from developing countries subject to binding restriction increased from 28 per cent to 35 per cent over the period covered. Thirdly, the proportion of restricted imports subject to binding quotas increased from 61 per cent to 71 per cent, suggesting that quotas were becoming more restrictive. Finally, the overall average quota utilisation rate increased from 69 per cent to 82 per cent in the four markets. Their conclusion was that, during the 1980s, far from becoming less restrictive, the MFA had tended to become more so.

Because restrictions on textile and clothing imports are source-specific, one effect is to cause diversion of trade from exporters whose goods are subject to restriction (that is, subject to quotas which have been largely utilised) to other countries not subject to restrictions (that is, either not subject to quotas or not having reached quota ceilings). These may comprise other developed countries or new or less established suppliers either not subject to quotas or with underused quotas. To the extent that this is true, we might expect less competitive developing-country exporters to favour the MFA as a means of providing them with a guaranteed share of the markets of developed countries. We might even regard such an effect as desirable if it served to promote the trade of smaller and relatively new developing suppliers. In fact, although some trade diversion has resulted, there is little evidence to show that any significant amount of trade was diverted from restricted to unrestricted developing-country suppliers (Erzan *et al.* 1989). (Noteworthy exceptions have been the Mediterranean associates of the EC and countries covered by the US Caribbean Basin Initiative (CBI).) One reason for this is that suppliers in unrestricted developing countries were not always able to take advantage of opportunities to export more: supply conditions in their own countries constrained them. Moreover, to the extent that newly established suppliers succeeded in expanding exports, they either came up against quota ceilings or became subject to restrictions. The risk of this happening was found to constrain producers from investing in capacity to take advantage of the situation. Erzan *et al.* similarly found little evidence for trade diversion towards suppliers in other developed countries. Instead, the main beneficiaries have been domestic producers in the developed countries who have seen their market share expand at the expense of suppliers in developing countries. The conclusion is that the MFA resulted in more trade destruction than trade diversion.

Although the MFA has restricted the volume of developing-country

175

exports of textiles, it has enabled developing-country exporters to raise prices and thereby acquire quota rents. Prices are also increased on account of the up-grading effect which characterises any form of voluntary export restraint (see Chapter 3). The quota rents enjoyed by exporters in developing countries are obtained at the expense of consumers in the developed countries. Much interest has been shown in the nature and extent of these rents as a possible source of offsetting gain to developing countries. What is clear is that established exporters in developing countries will always prefer negotiated restraints on exports to import restrictions imposed by developed countries. If developed countries impose quotas under Article XIX of the GATT, such quotas would have to be global and be administered by authorities in the importing country. Hence, the quota rent would accrue to importers in the developed country. Under a negotiated source-specific quota, the rent goes to the exporting country. However, it is not true that these rents are of sufficient magnitude to offset the loss of export revenues resulting from trade restrictions. For example, Balassa and Michalopoulos (1985) estimated that the value of forgone textile and clothing exports of developing countries exceeded the transferred rent by nine times in the case of the United States and seven times in the case of the EC. The value of these rents has also been found to be quite small in relation to the national income of the countries in question. For example, one estimate found that quota rents contributed about 4–6 per cent to Hong Kong's gross domestic product in the 1970s and much less in the 1980s (Wolf, 1989b). Another estimate put the rent transfer to Hong Kong for clothing products for the years 1981–2 at US$567 million or 1 per cent of Hong Kong's GDP (Hamilton, 1984b). However, what is important is that the rents create an important source of gain for particular interest groups within developing countries. Since export licences are usually allocated to existing firms on the basis of past export performance, the largest rents accrue to established suppliers. Therefore, there exists a strong incentive for these producers to bribe state officials to obtain larger quotas. Politicians, state officials and established producers have a strong interest in retaining these controls.

One attempt to analyse the combined welfare effect of reduced export revenues and higher export prices – due to both the upgrading effect and quota rents – has concluded that, in aggregate, developing countries lose substantially from the MFA (Trela and Whalley, 1989). Using a global general equilibrium model covering several major developed countries (the United States, Canada and the EC) and fourteen textile and clothing product categories plus one composite other good, Trela and Whalley estimated the effects of restrictions on developing countries as a whole using 1986 data. They found that developing countries together would gain around US$8 billion from the removal of *all* trade restrictions on textiles and clothing. The gain from improved market access more than offsets the losses from forgone rent transfers. If only quotas were eliminated and tariffs left in place, developing countries as a whole would gain only US$3 billion and there would be a few more losers among developing countries. However, these results do not capture all the effects of the MFA. Thus the MFA may have resulted in trade diversion from more restricted to less restricted developing countries, in which case the latter enjoy gains which partly offset the losses of the former. The upgrading effect referred to above may also constitute a further source of gain to developing countries. Increased foreign investment in nonrestricted or less restricted developing countries could give rise to another source of gain. Little is known about the nature and magnitude of these indirect effects. However, while they serve to complicate the picture, it seems improbable that they are sufficient to offset the loss to developing countries that has been estimated by other studies. Moreover, the adverse effects of the MFA go beyond the purely static. There are the retarding effects of trade restrictions on economic development, especially for the poorer developing countries who face limited access to developed-country markets. This makes it difficult for them to adopt export-orientated trade policies and to adopt the model of industrialisation established by the more advanced developing countries, particularly in South-East Asia. Furthermore, trade restrictions reduce investment opportunities in poorer developing countries, in particular by discouraging inward investment. On the other hand, the high growth rates enjoyed by the most successful Asian countries despite restrictive MFA quotas suggest that the effects on development of these restrictions is complex.

Next, what have been the effects of the MFA on developed countries? Here the issues are relatively more straightforward. A large number of studies have been carried out to estimate the costs to developed countries of textile and clothing protection. Greenaway and Hindley (1986) put the cost to the UK at £170 million in 1982. Silbertson (1989) estimated that the abolition of the MFA would benefit UK consumers by an estimated £980 million a year, equivalent to £29,700 for each worker displaced. This was about three or four times the average wage in the sector. Cline (1987) put the cost to the US consumer at US$40 billion or roughly US$500 per household per annum in 1985. Trela and Whalley (1989) estimated the combined gain to the United States, Canada and the members of the EC from removing all trade restrictions on textile and clothing products at nearly US$7.27 billion. If only quotas were removed, then these countries would jointly gain by US$1.08 billion. Abolishing the MFA would create adjustment problems for the developed countries. However, because of the declining importance of textile and clothing production in the developed countries, the cost of adjustment are not large. Silberstone (1989) estimated that the abolition of the MFA would result in a loss of 33,000 jobs in the UK, but this should be compared with the loss of 175,000 jobs which took place in the UK industry in the 1980s alone as a result of productivity growth. The adjustment costs are therefore clearly lower than the welfare gain which would accrue to developed countries as a whole.

Phasing out the MFA

The developed countries have always argued that the LTA/MFA amounted to a temporary departure from normal GATT rules and discipline. At some stage in the future, textiles would be brought back into the GATT. Yet for more than two decades, successive agreements were renewed. In some cases, more restrictive and often more extensive arrangements than those which existed before took their place. Why was this? To begin with, there was the relative strength of the protectionist lobby in the developed countries and the relative weakness of the consumer interest who were the main losers. This ensured that the case for trade restrictions was always heard more forcibly than the case against. The short-term need to conserve jobs in often economically depressed and therefore politically sensitive industries regardless of the long-term cost of doing so became the dominant concern of the politicians. At the same time, there were enough beneficiaries from quotas within the developing countries to weaken the resolve of the developing world to press for change. These included the established firms which had assured quotas and received quota rents. However, they also included state officials and politicians with responsibility for allocating quotas who shared in rents by accepting bribes from exporters. As far as the advanced developing countries were concerned, although the MFA denied them market access, there was some compensation from the rent transfers received. Moreover, it was not entirely clear to these countries how they might fare if restrictions were abolished. As one writer has put it, 'a restraint in the hand has seemed more valuable than export expansion in the bush' (Wolf, 1989). Rather than pressurising developed countries to end the MFA, some of these countries became preoccupied with seeking the highest quotas for themselves. At the same time, some of the poorer developing countries, which might have been expected to oppose the MFA, appeared to favour its continuation on the grounds that it gave them some guarantee of market access in the face of competition from lower-cost suppliers in the more advanced developing countries.

In the recent decade, however, various factors have been at work in both developed and developing countries which tilted the balance of debate in favour of liberalisation. In the developed countries, the declining importance of the textile industry meant that it could exert less influence on trade policy than was once the case. For example, the potential employment loss from abolishing restrictions was now much smaller than it had been. (This point should not be overplayed. Developed countries are still major players in textiles but have increasingly specialised in short runs of high value-added products produced with short time lags via computer-aided technology.) In addition, the fact that the MFA had originally been envisaged as only a temporary exception from normal GATT rules and discipline meant that it was becoming increasingly difficult to justify any further extension of the arrangements. In the developing world, the situation was also changing. In particular, a larger number of the poorer developing countries now enjoyed lower costs than the advanced developing countries and as a result came to view the MFA as a barrier to export expansion. Furthermore, as a result of rising labour costs in some of the more advanced developing countries, production was increasingly being shifted to cheaper locations in other parts of the developing world. These producers came to view the quota system as excessively rigid and restrictive.

The Uruguay Round created an opportunity to bring the MFA to an end. MFA 4 was in any case due to expire on 31 July 1991. The question of the future of the MFA was therefore necessarily subsumed within the negotiations. The Punta del Este Ministerial Declaration launching the Round had stated that

> negotiations in the area of textiles and clothing shall aim to formulate modalities that would permit the eventual integration of this sector into GATT on the basis of strengthened GATT rules and disciplines, thereby also contributing to the objective of further liberalisation of trade.

Many of the developing countries viewed the dismantling of the MFA as a major negotiating objective and a necessary price for any agreement in the newer areas, such as services, where developed countries wanted concessions. Since the developed countries were keen to make progress in the latter, there was a need to offer something meaningful in exchange. The context therefore very clearly favoured agreement being reached on the eventual phasing out of the MFA. In the actual negotiations, the main difference concerned the method to be employed for dismantling the MFA. Specifically, the developing countries plus the EC, Japan and the Nordic countries favoured a phase-out within the framework of the MFA, while the United States and Canada argued for a transitional structure based on global quotas. The US submitted a plan under which, when the MFA expired in July 1991, it would be replaced with global quotas on imports from all sources based on average imports in recent years. Within the global quotas, there would be country allocations for current quota holders based on actual import shares but not exceeding 15 per cent of the global quota in each category. The global 'basket' would expand each year by an agreed growth factor. Unlike the MFA, global quotas would be administered by the importing country although exporters would continue to administer their own quotas. The latter would be fully tradable among exporting countries. Finally, there would be 'special treatment' for least developed countries. After ten years, all quotas would end.

The most positive feature of the US proposals was that they put an end to the discrimination which characterised the MFA. In this respect, they would bring textiles and clothing swiftly back into the GATT framework as a prelude to subsequent liberalisation. However, the US proposals were seen by developing countries as having several drawbacks. Firstly, the adoption of global quotas based on the average volume of imports in recent years, even with country allocations for current quota holdings, would result in some loss of quota for current holders. There were two reasons for this. To begin with, actual shipments in recent years were often below permitted quotas, reflecting the fact that, for some countries, part of their quota had not been utilised. In addition, current quota holders could not obtain quotas equivalent to more than 15 per cent of the exporter's market. For some quota holders, this would mean that some of their existing quota would effectively be transferred to the unallocated basket. Erzan and Holmes (1990) estimated that, under the US proposals, current quota holders would lose up to 44 per cent of their initial quota holdings in the US market. Countries which would experience the biggest loss included major suppliers such as China, Korea, Japan, Taiwan and Hong Kong. On the other hand, the loss in guaranteed quotas for these countries need not imply a loss in export volume or even market share. Export volume could exceed the country's allocation provided that total imports did not exceed the global quota. Nevertheless, as Erzan and Holmes demonstrated, a transition to global quotas along the lines proposed by the US would have resulted in a major increase in the restrictiveness of the system because the unfilled portion of existing quotas would be excluded from the global quota. Subsequent modifications of the US proposals, however, did provide for an additional increment to quotas for each product; this could have eliminated the overall restrictiveness of the measures, but nevertheless it would still have resulted in a loss of quota for some major suppliers. Secondly, because global quotas would favour efficient over inefficient producers who receive guaranteed market shares under the MFA, there were distributional implications which were unacceptable to these countries which stood to lose. Thirdly, a switch to global quotas, which are operated by the importing and not the exporting country, would necessarily result in a loss of quota rent for exporting countries.

The developing countries plus the EC, the Nordic countries and Japan favoured a phasing out of the MFA within the existing framework. The EC plan favoured eliminating existing quotas in stages with a certain percentage of the total volume of quotas being abolished at each stage. Participants would have freedom to choose which quotas to liberalise first. At the same time, remaining quotas would be subject to accelerated growth. No period of phase-out was specified. The Nordic countries and Japan both proposed an eight-year phase-out period while favouring a similar approach to that of the EC. The opinions of the developing countries were split between smaller and larger exporters. The larger developing countries as represented by the International Textiles and Clothing Bureau (ITCB) proposed a four-stage phase-out over six years with immediate elimination of quotas on new products introduced by MFA 4, all restrictions on least developed countries, and accelerated growth of quotas before their total elimination. The smaller developing countries (for example, the Caribbean producers) favoured a much longer transitional period. A major issue concerned the exact rate at which quotas would grow during the transitional phase. Specifically, should there be a single fixed-percentage base-year growth rate (suggested by the developing countries) or should there be differentiation between products, suppliers and markets? In general, the proposals for MFA phase-out had the attraction that they were reasonably simple to manage given the existence of the MFA framework of quotas and quota growth rates which had been in place for many years. For the same reason, they were much easier to understand. They would also enable exporting countries to retain their quota rents for the time being, although these would be eroded with time as quotas were expanded. On the other hand, there was a risk that there would be too slow a phasing out of the MFA, especially if importing countries retained the right to choose which quotas could be withdrawn at each stage. The temptation would be to remove the least important quotas first, such that the most meaningful liberalisation would be postponed until the later stages of the transition.

In February 1992 agreement was reached on a draft accord. In essence, this came down in favour of the transitional approach favoured by most countries except the US and Canada. Subsequently, this agreement was incorporated in the Uruguay Round Final Act as the Agreement on Textiles and Clothing. The main elements of this are:

1 It contains provisions for a *transitional period* during which the textiles and clothing sector will be gradually integrated into the GATT. First, on 1 January 1995 countries are required to integrate into the GATT 'products which, in 1990, accounted for not less than 16 per cent of the total volume of imports in 1990' of the products listed in the Agreement. Integration means that these products will henceforth be governed by normal GATT rules and disciplines. In the second phase, on 1 January 1998 products which, in 1990, accounted for not less than 17 per cent of the total volume of 1990 imports are to be integrated. In the third phase, on 1 January 2002 products which in 1990 accounted for not less than 18 per cent of total 1990 imports are to be integrated. All remaining products are to be integrated at the end of the transitional period commencing 1 January 2005. At each of these stages, products to be integrated must be chosen from each of four categories, namely, tops and yarns, fabrics, made-up textile products, and clothing.
2 During this transitional period, all quantitative restrictions on imports

imposed as part of bilateral agreements under the MFA are effectively brought under the new Agreement until such time as the restrictions are removed or the products integrated into the GATT. In the case of products which remain subject to restriction, there is a complex formula for gradually reducing the level of restriction. In Stage 1, commencing on 1 January 1994, the level of any restriction in force must be increased annually by no less than the growth rate established for the previous MFA restriction plus 16 per cent. In Stage 2, commencing 1 January 1998, the formula is the growth rate under the MFA restriction plus 25 per cent. In Stage 3, commencing 1 January 2002, it is the growth rate under the MFA restriction plus 27 per cent. Flexibility provisions (that is, swing, carryover and carry forward) remain the same as those under the MFA.

3 There is a provision for special treatment of restrictions affecting 1.2 per cent or less of the total volume of restrictions applied by an importer on 31 December 1991. This is to take the form of 'advancement by one stage of the growth rates' set out above or through 'equivalent changes mutually agreed with respect to a different mix of base levels, growth and flexibility provisions'.

4 There is a recognition that some restrictions may be in existence which are not part of the MFA but which are inconsistent with the GATT. These must also be 'brought into conformity with the GATT 1994 within one year following the entry into force of the Agreement' or 'phased out progressively according to a programme not exceeding the duration of the Agreement'.

5 Bilateral restrictions on imports plus any restrictions introduced under the special safeguard provisions (see below) are to be administered as under the MFA by the exporting country.

6 There are special provisions to deal with the problems of transshipment, rerouting, false declaration concerning country or place of origin, and falsification of official documents.

7 The Agreement contains a special *safeguard mechanism* to apply during the transitional period called the 'transitional safeguard'. This applies to all products covered by the Agreement except those which have been integrated into the GATT (in which case these are covered by Article XIX of the GATT). Safeguard action may be taken if a product is being imported in such increased quantities as to cause or threaten serious damage to the domestic industry. The importing country must first consult with the exporting countries which might be affected by any safeguard measures adopted. If agreement is reached on the need for export restraint, the volume of exports must not be fixed at a lower level than the actual level during the twelve-month period which terminated two months before the request for consultation is made. Where no agreement can be reached after a period of sixty days, unilateral restrictions may be imposed by the importing country. In extreme cases,

where delay might cause damage, provisional restrictions may be imposed by the importing country prior to consultation. Safeguard measures can remain in force for up to three years without extension or until the product is integrated into the GATT, whichever comes first. If a restriction remains in force for more than one year, the level must be increased by a growth rate of not less than 6 per cent per annum. In the application of the transitional safeguard, it is also stated that 'particular account' should be taken of the interests of least developed countries, countries whose total volume of exports is small in comparison with other exporting countries and in relation to the total imports of the importing country, wool products coming from developing countries heavily dependent on the wool sector and reimports of products from another country for processing.

8 As part of the integration process, countries are required to take such actions as shall improve market access for textile and clothing products (including tariff reductions, tariff bindings, reducing or eliminating nontariff barriers, and so on), ensure fair and equitable trading conditions (for example, in relation to antidumping policy) and avoid discrimination against imports in the textiles and clothing sectors.

9 There are institutional provisions for the creation of a special Textiles Monitoring Body (TMB) to oversee the implementation of the various commitments and to prepare reports as part of regular reviews conducted by the Council for Trade in Goods at the end of each stage of the integration process.

In total, the Agreement represents a significant step towards the eventual phasing out of the MFA and the integration of the textiles and clothing sectors into the GATT. If, indeed, this is achieved according to the timetable set out in the Agreement, it will represent a significant step forwards. The fact that an agreement was reached to begin the phasing out of the MFA, while not unexpected, did constitute a major negotiating victory for developing countries. As stated above, attempts at estimating the likely effects of ending trade restrictions on textile and clothing products show major gains for developing and developed countries alike. There will be adjustment problems for textile producers in the developed countries. However, the potential loss of employment is now much less than before because of the rapid decline in recent decades of employment in the industry in developed countries. Moreover, the gradual phasing out of restrictions should provide sufficient time for developed countries to adjust. For the developing countries, a major victory was to secure a rejection of the global-quotas approach favoured by the US and Canada and strongly backed by the textiles lobby in the US. On the other hand, the major gain from liberalisation is unlikely to be reaped for some years to come, partly because the phasing out of quota restrictions is heavily back loaded, with most of the quota restrictions disappearing only in the later stages of the transitional period. Moreover, the Agreement allows the developed countries considerable freedom to choose which products to integrate into the GATT at the various stages. In theory, they could choose first to integrate products not currently subject to restriction or subject to relatively trivial restriction. If this were the case, many important quotas could remain in place until the end of the transitional period, namely, 1 January 2005. It should also be borne in mind that the textiles and clothing sectors will remain highly protected even after the phasing out of quotas. This is because the Uruguay Round did relatively little to reduce the high tariff rates which exist in developed countries on these products. Finally, there is the danger that many of the gains from phasing out the MFA will be undermined if developed countries resort too easily to the transitional safeguard mechanism. Although this cannot be used to reduce the level of imports below the base-period level, it may be used to reduce their rate of growth.

THE EFFECTS OF THE URUGUAY ROUND ON DEVELOPING COUNTRIES

What have been the effects of the Uruguay Round on developing countries? Although not all the results can be quantified, there have been attempts to estimate those which can be measured. The three main areas where quantification is possible are trade in manufactures, agriculture and textiles. Each of these is discussed below.

Trade in manufactures

There are three sources of potential benefit for developing countries: tariff reductions, tariff bindings, and a reduction of quantitative barriers. According to the Overseas Development Institute (ODI) (1995), the average fall in industrial-country MFN tariffs on goods exported by developing countries was 2.4 points, from 6.3 per cent to 3.9 per cent. However, the gain to developing countries is relatively small because most of them enjoy preferential access to developed-country markets. Where developed countries reduced tariffs to zero, developing countries have lost their entire preferential advantage. For these reasons, the gain from tariff cuts appears quite small. On the other hand, developing countries also gain from tariff reductions made by other developing countries. A substantial and growing proportion of developing-country exports now goes to other developing countries. According to the ODI (1995), the average tariff charged by all developing countries fell from 13.5 per cent to 9.8 per cent.

However, more important than tariff reductions is the gain from tariff bindings. Developed countries had already bound most of their industrial tariffs before the Uruguay Round. However, developing countries had on average bound only 13 per cent of their industrial tariffs. This was increased to 61 per cent as a result of the Round. Although in many cases tariffs have been bound at levels above the currently applied level, bindings are still seen as important in locking-in tariff reductions which many developing countries had made autonomously prior to the completion of the Round (WTO, 1995). While not directly increasing market access, tariff bindings increase certainty and predictability of future access.

Developing countries will also gain from the agreements reached on the removal of certain quantitative restrictions on trade. In particular, the provisions for the elimination within four years of all so-called 'grey area' measures such as voluntary export restraints should further improve access to developed-country markets for manufactures. Developing countries themselves have undertaken to accept more discipline in the use of quantitative restraints. In particular, a new Understanding on the Balance of Payments Provisions of the GATT will make it more difficult for developing countries to resort to quantitative restrictions for balance of payment reasons as provided for in Article XVIII of the GATT. As was noted above, these provisions of the GATT have been widely exploited by developing countries to introduce quantitative limits on trade.

Page and Davenport (1994) have estimated the *trade* effects of tariff reductions and bindings on developing countries (see Table 5.4). Overall, developing-country manufacturing exports fall by 1 per cent by the time the measures have been fully implemented and full adjustment allowed for. This is for the reasons given above, namely, that loss of tariff preferences offsets the benefit of improved access due to lower tariffs and increased bindings. The biggest reductions occur for those countries who have gained most from preferences, namely, Africa and the ACP (African, Caribbean and Pacific) countries. The latter group of countries includes signatories of the EU's Lomé Convention which gives to these countries additional preferences over and above the GSP from which most developing countries have benefited. However, these estimates do not measure the *welfare* effect from tariff reductions and bindings which is necessarily positive.

Agriculture

The most important aspect of the Agriculture Agreement for developing countries comprises the provisions for tariffication. This refers to the conversion of all nontariff border measures into tariff equivalents and their reduction by 36 per cent over a six-year period from their pre-Round 1986–8 level. In the case of developing countries, the tariff reduction is 24 per cent over ten years, while the least developed countries are exempt. In addition, all tariffs are to be bound at their current levels, which significantly increases the proportion of bound tariffs in agriculture. Tariffs on tropical foodstuffs,

Table 5.4 Trade effects of the Uruguay Round over the implementation period
(% 1992 exports)

	Temperate	Tropical	Mfr Tariff	MFA	Total
1995					
Africa	−0.24	−0.10	−0.29	0.00	−0.63
Latin America	0.01	0.03	0.03	0.00	0.07
Asia	0.01	0.01	0.01	0.00	0.03
South Asia	−0.07	0.01	0.06	0.00	−0.01
ASEAN	0.11	0.01	0.01	0.00	0.13
NICs	0.03	0.01	−0.01	0.00	0.03
Other	−0.03	0.01	0.01	0.00	−0.01
ACP	−0.29	−0.12	−0.23	0.00	−0.63
All developing	−0.02	0.00	0.00	0.00	−0.02
1998					
Africa	−0.30	−0.16	−0.48	0.00	−0.94
Latin America	0.03	0.05	0.06	0.00	0.12
Asia	0.01	0.02	−0.01	0.00	0.02
South Asia	−0.09	0.01	0.10	0.00	0.02
ASEAN	0.14	0.02	0.01	0.00	0.17
NICs	0.04	0.01	−0.02	0.00	0.03
Other	−0.03	0.01	0.02	0.00	0.00
ACP	−0.36	−0.20	−0.38	0.00	−0.94
All developing	−0.02	0.00	0.00	0.00	−0.02
2001					
Africa	−0.33	−0.23	−0.67	0.20	−1.03
Latin America	0.01	0.06	0.08	0.10	0.27
Asia	0.01	0.02	−0.02	0.50	0.52
South Asia	−0.10	0.01	0.14	1.12	1.18
ASEAN	0.15	0.02	0.02	−0.33	−0.13
NICs	0.04	0.01	−0.02	0.45	0.48
Other	−0.04	0.02	0.02	1.52	1.52
All developing	−0.02	0.00	−0.01	0.35	0.30
2005					
Africa	−0.36	−0.29	−0.87	0.80	−0.72
Latin America	0.02	0.08	0.12	0.40	0.62
Asia	0.02	0.02	0.01	2.00	2.05
South Asia	−0.11	0.02	0.19	4.50	4.59
ASEAN	0.16	0.03	0.02	−1.30	−1.08
NICs	0.04	0.01	0.02	1.80	1.88
Other	−0.04	0.02	0.02	6.10	6.10
ACP	−0.45	−0.37	−0.68	−2.20	−1.70
All developing	−0.02	0.00	−0.01	1.40	1.37

Source: Page and Davenport (1994)

which account for roughly one-half of all developing-country exports of agricultural products, are to be cut by an above average 43 per cent. In addition, reductions in the levels of domestic subsidies and both the volume and value of export subsidies, while mainly affecting the developed countries, will mean higher world prices. This will benefit those developing countries which are net exporters of temperate-zone foodstuffs, but will reduce the welfare of countries which are net importers. According to Page and Davenport (1994), because developing countries as a whole are net importers of food, the trade effects are negative (see Table 5.4). However, this is mainly accounted for by the African and ACP countries, many of whom are net importers of food. The ACP countries also suffer from the erosion of certain preferences which they enjoy on temperate-zone products. By way of contrast, there are positive effects for the Latin American and some of the Asian countries.

Countries which faced both high nontariff barriers and the least preferential access are among those which gain most. For example, Thailand gains from being able to export more rice, while Argentina and Brazil should benefit from increased exports of wheat and animal feed. However, some doubts have to be raised as to the extent of liberalisation that will result from the Agricultural Agreement (Ingco, 1995a, 1995b). Tariffication may prove less beneficial than it seems for one important reason. The base period chosen, 1986–8, was one in which extremely high levels of border protection prevailed. Consequently, tariff equivalents based on this period could conceivably be set at higher levels of protection than were in existence at the time of the completion of the Round. Estimates suggest that excessive tariffication has been widespread, especially for sensitive commodities such as grains, sugar and dairy products, with only Japan, among the developed countries, offering significantly lower levels of tariff equivalents.

Textiles and clothing

The major source of gain for developing countries from the Round appear to come from the phasing out of the MFA. This is not surprising because the tariff equivalent of MFA quotas far exceeds the level of tariffs applied by developed countries to these products. However, these gains are likely to take some time to come through because the arrangements for phasing out the MFA are heavily backloaded. As stated above, under the transitional arrangements, half of all quotas need not be lifted until the end of the transitional period in the year 2005. The transitional safeguard mechanism referred to above may also enable countries to introduce new restrictions during this period. Nevertheless, the trade effects for developing countries as a whole are potentially very great. Page and Davenport (1994) put the increase in net exports at 1.4 per cent by the end of the implementation period. However, most of the gain is only achieved towards the end of the transitional period. ACP countries and ASEAN will experience trade losses, while big increases in net exports will accrue to Southern Asia and certain other Asian countries. China, India, Pakistan and South Korea are among those countries which should gain most.

* * * *

Page and Davenport (1994) put the overall trade effect of all these measures at 1.37 per cent by the end of the ten-year transitional period, with most of the gain coming from the phasing out of the MFA (again, see Table 5.4). The biggest gains will be felt by the Asian countries mainly because their trading neighbours are making bigger tariff cuts, and because of the prospects which these countries will enjoy following the phasing out of the MFA and the fact that these countries have few preferences to lose. Significantly, the African countries gain the least. While they gain from the phasing out of the MFA, this is more than offset by the loss of tariff preferences on manufactured and agricultural products and their losses as net food importers from higher world food prices. The Latin American countries enjoy some small benefit from the overall package of measures. One noticeable result shown in Table 5.4 is that most of the trade effects come at the end of the implementation period. In fact, the trade effects in the first few years are negative. The reason for this is that the biggest source of gain comes from the phasing out of the MFA. Yet because this is heavily backloaded, the gain does not come until the end of the ten-year period. By way of contrast, the reduction of domestic and export subsidies in agriculture by the developed countries is more immediate, leading to some losses for developing countries which are net importers of food.

At face value, the effects of the Uruguay Round on developing countries seem at best quite small and for some countries (particularly the African countries) possibly adverse. Account should also be taken of the fact that, in a number of other areas, developing countries have assumed new obligations (such as tariff bindings, restrictions on the use of quotas, TRIMs, TRIPs and services). Viewed in this way, the results seem of questionable value for developing countries taken as a whole. However, this is where a narrowly quantitative evaluation of the Round breaks down. In several key respects, the Round has brought potentially important benefits to developing countries. Rodrick (1994) must be right in seeing the gain as residing in the areas of multilateral trading rules and rule enforcement. In a number of important respects, the Uruguay Round has strengthened trading rules in ways which should bring benefits for developing countries. Key areas in this respect are those of antidumping, subsidies and safeguards. These agreements have been examined in other chapters of this book. Although in several respects (particularly antidumping) the new rules are disappointing, few would deny that they represent some improvement on what existed beforehand. Reductions in tariff or nontariff barriers are of little value if developed countries can readily circumvent these measures by imposing antidumping duties or resorting to safeguards. Any progress made in strengthening these rules is therefore of great value to developing countries.

However, of arguably greater importance are measures which strengthen the rule-enforcement procedures of the GATT. Developing countries lack the powers of retaliation which the bigger developed countries enjoy. They are therefore dependent on multilateral dispute settlement mechanisms to remedy any breech of trading rules by the bigger countries. Yet the GATT disputes-settlement mechanism, relying as it does on consensus, has been widely criticised as too weak. Consequently, developing countries have in the past made very little use of it. Instead, they have tended to settle their disputes with developed countries 'out of court', for example, by offering price undertakings when threatened with antidumping measures or by agreeing to voluntary export restraints when faced with import quotas since these offer effective compensation from higher economic rents. However, the provisions of the Uruguay Round for the creation of the World Trade Organisation (WTO) include a new disputes-settlement mechanism which in several respects is considerably stronger than that which existed under the GATT. This is discussed in Chapter 9. In this chapter, it is sufficient to note the change which has occurred providing for a more automatic complaints procedure subject to a stricter timetable and punishment of a member state found by a panel to be in breach of WTO rules and which has failed to remedy the measure in question. As Rodrick (1994) rightly notes, much will depend on the willingness of the developing countries to make use of the new machinery. Nevertheless, on paper, the agreement is one of major importance for developing countries. If it lives up to the expectations of those who have long advocated a strengthening of rule enforcement mechanisms, it could prove of greater value than any of the more quantifiable gains of the Uruguay Round for developing countries.

CONCLUSION

Recent years have seen a significant change in the attitude of the developing world towards the multilateral trading system. In the early years of the postwar period, the developing countries viewed the GATT with some suspicion. At best, it was considered of little relevance to their needs. Influenced by the conventional wisdom of that time, most developing countries pursued inward-looking, import-substitution policies. Beginning in the late 1960s and early 1970s, disillusioned with such policies, a number of developing countries switched over to more outward-looking, export-orientated policies. In the main, the countries which did so achieved a high degree of success. One result of this has been the emergence of an expanding group of developing countries, the so-called newly industrialising countries, which are now important producers of manufactured goods. These countries have consequently come to share similar aims to those of developed countries, namely, the need to lower trade barriers. More importantly, import barriers have ceased to be regarded by them as necessary prerequisites for industrialisation. On the contrary, the lowering of these barriers is increasingly being seen as bringing substantial gains to their economies. Consequently, they now perceive it to be more valuable to offer such barrier reductions in the course of multilateral trade negotiations in order to gain concessions from the developed countries for their manufacturing exports than to play no role in such negotiations, as in the past.

The GATT rules do provide for 'differential and more favourable treatment' for developing countries. However, it is doubtful how much benefit this has brought them. The decision to waive the reciprocity requirement for developing countries in the 1960s was of little or no value to them. Although they received any concessions made by developed countries without having to offer anything in return, most of these concessions were of no value to developing countries. The decision to waive the MFN rule to allow developed countries to grant tariff preferences on goods coming from developing countries paved the way for a new form of 'differential and more favourable treatment'. However, the results of the GSP scheme have been disappointing, largely because of the limitations placed on preferences in terms of product coverage, country coverage and the degree of preference to which beneficiaries were entitled. Developing countries have faced a choice between pushing for improvements in the system of preferences or seeking from developed countries bigger nondiscriminatory tariff reductions. Although the latter erode the margin of preference, the benefit from improved access to developed-country markets is likely to more than offset this.

Even more important than extracting more tariff concessions from developed countries is the need to seek the removal of many of the nontariff barriers which have been erected. The importance of NTBs is most aptly illustrated by the arrangements which developed countries have put in place for managing trade in textile and clothing products. Although intended as a temporary aberration from GATT principles, the Multi-fibre Arrangement (MFA) has become a more or less permanent system of protectionism that allows developed countries to apply policies which would be entirely unacceptable if applied to any other trading sector. Nevertheless, the opportunities which quotas have opened up for developing-country exporters to raise prices and earn high economic rents has weakened opposition among certain developing countries to removing the MFA. However, there can be little doubt that the MFA has a harmful effect on developing countries as a whole. The decision, therefore, to phase

190

out the MFA over a ten-year transitional period commencing in January 1995 constitutes a major success for the developing countries in the Uruguay Round. Indeed, empirical estimates of the effects of the Round on developing countries suggest that the phasing out of the MFA should have the biggest impact on their trade. Nevertheless, some uncertainties remain because of the opportunities which the textiles agreement creates for backloading and for introducing new restrictions under the safeguard provisions.

Overall, the Uruguay Round is beneficial for developing countries even if, quantitatively, the gains look small. There is a possibility that the Agricultural Agreement may have an adverse effect on some poor developing countries, particularly in Africa, which are net importers of temperate zone foodstuffs and may therefore suffer if world prices rise. On the other hand, higher world prices should stimulate agricultural production in the developing world as a whole and cause more of these countries to become net exporters. However, the most important aspects of the Uruguay Round Final Act for developing countries concern changes made to trade rules and the system of rule enforcement.

New agreements covering antidumping, subsidies and safeguards could bring important benefits for developing countries if they are successful in restraining the spread of nontariff protection among the developed countries. In many respects, these agreements are deficient and developing countries will need to press for further improvements in future negotiations. The antidumping rules still give developed countries too much freedom to restrict imports from developing countries on the spurious grounds that mere price discrimination is in some sense 'unfair'. The new Code does not do enough to deal with this.

Perhaps of even greater importance is the creation of the new World Trade Organisation (WTO) equipped with a new and improved system for settling trade disputes, including procedures for forcing member states to abide by panel rulings. This is discussed further in Chapter 9. If developing countries are prepared to make use of the new procedures for making complaints, they may be better able to prevent developed countries adopting trade measures which are injurious to developing countries. Moreover, the existence of a new and improved multilateral system for settling disputes weakens arguments which developed countries may wish to employ in defence of unilateral action to safeguard their interests.

6

AGRICULTURAL PROTECTIONISM

INTRODUCTION

Perhaps the single most abject failure of the first seven rounds of the GATT was the inability to open up trade in agricultural goods. Throughout the past forty years and at a time when trade in industrial products was being progressively liberalised, trade in agricultural goods largely remained outside any agreed international rules or discipline. Governments were free to pursue whatever policies they wished. The result was that trade in agricultural goods was seriously impaired and distorted. In the light of this, the decision to give prominence to agriculture in the Uruguay Round represented a significant development. The background was a growing awareness of the cost of protectionist agricultural policies in the advanced industrialised countries and a recognition that agriculture could no longer be excluded altogether from normal GATT rules and disciplines. Governmental support for agriculture in the advanced industrialised countries was escalating and creating an increasing financial burden. At the same time, the international repercussions of such policies meant that they were becoming a source of growing friction between countries. Disputes involving agricultural trade policies threatened to spill over into other areas of trade and to undermine the liberalisation process in these sectors. Moreover, it had become clear that no further progress in liberalising world trade as a whole could be made without the inclusion of agriculture.

In theory, agricultural trade is subject to exactly the same disciplines as other products. GATT was intended to cover all trade in goods, not just industrial products. However, a distinction was made between industrial and primary products in certain respects. Firstly, in certain circumstances, agriculture was exempt from the general prohibition of quantitative trade restrictions contained in Article XI. Article XI:2 lists these as:

(a) export prohibitions or restrictions temporarily applied to prevent or relieve critical shortages of foodstuffs or other products essential to the exporting contracting party;

(b) import and export prohibitions or restrictions necessary to the application of standards or regulations for the classification, grading or marketing of commodities in international trade;

(c) import restrictions . . . necessary for the enforcement of governmental measures which operate:

    (i) to restrict the quantities of the like domestic product permitted to be marketed or produced . . .

    (ii) to remove a temporary surplus of the domestic product . . .

    (iii) to restrict the quantities permitted to be produced of any animal product the production of which is directly dependent, wholly or mainly, on the imported commodity . . .

(GATT, 1969)

Secondly, as we saw in Chapter 4, Article XVI provides for exceptional treatment for agriculture in applying GATT rules concerning subsidies. This declares that any form of subsidy on the export of any product is prohibited except for primary products. It states that

> contracting parties should seek to avoid the use of subsidies on the export of primary products. If, however, a contracting party grants directly or indirectly any form of subsidy which operates to increase the export of any primary product from its territory, such subsidy shall not be applied in a manner which results in that contracting party having more than an equitable share of world export trade in that product, account being taken of the shares of other contracting parties in such trade in the product during a previous representative period, and any special factors which may have affected such trade in the product.

(GATT, 1969)

The GATT Subsidies Code, which was negotiated as part of the Tokyo Round, also allowed export subsidies on primary products provided that market shares were not increased unduly or prices depressed.

Historically, the special treatment of agriculture in the GATT was greatly assisted by the decision in 1955 to grant the United States a waiver not to apply the GATT rules to a substantial part of its agricultural imports. The problem arose because the US wished to retain import quotas on certain products despite having a favourable overall trade balance in agricultural goods. This acted as a cue for other countries to engage in similar trading practices which were in conflict with the GATT rules but without seeking the formality of a waiver. Subsequently, when the US was keen to tackle subsidies and quotas which denied access to US farm exports, other countries were content to remind the US of the waiver granted in 1955.

The reason why it has proved so difficult to subject agricultural trade to the same approach as trade in industrial products is the extent of government intervention in agriculture. Governments in both developed and developing countries intervene in a wide variety of different ways and with several objectives in mind. Agricultural policies in developed countries adversely affect trade by restricting market access, by the overstimulation of domestic production leading to the accumulation of large structural surpluses in certain products, by depressing world prices as these surpluses are disposed of on the world market with the aid of export subsidies, and by destabilising agricultural markets and prices. Agricultural policies in developing countries may also distort trade although they generally do so by discouraging agricultural production (World Bank, 1986). Thus, whereas developed countries as a group tend to produce too much food, developing countries as a group produce too little.

This chapter begins with a discussion of the nature of agricultural policies in developed and developing countries. Firstly, the motives for government intervention are discussed. This is followed by an examination of the main forms of intervention. Secondly, the effects of these policies on trade are examined. Alternative methods of measuring the trade-distorting effects of agricultural policies are set out. Thirdly, the chapter discusses the likely effects of agricultural trade liberalisation. Reference is made to a number of the quantitative models used to simulate the effects of different liberalisation scenarios. Fourthly, the Uruguay Round negotiations covering agricultural trade are discussed. Finally, the outcome of these negotiations as represented by the Agreement on Agriculture set out in the Final Act is discussed.

THE NATURE OF AGRICULTURAL POLICIES IN DEVELOPED AND DEVELOPING COUNTRIES

Why do governments intervene in agriculture? There are a number of different reasons. Firstly, to stabilise the market for agricultural produce and, in particular, to stabilise farm incomes and prices. It is argued that the market for many agricultural products is inherently unstable, with prices and hence farm incomes fluctuating a great deal year by year. The economic explanation for this is usually given in terms of the dependence of agriculture on the weather with the result that the supply is subject to large unplanned changes and the short-run inelasticity of both the demand for and supply of food. (Agricultural goods that are inputs into other agricultural sectors are also subject to derived demand fluctuations.) The justification for intervening to stabilise the market is that unstable prices lead farmers to make suboptimal production decisions. Where prices are subject to large fluctuations, producers will tend to underinvest, resulting in a lower level of production than otherwise. Thus, governments in most developed countries intervene to iron out temporary fluctuations. Where the product is nonperishable, this is achieved by creating buffer stocks of the product: in periods of temporary glut, the authorities buy up surpluses and, in periods of temporary shortage, they unload stocks on to the market. The aim is to stabilise the price around some trend value.

Secondly, governments intervene to guarantee farmers some minimum level of income on the grounds that, in the absence of intervention, farm incomes would fall behind incomes in other sectors of the economy. It is argued that there exists a secular tendency for farm prices and incomes to fall relative to nonfarm prices and incomes. The reasoning is as follows. To begin with, the income elasticity of demand for food is low so, as per capita incomes rise, consumers spend less of their income on food and more on nonfarm products. This means that the demand curve for agricultural products is, at best, moving only slowly to the right over time. Next, technological improvements in methods of agriculture (such as mechanis-ation, new scientific techniques of farming, modern management methods) make it possible to produce the same output with fewer resources. The result is a large rightward shift in the supply curve for agricultural goods over time. When combined with the highly limited rightward shifts in the demand curve, the result is, in the absence of government intervention, a secular decline in the price of agricultural goods. Finally, the specificity of many of the resources employed in farming means that, in the short run, they are 'trapped' in agriculture and unable to move out in response to declining returns. This is particularly true of much capital and land used in agriculture which have few, if any, alternative uses. In the case of labour, the problem is often a reluctance to seek employment elsewhere. Put another way, the supply curve for agricultural resources is upward-sloping (inelastic) in the short run. In the absence of government intervention, the result is a fall in the price received by agricultural resources both in a relative sense and, conceivably, in an absolute sense. Arguments about the need to support farm incomes often get muddled with arguments about intervention to stabilise markets.

Thirdly, government intervention is justified in terms of the need to ensure regular supplies of food. There are two different parts to the argument although they are often not distinguished. The first emphasises the need to reduce dependence on imports and increase self-sufficiency to safeguard the country against a rise in world agricultural prices. Parallels with the world oil crises of the 1970s and early 1980s are often drawn. In the mid-1970s, there were a number of forecasts by bodies such as the Club of Rome which predicted world food shortages of Malthusian proportions which reinforced such thinking. In fact, the trend since then has been for world agricultural prices to fall in real terms. An alternative argument emphasises the need for countries to avoid sudden food shortages caused by international events outside its control (for example, wars). However, in most conceivable situations, it should be possible to obtain supplies from somewhere. If there were a global catastrophe, not only food supplies but the inputs needed for food production (oil, fertilisers, pesticides, and so on) would be unobtainable. So complete food security is clearly not achievable.

Finally, noneconomic arguments often play an important role in support of government intervention in agriculture, such as the need to preserve the countryside or prevent the decline in family farming. In reality, agricultural policy in developed countries typically has the opposite effect, bringing disproportionate benefit to larger, richer farmers and encouraging the replacement of small-scale, family farms with large-scale, capital-intensive methods of farming. In some countries, dietary considerations motivate certain aspects of agricultural policy. For example, in Japan, government policies have deliberately sought to keep the price of beef high by international standards in order to discourage meat consumption.

Governments use a wide variety of measures to achieve their objectives. Broadly speaking, five categories of measures can be distinguished:

1 measures to reduce farm costs, which include input subsidies (e.g. fertiliser subsidies, low-cost loans, etc.) and help farmers to improve agricultural productivity;
2 measures designed to increase farm revenues, which include policies for raising farm output, policies which subsidise farm product prices (e.g. deficiency payments), policies to reduce the quantity of imports (e.g. import quotas, tariffs, etc.) and policies which control domestic supplies (e.g. production quotas, land retirement schemes, the use of intervention agencies to buy up 'surpluses');
3 government expenditure directed specifically towards rural areas (e.g. on rural infrastructure, the provision of social services, transport subsidies, etc.);
4 policies to develop farm-based nonfarm occupations (e.g. tourism);
5 direct income supplementation.

It is clear, however, that not all these measures distort trade. Those which most obviously affect trade are the measures imposed at a country's border whether they affect imports or exports. Firstly, there are *tariffs*. However, tariffs on agricultural trade are comparatively low. Table 2.5 (p. 47) showed the post-Tokyo average MFN tariff rate for food items to be 6.4 per cent compared with 7.0 per cent for manufactures. The average MFN tariff rate for agricultural raw materials was just below 1 per cent. Generally speaking, developed countries prefer other means of restricting imports. One reason is that tariffs are ineffective in achieving the aim of price stability since internal prices vary with world prices. However, tariffs are still quite high on certain tropical products (e.g. fruit and vegetables, tobacco) and on processed agricultural goods. This gives rise to the phenomenon of tariff escalation discussed in Chapter 2.

More important than tariffs as a trade barrier are nontariff barriers. Firstly, there are *import quotas*. Quantitative restrictions on trade in agricultural goods are a major source of trade distortion. Unlike tariffs, import quotas have the advantage that they can isolate the importing country from fluctuations on the world market. (Of course, this will not be so if a bad harvest elsewhere curtails world supply.) The reasons for imposing import quotas are not always to protect domestic producers. In some cases, they may be set to guarantee to a developing country a fixed share of the market of a developed country. For example, the EU's quota on banana imports is designed to protect the market of ACP (African, Caribbean and Pacific) countries which are signatories of the Lomé Convention. Likewise, under the Sugar Protocol the EU guarantees to buy a fixed quantity of sugar at a predetermined price from ACP sugar-producing countries. One country which relies heavily on quotas to control imports is Japan. Tight restrictions are maintained on imports of rice (grown on about one-half of all arable land in Japan) such that domestic producer prices are around three times the world price. The reasons given are to protect domestic producers and to increase self-sufficiency. In the case of beef quotas, the aim is to keep beef prices high to discourage beef consumption and maintain the traditional Japanese diet.

A second type of nontariff barrier is *variable import levies*, which have been a central element of the EU's Common Agricultural Policy. In the case of cereals, this worked as follows: the EU fixed annually a 'target price' for the region of greatest deficit (Duisberg in the Ruhr district of Germany). From this, 'derived prices' were obtained for other regions by deducting transport costs. The derived price for the port of Rotterdam, where most imports of cereals enter the EU, determined the EU's so-called 'threshold price'. No cereals could be imported at a price lower than this threshold price. This was achieved by imposing an import levy on consignments arriving at Rotterdam equal to the difference between the value of the imported consignment and the EU threshold price. Thus, if world cereal prices fell, the import levy was increased to ensure that EU internal prices were not undermined. On the other hand, if world cereal prices rose, the import levy was reduced. This ensured that EU prices were unaffected by fluctuations in world cereal prices and that price stability was thus guaranteed. A similar regime operated for other products covered by the CAP. Not only are such measures more protectionist than fixed tariffs, because they prevent production and consumption in the protected country from responding to changes in world costs and prices, they also increase the instability of prices on world markets. For example, in an uncontrolled world market, if world maize production increases in any particular year, causing a sharp fall in world maize prices, world demand will rise. The more elastic the demand for maize, the less the fall in the world price. If, however, importing countries prevent internal prices falling in line with world prices, demand will not increase. The result is that the world maize price falls more than is necessary.

Finally, there exist a number of other types of import restriction although the intention may not be to control imports. The need to ensure that imports conform with *health and sanitary requirements* in the importing country may result in imports being restricted. Although such controls are needed, governments may make excessive use of them or use them to discriminate against particular suppliers. This is apparent from the fact that the proportion of imports controlled in this way varies considerably from one country to another (World Bank, 1986). *State trading organisations* in both developed and developing countries may give rise to another type of import restriction. For example, Japan uses state trading agencies to restrict imports of rice.

In Chapter 3, the importance of nontariff barriers was shown to be much higher for agricultural trade than for manufactures. Table 3.3 (p. 58) shows that 44 per cent of the agricultural imports of developed countries were covered by NTBs, compared with 14 per cent for industrial products. Laird and Yeats (1990) have also demonstrated that the frequency of NTBs increased fastest between 1966 and 1986 for imports of food products. The share of all imported food product groups which were subject to NTBs rose from 36 per cent in 1966 to 89 per cent in 1986.

Table 6.1 shows the results of another study of the extent of NTBs in agricultural trade. This shows the number of imported items of eight industrialised countries subject to particular kinds of NTBs (tariff quotas and seasonal tariffs, quantitative restrictions and minimum-price policies) as a percentage of the total number of import items. As with the frequency ratios used in Chapter 3, the figures do not state the value of imports affected by NTBs or how much of each import item affected by NTBs is restricted. They are simply a measure of the presence or absence of nontariff barriers. The table reveals that nearly 30 per cent of all agricultural imports, compared with only just over 9 per cent of manufacturing imports, were affected by NTBs. It also shows some interesting differences between agricultural product groups. The frequency of nontariff barriers is very low for raw materials and for tea, coffee and cocoa, but on the other hand is very high for sugar and confectionery imports and quite high for meat and live animals and for dairy products. Quantitative restrictions were common in meat and live animals and in dairy products; variable import levies were most apparent in sugar and confectionery.

Finally, agricultural trade is distorted by a variety of different types of *export incentives* or subsidies. One of the most important types of export incentive used by the EU and other developed countries to facilitate the disposal of food surpluses has been the export restitution. In the case of the EU, these were paid to exporters on the difference between the EU's internal price and the world price of the product in question. In the case of cereals, export restitutions were equal to the difference between the EU intervention price and world market prices. If world market prices fell, the amount of the export restitution was increased. Typically, export restitutions emerge as the consequence of other measures (including import levies) which, by artificially raising domestic prices, regularly cause domestic production plus imports to exceed domestic consumption. Rather than cut domestic prices, governments prefer to dispose of surpluses abroad by granting exporters subsidies on every sale made on world markets at a price which is below the domestic price. This scenario is illustrated by the manner in which the EC switched from being a net importer of cereals in the 1960s to being a net exporter in the 1980s. This had nothing to do with developing a new comparative advantage in cereals (World Bank, 1986). In 1985, the US introduced its own system of export subsidies known as the Export Enhancement Program (extended in 1990) to enable US exporters to win back markets purportedly lost due to the increase in the EC's export restitution payments.

Nonborder measures may also distort trade. One method is the setting of *target or minimum prices* for agricultural goods. This is common in most industrialised countries. In the EU, in the past a target price was fixed

Table 6.1 Frequency of application of various nontariff barriers in industrial countries, 1984 (%)

	(1)	(2)	(3)	(4)	(5)
	Tariff quotas & seasonal tariffs	Quantit. restrictions	Minimum price policies		Total[a]
			All	Variable levies	
Meat & live animals	12.3	41.0	26.0	23.8	52.2
Dairy products	6.9	29.6	28.6	25.6	54.6
Fruits & Vegetables	15.7	18.8	4.9	0.8	33.1
Sugar & Confectionery	0.0	21.7	58.0	58.0	70.0
Cereals	1.7	10.9	21.7	21.7	29.0
Other food	0.8	16.3	13.5	13.2	27.0
Tea, coffee, cocoa	0.4	4.0	2.5	2.5	6.6
Other beverages	18.5	22.9	18.4	0.6	42.3
Raw materials	0.0	7.5	0.3	0.3	7.8
All agriculture	8.2	17.2	11.5	8.2	29.7
Manufactures	2.2	6.7	0.6	0.0	9.4

Source: World Bank (1986)

Notes: Data are the number of import items subject to the nontariff barriers, shown as a percentage of the total number of import items. The industrial-country markets considered are Australia, Austria, the EC, Finland, Japan, Norway, Switzerland and the United States.
[a] This column will be less than the sum of columns (1), (2) and (3) if some import items are subject to more than one barrier.

annually for cereals. Official intervention agencies undertook to buy cereals from farmers at a price which was 90 per cent of the target price. Thus, if the market price dropped below 90 per cent of the target price, it became more profitable for farmers to sell their cereals into intervention. This ensured that the internal market price could never fall lower than 90 per cent of the target price for any length of time. A similar system operated for several other farm products. The effect of fixing target prices is to encourage overproduction of the products. As and when the resultant surpluses are dumped on world markets, the world market price is depressed, to the detriment of other exporting countries. The US has also set target prices. In the case of wheat, it determined the minimum price paid to farmers by undertaking to lend cash to them through the federal Commodity Credit Corporation (CCC) using grain as collateral. If the market price fell below the loan rate, farmers prefered to borrow cash from the CCC rather than sell grain on the market. If the market price did not rise subsequently, farmers kept the cash and allowed the government to keep their grain stocks. If, on the other hand, the market price rose, they retrieved their stocks and sold them at the higher price. At the same time, since the US was the world's largest grain exporter, the CCC loan rate determined the world price of grain, for, if the world price should fall below this level, US grain exporters would prefer to borrow cash from the CCC against grain. US exports would fall, driving up the world price.

A number of countries give support to their farmers by means of a system of *deficiency payments*. This method of support was operated by the UK before joining the EC in 1973. Under this system, an annual guarantee price is determined for each product and, if the market price should fall below this level, the farmer is entitled to a deficiency payment equal to the difference. This shifts the cost of agricultural support from the consumer to the taxpayer. In the case of the UK, this system enabled consumers to buy food at low world prices from the cheapest source. To this extent, trade was less distorted than when high support prices are enforced through intervention buying and import levies. However, trade is indirectly distorted since domestic production is artificially boosted. In the US, deficiency payments are conditional upon farmers agreeing to set aside part of their farming land. This is part of the US Acreage Reduction Program designed to prevent deficiency payments stimulating excess domestic production. One of the issues which has divided countries in the GATT negotiations has been disagreement about the effects of US deficiency payments on trade. Specifically, do they distort trade by artificially boosting domestic production? The US often claims that they do not since they are conditional on farmers setting aside part of their acreage. On the other hand, since the amount of deficiency payment depends on the volume of production, it is clear that they do. By how much depends on how responsive domestic output is to the receipt of such payments.

The EU operates a deficiency payments system for certain products. One example of this concerns *oilseeds* which was the source of a US complaint to the GATT in 1987. In 1962 as part of the Kennedy Round, the EC agreed to bind its tariff on imported soya beans at a zero rate. Instead, the EC pays a subsidy to its processing industries if they use EC-grown products. This payment is similar to a deficiency payment since it is set equal to the difference between the EC price and the price of imports coming in. The ground for the US complaint was that the EC subsidies 'nullified and impaired' the 1962 commitment to allow duty-free access for US exporters. In March 1992 the GATT panel set up to investigate the complaint ruled against the EC oilseeds programme.

A number of countries operate a system of *output quotas* on specific products which seek to limit the amount of production entitled to a guaranteed price. These tend to be introduced when the budgetary costs of surpluses become excessive. One example is the system of *milk quotas* introduced by the EC in 1984. As with most quota systems, they were introduced as a method of controlling the rising costs caused by mounting milk surpluses. Quotas were allocated to each country based on 1981 deliveries plus 1 per cent (except Italy and Ireland whose quotas were set equal to 1983 deliveries). The aim was to cut milk production from 103 million tons in 1983 to 99 million tons in 1984. Member states are free to distribute quotas either on the basis of farms or collectively for dairies. (Thus, by way of example, quotas are allocated on the basis of farms in Germany and on the basis of dairies in France.) If a quota is overrun, farmers are subject to a superlevy of 75 per cent (100 per cent in the case of dairies). In 1988–9, the quota system was extended for a further three years. However, because the quotas originally set were well above consumption, the Community 'bought back' part (3.5 per cent) and 'suspended' a further 5.5 per cent of the reference quantities in return for compensation. Quotas were cut by a further 2 per cent in 1991–2 and 3 per cent in 1992 (Commission of the EC, 1991). Although milk production has declined under quotas, it has not fallen sufficiently to match declining milk consumption.

Similar to quotas are the *guarantee thresholds* which the EC introduced for cereals in 1981 and subsequently a number of other crop products (oilseeds, protein crops, olive oil, cotton, tobacco, certain fruit and vegetables, and wine), as well as for sheepmeat and goatmeat. In May 1992 these were replaced by a new regime brought in as part of the MacSharry Plan for reforming the CAP. The new regime is described later in this chapter. The quotas for cereals involved penalising producers if they exceeded certain maximum guaranteed quantities (MGQs). This took the form of a price or aid reduction. However, unlike milk quotas, the MGQs related to the *total* output of the sector and not *individual* levels; so, if these were exceeded, all producers suffered. In cereals, there was an automatic 3 per cent reduction in price if the MGQ was exceeded in any particular year.

The US also has quota schemes for certain products, such as tobacco. Japan sets similar limits on rice production. Quotas may succeed in reducing the budgetary costs of agricultural policies but, by raising retail prices, they penalise consumers. Moreover, they may simply cause farmers to switch their resources into other products, causing overproduction in these sectors. For example, milk quotas in the EU have had the effect of increasing the number of cattle slaughtered, aggravating the overproduction problem in the beef sector. Also, unless quotas can be traded, production patterns become rigid. (In the case of the EU's milk quotas, these are tradable in the UK but not in other parts of the EU.) Finally, they are extremely costly to administer.

Quantitative restrictions on inputs are other devices used to reduce output. The most common forms of input control are land set-asides and acreage reduction programmes. In 1988 the EC introduced a land set-aside scheme under which EC farmers who took at least one-fifth of their arable land out of production for five years received a premium the amount of which depended on the quality of the land set aside and the average crop yield. In addition, farmers who set aside at least 30 per cent of their arable land were exempt from the corresponsibility levy which large-scale cereal producers were required to pay. The US has a long history of set-aside and acreage reduction schemes, the most recent of which is the payment-in-kind scheme introduced in 1983. Input control schemes are generally less costly to administer than production quotas but their effects on the volume of production are much less predictable. There is a danger that farmers will take their least productive land out of farming. In addition, producers respond by farming their remaining land more intensively. If producers expect prices to rise, there is the added problem that some farmers may not choose to participate. Unlike output quotas, input controls tend initially to increase rather than reduce budgetary expenditures on agriculture. On the other hand, this may be preferred to paying farmers to produce a crop for which there is no demand. Nevertheless, they add to farming costs by encouraging farmers to adopt a suboptimal input mix. They may even encourage farmers to plough up land that would otherwise not be farmed in order to take advantage of the scheme in the next qualification period. Finally, their impact is often counteracted by the input subsidies which governments grant to farmers. In this case, two different measures for assisting farmers work in totally opposite directions.

Lastly, there are *direct income supports*. These have been defined as 'all explicit (monetary) transfers provided by public budgetary funds to all or a specific group of agricultural households, not based on past, present or future production or factors of production and with no conditions or stipulation concerning the use of the transfers' (OECD, 1990). Their distinctive feature is that, in their pure form and unlike other forms of assistance to farmers, they are not related to production and so do not distort trade. This makes them attractive as a method of assisting farmers if for social reasons this is thought to be desirable. Since they are less distorting than other measures, they may be a way in which governments can continue to help farmers while reducing or eliminating other forms of trade-distorting measures. However, in practice there are few forms of direct income support that have no effect on production. There is a danger that they could become backdoor measures for granting support to farmers which, like price support, is related to production. In this case, production and hence trade might still be distorted. Moreover, they are likely to be expensive to administer and lead to excessive budgetary costs. There is a need to decide which farmers should be entitled to assistance. Furthermore, since they are nothing more than a payment designed to supplement the incomes of certain farmers, they carry the stigma of being mere welfare payments which may make them unattractive to farmers. Alternatively, payments could be linked to structural reform (for example, early retirement of farmers, retraining, and so on) so that wider objectives can be attained.

Although most of the policies discussed so far apply to the developed countries, it should not be supposed that *developing countries* are any different in this respect. Governments in most developing countries adopt highly interventionist policies towards agriculture. However, the basic difference between the two is that, whereas policies in the developed countries subsidise agriculture, in developing countries policy is biased against agriculture. In its 1986 World Development Report, the World Bank examined the nature of agricultural policies in developing countries and found that they effectively penalised farming both at the macroeconomic and the sectoral level (World Bank, 1986). At the macroeconomic level, policies implicitly tax agriculture by favouring industrial production and by overvaluation of the exchange rate. In the past, the emphasis of development strategies in many developing countries has been on promoting industrialisation by a policy of high import barriers. This has raised both the price of industrial products relative to agricultural goods and the costs of industrial inputs to farmers, thus reducing the profitability of the agricultural sector relative to that of the industrial.

Overvaluation of the real exchange rate happens partly through failure to adjust the nominal exchange rate as prices at home rise faster than those abroad. The latter is often the result of an overexpansionary monetary and fiscal policy. An overvalued exchange rate renders traded agricultural goods less profitable than nontraded goods. At the sectoral level, governments in developing countries often impose taxes on agricultural export crops and import substitutes. These depress the farmgate price relative to the world price. A major reason given is the need to generate sufficient revenues to finance costly public expenditure programmes. However, when combined with overvaluation of the exchange rate, the effect of such policies is highly damaging for agriculture. (In a similar manner, monopsonistic marketing boards in developing countries often generate fiscal revenues for the government by buying from farmers at prices below world market prices.) Input costs are often reduced through the subsidisation of farm inputs but these largely benefit the bigger, more affluent farmers. Governments also intervene at the marketing stage by setting up public marketing agencies. However, the conclusion of the World Bank was that none of these measures was sufficient to offset the punitive effects of high taxation. It concluded that agricultural policies in developed and developing countries have opposite effects: in developed countries they overencouraged production, while in developing countries they had a discouraging effect. The overall result was a distortion in the patterns of world agricultural production and trade.

THE EFFECTS OF AGRICULTURAL PROTECTIONISM

Because agricultural protection involves both tariff and nontariff barriers and nonborder as well as border measures, the calculation of the costs of agricultural protection to industrial countries is a complex exercise. Since the effect of any form of import protection is to raise the price of domestically produced substitutes relative to the world price, one approach is to express the domestic price in the importing country as a ratio with the world price. The most common practice is to take the price with the same product at the border where it is imported. This is known as the *nominal protection coefficient* (NPC). Estimates of the NPC for various commodities in several industrial countries for the period 1980–2 are shown in Table 6.2.

The NPC for producer prices measures the implicit subsidy to domestic producers, while the NPC for consumer prices measures the implicit tax on domestic consumers. As Anderson and Tyers (1991) explain, estimates of NPCs are not exact for various reasons. Firstly, there are differences in the quality of the good produced and consumed. Secondly, fluctuations in world prices affect the calculation of NPCs. Since domestic prices tend to be relatively more stable than world prices, when world prices fall, the NPC increases and vice versa. Because the period 1980–2 was one of relatively high international prices, the figures in Table 6.2 are an underestimate of the extent of agricultural protection.

Bearing these qualifications in mind, a number of conclusions can be drawn from Table 6.2. Firstly, the highest rates of protection are found for rice, dairy products and sugar. Secondly, the countries which have the highest rates of protection are Japan and those in Europe (both the EC and the rest of Western Europe). These are both net importing regions whereas the other countries are mainly net exporters. Thirdly, there are considerable variations between countries and commodities. It is interesting to compare the above figures with estimates of NPCs for developing countries. If agricultural policies in developed countries have been biased towards

Table 6.2 Nominal protection coefficients (NPCs) for producer (PR) and consumer (C) prices of selected commodities in industrial countries, 1980–2

Country or region	Wheat		Coarse grain		Rice		Beef & lamb		Pork & poultry		Dairy products		Sugar		Weighted average[a]	
	PR NPC	C NPC	PR NPC	C NPC	PR NPC	C NPC	PR NPC	C NPC	PR NPC	C NPC	PR NPC	C NPC	PR NPC	C NPC	PR NPC	C NPC
Australia	1.04	1.08	1.00	1.00	1.15	1.75	1.00	1.00	1.00	1.00	1.30	1.40	1.00	1.40	1.04	1.09
Canada	1.15	1.12	1.00	1.00	1.00	1.00	1.00	1.00	1.10	1.10	1.95	1.95	1.30	1.30	1.17	1.16
EC[b]	1.25	1.30	1.40	1.40	1.40	1.40	1.90	1.90	1.25	1.25	1.75	1.80	1.50	1.70	1.54	1.56
Other Europe[c]	1.70	1.70	1.45	1.45	1.00	1.00	2.10	2.10	1.35	1.35	2.40	2.40	1.80	1.80	1.84	1.81
Japan	3.80	1.25	4.30	1.30	3.30	2.90	4.00	4.00	1.50	1.50	2.90	2.90	3.00	2.60	2.44	2.08
New Zealand	1.00	1.00	1.00	1.00	1.00	1.00	1.00	1.00	1.00	1.00	1.00	1.00	1.00	1.00	1.00	1.00
United States	1.15	1.00	1.00	1.00	1.30	1.00	1.00	1.00	1.00	1.00	2.00	2.00	1.40	1.40	1.16	1.17
Weighted average	1.19	1.20	1.11	1.16	2.49	2.42	1.47	1.51	1.17	1.17	1.88	1.93	1.49	1.68	1.40	1.43

Source: World Bank (1986)

Notes: [a] Averages are weighted by the values of production and consumption at border prices.
[b] Excludes Greece, Portugal and Spain.
[c] Austria, Finland, Norway, Sweden, Switzerland.

agriculture, those in many developing countries have worked in the opposite direction. Estimates of NPCs for cereals and export crops in thirteen African countries over the period 1972–83 found that protection was negative (World Bank, 1986). Table 6.2 says nothing about the trend in agricultural protection. However, later estimates by Anderson and Tyers (1991) suggest that the rate of protection has been increasing in recent decades. They estimated that the average rate of protection in industrial countries for grain, livestock products and sugar was 21 per cent in the decade 1965–74 and 28 per cent during 1975–83.

An alternative approach to measuring the effects of agricultural protectionism is to employ the concept of *producer subsidy equivalents* (PSEs). The concept was originally developed by Josling (1973, 1975) and then later expanded and applied by the OECD in a four-year study of the effects of national agricultural policies on trade (OECD, 1987). Its great attraction is that it seeks to take into account the effects of a wide variety of policy measures and not just border measures. Tangermann *et al.* (1987) define producer subsidy equivalent as 'the subsidy that would be necessary to replace the array of actual farm policies employed in a particular country in order to leave farm income unchanged' or as 'the "cash" value of policy transfers occasioned by price and nonprice means'. Ideally, the aim should be to include the effects of all government policies which transfer incomes to farm producers. In practice, inadequate information frequently makes it necessary to settle for something less than this. If, also, the concern is to measure the impact of agricultural policies on trade flows, those measures which have no direct impact are excluded. To begin with, a calculation is made of the transfers effected by domestic price support systems. Where these take the form of straightforward subsidies to producers, as under a deficiency payments system, this is obtained directly from the figures for government expenditure. Where, however, price support is achieved through government intervention in agricultural markets combined with import restrictions, as under the EU's CAP system, the amount of transfer brought about has to be derived indirectly. Some estimate is made of the price-enhancing effects of intervention buying combined with variable import levies for domestic sales. To this is added the restitution payments made on export sales. In addition, the transfers to farm producers effected through input subsidies is generally included. Account might also be taken of the effects of any factor subsidies and taxes.

PSEs are generally calculated by commodity and expressed as the amount of money transferred to producers of that commodity. These amounts can then be aggregated to obtain an estimate of the total transfer of incomes to the farming sector as a whole. It is also possible to express the total amount of PSE to the producers of a particular product as a percentage of the value of domestic production valued either at domestic or world prices. If domestic production is valued at world prices, the percentage value is equivalent to an *ad valorem* tariff. Thus, PSEs could be used as the basis for agricultural trade negotiations in a similar manner to tariffs (see Tangermann *et al.*, 1987). As with tariffs, commitments could be made by countries to bind PSEs at existing levels as well as making actual reductions of an agreed proportion.

In addition to producer subsidy equivalents, the OECD in its study of the effects of agricultural policies separately calculated the *consumer subsidy equivalent* (CSE). In an analogous way to the producer subsidy equivalent, this measures the transfer effected by government policies to consumers of farm products. In developed countries, this is normally a negative amount. Under the EU's CAP system, this is definitely the case and there exists an obvious link between the transfer *to* producers and the transfer *from* consumers. In the case of a deficiency payments system, however, this does not happen because producer prices are raised relative to consumer prices. Rather, the transfer occurs to producers from taxpayers and not from consumers *per se*.

Table 6.3 sets out the OECD's estimates of producer subsidy equivalent for different commodities and countries. For the period 1984–6, the average level of PSE for all OECD countries was 38 per cent compared with 29 per cent for the period 1979–81. Japan had the highest average PSE (69 per cent) followed by the EC (40 per cent). At the other extreme were Australia and New Zealand (19 per cent). The products with the highest level of PSE were rice, sugar and milk. Significant differences existed between countries. Japan had higher PSEs for crop products, notably wheat, coarse grains, rice and soyabeans. The EC had higher PSEs for livestock products, notably sheepmeat, milk and beef, and veal. The USA had the highest PSEs for sugar, wool, milk and rice. In 1987, the average level of PSE for the OECD countries rose further to 50 per cent before falling back slightly to 44 per cent in 1990 (OECD, 1991).

Although both the measures used above are useful in showing differences in the degree of agricultural protection between countries and commodities and in demonstrating the trend towards increasing protectionism in the developed countries, they do not provide any estimates of the actual cost of such policies either for developed or for developing countries. For this purpose, the welfare loss created by such policies must be measured. Since a number of commodities are involved, it is not possible to use a simple single-commodity partial equilibrium approach. Anderson and Tyers (1991) have sought to estimate the effects of protection on the developed countries using a multicommodity model of world markets, which included seven commodities that together account for roughly one-half of world food trade. These were grain (wheat, coarse grain, rice), sugar and livestock products (ruminant meat, nonruminant meat and dairy products). Hence, they named their model the GLS (grain, livestock products and sugar) model. It has the disadvantage that it is not a general equilibrium model which includes all

Table 6.3 OECD: producer subsidy equivalents (PSEs) by commodity and country, 1979–86 (%)

	United States		Canada		European Community		Japan		Australia & New Zealand^a		Total OECD^b	
	1979–81	1984–6	1979–81	1984–6	1979–81	1984–6	1979–81	1984–6	1979–81	1984–6	1979–81	1984–6
Eggs	5	7	26	5	20	18	20	19	27	25	16	14
Milk	55	66	74	97	67	56	79	82	27	33	63	63
Wheat	14	44	15	41	28	36	97	98	4	13	21	41
Coarse grains	9	30	15	42	24	26	96	98	8	8	15	30
Beef and veal	9	9	11	16	42	53	53	55	10	11	25	30
Pigmeat	5	6	8	5	7	6	22	40	19	9	9	11
Poultry	5	10	29	17	24	27	19	16	24	12	16	16
Sugar	15	76	15	37	34	75	46	72	-1.4^c	21^c	28	71
Rice	7	61	–	–	15	68	71	86	16^c	25^c	63	84
Sheepmeat	7	8	–	–	55	63	–	–	13	37	40	53
Wool	41	69	–	–	–	–	–	–	12	9	11	12
Soya beans	6	10	–	–	43	59	82	84	–	–	8	13
Other oilseeds	–	–	15	30	40	36	–	–	4^c	9^c	28	24
Crops	10	31	15	40	27	38	71	86	6	12	25	44
Livestock products	21	26	31	39	41	41	40	46	15	19	32	35
Average (all above)	16	28	24	39	37	40	57	69	14	19	29	38

Source: OECD (1991)

Notes: ^a Arithmetic average.
^b Includes all OECD countries.
^c Australia only.

tradable and nontradable goods and factor markets. This may not matter too much given the relative smallness of the agricultural sector within the economies of developed countries as a whole. Moreover, the model has the special attraction that it can be used to determine the extent to which agricultural policies create instability on world markets as well as the more conventional protectionist effect on welfare.

Their estimates of the costs of agricultural policies for the developed countries are set out in Table 6.4. These show the welfare costs to the developed countries of their existing agricultural policies. This is roughly the difference between the consumer trading loss plus the government budgetary cost less the producer gain. For both the EC and Japan, this amounted to about US$9 billion per year. Expressed on a per capita basis, the cost was US$75 for Japan compared with US$25 for the EC. The per capita cost to the EFTA countries was even higher than for the EC countries. By way of contrast, the welfare cost to the US was much lower at US$3.2 billion or US$14 per capita. Table 6.4 also shows how agricultural policies give rise to substantial transfers from consumers/taxpayers to farm producers. The effective 'tax' on consumers/taxpayers in the EC and Japan amounted to US$800 and US$1,120 respectively and came mainly in the form of higher prices. For every dollar received by farm producers in the EC and Japan, consumers/taxpayers paid US$1.19 and US$1.44 respectively. In the US and Canada, the ratios were roughly the same as for the EC. These constitute *minimum* estimates of the costs of agricultural protectionism. The true cost is almost certainly much greater. Moreover, the benefits to farm producers are unequally distributed, with the poorest farmers receiving a

Table 6.4 The domestic effects of the food policies of various industrial market economies, 1980–2 (1985 US$ billion per year)

	EC (12)	EFTA (5)	Japan	USA	Canada
Domestic consumer cost	55.0	11.7	35.6	17.5	3.0
Government revenue cost	1.2	0.6	–6.0	2.6	0.9
Domestic producer benefit:					
(a) Total	47.3	9.6	20.6	16.9	3.3
(b) As % of gross GLS receipts	23.0	35.0	63.0	11.0	17.0
Net domestic cost:					
(a) Total	8.9	2.7	9.0	3.2	0.6
(b) Per capita	25.0	85.0	75.0	14.0	24.0
Transfers from consumers/ taxpayers:					
(a) Per nonfarm households	800	1,710	1,120	370	680
(b) Per dollar received by producers	1.19	1.28	1.44	1.19	1.18

Source: Anderson and Tyers (1991)

relatively small amount of the gain. This is because the poorest 30 per cent of farmers in developed countries produce only about one-tenth of all output. So roughly 90 per cent of the transfers are going to producers who do not need support. If the purpose of protectionist agricultural policies is to help the poorest farmers, these policies are extraordinarily inefficient. Moreover, as the World Bank (1986) has shown, much of the gain to producers is in fact being mopped up by the owners of fixed assets employed in agriculture, in particular landowners. Because the supply of agricultural land in most developed countries is in fixed supply, increased agricultural production stimulated by artificially high food prices simply drives up land rents which in turn forces up land prices. The end result may be no change in the rate of return enjoyed by farm producers but a big rise in incomes to landowners.

In addition to the costs of agricultural protection to the developed countries, Anderson and Tyers (1991) estimated the costs of such policies to other countries, in particular other farming-exporting countries and the developing countries. Agricultural exporting countries such as Australia and New Zealand were found to have experienced a substantial welfare loss, most of which was caused by the EC's CAP. Australia's net welfare loss due to the CAP was put at US$55 per capita and that of New Zealand at US$185 per capita. This is due primarily to the effect which policies such as the EC's CAP have in depressing world prices. Food-exporting developing countries are similarly affected. On the other hand, food-importing developing countries benefit in comparison with a situation where world prices are higher. Anderson and Tyers (1991) estimated that agricultural protection in the developed market economies of the world depressed grains, livestock products and sugar prices by as much as 14 per cent. The EC's CAP alone reduced world prices by 10 per cent.

In addition, these policies are a major source of international price instability. Domestic markets are effectively insulated from the effects of fluctuations in world supply. For example, a sudden world shortage of sugar will cause the world price to rise. In the EU, reduced variable import levies ensure that the rise in price is not transmitted to the EU market. Instead, world prices must rise by more than they otherwise would to bring about the required fall in world demand. The CAP may also ensure that any domestically generated supply fluctuations cause bigger world price fluctuations than otherwise. This is because the effects of over- or undersupply take the form of changes in trade flows rather than in domestic prices. For example, the effect of a grain surplus takes the form of an increase in EU exports rather than a fall in the EU grain price. The result is a larger fall in world grain prices than otherwise. Anderson and Tyers (1991) estimated that, if all agricultural policies in developed and developing countries were liberalised, the fluctuation in world wheat and rice prices would be only a quarter of what it was over the period 1961–83.

THE EFFECTS OF WORLD AGRICULTURAL TRADE LIBERALISATION

Before discussing the agreement on agriculture reached as part of the Uruguay Round, it is useful to examine some of the attempts which have been made to estimate the likely effects of world agricultural trade being liberalised. Liberalisation could take one of several different forms and it is interesting to compare the outcomes of each of these alternatives. Firstly, one or more countries could liberalise on their own (unilateral liberalisation) or all countries could agree to liberalise simultaneously (multilateral liberalisation). Secondly, liberalisation could be confined to the industrialised economies only or could include developing countries. Thirdly, there could be a total elimination of all trade-distorting measures or a partial removal of some trade-distorting measures or a reduction in their trade-distorting effects. As we shall see, the Uruguay Round agreement took the form of a negotiated partial liberalisation involving (to varying degrees) both developed and developing countries.

Anderson and Tyers (1991) simulated the effects of a total liberalisation of all trade-distorting policies in industrialised economies only. The procedure was to insert into the model, which was initially constructed using 1980–2 data, additional information about trends in world agricultural markets in subsequent years and thereby obtain projected domestic and border prices for different groups of commodities and countries. In this way, nominal protection coefficients could be calculated for these years. The effects of liberalisation were obtained by assuming that international prices fully adjust to the total elimination of all agricultural protection in the industrial countries. This exercise was performed for the years 1990 and 2000. The results obtained by the Anderson and Tyers study are summarised in Tables 6.5 and 6.6.

Firstly, liberalisation has a significant upward effect on the international price level for all products included in the model. On average, international prices would rise by 28 per cent by the year 2000 in comparison with the levels prevailing in 1980–2. The increases are especially large for dairy products and beef. The EC makes by far the biggest contribution to this price rise. Although the *international* price level rises following liberalisation, *domestic* price levels in the industrialised countries fall. It is this fall in the domestic price level which is resisted by farming interests in the industrialised countries. One interesting result of the Anderson–Tyers model is that, where one country (say, the US) unilaterally liberalises, the required fall in the domestic price level of that country is much greater than when all countries liberalise simultaneously. This means that political opposition to liberalisation in any one country (such as the US) is likely to be greater if unilateral as opposed to multilateral liberalisation is pursued.

Secondly, liberalisation has a major impact on international trade flows in

Table 6.5 The international price and trade effects of agricultural trade liberalisation

Country	Wheat	Coarse grain	Rice	Ruminant meat	Nonrumi-nant meat	Dairy products	Sugar	Weight (average)
Percentage change in international prices following liberalisation								
EC(12)								
1980–2	6	5	3	22	4	33	8	11
1990	12	6	6	33	4	64	16	18
2000	15	9	9	33	4	72	15	19
EFTA(5)								
1980–2	1	1	1	3	0	6	0	1
1990	1	0	0	3	0	6	1	1
2000	1	0	0	5	1	13	3	2
Japan								
1980–2	1	1	6	5	4	11	2	3
1990	1	1	10	15	5	30	3	6
2000	1	1	10	16	6	33	2	7
USA								
1980–2	1	–4	0	3	–1	28	3	4
1990	–3	–7	–2	6	–2	35	3	1
2000	–3	–5	–1	7	–1	30	3	1
All DMEs								
1980–2	10	3	11	27	8	61	11	16
1990	12	2	16	49	9	104	22	25
2000	16	6	18	50	10	117	22	28
Change in net exports following liberalisation (in million tonnes)								
W. Europe & Japan								
1980–2	–4.5	–4.0	–3.8	–5.6	–1.7	–14.0	–2.3	
2000	–30.5	3.5	–9.8	–13.1	–4.0	–67.1	–8.4	
Australasia & N. America								
1980–2	–3.0	8.6	–0.2	2.1	0.9	–14.4	–0.7	
2000	10.8	6.5	0.0	2.5	2.3	–12.3	–1.6	
Centrally planned E. Europe								
1980–2	2.6	–1.9	0.0	0.5	0.0	6.2	0.0	
2000	4.5	–4.1	0.1	0.9	0.1	13.7	0.0	
Developing countries								
1980–2	4.9	–2.3	4.0	2.9	0.7	22.0	2.9	
2000	31.3	–11.1	12.6	2.5	0.3	46.2	6.7	

Source: Anderson and Tyers (1991)

Table 6.6 Global welfare effects of liberalising food policies of all industrial market economies by the year 2000 (1985 US$ billion per year)

Country/region	Effects of liberalisation by all industrial market economies on:	
	Producer welfare	Net economic welfare
EC (12)	−78.6	15.1
EFTA (5)	−14.2	3.3
Japan	−44.4	25.1
United States	7.5	4.5
Canada	−1.9	1.1
Australia	3.4	1.8
New Zealand	1.7	1.1
All industrial countries	−126.6	52.0
All developing countries	34.9	1.5
Centrally planned E. Europe	14.6	3.5
Global total	−77.1	57.0

Source: Anderson and Tyers (1991)

food products. Table 6.5 shows that the net exports of Western Europe and Japan for most products fall following liberalisation. This is due to increased imports of these products. In contrast, the traditional food exporters of Australasia and North America experience an increase in the net exports of most products. The developing countries and East European economies also enjoy an increase in the net exports of most products.

Thirdly, liberalisation significantly increases economic welfare in all industrialised economies. Anderson and Tyers put the global welfare gain by the end of the decade at $57 billion at 1985 prices. This represents a gain per nonfarm household of US$1,500 in the EC and almost US$3,000 in other West European countries and Japan. Nevertheless, in these countries farm producers will experience a substantial welfare loss although this is still less than the gain to consumers/taxpayers. Developing countries also gain overall although by much less than the industrial countries. The reason is that many developing countries are net food importers and lose from higher international prices. However, this is just offset by the gain to developing countries which are net food exporters and who gain from better terms of trade.

An earlier study by Anderson and Tyers (World Bank, 1986) reckoned that developing countries would lose on account of the fall in their terms of trade because they were net importers of food. Only if developing countries also liberalised their own farm trade policies would they also benefit.

Subsequently, Loo and Tower (1988) demonstrated that, when allowance is made for the effects of liberalisation on other parts of the economy, developing countries do in fact gain. Firstly, higher world prices cause an expansion of farming in developing countries relative to other sectors of the economy. The resultant improvement in resource allocation represents an additional welfare gain for developing countries. Secondly, expansion of the agricultural sector causes an increase in government tax revenues because the farm sector is relatively highly taxed. This permits tax cuts while at the same time improving the budget balance. Lower tax rates have a beneficial effect on efficiency in the rest of the economy. Moreover, if a larger number of products are included, the terms-of-trade effect becomes positive. The reason why Anderson and Tyers (1991) have since obtained a positive result for developing countries from liberalisation solely by developed countries is because their calculations are for the year 2000. This gives time for developing countries to adjust. Specifically, higher international farm prices encourage an expansion of the farm sector in developing countries such that developing countries eventually become net exporters of food. This means that the terms-of-trade effect becomes positive not negative.

Loo and Tower (1988) employed a general equilibrium approach and this was the main reason they obtained a different result to that of earlier studies. This has the advantage that it catches the follow-through effects of trade liberalisation to other parts of the economy. McDonald (1991) provides another example of such an approach. He uses a general equilibrium model which includes four regions (the US, the EC, Japan and the rest of the world) and nine commodities (eight of which are agricultural commodities and the ninth represents all other goods and services). The model has other attractions. Firstly, it uses 1989 data; other models have tended to use much earlier data. Secondly, there is an allowance for imperfect substitutability in both capital and land markets. Thirdly, it is assumed that commodities are imperfect substitutes for one another, allowing for the possibility of two-way trade in commodities. A particularly interesting feature of the model is the attempt which is made to incorporate separately a variety of different agricultural policy instruments including tariffs, quotas, export subsidies, production subsidies and land set-asides. This makes it possible to simulate a number of different liberalisation scenarios. Specifically, McDonald simulates five complete liberalisation scenarios: three unilateral scenarios (one by each of the US, the EC and Japan) and two multilateral scenarios (one by the US and the EC and a second by the US, the EC and Japan) and a further four partial liberalisation scenarios.

With regard to the case of *complete* liberalisation, the most important effects may be summarised as follows. Firstly, where one country or region liberalises *unilaterally*, agricultural output and prices fall in that country but increase in other regions. Returns to factors of production employed in

214

farming are similarly affected. For example, if the EC liberalises, agricultural output and prices fall in the EC but rise in the US. Returns to factors employed in farming also fall in the EC but rise in the US. One of the particularly striking aspects of this is that the US agricultural sector benefits much more from the EC liberalising its agricultural policies than vice versa. This suggests that US agriculture stands to gain more from persuading the EC to liberalise its policies than vice versa, and helps to explain the different negotiating positions adopted by the two regions in the Uruguay Round. Economic welfare is increased in all countries by unilateral liberalisation with one exception: Japanese welfare falls in the case of the US liberalising its trade policies because Japan is a large net importer of food. Secondly, where all countries *multilaterally* liberalise, the gain in economic welfare for all countries is greater. On the other hand, there are slightly different effects on the farm sectors of the different countries. In particular, the drop in farm returns in the US is much less in this case than when the US liberalises alone. Farmers in the EC and Japan, by contrast, are only slightly better off under multilateral as opposed to unilateral liberalisation.

More interesting is the case of partial liberalisation based on a negotiated package involving the US, the EC and Japan. The results obtained by McDonald for three *partial* liberalisation scenarios were based upon certain assumptions about the outcome of the Uruguay Round negotiations. McDonald considered four possible scenarios. Firstly, the model considered the effects of implementing the US proposals for the elimination of all farm subsidies which distort production and trade. Only subsidies which are 'decoupled' from production would be permitted. As a proxy for decoupling, the model substituted a farmland input subsidy. This had much the same effect as the case of complete multilateral liberalisation except that the returns to farm factors remained closer to their preliberalisation levels.

Secondly, the model examined the effects of implementing the EC proposals favouring a more gradual approach in which agricultural support was initially reduced by only a limited amount and using an aggregate measure of support (AMS). McDonald proposed as a proxy for EC proposals a 30 per cent reduction in levels of agricultural support. This had effects that are similar to but smaller than the case of complete multilateral liberalisation. However, one interesting result was that EC welfare increased more under its own (30 per cent) proposal than under the US (100 per cent) proposal.

Thirdly, the model considered what would happen if the 'rebalancing' favoured by the EC but opposed by the US was allowed. Under this, tariff rates on oilseeds and nongrain feeds were increased to offset the effects of lower tariffs on feed grains and food grains (see p. 218). The results obtained showed that rebalancing serves to spread the effects of liberalisation more evenly across commodity groups and may therefore be important for obtaining political acceptance for such measures.

Finally, the model considered the case where countries agree to the elimination of all export subsidies (strongly favoured by the US) but with the continuation of domestic price supports. To control production, this is combined with land set-asides. The result was a smaller gain in world welfare than with any of the other multilateral approaches.

One of the interesting conclusions which emerged from the model was that, whichever approach was used, the adjustment pain was always greater for EC farmers than US farmers. Japanese farmers were the hardest hit in all the multilateral scenarios considered. This helps to explain the greater reluctance of the EC to contemplate substantial liberalisation. It also supports the view that some rebalancing could help to ease the adjustment pain in the EC by spreading the effects of liberalisation across product groups. Finally, any package which continues to allow decoupled payments to farmers would also help farmers to adjust by providing some income support.

AGRICULTURAL NEGOTIATIONS IN THE URUGUAY ROUND

The inclusion of agriculture as a major item on the agenda for the Uruguay Round negotiations constituted an important breakthrough. Previous GATT rounds had generally failed to tackle the problem of agricultural protectionism. The background to these negotiations was a growing imbalance in world agriculture trade largely brought about by misguided policies pursued in both developed and developing countries (see Miner and Hathaway, 1988, for a fuller discussion of these problems). These problems arose because of a massive increase in agricultural supplies at a time when world demand for agricultural goods was weakening. Production in the developed countries increased as a result of high support prices aided by improved yields brought about by technological improvements in farming methods. By contrast, production in many developing countries was held back by policies which in effect discriminated against the farming sector. At the same time, the debt crisis of the early 1980s meant that many developing countries, experiencing stagnant or even declining real incomes, were less able to pay for imports. The result was a significant fall in the volume of world agricultural trade, leaving the developed countries with excess capacity and accumulating stocks. In an effort to find markets for unwanted output, governments (in particular, the EC and the US) increased their subsidies to exporters. One result was an escalation in the costs of such policies in developed countries. If for no other reason, this meant that governments in these countries were keen to negotiate some new restraints on measures distorting trade in agricultural goods. In addition, there was the need to prevent the growing number of agriculture-related trade disputes coming before the GATT from undermining the credibility and authority of the GATT in other areas. Not only was the number of such disputes increasing but, in many cases, the GATT seemed unable to bring about a settlement. Partly this was because of deficiencies in the GATT dispute-settlements process itself. Partly, too, it reflected the vagueness of the GATT rules which governed trade in agricultural goods.

The ministerial declaration which launched the Uruguay Round at Punta del Este in September 1986 set out the aims:

> Contracting Parties agree that there is an urgent need to bring more discipline and predictability to world agricultural trade by correcting and preventing restrictions and distortions including those related to structural surpluses so as to reduce the uncertainty, imbalances and instability in world agricultural markets. Negotiations shall aim to achieve greater liberalisation of trade in agriculture and bring all measures affecting import access and export competition under strengthened and more operationally effective GATT rules and disciplines, taking into account the general principles governing the negotiations, by:
> (i) improving market access through, inter alia, the reduction of import barriers;
> (ii) improving the competitive environment by increasing discipline on the use of all direct and indirect subsidies and other measures affecting directly or indirectly agricultural trade, including the phased reduction of their negative effects and dealing with their causes;
> (iii) minimising the adverse effects that sanitary and phytosanitary regulations and barriers can have on trade in agriculture, taking into account the relevant international agreements.
>
> (Finger and Olechowski, 1987)

At the start of the negotiations, a vast gulf appeared to separate the positions of the two major blocs. On the one hand, the United States and the so-called Cairns Group (fourteen independent agricultural exporting countries including Australia, New Zealand, Canada, Brazil and Argentina) were keen to make rapid and significant progress towards liberalising agricultural trade. On the other hand, the EC, the other West European states and Japan, all of whom operated highly protectionist policies, preferred a much more gradual process. To begin with, there seemed to be little common ground between the position of the two dominant negotiators, the United States and the EC. The US called for the phasing out over a ten-year period of all agricultural subsidies and import barriers using some agreed measure of aggregate support. This was the so-called 'zero option' which was supported by the Cairns Group but totally rejected by the EC. Instead, the EC proposed a two-stage approach. In the first stage, measures should be adopted to restore balance in those sectors with the worst surpluses (notably, milk, sugar and cereals), including price discipline and quantitative restrictions. In the second stage, there would be 'progressive reduction' in support levels and the level of external protection. However, so-called 'rebalancing' should be allowed in sectors characterised by structural surpluses. This was stated to mean imposing tariffs on corn gluten feed and other cereal substitutes which at the time enjoyed free entry to the EC if, at the same time, domestic suppport prices and hence variable import levies on cereals were to be reduced.

At the Mid-term Review in December 1988, negotiations broke down with the sides unable to agree a negotiating framework to cover the remaining two years of the Round. A deadline was set of April 1989 to resolve the issues. What emerged was an agreement between the US and the EC to cover both the short and long term. Both sides agreed not to increase farm supports for eighteen months and to elaborate a programme of long-term reforms which would include reductions in both export subsidies and domestic supports (see *The Financial Times*, 7 April 1989).

In October 1989, the US unveiled a new set of proposals containing four elements. Firstly, all export subsidies on farm products should be eliminated within five years. Food aid should be exempt but subject to new rules. Secondly, domestic supports directly affecting farm production and prices would be phased out over seven years. Income supports which were not linked to production were specifically excluded. It was proposed that, as a concession to the EC, an aggregate measure of support should be used as the basis for reducing domestic supports. Thirdly, all nontariff barriers affecting imports of agricultural products should be converted into tariffs – a process known as 'tariffication' – and then cut over ten years to zero or very low rates. Variable import levies would be prohibited as would voluntary export restraints and minimum import pricing of any kind. A special safeguard mechanism would protect countries from import surges during the ten years. Tariffication would be brought about by deducting the world price from the domestic price to determine the equivalent tariff. Because this would result in certain cases in very high and prohibitive rates of duty, it was proposed that a zero or very low tariff would be charged on a fixed amount with the full tariff applying only to imports in excess of this amount. The low-tariff quota would then be gradually raised and the higher full tariff lowered so that by the year 2000 the duty would be close to zero. Finally, efforts would be made to ensure that import measures designed to protect health, human, animal or plant life were consistent with 'sound scientific evidence' and recognised 'the priniciple of equivalency' (see *The Financial Times*, 25 October 1989).

Although aspects of these proposals were acceptable to the EC, major differences still existed. The EC made clear that it was willing to accept some tariffication of import barriers subject to two conditions: (a) tariffs should be specific and not *ad valorem* tariffs; (b) the tariff should contain some variable component (as with their existing system of variable import levies) to allow for exchange-rate fluctuations (such as a sudden drop in the value of the US dollar) or abrupt changes in world prices due to a drought or other natural disaster. The US saw the latter as an attempt by the EC to keep its variable import levy system. The EC also insisted that tariffication should be applied to the US deficiency payments system and should allow the rebalancing of cuts in internal supports to farmers with higher border tariffs. Japan was also willing to accept tariffication provided that imports of rice were exempt. The EC was also willing to reduce domestic supports but wanted the use of an Aggregate Measure of Support (AMS). It proposed the freezing of all AMSs at current levels and then an annual trimming back by some agreed percentage. However, the EC wanted a slower rate of reduction than that proposed by the US. The US had proposed dividing aids into three categories: a 'red-light' group to be phased out immediately; an 'amber-light' group to be kept under discipline and to which the AMS concept would be applied; and a 'green-light' group which would be permitted because they do not distort trade. A crucial question was which aids would be put in the so-called 'green box' and thus be allowed after liberalisation. But the biggest differences existed over export subsidies, which the US wanted eliminated within five years. The EC took the view that there was no need for a separate set of reductions for export subsidies since these would be automatically cut as domestic price supports were lowered (see *The Financial Times*, 26 April 1990).

With the deadline for concluding the Round fast approaching, it became crucial to achieve a breakthrough on the issues still dividing the US and the EC over agriculture. At the Houston Summit in July 1990, agreement was reached between the G7 countries on a way forward. The agreement was widely regarded as a victory for the EC; its insistence on using an ASM formula for reductions in levels of support was conceded. On the other hand, it was made clear that these should include export subsidies and import protection and not just domestic supports. The wording of the agreement spoke of 'substantial and progressive reductions in support and protection' of agriculture with specific reference being made to 'internal regimes, market access and export subsidies' (see *The Financial Times*, 13 July 1990).

In October 1990, the EC published its new proposals for agricultural reform. These proposed cuts of 30 per cent in internal price supports over a ten-year period from 1986 to 1996 with provisions for 'rebalancing' and for protecting farmers against commodity price volatility caused by exchange-rate movements. There was also no firm commitment to curb export subsidies. When the US published its revised set of proposals in October 1990, it was clear that the two sides were still no nearer agreement than when the negotiations first commenced. The US demanded a reduction in export subsidies of 90 per cent over ten years (instead of their total elimination over five years, as previously). Secondly, domestic subsidies affecting production and prices were to be reduced by 75 per cent a year over ten years (instead of their complete phasing out within ten years). Thirdly, with regard to import access, they proposed the introduction of a 'corrective factor' to shield farmers from swings in prices or exchange rates. Governments would be able to impose a surcharge if the import price of a product fell below 75 per cent of the average import price for the product over the preceding three years. But there was no concession made on the EC's rebalancing demands. Disagreements also remained over the appropriate base period to use for reducing the level of internal supports and border protection. The US did not accept the EC's plan for taking 1986 as the base year but instead proposed 1986–8 for internal support and border protection and 1987–9 for export subsidies. Finally, the US reiterated its demand for all NTBs to be converted into tariff equivalents. They would then be subject to annual cuts up to 50 per cent after ten years.

So great were the differences between the two sides that talks broke down in December 1990 with neither side showing much willingness to compromise. Following the collapse of talks, it was agreed to recommence negotiations on the basis of the formula agreed at the Houston Summit; namely, 'specific and binding commitments' to reduce farm support in each of the three areas of internal assistance, border protection and export subsidies (the so-called Dunkel Formula). This commitment to negotiate on each of the three areas pleased the US and the Cairns Group. On the other hand, there were no other prior conditions stipulated for resuming talks, which suited the EC (see *The Financial Times*, 22 February 1991). In November 1991, hopes were raised by the willingness of the US to scale down their target reductions for farm subsidies, announced at The Hague Summit. Specifically, the US indicated that it was prepared to make reductions of only 35 per cent in export subsidies (compared with 90 per cent in November 1990) and 30 per cent in border protection and domestic supports (compared with 75 per cent in November 1990) but over a period of five years (instead of ten).

But deep differences still remained on how such reductions would be made. Firstly, the US still wanted to use 1986–8 as the base period while the EC favoured 1988–91. The difference was important because subsidies rose sharply after 1986–8. Secondly, it was not agreed which measures should be put in the 'green box' as being permissible when domestic supports were cut back. The EC wanted to include all compensatory payments to farmers which were a key part of the package of reforms to the CAP then being proposed by Raymond MacSharry, the Agricultural Commissioner. Thirdly, there were differences over how tariff equivalents would be calculated when border protections were converted into tariffs and on the safeguard mechanisms for dealing with unexpected surges of imports. Finally, the EC was continuing to insist on rebalancing – specifically, to impose tariffs on imports of animal feedstuffs and oilseeds currently entering the EC duty-free in return for concessions in other areas. This was totally opposed by the US (see *The Financial Times*, 20 November 1991).

As the previously extended five-year deadline for completing the Round approached, the two sides still appeared deadlocked. In a last-minute effort to secure an agreement, Arthur Dunkel, GATT Director-General, put forward a 436-page draft agreement containing some twenty-six accords on various matters, including agriculture. In the case of agriculture, the stumbling block was still the issue of export subsidies. The Dunkel proposals were for cuts of 36 per cent in the value of export subsidies and 24 per cent in the volume of subsidised exports over a six-year period from 1993 using 1986–90 as the base period. The US wanted ceilings to be set on the tonnage of subsidised EC farm exports as well as on the actual budgetary outlays of governments. The proposals ignored the EC demand for rebalancing and stipulated that neither US deficiency payments nor EC compensatory payments could be included in the 'green box' as nontrade-distorting measures. Modest reductions in domestic supports of 20 per cent by 1999 using 1986–8 as the base period were also proposed. Next, the agreement provided for tariffication of all border controls, and tariffs to be reduced by an average of 36 per cent over six years with a minimum reduction of 15 per cent on each product. To deal with the possibility that some tariffs might be very high immediately after conversion, there was also a requirement that countries allow minimum access for imports initially equivalent to 3 per cent of domestic consumption but then rising to 5 per cent in 1999 (see *The Financial Times*, 23 November 1991).

The package was clearly a difficult one for the EC to accept, given the position which it had adopted in the negotiations, and accordingly it was rejected. Two issues stood out as being the most contentious: rebalancing, and EC demands that its compensatory payments to farmers, which were a centrepiece of its plans for reforming the CAP, should be treated as nontrade-distorting, green-box measures. However, the Dunkel proposals supplied the basis for the new set of negotiations which subsequently took place. A precondition for any GATT agreement on agriculture was for the EC to agree on a set of internal reforms to the CAP. The failure of the EC Council of Ministers to approve measures proposed by the Commission created some uncertainty about the ability of the EC to deliver any deal struck internationally.

In May 1992, this hurdle was at last crossed when the EU Council of Ministers voted to adopt an amended version of the MacSharry measures proposed by the Commission. The measures went much further than any previous attempts at reforming the CAP. Cereal intervention prices were to be cut by about one-third from their 1992 levels with compensatory payments to offset the effects of price reductions. Except for small farmers, these payments were to be subject to 15 per cent rotational set-aside. For oilseeds and protein crops, price support was to be eliminated altogether.

Intervention prices for beef were to be reduced by 15 per cent from July 1993 in three steps, and normal intervention ceilings were to be scaled down from 750,000 to 350,000 tonnes by 1997. Livestock farmers would receive compensation through direct headage payments and increased male bovine and suckler (beef) cow premiums. In addition, there were accompanying measures to encourage the earlier retirement of farmers and farm workers, aid for forestry investment and management, and an agri-environmental package with up to 50 per cent of the costs of these measures being borne by the CAP budget. In total, the measures amounted to a very substantial reduction in the market price for cereals and oilseeds which would bring EU support prices much closer to the world price level. This, in turn, meant a lower level of variable import levies and export subsidies, so reducing the trade-distorting impact of the CAP. Cuts in cereal prices meant lower costs for livestock farmers and thereby made possible a reduction in beef prices.

Criticisms of the measures centred on the failure to include certain other major product sectors such as sugar, olive oil, wine, fruit and vegetables, and milk. Also, the new set-aside arrangements were criticised as needing additional bureaucracy to implement them and for creating other potential economic inefficiencies. From the standpoint of the GATT negotiations, a more important issue concerned whether the measures were adequate to implement the kind of GATT agreement being sought by the US and the Cairns Group of countries (see Swinbank, 1994, for a discussion of some of these issues). These uncertainties aside, the fact that the EU had succeeded in reaching agreement on a major reform of the CAP did help to enhance the prospect of a GATT deal being struck.

A further stumbling block was created by the long-standing dispute between the EC and the US over oilseeds which, at the time the GATT negotiations were reaching their climax, threatened to spill over into a full-blooded trade war. The dispute dated to the Dillon Round when, in different circumstances, the EC made a concession to the US binding her tariffs on soya beans and meal at a zero rate. At the time, this made sense for the EC. There was virtually no domestic production of oilseeds and low tariffs benefited the EC's crushing and refining sectors. The situation soon changed, however, as high grain prices in the EC drove processors to seek out nongrain substitutes and soya bean sales rocketed. EC policy changed to one of stimulating production by fixing prices at levels often double the world price. Partly, the aim was to draw EC farmers away from surplus grain production. At the same time, the EC paid generous subsidies to crushers using home-grown oilseeds. High internal oilseed prices combined with subsidies to crushers buying home-grown oilseeds served to boost EC production of oilseeds (particularly rapeseed and sunflower seed) damaging US exporters (mainly of soya beans). In 1987, the American Soyabean Association filed a case against the EC and the US took the matter to the GATT on the ground that the EC had 'nullified and impaired' their original concession to the US. In 1990, a GATT panel concluded that the EC programme had indeed impaired the advantage which it had granted in 1962 when it bound import tariffs at a zero level. After some delay, the EC revised its oilseed programme but in a way which failed to tackle the violation. Instead of making payments to oilseed processors using EC oilseeds, the new arrangements proposed making direct income payments to farmers. This ended the overt discrimination against foreign producers of the previous regime but failed to satisfy US producers since EC production was still subsidised. Hence, the US lodged a second complaint with the GATT. In March 1992, a reconvened panel found against the EU's oilseed regime. In the following month, the EU blocked adoption of the panel's report but promised to introduce new measures in an effort to settle the dispute. US patience ran out and a plan for sanctions against the EU was drawn up. On 5 November the US announced the imposition of punitive tariffs of US$300 million-worth on agricultural imports from the EU. Specifically targeted were EU exports of white wine, mainly from France and Italy.

The danger existed that a trade war over oilseeds would finally destroy the delicately poised attempts of the US and the EU to reach an agricultural trade agreement. A breakthrough came on 20 November 1992 with what came to be known as the *Blair House Accord*. It had two aspects. Firstly, a settlement of the oilseeds dispute. The EU agreed to create a separate base area for subsidised oilseed production equal to 5.128 million hectares from 1995–6. This was preferred to a formal tonnage limit which the US had originally sought in the negotiations leading up to the Accord. Each year, the area would be reduced by a set-aside rate not less than 10 per cent (compared with 15 per cent under the CAP) with penalties if the area was exceeded. This would exclude oilseeds grown for industrial purposes which would be subject to a 1 million-tonne soya meal equivalent. Secondly, the Uruguay Round negotiations: on the issue of export subsidies, it was agreed that export subsidies would be cut by 36 per cent over six years and the volume of subsidised exports by 21 per cent over the same period with 1986–90 the base period. Internal supports would be reduced by 20 per cent with 1986–8 as the base period. All border measures would be converted to tariffs and reduced by 36 per cent over six years with minimum reductions of 15 per cent for each tariff. All this was much the same as proposed in the Dunkel Draft Final Act. However, it was agreed that direct CAP aids such as the compensatory payments of the May 1992 reforms *could* be counted as nontrade-distorting, green-box measures. On rebalancing, it was agreed that, if EU imports on nongrain feed ingredients increased to a level which threatened CAP reform, the EU and the US would consult with each other to find a solution. Finally, under a special 'peace clause', both sides agreed that internal support measures and export subsidies would be considered exempt from any actions or claims under Article XVI (the GATT Subsidies

Article). Despite later attempts by France to reopen the negotiations which took place at Blair House, the agreement more or less held solid, subject to only minor clarifications.

THE URUGUAY ROUND AGREEMENT ON AGRICULTURE

The Agreement on Agriculture comes in four main parts. Firstly, there is the Agreement on Agriculture itself (some twenty-one articles and five annexes), a list of the concessions and commitments which countries have undertaken on market access, domestic support and exports subsidies, a special Agreement on Sanitary and Phytosanitary Measures, and a ministerial decision concerning Least Developed and Net Food-importing Developing Countries. These various aspects of the Agreement are summarised below.

Market access

Nonborder measures are replaced by tariffs that provide substantially the same level of protection (tariffication). Tariffs must then be reduced by an average of 36 per cent over six years in the case of developed countries and by 24 per cent over ten years in the case of developing countries. Countries have flexibility in determining how much to cut tariffs on individual products as long as each tariff is reduced by at least 15 per cent over the six-year implementation period. Developing countries must make reductions of at least 10 per cent over the implementation period. Least developed countries are not required to undertake reduction commitments. There is a further requirement that, following tariffication, countries maintain current access opportunities, recognising the possibility that tariffication could lead initially to some very high tariffs. For this purpose, minimum tariff quotas at reduced tariff rates must be established where current access is less than 3 per cent of domestic consumption. These are then to be increased to 5 per cent over the implementation period.

Special safeguard provisions (SSGs) are also included which allow for the imposition of additional duties in certain circumstances. These require that either the volume of imports in any year exceeds a 'trigger level' (a formula based on existing market access opportunities) or the prices of imports fall below a trigger price equal to the average 1986–8 reference price for the product concerned. The additional duty may only be imposed until the end of the year in which it is imposed and may not exceed one-third of the level of the then-existing tariff. There are further provisions for 'special treatment' of certain products where tariffication might create difficulties but these are subject to certain clearly specified conditions.

Lastly, under a special last-minute adjustment and in order to secure

Japanese assent to the overall Uruguay Round Agreement, it was agreed that Japan and South Korea should be allowed to postpone tariffication of their rice imports until the end of the implementation period (2001). However, Japan is required to maintain a minimum access quota equal to 4 per cent of domestic consumption, rising to 8 per cent by the year 2000, and Korea a 1 per cent quota rising annually by 0.25 per cent over four years and then by 0.5 per cent in the final year to a level of 4 per cent in 2004.

Domestic support

The domestic support commitments contained in the Agreement are expressed in terms of the *aggregate measurement of support* (AMS) and apply to all domestic support policies except those given specific exemptions. The latter are defined as supports 'not involving transfers from consumers' but 'provided through a publicly funded government programme' and which do not 'have the effect of providing price supports to producers'. These include such policies as: general government services (in areas such as research, pest and disease control, and so on); public stockholding for food security purposes; domestic food aid; direct payments to producers; 'decoupled' income support (that is, support not related to or based on production); structural adjustment assistance; payments under environmental programmes; and payments under regional assistance programmes.

In addition, measures of assistance to encourage agricultural and rural development in developing countries, investment subsidies in developing countries and agricultural input subsidies to low-income or resource-poor producers in developing countries are exempt from domestic support reduction commitments. Other support which makes up a low proportion of the value of production (up to 5 per cent in a developed country and 10 per cent in a developing country) and which otherwise would be included in the calculation of a country's AMS can be omitted. Finally, direct payments under production-limiting programmes are not subject to the reduction commitment.

Total AMS is to be reduced by 20 per cent (13.3 per cent in the case of developing countries) over a six-year period (ten years for developing countries) commencing in 1995. AMS is defined as 'the annual level of support, expressed in monetary terms, provided for an agricultural product in favour of the producers of the basic agricultural product or nonproduct-specific support provided in favour of agricultural producers in general, other than support provided under programmes that qualify as exempt from reduction'.

Export subsidies

These are defined as 'subsidies contingent upon export performance'. Developed countries must reduce the value of export subsidies to a level 36 per cent below the 1986–90 base period and the quantity of subsidised exports by 21 per cent over the six-year implementation period. The reductions for developing countries are two-thirds those of developed countries and cover a ten-year period, with least developed countries being subject to no reductions at all. Developing countries are also not required to undertake commitments in respect of subsidies to reduce the costs of marketing exports of agricultural products and the provision of favourable internal transport and freight charges on export shipments. Where subsidised exports have increased since the 1986–90 base period, 1991–2 may be used as the starting point of reductions, but the end point remains that based on the 1986–90 base period level. There is some flexibility allowed in implementing the reductions, this may mean that, under strict conditions, the level of export subsidies in any one year can exceed the annual commitment levels.

Other provisions deal with the possibility that exempt export subsidies might be used to circumvent commitments; they also contain a commitment to agree new international disciplines regulating export credits and include new criteria for the granting of food aid internationally.

Peace provisions

It was agreed that, during the implementation period, domestic support measures which are exempt from reduction commitments (the so-called 'green-box' measures) count as nonactionable subsidies for purposes of countervailing duties, actions under Article XVI of the GATT and the Subsidies Agreement and actions based on 'nullification and impairment' of tariff concessions previously granted by one country to another. Other domestic support measures which may be excluded from the calculation of the ASM, such as direct payments under production-limiting programmes and domestic support within *de minimis* levels, are covered by similar 'due restraint' provisions.

Sanitary and phytosanitary measures

These measures are concerned with food safety and animal and plant health regulations. They recognise that countries have the right to take such measures as are necessary to protect human, animal or plant life or health but that they should be applied only to the extent necessary as determined by scientific principles and should not be used to discriminate arbitrarily against goods coming from other countries where identical or similar conditions prevail. The Agreement provides for harmonisation of sanitary and phytosanitary measures 'on as wide a basis as possible', using 'international standards, guidelines or recommendations, where they exist'. Higher standards may be introduced where there is scientific justification or, as a consequence of consistent risk, decisions based on an appropriate risk assessment.

Countries must follow carefully specified procedures and criteria in assessing risk and determining the appropriate level of protection. They are required to accept the measures of other countries as equivalent even if they differ from their own, provided that the importing country demonstrates that its measures are required to achieve the appropriate level of protection. In these cases, there is provision for inspection, testing and other relevant procedures. Finally, there are provisions for transparency that cover changes in such measures and the provision of information about such measures.

Least developed and net food-importing developing countries

The Agreement is also affected by the Decision on Measures Concerning the Possible Negative Effects of the Reform Programme on Least Developed and Net Food-importing Developing Countries. This recognises that the Agricultural Agreement could have negative effects on this group of countries. Therefore, it was agreed that ministers would set up a mechanism for ensuring that the availability of food aid was not negatively affected and that any agreement relating to agricultural export credits 'makes appropriate provision for differential treatment in favour of' this group of countries. It also recognises that the Agreement might create financial difficulties for certain developing countries. Consultations with the IMF and World Bank will seek to ensure that these problems are addressed.

Implementation and review

A Committee on Agriculture is to be set up to monitor the implementation of the Agreement and to review progress. The Agreement is viewed as the first stage in a continuing reform process with the long-term objective of 'substantial and progressive reductions in support and protection resulting in fundamental reform'. Therefore, one year before the end of the implementation period (that is, after five years), negotiations will be initiated which will take into account how well the current Agreement has worked. Specific mention is made of 'nontrade concerns, special and differential treatment to developing country Members, and the objective to establish a fair and market-oriented agricultural trading system' as matters to be taken into account in this next stage of negotiations.

* * * *

How is the Agreement for Agriculture to be evaluated? The liberalisation measures agreed represent an unimportant first step towards freeing trade in agricultural goods and bringing agriculture under the same trading rules as apply to other sectors of world trade. However, the degree of actual liberalisation is disappointing and much less than was at one stage hoped for. In particular, it falls a long way short of the initial US and Cairns Group proposals which called for the complete elimination of all trade-distorting subsidies over an agreed period of time. It follows that the potential gain in global economic welfare from such measures is significantly less than would otherwise have been possible. On the other hand, it is clear that the alternative was no agreement at all. The fact that the EU was prepared even to contemplate some reduction in the high levels of support which its farmers enjoy under the CAP amounted to some shift in outlook. In the same way, the willingness of the Japanese government, in the face of fierce domestic opposition, eventually to open up its heavily protected rice market to a limited volume of imports was important. Even if the degree of liberalisation that has been achieved in this first attempt is less than economic logic would deem desirable, a basis has been established which can be built upon. The provision for negotiations to be reopened by the turn of the century with a view to bringing about further liberalisation may be the most significant aspect of the entire Agreement.

The Agreement may be evaluated in terms of its three main liberalisation elements. Firstly, there are the provisions regarding *market access*. The provisions for tariffication are to be welcomed because they bring an element of increased transparency to agricultural trade. On the other hand, they are disappointing in the extent to which they will actually reduce levels of agricultural protection. There are several reasons for this. To begin with, the provisions for tariffication are widely regarded as being too loose (see Ingersent *et al.*, 1995, and Ingco, 1995a, 1995b). The provisions in the Agreement for calculating tariff equivalents require countries to take the difference between internal and external prices *in the base period 1986–8*. This period appears to have been one of low world prices so that 'tariff equivalents' derived using these data are necessarily higher than if another more representative period had been chosen. As a result, the base-period tariff rates shown in countries' actual tariff schedules submitted after the conclusion of the Round are high and, in many cases, significantly in excess of both the tariff equivalent of border measures in the base period and the pre-Uruguay Round applied rates (Ingco, 1995a, 1995b). To the extent that this is so, a 36 per cent reduction in tariffs to be achieved by the year 2001 (and as little as 15 per cent in the case of some products) will leave them at extremely high levels and conceivably higher than the rates applying prior to the Agreement. So-called 'dirty tariffication', in which the tariff equivalent has been set higher than the level of NTBs applying immediately prior to the Round, has been common in 'sensitive commodities' such as grains, sugar, meat and dairy products. Furthermore, most countries appear to have reduced their highest tariffs the least and their lowest tariffs the most. Once again, 'sensitive commodities' have been subject to the minimum 15 per cent tariff reduction, so these sectors will remain highly protected.

In theory, the provisions for ensuring minimum access will provide some protection against import access being blocked by high tariff levels. In practice, it is doubtful that these provisions will amount to very much. For example, due to the special import quota arrangements which the EU operates for certain agricultural products coming from third countries, such as the Sugar Protocol of the Lomé Convention, current EU access levels for many products already exceed the 3–5 per cent minimum stipulated by the Agreement. In general, it appears that countries will be allowed to count imports under existing special arrangements within the calculation of global quotas under the minimum-access provisions. Only in the case of rice are the minimum-access commitments likely to be important. A further issue concerns the special safeguard provisions (SSGs). Although these may have been politically necessary to gain acceptance for tariffication, there is a danger that their application could undermine the objective of increasing market access. (The EU schedule of tariff-reduction commitments, for example, has indicated that SSG provisions will be applied to most products.)

Secondly, there are the provisions for reducing the level of *domestic supports*. Although on paper these provide for a seemingly significant reduction in levels of subsidy, they are unlikely to amount to much in practice. Firstly, several kinds of subsidy are to be excluded from the calculation of the AMS, including the US deficiency payments system and the EU's system of compensation payments under the 1992 CAP reforms. By switching domestic subsidies towards these excluded types of support, governments can clearly achieve the Uruguay Round objectives without reducing the actual level of subsidy paid to farmers. The only constraint may prove to be the need to control government spending at a time of budgetary restraint. This might not have mattered so much if these other forms of domestic support had no production- or trade-distorting effects. However, it is by no means clear that the above-mentioned schemes represent a genuine 'decoupling' of systems of support (Ingersent *et al.*, 1995). To the extent that both the US and EU systems of deficiency payments and compensatory payments increase domestic production, trade is indirectly distorted. Secondly, a further problem with these provisions is that, because the arrangements for reducing domestic supports are expressed in aggregated terms, support for individual commodities can be cut by less than the stipulated 20 per cent or not at all. Thirdly, the required reduction in domestic supports are based on prices in the base period 1986–8, as with the provisions for tariffication. As we noted above, this period appears to have been one of historically low world prices. The EU has already made reductions in support levels under the 1992 CAP reforms (and indeed under some measures which preceded these reforms) and therefore will be under little pressure to make any further reductions. Th EU's system of direct compensatory payments to farmers is in any case exempt from the reductions. The US can similarly exempt its deficiency payments system, so levels of domestic support are unlikely to be affected. All in all, the provisions for cutting domestic subsidies are disappointing.

Thirdly, there are the provisions for cutting back the level of *export subsidies*. There is widespread agreement that these represent the most important aspects of the package, being more likely than the other provisions to stimulate trade. Of course, the cuts fall a long way short of the demands of the US and the Cairns Group in the earlier stages of the Round for the total elimination of such subsidies. Moreover, they mean that agricultural trade will continue to be treated differently from trade in other goods for some time to come. Nevertheless, they do provide for substantial reductions in both the value of export subsidies *and* the volume of subsidised exports. This will ensure that it is not possible to shift subsidies between different products. Furthermore, the fact that the reductions in budgetary outlays are expressed in nominal terms means that, in view of inflation, the *real* value of subsidies will fall even further. A weakness is that certain kinds of export subsidy such as export credits are exempt. Nevertheless, most attempts to simulate the effects of the export subsidy provisions show that substantial reductions in export subsidies will be required in both the EU and the US (Ingersent *et al.*, 1995). In the case of the EU, this is likely to bring forward the need for further reforms of the CAP.

CONCLUSIONS

From the very beginnings of the GATT, trade in agriculture was treated differently to trade in most other products. The General Agreement provides for some special treatment for primary products particularly in the areas of quantitative restrictions and subsidies. More importantly, GATT rules and disciplines have never been fully applied in the case of agriculture. Until the Uruguay Round, successive GATT rounds largely failed to tackle the problem of agricultural protectionism. The reasons for this lay in the unwillingness of governments, especially in the developed countries, to expose agriculture to the same forces of competition as exist in other sectors. Instead, nearly all governments engage in costly forms of intervention designed to aid farmers, giving rise to huge trade distortions. Intervention is also common in developing countries except that, in these countries, the effect has been mainly to discourage the development of agriculture by lowering the prices of agricultural goods relative to industrial products.

In recent decades the costs of these policies have become more apparent than ever. In the developed countries, the costs for consumers and taxpayers have risen noticeably. High support prices and massive subsidies have resulted in a build up of excess capacity and surplus stocks. The result has been a frantic search for new markets on which to unload this unwanted output. Countries have engaged in mutually destructive subsidy wars in an effort to steal third markets from one another. A growing number of trade disputes arising between developed countries came to involve agricultural trade. The GATT Dispute Settlements Mechanism proved unable to cope. The result was an undermining of the credibility of the GATT, and disputes involving agricultural trade threatened to spill over into other areas. These pressures forced countries, for the first time ever, to address seriously the issue of agricultural protectionism in the Uruguay Round.

The Round began with high hopes. At long last, new, stricter rules could be established that would provide a disciplined framework for agricultural trade comparable to that which existed for other goods. There was hope, too, that a substantial measure of trade liberalisation would be achieved. As the Round progressed, it became apparent that much more limited progress was the best that could be hoped for. At times it became uncertain whether any agreement would be achieved. Indeed, on several occasions, disagreements over agriculture threatened to bury the entire Round. It was therefore a cause for celebration when the negotiations were successfully concluded just in time to meet the final deadline. The Agreement is a disappointment when judged by what is required if trade in agricultural goods is to be put on the same basis as trade in other goods. However, it does constitute a starting point, establishing a framework for future negotiations. Perhaps the most important result of the new Agreement is the clear commitment which it contains for countries to enter into a second round of negotiations by the turn of the century. The implication is that the Agricultural Agreement is to be regarded as the first stage in an ongoing process of reform. It remains to be seen whether verbal undertakings will be matched by equivalent actions.

7

REGIONALISM

INTRODUCTION

Regionalism has been defined as 'the promotion by governments of international economic linkages with countries that are geographically proximate' (Hine, 1992). Its primary manifestation is the formation of regional free-trade areas, customs unions and common markets, known generically as 'regional trading blocs' or 'regional trading arrangements'. Regionalism can be contrasted with globalism or multilateralism, which seek to increase integration between countries at a worldwide level. Since the latter is one of the aims of the GATT, there exists a potential conflict between the attempts of the GATT/WTO to create a more open, multilateral trading order and the proliferation of regional trading blocs or arrangements. In the past, the potential for conflict was not considered a matter of great concern. Except in Western Europe, most developed countries showed little interest in seeking closer regional linkages. Where free-trade areas or customs unions were formed (for example, the EC and EFTA in the late 1950s), it happened in a manner which had no serious consequences for multilateralism. Indeed, some would say it spurred on the process of global trade liberalisation by compelling other countries (in particular the US) to seek fresh multilateral negotiations. Most of the early regionalist experiments involved developing countries and were largely unsuccessful. Their effects on world trade were at worst marginal.

More recently, however, the situation has changed. The 1980s and 1990s have witnessed a new enthusiasm for establishing regional trading arrangements which has not been confined to the West European countries. A significant development has been the conversion of the United States, formerly the custodian of multilateralism, to the regionalist cause. In the Asian/Pacific region, too, there have been several attempts to foster closer regional linkages. Indeed, some have talked of a growing tripolarisation of the world trading system with the emergence of regional trading blocs in Europe, the western hemisphere and the Pacific region. Whether or not this is so, regionalism has clearly become a force to be reckoned with. There are

232

some obvious implications of this fascination with regional trading arrangements for the attempts of the GATT/WTO to promote a more open, multilateral trading order.

This chapter begins with an examination of the existing GATT rules on regional trading blocs. We shall then proceed to discuss the theory of regional integration to see whether there exist any theoretical grounds for regarding regional trading blocs as harmful. Next, we discuss the various attempts at regionalism since the GATT came into being in 1947. Two distinct waves of regionalism have been identified, giving rise to the expressions 'old regionalism' and 'new regionalism'. We need to consider how far the experience of regionalism has conformed to theoretical expectations. This is followed by an empirical examination of the extent to which world trade has become more or less regionalised. If trade has become more regionalised, we need to know whether this has been at the expense of multilateralism. The chapter finishes with a discussion of the implications of the current wave of regionalism for the GATT/WTO and any changes which might be necessary to the existing GATT rules on regional trading blocs. This includes a discussion of the adequacy/sufficiency of the changes recently made in the Uruguay Round.

UNCONDITIONAL MFN – THE GATT APPROACH

The GATT approach to trade liberalisation has been essentially a multilateral approach. This has two aspects. Firstly, countries simultaneously negotiate reductions in tariffs. What happens is that countries conduct a series of bilateral negotiations with other contracting parties which all take place at the same time. Secondly, any tariff cut agreed between any pair of countries is automatically applied to all other contracting parties. Equally, any tariff increase imposed on imports from one particular country is applied equally to the same imports from all other countries. The essence of this approach is contained in Article I of the GATT, the famous *Unconditional Most-favoured-nation* Clause. Paragraph 1 states:

> With respect to customs duties and charges of any kind imposed on or in connection with importation or exportation or imposed on the international transfer of payments for imports or exports, and with respect to the methods of levying such duties and charges, and with respect to all rules and formalities in connection with importation and exportation . . . any advantage, favour, privilege or immunity granted by any contracting party to any product originating in or destined for any other country shall be accorded immediately and unconditionally to the like product originating in or destined for the territories of all other contracting parties.

It should be noted that Article I stipulates *unconditional* MFN.

A policy of *conditional* MFN offers nondiscrimination to a trading partner on condition that the partner reciprocates. Specifically, suppose two countries, A and B, sign a trading agreement in which A offers B conditional MFN treatment. Suppose A subsequently enters into another agreement with a third country, C, and that, as part of that agreement, A offers C tariff cuts on certain goods in return for equivalent concessions made by C on A's goods. Under the conditional MFN policy granted by A to B, A must extend to B those tariff cuts offered to C but *on condition that* B offers equivalent concessions to those given to A by C in return. Such a policy may have the attraction for countries entering into trade agreements with third countries that the second country cannot 'free ride', that is, enjoy all the benefits of tariff cuts which its partner country subsequently offers to third countries with no obligation to offer anything in return. On the other hand, a policy of conditional MFN inevitably results in discrimination. Since 1932, US trade policy has been based on unconditional MFN. After the Second World War the US was keen to establish this principle as the basis for postwar trade policy. To an extent, the free-rider problem was tackled by requiring contracting parties to agree to general or multilateral reciprocity. Thus, Article XXVIII of the GATT states that tariff negotiations should take place on 'a *reciprocal and mutually advantageous* basis, directed to the substantial reduction of the general level of tariffs and other charges on imports and exports' (GATT, 1969; my emphasis). It goes on: 'the contracting parties recognise that in general the success of negotiations would depend on the participation of all contracting parties which conduct a substantial proportion of their external trade with one another' (ibid.). This has generally been taken to mean that all countries should offer tariff cuts in return for concessions received from other contracting parties

In fact, the GATT Treaty contains a whole number of exceptions to the principle of nondiscrimination. One major exception, and the one which is of immediate concern, is Article XXIV permitting countries to set up regional free-trade areas and customs unions. A regional free-trade area is a tariff-free area in which goods originating within the area may pass freely from one member to another with no tariff imposed. (Because a product may be partially produced in a country outside the area, free-trade areas normally require complex origin rules which specify how much of the transformation process or the value added must have taken place within the area for a product to enjoy tariff-free treatment.) Customs unions similarly create an internal tariff-free area for goods produced within the union. However, they go further and involve the creation of a common external (or customs) tariff on all goods coming from outside the union, this is achieved by the members harmonising their tariffs at some agreed level. By removing all tariffs on trade between the member states while maintaining tariffs on imports from nonmember states – which in the case of a customs union is a common tariff – such arrangements necessarily entail discriminatory or preferential treatment of imports coming from fellow member states and against imports coming from the rest of the world.

Article XXIV makes it quite clear that the exception only applies to the case of preferential trading arrangements which result in the complete abolition of tariffs on trade between the member states. Paragraph 8 states that

> a customs union shall be understood to mean the substitution of a single customs territory for two or more customs territories, so that (i) duties and other restrictive regulations of commerce . . . are eliminated with respect to *substantially all the trade* between the constituent territories of the union or at least to substantially all the trade in products originating in such territories, and, (ii) . . . substantially the same duties and other regulations of commerce are applied by each of the members of the union to the trade of territories not included in the union.
>
> (GATT, 1969; my emphasis)

A free-trade area is taken to mean 'a group of two or more customs territories' and there is a similar requirement that 'duties and other restrictive regulations of commerce' are eliminated on 'substantially all the trade between the constituent territories in products originating in such territories' (GATT, 1969). It follows that preferential trading arrangements which result in anything less than 100 per cent tariff preferences are not permissible. In fact, the use of the wording 'substantially all the trade' creates a degree of ambiguity which can be exploited by countries to justify less than 100 per cent preferences. Article XXIV does refer to 'interim agreements', which are transitional arrangements for bringing about the formation of CUs/FTAs over a period of time and clearly these will entail less than 100 per cent preferences until such time as the process of transition is complete. It is, however, stated that these should include 'a plan and a schedule for the formation of such a customs union or of such a free trade area within a reasonable length of time' (ibid.). It should also be pointed out that, for some time after the creation of the GATT, various schemes of tariff preference which did not conform with GATT rules remained in existence. These included the UK's system of Imperial Preference. There was a let-out in paragraphs 2,3 and 4 of Article I which did not require the immediate elimination of all existing preferences although the margin of preference was not to be increased. Subsequently, most of these preferences were eroded by nonpreferential tariff reductions brought about through the various GATT rounds and were eventually abandoned by the countries concerned. For example, the UK abandoned its system of Commonwealth preferences when it joined the European Community in 1973.

Other conditions for the formation of customs unions/free-trade areas were specified in Article XXIV. There is a requirement that the external tariff applied to imports from countries not belonging to the customs union/free-trade area should not be any higher or more restrictive than the tariffs applied to such imports by the member states before the customs union/free-trade area was formed. Paragraph 5a states that:

> with respect to a customs union . . . the duties and other regulations of commerce imposed at the institution of any such union . . . in respect of trade with contracting parties not parties to such a union . . . shall *not on the whole be higher or more restrictive* than the general incidence of the duties and regulations of commerce applicable in the constituent territories prior to the formation of such union . . .
>
> (GATT, 1969; my emphasis)

The same requirement is stipulated for free-trade areas. It is not, however, made clear how this to be determined. For example, is it the average level of tariff which is to be used and, if so, should a weighted or unweighted average be used? Should account be taken of nontariff bariers as well as tariffs and, if so, how are these to be quantified? It is, however, stated that, if any member of a customs union/free trade area, consequent upon the formation of the CU/FTA, increases any rate of duty on imports from another GATT party, then the latter is entitled to compensation. It follows that, if the members of a customs union agree on a common external tariff which is an average of the rates of tariff applied by the member states before the formation of the union, this may necessitate certain formerly low-tariff member states raising their tariffs on imports from nonmember states. The level of tariff is no higher or more restrictive than the corresponding tariff before the union was formed but other GATT parties which are not part of the union may find their access to the markets of some members of the union now rendered more restricted and therefore be entitled to compensation. The GATT treats any such increase in tariff rates as a 'modification of schedules' which is covered by Article XXVIII. If the parties concerned cannot negotiate compensation, the country adversely affected is entitled to withdraw 'substantially equivalent concessions'. Finally, there are certain procedural rules to which countries are supposed to adhere. These require that countries entering into a CU or FTA 'promptly notify' the GATT and make available 'such information as will enable them to make such reports and recommendations' as they consider appropriate. In the case of interim agreements leading to the formation of a CU/FTA, the GATT is supposed to have the role of scrutinising the arrangements and, if necessary, requiring modifications to be made.

These conditions were designed to provide some control over the formation of CUs/FTAs and more specifically to ensure that this blanket exception to the nondiscrimination rule was not abused. Moreover, there was a need to ensure that it did not lead to an uncontrolled proliferation of various kinds of preferential trading arrangements which might have undermined the GATT's aim of multilateral trade liberalisation. In allowing this exception to the nondiscrimination principle, there was an implicit statement that free-trade areas and customs unions need not be opposed to the goal of global free trade but could indeed be useful stepping stones in that direction, provided that certain conditions were met. For example, a situation might arise in which some countries want to move at a more rapid pace than others towards complete free trade. Rather than wait until all countries are ready, it might be preferable to allow free trade on a regional basis. With hindsight, many of the conditions stipulated in Article XXIV were woefully inadequate, open to varying interpretations and inviting abuse. Thus, many arrangements have come into being which clearly involve less than 100 per cent preferences on substantially all trade. Some products and sectors have been excluded from the arrangements and different degrees of preference applied for different sectors. In some cases, interim arrangements have enjoyed a more or less permanent existence as timetables have not been met. In the absence of any definite criteria for determining whether external tariffs are more restrictive after rather than before the formation of a CU/FTA, it has not always been possible to monitor the position. Finally, the procedural provisions have been rendered ineffective by the absence of any requirement for advance approval for an arrangement. In practice, once entered into, all CUs/FTAs have gone ahead but many have failed to comply with the conditions of Article XXIV.

THE THEORY OF REGIONAL INTEGRATION

We shall return to some of the issues raised in the last section towards the end of the chapter. Before doing so, however, it is necessary to consider what economic theory has to say about the effects of such arrangements. The basic theory of free trade areas/customs unions was first expounded by Jacob Viner in 1950. The theory was elaborated by Meade (1956) and Lipsey (1957). Viner explained how free-trade areas/customs unions have two effects: trade creation and trade diversion. The removal of tariffs on intra-area imports causes *trade creation*, defined as a shift in production of a product from a high-cost domestic source to a lower-cost source in a partner country. For example, suppose country A can supply widgets at a cost price of 100, B at a cost price of 80 and C at a cost price of 50. Suppose that A imposes a nondiscriminatory tariff on imported widgets of 100 per cent. Such a tariff is sufficient to price all foreign sources of supply out of the market. Suppose now A and B form a customs union and apply a common external tariff of 100 per cent on imported widgets. Imports from B are now cheaper than domestically produced widgets. Therefore, production will shift from higher-cost producers in A to lower-cost producers in B. Such a change results in an improved allocation of global resources and is therefore

237

desirable from an efficiency point of view. As Viner put it, it represents a move in the direction of free trade.

On the other hand, the removal of tariffs on intra-area imports *combined with* the retention of a tariff on extra-area imports results in *trade diversion*. This is defined as a shift of production away from a lower-cost producer outside the customs union to a higher-cost source of supply within it. Using the example above, suppose that, to begin with, A imposes a nondiscriminatory tariff of 80 per cent on imported widgets. Such a tariff is sufficient to price B's imports out of A's market, but not C's imports. Imports from C are still cheaper than domestically produced widgets. Therefore, production will be concentrated in C, the world's lowest-cost supplier. However, if A and B form a customs union, imports from B are now cheaper than imports from C so that some higher-cost production of widgets in B will displace lower-cost production in C. Such trade diversion results in a worsened allocation of global resources. It is therefore undesirable from an efficiency point of view and represents a move in the protectionist direction.

Viner concluded that the effects of customs unions/free trade areas on economic welfare depend on the relative size of the two effects. If trade creation exceeds trade diversion, the formation of the customs union/free-trade area will result in an improvement in economic efficiency and therefore an improvement in economic welfare. But if, vice versa, trade diversion exceeds trade creation, the effect will be harmful to economic efficiency and therefore will reduce economic welfare. Viner went on to show that a customs union was more likely to have a favourable effect on economic efficiency if a number of conditions were satisfied:

1 If the customs union covers a large economic area, the scope for trade diversion is decreased and opportunities for trade creation increased.
2 If the common external tariff is low in comparison with the level of external tariffs that would have existed had a union not been formed, trade diversion will be less.
3 Where the degree of complementarity is low (and therefore the degree of rivalry great) between members of the union with respect to the industries protected by high tariffs before the union is formed, the scope for trade diversion is less. Where two countries have similar economic structures, they will continue to import goods in which neither has a comparative advantage from the rest of the world after the formation of the union.
4 Where the difference in unit costs for protected industries of the same kind as between partner countries is great (that is, they are potentially complementary), the scope for trade creation is increased.
5 A high level of tariffs in potential export markets outside the union with respect to products in which the members have a comparative advantage

under free trade will be beneficial. This will mean less damage from a reduction in the degree of specialisation between the union and the outside world following the formation of the union. At the extreme, if tariffs in the rest of the world were high enough to prohibit all trade before the formation of the union, there will be no trade to be diverted.

In addition, Viner identified two other possible effects of customs unions. Firstly, in industries where unit costs fall with output, small countries that have a limited domestic market and face high foreign tariffs which prevent them from finding outside markets may be unable to reach a scale of production large enough to achieve minimum unit costs of production. By forming a customs union with another country, it may be possible to create a domestic market of sufficient size for an optimum scale of production to be achieved. Viner rather dismissed this source of gain as being of any great importance, arguing that there were few industries which could not achieve optimum size even in small countries. Secondly, there existed the possibility that the members of a customs union might enjoy an additional welfare gain through an improvement in their terms of trade, albeit at the expense of the rest of the world. The argument is similar to the large-country model for an ordinary tariff (see Chapter 2). Just as a large country may be able to shift the terms of trade in its favour by imposing a tariff, so a group of countries, by forming a customs union and thereby creating a larger tariff area, may be able to improve the efficacy of the tariff in achieving this effect. Although there is a gain accruing to the members of the union, this is offset by the loss to the rest of the world. Thus, global welfare is not increased.

The significance of Viner's contribution was in showing that the establishment of a customs union or free-trade area was not necessarily welfare-improving. The possibility existed that it could result in a worsened allocation of resources and hence a reduction in economic efficiency. Everything would depend on the strength of the trade-creating and trade-diverting effects. Meade (1956) showed that the Vinerian theory failed to provide a precise criterion for estimating the net economic gain or loss from the formation of a customs union. One of the main reasons was the failure to take into account *consumption effects*. The change in the relative prices of goods following the formation of a customs union will affect the demand for different goods and hence the pattern of consumption. The Viner analysis holds only if the elasticity of demand for all goods is zero, which it obviously is not. In the example of trade diversion above, the price of widgets in A fell following the formation of a customs union with B (from 90 to 80). If the demand for widgets is elastic, the fall in price will cause increased demand and hence increased imports of widgets from B. Such trade expansion constitutes an *additional* source of welfare gain for A which might be sufficient to offset the welfare loss from trade diversion. Before the formation of the union, consumers of widgets in A were prevented by the high (tariff-affected) price from buying as many as they would like. The subsequent fall in price enables them to do so. The value of this extra consumption depends on the value consumers place on each extra unit they now can buy. On the other hand, account must be taken of the loss of tariff revenue to country A in order to deduce the net welfare gain or loss from forming a customs union. Nevertheless, what is clear is that, if consumption effects are included in the analysis of customs unions (as they clearly must be), the welfare gain (loss) from a customs union is likely to be greater (smaller) and a stronger case can be made out for customs unions. Lipsey (1957) made a further useful contribution along similar lines to Meade by demonstrating that, where favourable consumption effects outweigh unfavourable production effects, the theoretical possibility exists that a *trade-diverting* customs union could still improve the welfare of the members of the union and even of the world.

These effects can be illustrated by a diagram using the partial equilibrium approach that we used for the analysis of the effects of a tariff. Figure 7.1 shows the effects of the formation of a customs union on the home country H and the partner country P. The world (free-trade) price of widgets is OP_W. Before the formation of a customs union, country H applies a nondiscriminatory tariff of P_WT_H and country P of P_WT_P. In country H, the price of widgets will be OT_H. Domestic production is OQ_2 and consumption is OQ_3. Imports are Q_2Q_3, all of which come from the rest of the world. In country P, the price of widgets is OT_P. Demand equals supply so that imports are zero. Next, H and P form a customs union and adopt a common external tariff of CET which is a (weighted) average of P_WT_H and P_WT_P. In country H, the price falls to OCET. Demand increases by Q_3Q_4 and domestic production falls by Q_1Q_2. Imports increase by $Q_1Q_2 + Q_3Q_4$. However, all these now come from the partner country, P. Elements of trade creation and trade diversion are both present. The expansion of H's imports represents trade creation since P can produce the product at lower cost than H. Such trade creation has both a (Viner) production effect and a (Meade) consumption effect. BDE represents the resource-saving from producing these goods in P rather than H. CFG is the consumption gain from consumers who are able to buy more widgets at the lower price. So the welfare gain to H from trade creation is (BDE + CFG). On the other hand, the diversion of imports to P from the rest of the world results in an efficiency loss since the rest of the world could produce the product at lower cost than P. The loss from trade diverted is EFIJ. If EFIJ exceeds (BDE + CFG), the home country suffers a net welfare loss. Conversely, if areas (BDE + CFG) exceed area EFIJ, the effect is a net welfare gain.

In country P, the price rises to OCET. Demand falls by Q_1Q_2 and domestic supply increases by Q_2Q_3. The difference between supply and demand (UY which equals DG) is exported to country H at the union price

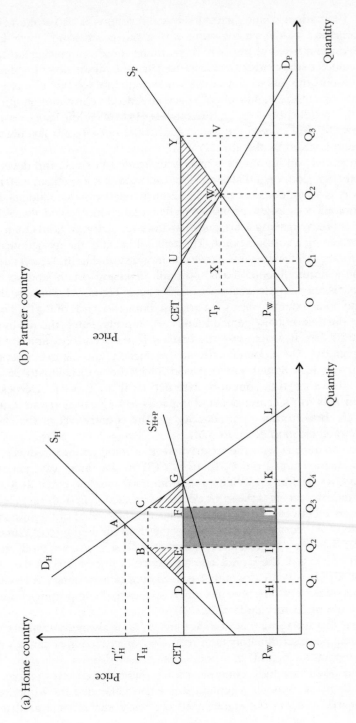

Figure 7.1 The effects of a customs union on the home and partner countries

of OCET. The partner country gains increased revenues of UYVX as a result of the formation of the customs union. On the other hand, there is a consumption loss because prices have risen and there is a production loss due to the need to draw additional resources into the production of widgets. UXW represents the loss to consumers who are not able to buy as many as they would like at the higher price. This is the Meade consumption effect. WVY is the production loss or Viner effect. However, the gains to the partner country will exceed the losses so that the net effect is favourable. The net gain is given by the area UYW.

Subsequently, various attempts have been made to extend and develop the basic theory. Cooper and Massell (1965) showed that a problem with the basic theory is that it does not provide a convincing economic rationale for customs unions because the economic welfare of a country could always be increased more by making a nondiscriminatory reduction in tariffs than by forming or joining a customs union. This will hold if, after the reduction, the nonpreferential tariff is the same as the common external tariff. Where tariffs are cut on a nonpreferential basis, no trade diversion occurs and so the entire effect is one of trade creation. Consider again Figure 7.1. Suppose that initially the home country imposes a nondiscriminatory tariff of $P_W T_H''$. Then home production equals demand and no imports enter the country. Equilibrium exists at A. Suppose the country forms a customs union with another country. The combined home production and partner country supply curve is S_{H+P}''. Equilibrium occurs at G with the price falling to OCET. Suppose also that the common external tariff is $P_W CET$. Domestic production falls to OQ_1 and demand expands to OQ_4. Imports are $Q_1 Q_4$ all of which come from the partner country. The country enjoys a welfare gain from trade creation equal to ADG.

Now, compare this with the case where the home country reduces its nondiscriminatory tariff from $P_W T_H''$ to $P_W CET$. In the same way, imports expand to $Q_1 Q_4$ yielding a welfare gain from trade creation equal to ADG. Domestic industry receives the same degree of protection in both cases. The only difference between the two cases concerns the source of the imports. In the case of the customs union, they come from the higher-cost partner country. In the case of the reduction in the nondiscriminatory tariff, they come from the rest of the world. The difference in price between the two sources of supply is $P_W CET$, so the loss to the importing country is DGHK. This is equal to the customs revenue which accrues to the importing country from a nondiscriminatory tariff of $P_W CET$.

It is clear that the formation of a customs union is always *second best* to an equivalent nondiscriminatory tariff reduction. Since a country can always do better by cutting its tariff in a nondiscriminatory manner, it is not clear why, on economic grounds, countries should enter into customs unions.

The Cooper and Massell argument was later challenged by Wonnacott and Wonnacott (1981). The significance of their contribution was that it drew attention to the role which customs unions can play in meeting the interests of *exporters*. Countries may enter into customs unions in order to gain beneficial export effects rather than to obtain welfare gains from conventional trade creation in the manner postulated in the orthodox model. The problem with the latter, they argued, is that it ignores any tariff which the rest of the world may impose on the exports of either of the two countries forming the customs union. The latter are assumed to be too inconsequential for such a tariff to serve any purpose. This follows from the assumption that the countries forming the customs union are small and face a perfectly elastic world supply curve. The Wonnacotts referred to this as the case of the 'missing' third-country tariff. One reason why third countries may impose tariffs is as bargaining counters which they hope to use to gain better access for their exports. If this is acknowledged, a rationale may exist for the formation of a customs union. This is illustrated in Figure 7.2.

The partner country, P, is assumed to be a low-cost producer of a good for which (for simplicity) there exists no domestic demand. However, it cannot fully exploit its comparative advantage because it faces a third-country (rest-of-the-world) tariff of $P_W P_1$, the world price being OP_W. The home country, H, imposes a still more prohibitive tariff of $P_W P_2$ such that imports are zero. If the partner and home country now form a customs union and adopt a CET which is sufficient to shut out all imports from the rest of the world, the price will be determined by the combined demand and supply in the two markets. Suppose this gives a price of OP_1. The home country will enjoy trade creation of $Q_1 Q_3$, yielding a welfare gain of area A + B. This it could have obtained by a unilateral, nondiscriminatory tariff reduction of $P_1 P_2$ as argued by Cooper and Massell. However, the gain to the partner country is different. It enjoys a net welfare gain of area D, area E being the costs of producing the increased output of $Q_1 Q_2$. The partner country has been able to obtain beneficial export effects by persuading the home country to form a customs union. Presumably, it must have been in a position to offer something in return. This would be the case if there were other industries in which the home country enjoyed equivalent export interests which it could not satisfy through unilaterally dismantling its tariffs.

Having questioned the usefulness of the Vinerian theory in providing an explanation for the formation of customs unions, Cooper and Massell (1965) proposed a departure from the traditional framework. Governments may have *noneconomic* reasons for wishing to protect their domestic market. A customs union may enable each country to maintain a protected market at less cost than would result from a nondiscriminatory tariff. Independently, Johnson (1965) proposed a similar extension to the conventional theory. The conventional theory assumes that economic welfare is maximised by maximising the satisfaction which households derive from the *private* consumption of goods. If, however, the welfare function is defined to

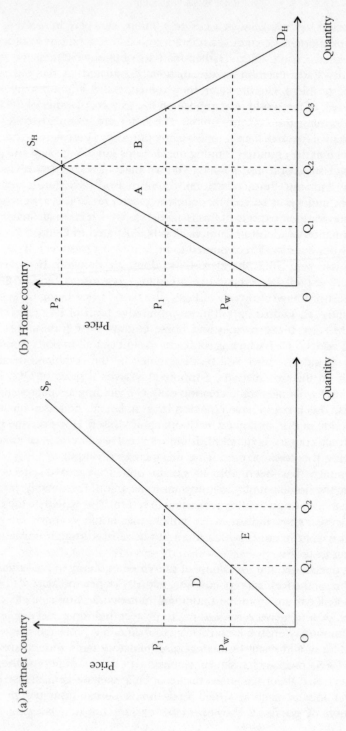

Figure 7.2 The effects of a customs union when the rest of the world imposes a tariff

include collective consumption of certain '*public* goods', a rationale exists for customs unions. Johnson considered the case in which there exists a collective preference within countries for industrial production. This may explain why governments impose tariffs. Although a tariff will impose a private cost, this will be offset by the welfare gain from collective consumption of increased industrial activity. Johnson postulated that, if governments act rationally, protection will be carried to the point where 'the value of the marginal collective utility derived from collective consumption of domestic industrial activity is just equal to the marginal excess private cost of protected industrial production'. In the case of a country which is a net exporter of industrial goods, the same considerations would necessitate the granting of an export subsidy coupled with a tariff sufficient to prevent reimportation. However, GATT rules prohibit overt export subsidies and therefore make it difficult for industrial exporting countries to satisfy fully their preference for industrial production.

Johnson went on to show that the same objective could be achieved more efficiently by any two countries making preferential tariff reductions. If both countries have a collective preference for industrial production, the reciprocal reduction in tariffs on imports from each other enables both countries to increase their exports and industrial production without suffering any loss of their own production. This is because discriminatory tariff reductions between any two countries result in trade diversion. Imports are diverted from third countries to the partner. Such trade diversion, of course, entails a cost for the tariff-reducing country which is equal to the difference between the cost of imports from the partner country and from the rest of the world. However, provided that is less than the 'marginal collective utility' derived from increased industrial production, the country gains. If, however, tariff reductions are carried sufficiently far, some trade creation may result, in which case the partner may experience some fall in domestic production. But, even in this case, it is the partner country, not some third country, which gains.

Johnson wanted to show why preferential tariff reductions may be preferred to nondiscriminatory tariff reductions. With a nondiscriminatory reduction, the partner's exports would expand by less than the tariff-reducing country's imports. In the case of a customs union, the two countries totally eliminate tariffs on their trade with each other. This is similarly preferable to a policy of nondiscriminatory tariff reductions where the two countries have a collective preference for industrial production for the same reasons. Hence, a rationale for customs unions is established. Such an arrangement is particularly beneficial to an exporting industrial country which is prevented by GATT rules from expanding industrial exports through a policy of subsidies. Interestingly, however, a *partial* preferential tariff arrangement will be more effective in meeting the collective preferences of the two countries than a 100 per cent preferential arrangement. This is because the costs to the tariff-reducing country from trade diversion will be less.

Johnson's approach differs markedly from the conventional theory in viewing trade diversion as a source of gain. Trade diversion is positively desirable because it enables the partner countries both to increase their industrial production and to realise their respective collective preferences for industrial goods. In the conventional theory, trade diversion is viewed as a loss except where it yields a significant terms-of-trade gain. This might suggest that the conventional, classical distinction between trade creation and trade diversion is unhelpful, but various criticisms have also been levelled at the public-goods argument. Firstly, it is argued that, under the auspices of 'public goods', essentially political arguments are being introduced which only serve to reinforce the oft-cited argument that the rationale for customs unions is noneconomic. Secondly, the public-goods argument for customs unions is still second best since the collective preference for industrial goods can always be more efficiently satisfied by a production subsidy. However, it is true that, in the special case of an industrial exporting country, this would involve the country in a conflict with GATT rules on export subsidies. Thirdly, even if the main thrust of the public goods argument is accepted, it is clear that it does not have a general application. For example, it is likely to be more applicable to a developing country just embarking on a policy of industrialisation. It is of little relevance to mature industrialised economies such as those of Western Europe or North America. One interesting aspect of the Johnson approach is the additional support it gives for the prediction that customs unions will tend to be formed between countries at roughly similar stages of development. If one partner country is economically more advanced than the other, the possibility exists that the reduction of tariffs will cause all industries to locate in the more advanced partner at the expense of the less advanced.

Earlier, reference was made to two effects of customs unions identified by Viner but which were omitted from his basic theory, namely, *economies-of-scale* and *terms-of-trade* effects. It is possible that there may be further gains to the countries forming the customs union from an increase in the size of the market in which goods are sold. This will occur in those industries where goods are sold under conditions of increasing returns (decreasing costs) and will be the case if the domestic market is too small to permit full exploitation of all available economies of scale *and* if the country in question faces high tariffs in the rest of the world. If the latter were not the case, economies of scale could be reaped by exporting more to the rest of the world and a customs union would have no rationale as a means for exploiting them. In this case, the potential welfare gain is quite large. Increased exports result in lower unit costs which apply to the *total* production of the good in question. By way of contrast, the static gains from net trade creation are quite small since they apply only to the increase in the

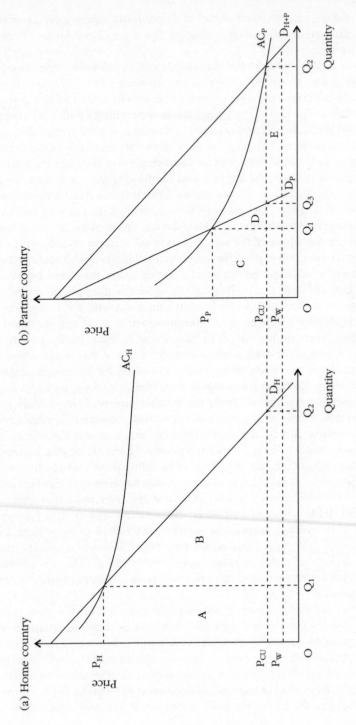

Figure 7.3 The effects of a customs union under decreasing costs

quantity of the product which is traded. Economists disagree on the extent to which the size of the market constrains the scale of production even in small countries.

A formal analysis of the effects of a customs union under conditions of decreasing costs was first provided by Corden (1972). Consider two countries, home country (H) and partner country (P), which form a customs union. In Figure 7.3, $D_H D_H$ represents the home country's demand curve for widgets and $D_P D_P$ the partner country's demand curve for widgets. D_{H+P} is the combined demand curve for widgets in the home and partner country. OP_W is the world supply price. Before the formation of the customs union, P imposes a tariff of $P_W P_P$ on imports and H of $P_W P_H$. AC_H and AC_P are the two countries' falling average cost curves. The tariffs are fixed so as to make production of widgets just viable in both countries. Country H produces OQ_1 and country P produces OQ_1. After the formation of the union, country P will capture the whole of the union market on account of its lower price. Country P's output will expand, resulting in a fall in average costs. It follows that production will now be viable at a lower union price and hence the common external tariff can be fixed at a level below the pre-union tariff. At price OP_{CU}, it is possible to satisfy total union demand for widgets from internal production. Hence, the common external tariff can be fixed at $P_W P_{CU}$. The effects on the two countries are as follows. Firstly, country H experiences straightforward trade creation of the conventional kind as higher-cost domestic production is now displaced by lower-cost imports from country P. Demand for widgets increases from OQ_1 to OQ_2, all of which is satisfied by imports from the partner country. The welfare gain accrues to consumers in the form of increased consumer surplus and is given by the areas A + B. The gain is divisible into a *production effect* (area A) as cheaper imports displace more expensive domestic production and a *consumption effect* (area B) as prices fall enabling consumers to buy more widgets. Secondly, consumers in country P gain because they can buy more widgets at a lower price. Corden called this the '*cost reduction effect*'. It arises from trade creation but it is different in that it arises from a cheapening of *existing* sources of supply rather than a movement to a *cheaper* source of supply. Demand increases from OQ_1 to OQ_3. Consumers gain increased consumer surplus, given by areas C + D. In addition, producers gain from increased sales to country H in excess of world prices, equal to area E.

A second possibility exists in which initial production of widgets takes place in one country only. Suppose that, before the formation of the customs union, there was no production of widgets in country H. If country H has no production, it may be assumed that the level of the tariff is zero (if the purpose of a tariff is to grant protection rather than raise revenue). Then, following the formation of the union, a common external tariff on imported widgets equal to the pre-union tariff of country P will now apply. This will enable country P to capture the whole of country H's market. However, consumers in country H will now lose from the rise in price. This loss contains two elements. Firstly, orthodox trade diversion has occurred as higher-cost widgets from P have displaced lower-cost widgets from the rest of the world. Secondly, consumers in H must now buy fewer widgets because of the higher price. On the other hand, country P enjoys the same favourable cost-reduction effect as in the first case discussed above. A further (but less likely) possibility is that initial production takes place in country H with no production in P, the lower-cost producer. In this case, the formation of the union may cause production reversal, with production in P driving out H. Country H thus gains on account of country P's lower costs and prices. On the other hand, country P loses because domestic production will still be more expensive than imports from the rest of the world. Following Viner, Corden called this *trade suppression*. It is similar to trade diversion, yet different because the more expensive source of supply which displaces imports from the rest of the world is a newly established domestic producer, not a partner country.

Thus, the occurrence of decreasing average costs opens up the possibility of additional gains over and above the conventional resource reallocation effects which orthodox theory predicts. Robson (1987) makes clear that this does not render the orthodox theory invalid but merely necessitates its extension to include trade-suppression and cost-reduction effects. However, the opportunity for exploiting economies of scale does not itself ensure that the formation of a customs union will have a beneficial effect. Trade diversion plus trade suppression may equally well outweigh trade creation plus the cost-reduction effect. Hence, the inclusion of economies of scale fails to provide a clear rationale for the formation of customs unions. Moreover, as was argued above, if opportunities for economies of scale do exist, these could be equally well obtained through increased exports to the rest of the world. Only if this is prevented by high tariffs imposed by the rest of the world on the products in question would there exist a clear rationale for a customs union.

The second effect of customs unions which Viner (1950) acknowledged may yield additional benefits to the partner countries arises from a favourable shift in the terms of trade of the newly formed union. Viner recognised the possibility that the countries forming the union by imposing a common external tariff which leads to trade diversion may be able to alter the terms of trade in its favour. Any gain accruing to the members of the union is of course at the expense of the rest of the world. Global economic welfare is not increased but is merely redistributed in favour of the members. This is analogous to the terms-of-trade argument for a tariff where the tariff-imposing country is large enough to exert monopsony power. As with the optimum-tariff argument, it rests on the assumption that the rest of the world does not retaliate.

Subsequently, the terms-of-trade effects were further explored by Mundell (1964) and Arndt (1968). Terms-of-trade effects have also been incorporated into general equilibrium approaches to customs union theory such as those of Vanek (1965) and Kemp (1969). At this point, it is appropriate to mention the work of Ohyama (1972) and Kemp and Wan (1976). They extended the basic theory of customs unions to show that, if the common external tariff is fixed at a certain level and lump sums are transferred among members, any customs union need result only in trade creation and no trade diversion. The common external tariff could be fixed at a level which leaves unchanged the member countries' trade with the rest of the world in terms of both quantities and proportions. Hence, the rest of the world is not affected at all while the members benefit from trade creation. Indeed, the external tariff could conceivably be set at a lower rate so that the rest of the world benefits also. It follows that no customs union need be harmful to the rest of the world and yet can benefit all or some of its members. While this may be true in theory, not all customs unions in practice meet these conditions, nor would it be easy to ensure that, whenever a customs union is set up, the conditions are met. On the other hand, an attraction of this approach is that it demonstrates that customs unions need not be incompatible with multilateral trade liberalisation. Any given customs union could be enlarged by adding new members in such a way as to improve the welfare of all members without harming the rest of the world. In this way, customs unions could provide a route towards multilateral liberalisation (see McMillan, 1993, for a good discussion).

A major weakness of all these approaches is that they use a comparative statics method of analysis. This was also true of Corden's analysis of the effects of customs unions in the presence of unexploited opportunities for economies of scale. A more useful approach is to consider the *dynamic* effects which enlargement of the market has on factors such as the rate of economic growth, the rate of capital investment and the rate of technological innovation. The possible gains to members of the union as a result of the fuller exploitation of economies of scale may be regarded as one type of dynamic gain. In addition to the static economies of scale which may result from increasing the size of the plant and of the firm, there may be unexploited dynamic economies which result from an increase in the cumulative volume of production. The existence of a learning curve whereby efficiency increases with cumulative output has been demon-strated for industries such as aircraft production, electrical goods, steel manufacture and paper production. In addition, there are external economies to the firm whereby the expansion of a particular industry causes a downward shift of the cost curves of every firm thereby causing a fall in the industry's long-run supply curve. It is frequently argued that such linkages or spillover effects exist in the electronics industry as research carried out in one branch of the industry (for example, consumer electronics) benefits firms in other parts of the industry (for example, semiconductors).

The effects on competition of the enlargement of the market has also attracted a good deal of interest. This may be related to arguments about scale economies in particular industries which, given the size of national markets, leave room for only one or a small number of producers. By enlarging the market in which firms sell, the number of firms can be increased without losing opportunities for economies of scale. Leibenstein (1966) introduced the concept of 'x-efficiency' to identify the output loss from managers' failure to minimise costs due to the absence of competition. This must be distinguished from the lost efficiency resulting from misallocation of resources, which is the main concern of the orthodox theory. The benefit to countries in terms of more rapid growth due to the elimination of nonallocative inefficiency may well exceed any gain from achieving optimum resource allocation. On the other hand, the formation of a customs union may fail to go far enough for this to be the case. If the removal of tariffs merely results in their replacement with nontariff barriers, competition may not be significantly increased. Certainly, the experience of the European Union supports this. Large differences in the pre-tax prices of identical goods in different EU member states are a reflection of this. Finally, with an enlarged home market, unions may increase the rate of technological innovation. The results of most empirical research into the effects of market structure on the rate of innovation largely support the view that competition has a beneficial effect on innovation. In addition, increased market size may stimulate research and development in research-intensive industries such as pharmaceuticals, where firms typically face heavy fixed R&D costs and comparatively short market lives during which these costs have to be recuperated. The bigger the home market, the larger the output, and the easier it is to recover these costs. The risks of investing funds in the development of a new product are accordingly lowered.

A HISTORY OF REGIONALISM

The First Regionalism

Bhagwati (1992) has suggested that a distinction be drawn between two waves or phases of regionalism which have occurred in the post-Second World War era. The 'First Regionalism' occurred in the late 1950s and early 1960s and spread to both developed and developing countries.

Among developed countries, regionalism was largely confined to Western Europe. In 1957, the signing of the Treaty of Rome led to the formation of the *European Community* (EC) comprising France, Germany, Italy, Belgium, the Netherlands and Luxembourg. The Treaty provided for the establishment of a customs union covering industrial and agricultural goods and leading to the abolition of all internal tariffs and the adoption of a common external tariff. In addition, it included provisions for the free movement of labour and capital and the creation of a common market. This was followed two years later by the signing of the Stockholm Convention and the establishment of the *European Free Trade Area* (EFTA). EFTA initially comprised seven countries: the United Kingdom, Austria, Switzerland, Sweden, Norway, Denmark and Portugal. Unlike the EC, EFTA involved only the elimination of internal tariffs with no common external tariff and was confined to industrial goods. In 1965, the UK and Ireland signed a free-trade agreement. Subsequently, in 1973, both the UK and Ireland joined the EC, along with Denmark. In 1975, the EC and EFTA signed a new free-trade agreement providing for the elimination of tariffs on trade in manufactured goods between the two blocs. Other examples of regional trading blocs among industrialised countries during this period included a free-trade agreement set up in 1965 between Australia and New Zealand, creating the *New Zealand and Australian Free Trade Area* (NAFTA). In 1983, this became the *Australian and New Zealand Closer Economic Relations and Trade Agreement* (ANZCERTA).

Most of these earlier forms of regionalism were also to be found among developing countries. Firstly, in South America, a number of arrangements came into being. In 1960, under the Treaty of Montevideo, the *Latin American Free Trade Association* (LAFTA) was formed between Mexico and all the countries of South America (except Guyana and Surinam). LAFTA came to an end in the late 1970s and was replaced in 1980 by the *Latin American Integration Association* (LAIA). In 1969, under the Cartagena Agreement, several South American countries including some LAFTA countries signed the *Andean Pact*, providing for closer economic relations. In Central America, the Managua Treaty of 1960 established the *Central American Common Market* (CACM) between Costa Rica, El Salvador, Guatemala, Honduras and Nicaragua. A *Caribbean Free Trade Association* (CARIFTA) was also set up which in 1973 was formed into the *Caribbean Community* (CARICOM). Its members were Antigua, Barbados, Belize, Dominica, Grenada, Guyana, Jamaica, Montserrat, St Kitts-Nevis-Anguilla, St Lucia, St Vincent, and Trinidad and Tobago.

In Central Africa, a *Central African Customs and Economic Union* (CACEU) was set up in 1964 comprising Cameroon, Gabon, Congo, Chad, the Central African Republic and, later, Equatorial Africa. In 1976, the *Economic Community of the Countries of the Great Lakes* (CEPGL) was formed between Rwanda, Burundi and Zaire. In West Africa, the *Mano River Union* (MRU) was established in 1973 between Liberia and Sierra Leone (and later Guinea). In 1974, the *West African Economic Community* (WAEC) was created comprising Côte d'Ivoire, Mali, Mauritania, Niger, Upper Volta (now Burkina Faso) and Senegal. In 1975, the *Economic Community of West African States* (ECOWAS) was formed under the Treaty of Lagos from some sixteen countries including WAEC and MRU members. In East Africa, the *East African Community* (EAC) was set up in 1967 between Kenya, Tanzania and Uganda but collapsed ten years later. In 1969, the *Southern African Customs Union* (SACU) was established between Botswana, Lesotho, Swaziland and the Republic of South Africa. Then, in 1981, the *Preferential Trade Area of Southern African States* (PTA) was set up consisting of fifteen countries drawn from the eastern and southern regions of the continent.

In Asia, there were fewer examples of regional integration. In 1967, an *Association of South-East Asian Nations* (ASEAN) was set up, consisting of Brunei, Indonesia, Malaysia, the Philippines, Singapore and Thailand. Also, in 1964, the *Arab Common Market* (ACM) was formed between Egypt, Iraq, Jordan and Syria. In 1981, the *Gulf Co-operation Council* (GCC) was established between Bahrain, Kuwait, Oman, Qatar, Saudi Arabia and the United Arab Emirates.

What were the effects of the first experiments in regionalism? Firstly, with regard to the *developed countries*, the main arrangements in question were the EC and EFTA in Europe and NAFTA/ANZCERTA in the Pacific. The EC differed in being a customs union and not a free-trade area. In the case of the EC, tariffs and all quantitative restrictions on trade were eliminated by July 1968, eighteen months ahead of schedule. At the same time, a common external tariff came into being through a process of tariff harmonisation. The Treaty of Rome provided for the external tariff to be fixed at the unweighted arithmetic average of the pre-union tariffs of the Six. In the case of EFTA, tariffs were also eliminated on intra-area trade within the stipulated period of six and a half years. However, being in a free-trade area, EFTA countries were free to determine their own tariffs on extra-area imports. In the case of NAFTA, tariffs were to be eliminated on 'nonsensitive' products (most of which were in any case subject to zero or very low tariffs). However, with the signing of ANZCERTA in 1983, tariffs and quantitative restrictions on trade were eliminated on all products. This was achieved by July 1990, five years ahead of schedule. In the case of EFTA, tariff liberalisation was confined to industrial goods. Although the EC included agriculture in the process of internal trade liberalisation, the Common Agricultural Policy provided for a highly comprehensive form of external protection. Thus, although the EC's tariff on trade with the rest of the world was no higher than the pre-union average tariff of the Six (and was reduced further in subsequent GATT rounds), trade barriers erected against agricultural imports from the rest of the world were indeed higher. The EC also went further than EFTA or NAFTA/ANZCERTA in providing for the removal of other nontariff barriers and distortions to trade between member states. The Treaty of Rome committed the member states to achieving free trade in both goods and services and free movement of the factors of production (labour and capital). It also contained provisions for the creation of various institutions and decision-making procedures of a supranational kind. However, it has to be said that the EC's aim of creating a common market was not realised. Moreover, in recent years, both ANZCERTA and EFTA have gone some way towards tackling the problems of nontariff barriers. In particular, recent changes to ANZCERTA include provisions for extending free trade to services and for the elimination of trade-distorting subsidies, for harmonising technical standards and regulations and customs process procedures, and for reducing discrimination in government procurement practices.

The effects of regional trading blocs can be analysed by examining their effects on the structure of a region's trade. Specifically, regional integration would be expected to increase the share in total trade of *intra-area* or intra-regional trade and therefore to decrease the share of *extra-area* or extra-regional trade. However, this tells us nothing about whether this was due to trade creation or trade diversion. One way of taking this into account is to look at the share of a region's extra-area trade in world trade and to compare this with the share of its total trade (intra- and extra-area) in world trade. If the share of a region's extra-area trade in world trade is falling at the same time as its share of total trade in world trade is rising, this might suggest trade diversion was occurring. Of course, many factors other than integration could cause shifts in these shares and therefore caution must be exercised in the interpretation of such measurements. Some figures for various kinds of regional trading blocs are given in Table 7.1.

For the moment, our focus is on the developed countries and the first wave of regionalism. The figures show a significant increase in the share of intra-area exports in total exports in the case of both the EC and EFTA. By contrast, the share of intra-area exports in NAFTA exports was much lower and barely increased at all. The fall in the share of extra-regional exports in world exports in all three cases could suggest some trade diversion. On the other hand, the share of total exports in world exports was also falling in all three cases. We can gain further insight by examining the trend in the ratio of extra-area trade to GDP. A decline in this ratio would suggest trade diversion. Some estimates are provided in Table 7.2.

In the EC(6), between 1960 and 1970, it rose by 1.5 points and, in the EC(10), by 5.2 from 1970 and 1985. In the case of EFTA, it fell very slightly by 0.6 points in 1960–70 but rose by 3.8 points in 1970–5 and by 9.4 points in 1975–85. Moreover, the ratio of total imports to GDP grew strongly during this period. However, in the case of NAFTA, the ratio of extra-area trade to GDP fell by 2.6 points while the ratio of intra-area trade to GDP barely increased. This suggests that the formation of the EC led to external trade creation rather than trade diversion. In the case of EFTA, although some trade diversion may have resulted, it was clearly quantitatively less significant than trade creation. However, in the case of NAFTA/ANZCERTA, trade diversion clearly exceeded trade creation. This perhaps was

Table 7.1 The share of intra-regional exports in total regional exports in various developed- and developing-country regional trading arrangements, 1960–90 (% share)

Trading bloc	1960	1970	1975	1980	1985	1990
A. Intra-regional/total exports						
NAFTA/ ANZCERTA(1965)	5.7	6.1	6.2	6.4	7.0	7.6
EC(6) (1958)	34.5	48.9	–	–	–	–
EC(10)	–	51.1	50.1	53.5	52.1	–
EC(12)	–	–	–	–	54.5	60.4
EFTA (1960)	21.1	28.0	35.2	32.6	31.2	28.2
US–CANADA (1986)	26.5	32.8	30.6	26.5	38.0	34.0
ASEAN (1967)	4.4	20.7	15.9	16.9	16.5	18.6
ANDEAN PACT (1969)	0.7	2.0	3.7	3.8	3.4	4.6
CACM (1960)	7.0	25.7	23.3	24.1	14.7	14.8
LAFTA/LAIA (1960/80)	7.9	9.9	13.6	13.7	8.3	10.6
ECOWAS (1975)	–	3.0	4.2	3.5	5.3	6.0
PTA (1981)	–	8.4	9.4	8.9	7.0	8.5
B. Total exports/world exports						
NAFTA/ANZCERTA	2.4	2.1	1.7	1.4	1.6	1.5
EC(6)	24.9	30.5	–	–	–	–
EC(10)	–	39.0	35.9	34.9	33.9	–
EC(12)	–	–	–	–	35.6	41.4
EFTA	16.7	14.9	6.3	6.1	6.3	6.8
US–CANADA	21.9	20.5	16.8	15.1	16.7	15.8
ASEAN	2.6	2.1	2.6	3.7	3.9	4.3
ANDEAN PACT	2.9	1.6	1.6	1.6	1.2	0.9
CACM	0.4	0.4	0.3	0.3	0.2	0.1
LAFTA/LAIA	6.0	4.4	3.5	4.2	4.7	3.4
ECOWAS	–	1.0	1.4	1.7	1.1	0.6
PTA	–	1.1	0.6	0.4	0.3	0.2
C. Extra-regional/world exports						
NAFTA/ANZCERTA	2.3	1.9	1.6	1.3	1.4	1.3
EC(6)	16.3	15.6	–	–	–	–
EC(10)	–	19.1	17.9	16.2	16.2	–
EC(12)	–	–	–	–	16.2	16.4
EFTA	13.2	10.8	4.1	4.1	4.4	4.9
US–CANADA	16.1	13.8	11.6	11.1	10.4	10.5
ASEAN	2.5	1.7	2.2	3.1	3.2	3.5
ANDEAN PACT	2.8	1.6	1.5	1.5	1.2	0.8
CACM	0.3	0.3	0.2	0.2	0.2	0.1
LAFTA/LAIA	5.5	4.0	3.1	3.6	4.3	3.0
ECOWAS	–	1.0	1.3	1.7	1.0	0.6
PTA	–	1.0	0.5	0.4	0.3	0.2

Source: Adapted from de la Torre and Kelly (1992)

Table 7.2 Changes in trade to GDP in selective industrial country regional arrangements (%)

Trading bloc		Total	Intra-regional	External
NAFTA/ANZCERTA	1980–90	–2.4	0.2	–2.6
EC-6	1960–70	11.6	10.1	1.5
EC-10	1970–85	12.0	6.8	5.2
EC-12	1985–90	–5.1	–0.2	–4.9
EFTA	1960–70	2.6	3.2	–0.6
	1970–75	8.4	4.6	3.8
	1975–85	10.7	1.3	9.4
US–CANADA	1985–90	2.1	0.3	1.9

Source: de la Torre and Kelly (1992)

unsurprising in view of the fact that the level of trade taking place between Australia and New Zealand was quite small at the time NAFTA was set up.

With reference to the EC and EFTA, there have been a large number of empirical studies carried out to estimate the extent of trade creation and trade diversion resulting from integration. Balassa (1974) used estimates of the income elasticity of import demand before and after integration to estimate net trade creation/trade diversion for the EC. His results also found evidence for substantial internal and external trade creation in manufactured goods but possible trade diversion in agricultural goods. Nevertheless, net trade creation amounted to US$11,400 million. Kreinin (1979) took the share of imports in apparent consumption before and after integration for both the EC and EFTA for the two stages of European integration but for manufactured goods only. He found that, in the first stage (1959–60 to 1969), annual trade creation amounted to US$11–15 billion for the EC plus EFTA and annual trade diversion US$2–3 billion. For the second stage (1970–1 to 1977), annual trade creation amounted to US$11–17 billion and annual trade diversion to US$2 billion. Combining the results of the many different studies carried out, Mayes (1978) estimated that, by 1970, the formation of the EC had resulted in net trade creation of US$8–15 billion. When expressed in terms of EC GNP, however, the welfare gain was found to be under 1 per cent. More recently, Jacquemine and Sapir (1988) have drawn attention to a tendency for extra-EC trade in manufactures to grow faster than intra-EC trade in recent decades. From 1963–72, the share of intra-EC trade in total trade rose from 51 per cent to 61 per cent, but by 1982 the share had fallen back to 58 per cent. They explained this in terms of, firstly, declining competitiveness in certain branches of manufacturing resulting in an increase in the share of extra-area imports in total EC imports and, secondly, a slowing down in the internal integration effect.

If account is taken of the dynamic effects, the gains to the EC from integration are almost certainly much larger. Owen (1983) reckoned that, by 1980, taking the dynamic effects into account, the GDP of the original Six was approximately 3–6 per cent higher. This was substantially more than the purely static gains of US$10–12 billion, equivalent to only ⅔ per cent of EC GDP. Marques-Mendes (1986) adopted a different approach focusing on the macroeconomic effects of the EC on internal economic growth. He estimated that, by 1972, the GDP of the EC was 2.2 per cent higher than it would have been without integration and, after enlargement in 1981, the GDP was 5.9 per cent higher. The positive effects of integration on economic growth may also explain why, following the formation of the EC, external trade creation rather than trade diversion took place in manufactured products.

If the experience of regional trading blocs among developed countries has been reasonably encouraging, the opposite was true of most of the early experiments involving *developing countries*. There is very little evidence to show any significant increase in the share of intra-regional trade in the total trade in these regions (see Table 7.1). One exception was CACM, in which intra-regional exports rose from 7 per cent of total exports in 1960 to 25.7 per cent in 1970 but fell in subsequent years. To a lesser extent, intra-regional trade in LAFTA also increased as a share of total trade following integration (that is, in 1960–80). The high share of intra-regional trade in ASEAN total trade is explainable largely in terms of significant transshipments. Moreover, it declined in the 1970s following the formation of ASEAN in 1967.

Most of these early attempts at regional integration were inspired by the prevailing development theories which argued that developing countries needed to create large regional markets if they were to overcome the constraints on industrial development posed by small domestic markets. It was argued that, by reducing trade barriers on trade with each other while erecting high barriers against imports from the already industrialised countries, developing countries could promote the development of their own indigenous industries and eventually achieve the necessary scale of production to be able to compete with the established firms of the developed countries. However, it is clear that, judged by the failure to increase the share of intra-regional trade in total trade, they failed dismally.

One reason for this was an almost universal failure to meet the deadlines for removing trade barriers. In some cases, each stage of barrier reduction necessitated fresh negotiations, resulting in excessive delays. The product coverage of intra-area trade liberalisation was also limited with each country negotiating different exclusions. In some cases, strict rules of origin meant that many products failed to qualify for tariff-free treatment. De la Torre and Kelly (1992) explain this failure in terms of the incompatibility between the goals of the partner countries, each of which sought to enlarge the market for its own protected industries. They could not all do so at the same time. Strong vested interests in import-competing industries in each country were unwilling to allow barriers to be lowered. A further reason for the failure of most of these schemes was that the economic structure of the countries was too often *competitive* rather than potentially *complementary*. The countries possessed similar factor endowments which limited the scope for increased inter-industry trade based on comparative advantage, while small markets and low per capita income meant that the opportunities for increased intra-industry trade were similarly unfavourable. In many cases, the effectiveness of regionalist trade strategies was further undermined by the failure of developing countries to pursue appropriate macroeconomic policies. By the 1970s, it was apparent that development strategies which emphasised import substitution, whether through the creation of regional trading blocs or otherwise, suffered from major weaknesses. These were further exposed when the external economic environment (in the 1970s higher oil and commodity prices, in the 1980s declining commodity prices, higher real interest rates and the debt crisis) began to deteriorate.

Not only did most of these arrangements fail to bring about a significant increase in the share of intra-regional exports in total exports, there was also evidence to suggest that some trade diversion may have occurred. In some cases (such as LAFTA), such trade diversion accounted for most, if not all, of the expansion in intra-regional trade. However, evidence for substantial trade diversion appears to be absent from most cases. Indeed, in some cases (for example, ASEAN), extra-regional trade increased as a share of total trade, although this probably had little to do with regional integration itself. This rather supports the view that most of the regional trading arrangements involving developing countries during this period in fact had very little measurable impact on trade flows at all. If anything, they were net trade diverting. Certainly, if their aim was to expand the share of intra-regional trade in total trade through trade diversion, they were largely unsuccessful.

Hence the largely neutral conclusion of Langhammer (1992), to the effect that all these early attempts at regional integration involving developing countries were 'too limited and fragile to have much impact on the world trade system'. He therefore concludes that they were not 'spearheads for regionalism' threatening multilateralism. The static effects were probably negative because they were net trade diverting. However, if anyone was harmed, it was the participating countries themselves. Furthermore, although little empirical work has been done on the dynamic effects of these various arrangements, the conclusion of such research as has been done suggests that no significant economies of scale were reaped (de la Torre and Kelly, 1992).

The Second Regionalism

By the end of the 1960s, many of the former regionalist experiments had collapsed, having failed to yield the gains once hoped for. Among developed countries, the enthusiasm for integration in Europe remained alive, but elsewhere no new schemes were forthcoming. Indeed, a proposal put forward by the US in the early 1960s for extending an enlarged EC (one which incorporated the UK) into a North Atlantic free-trade area covering all industrial goods failed to materialise. The 1980s, however, witnessed a revival of so-called regionalism, christened by Bhagwati (1992) the 'Second Regionalism'. A distinctive feature of this second wave has been its concentration on the developed countries. Closer regional integration has been taking place in each of the three major regions of the world: Europe, the western hemisphere (or the Americas) and Asia.

In *Europe*, regional integration was deepened by the signing of the *Single European Act* (SEA) in July 1987, which provided for the extension of the EC customs union into a common market in which the 'four freedoms' – goods, services, persons and capital – would prevail. The EC's 1985 White Paper on *Completing the Internal Market* (the Cockfield Report) identified three broad types of barrier impeding the internal market. Firstly, physical barriers affecting both people (immigration and passport controls) and goods (remaining import quotas, health regulations, transport controls and the special border taxes and subsidies known as 'monetary compensation amounts' applied to agricultural goods under the Common Agricultural Policy's green money system). Secondly, fiscal barriers arising from different levels and incidence of indirect taxes such as VAT, excise duties, and so on. Thirdly, technical barriers, including technical regulations and standards, public procurement policies, and so on that affect goods; lack of mutual recognition of national professional qualifications, impeding free movement of labour; and controls impeding the free movement of capital. The SEA proposed a programme of legislation involving over 300 separate measures required to eliminate most of these barriers by the end of 1992.

Following the passage of the SEA, the EFTA countries, fearful of being marginalised by the development of the Single Market, sought a closer relationship with the EC. After EC enlargement in 1973, the EFTA countries had signed a free-trade agreement with the EC covering industrial products, which provided for the elimination of tariffs on all trade in industrial goods between the EC and EFTA countries. After the SEA came into force, however, the EFTA countries desired equivalent access to the EC market for industrial goods to that enjoyed by EC member states. Hence, in October 1991, agreement was reached between the members of the EC and EFTA on the establishment of a *European Economic Area* (EEA), extending many of the aspects of the Single Market to EFTA countries also. Following ratification by national parliaments, the EA took effect from 1 January 1993 (although without Switzerland). It required EFTA countries to apply EU Single Market laws but left them with no say in the making of such laws. It was therefore logical that several of these countries should seek full EU membership. In January 1995 three – Austria, Finland and Sweden – became full members of the EU.

European regionalism received a further boost with the signing of the Maastricht Treaty in December 1991, which provided for full economic and monetary union between the Twelve by no later than 1 January 1999 and possibly earlier, although this may initially include only those member states which have met the convergence conditions. Together, the EU (as it is now known) and EFTA countries account for just under 40 per cent of world trade. This makes it an extremely powerful trading bloc in the world. This has been strengthened further by the complex web of other preferential trading agreements which the EU has entered into with a variety of other countries. In addition to the agreement between the EU and the EFTA countries, the EU has a trading agreement with seventy African, Caribbean and Pacific (ACP) countries which are signatories of the Lomé Conventions (first set up in 1975), a series of trading agreements with a further fourteen Mediterranean countries which have close trading relationships with the EU and, more recently, a series of trading agreements with various East European countries. Most of the latter were replaced by a new association agreement signed between the EU and six East European countries (Poland, Hungary, the Czech Republic, Slovakia, Romania and Bulgaria) in December 1991 which came into effect in March 1992. These so-called Europe Agreements involved the EU granting tariff preferences on mainly industrial goods from these countries, usually with no reciprocity requirement but subject to various safeguards and other provisions for so-called 'sensitive' products. In December 1994, the EU declared its commitment to admitting these countries to full membership by the turn of the century.

In *North America*, the most important development has been the conversion of the United States to regionalism. Since the signing of the GATT, the US has been the main advocate of multilateralism. In the mid-1980s, however, disillusioned by her efforts to achieve her trade policy objectives through the GATT, the US began to seek regional solutions. These were intended to complement rather than substitute for her efforts to achieve further multilateral trade liberalisation through the GATT. In 1985 the *United States* signed a Free Trade Agreement with *Israel*. This provided for the elimination of all tariffs on bilateral trade within ten years. The effects were minimal because Israel already enjoyed preferential access to the US market under the US Generalised System of Preferences. On the other hand, the FTA offered Israel more permanent access to the US market than the GSP. The US also gained from being able to export to Israel on the same terms as EC suppliers who enjoyed preferential access under a trading agreement signed in 1975. In May 1986 the US entered into negotiations with *Canada* for the creation of a Canadian–US Free Trade Area. In this case, the initiative lay with the Canadians, who feared that the US would raise import barriers in response to internal pressures to do something about the widening trade deficit. A particular concern of the Canadians was the possibility that their exports might be subject to stricter US countervailing and antidumping laws. The US, by contrast, was initially less keen on a fully fledged regional trading agreement and preferred a more pragmatic attempt to resolve a number of outstanding cross-border problems (for example, restrictions on US companies wishing to invest in Canada) that went back over a number of years. However, as the negotiations proceeded, the list of areas to be included lengthened.

In October 1987 the US and Canada signed an agreement to create a *Canada–US Free Trade Area* (CUSFTA). All bilateral tariffs and quantitative restraints were to be eliminated over a ten-year period starting in January 1989, even though average tariffs were already quite low. The average tariff on Canadian exports to the US prior to the agreement was roughly 1 per cent and less than 5 per cent for US exports to Canada, but the average concealed high tariffs on certain items such as timber and clothing. However, the agreement covered more than just tariffs: nontariff barriers were also included. Important aspects were the provisions for opening up public-service contracts. A special chapter on government procurement ended national preference on government contracts worth more than US$25,000 (the ceiling under the GATT procurements code was US$171,000) although it did not cover state and provincial contracts. There were also provisions for the elimination of all quantitative restrictions on trade, some of which impeded trade in agricultural products.

Initial attempts were made to liberalise trade in services and investment. With regard to investment, the agreement ended all restrictions on establishing new firms. This was mainly of benefit to the US, which had an estimated US$50 billion of direct investment in Canada in comparison with Canada's US$18 billion of direct investment in the US. Most of the restrictions applied by Canada on US investment were to be abolished. With regard to services, the agreement provided for the liberalisation of trade in commercial services, including the right of establishment and the right to national treatment for service firms in partner countries. However, this was weakened by the fact that all existing service arrangements would enjoy 'grandfather rights'. A special chapter on financial services would enable banks in either country to operate either side of the border without discrimination.

Next, the agreement provided Canada with some protection against new trade restrictions introduced by the US. In the past, Canada had often been affected by US protective measures targeted at other countries. Henceforth, any such measures would not be applied to Canadian exports unless specifically stated and only after bilateral discussions.

Finally, the agreement contained what is widely regarded as being an innovative general disputes-settlement mechanism. It had two aspects: Chapter 18 was similar to the GATT mechanism in providing for a panel system for settling general disputes but was arguably superior in that it included the right to initiate a panel and had strict procedural deadlines to establish an orderly timetable; Chapter 19 contained a mechanism for setting up panels to act in the place of domestic courts to review whether the imposition of antidumping and countervailing duties were consistent with the law of the country in which they were made. Decisions were to be reached within 315 days and were to be binding. However, Canadian exports would still be subject to US antidumping and countervailing laws. The US only conceded to Canada's demand for bilateral tribunals with binding powers to settle disputes at the last minute when Canada threatened to withdraw from the talks.

In March 1990 Mexico approached the US for a free-trade agreement. There were several reasons behind this approach. Firstly, like Canada, Mexico was anxious to secure unimpeded access to the US market for her exports at a time when protectionist pressures in the US were growing. Secondly, it was hoped that a free-trade agreement with the US would stimulate much-needed inward foreign investment in the Mexican economy and help to speed up economic growth. Thirdly, the Salinas Administration in Mexico was anxious to gain further support for its economic reform programme, including Mexico's admission to the GATT and her programme of unilateral trade liberalisation. In January 1991 a decision was reached to include Canada in formal negotiations, and in August 1992 a draft accord between the US, Mexico and Canada was announced. However, following President George Bush's electoral defeat in that year and the pledge of the incoming Clinton Administration to seek new side agreements covering labour and environmental standards, it was another twelve months before the proposal for a *North American Free Trade Area* (NAFTA) was ready for Congressional approval. (This should not be confused with Australia–New Zealand Free Trade Area of the same name which was set up in 1965 but which subsequently became ANZCERTA.)

NAFTA is modelled along similar lines to CUSFTA. Firstly, it provides for the complete elimination of all tariffs and export duties on trade among the three but with a slower timetable for Mexican–US and Mexican–Canadian trade than under CUSFTA. One aspect of NAFTA which has attracted criticism has been the much stricter rules of origin, especially for sectors such as textiles and apparel, automobiles and computers. In textiles and apparel, a 'yarn-forward' agreement means that all textiles and apparel from yarn through to the finished product must be of North American origin to gain tariff-free access to the market. (However, because Canadian manufacturers utilise fabrics from offshore sources, as under CUSFTA, they have been granted tariff-rate quotas for exports of garments to the US.) These arose because of the restrictions which both the US and Canada imposed on textile imports and the concern that, following the formation of NAFTA, substantial trade diversion might result which would undermine the restrictions then in place. In the automotive industry, vehicles must have 50–70 per cent local content to avoid tariffs, this is more severe than under CUSFTA. Under CUSFTA, there had been a long-standing dispute between the US and Canada over rules of origin for automotive products. The US wanted tougher restrictions but this was resisted by Canada and Mexico on the grounds that it would reduce their ability to attract investment by Japanese assembly plants. Under NAFTA, the content requirement was set at 50 per cent for four years, but rising to 56 per cent for the next four years and then to 62.5 per cent. This compares with 50 per cent under CUSFTA but the basis is to be net cost rather than direct cost of manufacturing.

Thirdly, as with CUSFTA, there is a chapter which contains provisions for national treatment and MFN treatment for service-providers except where countries have requested that particular services be excluded or specific derogations have been granted for particular policy measures. Land and air transport were included in NAFTA but were not covered by CUSFTA. There are separate chapters covering financial services and telecommunications. In the case of financial services, Mexico will gradually open up its financial sector to US and Canadian investment, eliminating barriers by 2007.

Fourthly, investment restrictions are to be eliminated in most sectors with certain exceptions (oil in Mexico, culture in Canada, and airline and radio communications in the US).

Fifthly, the general disputes-settlement mechanism under Chapter 18 of CUSFTA is to be adopted for NAFTA. The special binational appeal mechanism for antidumping and countervailing duty under Chapter 19 of CUSFTA is also extended to Mexico, but some special arrangements had to be made to take account of differences between Mexico's legal system and those of the US and Canada.

Finally, two important side agreements were negotiated covering environmental and labour standards to meet US concerns about so-called 'social dumping'. These include measures which spell out principles of labour and environmental protection (for example, commitments to equal pay for men and women; restrictions on child labour; and the right to strike) and provide for complaints against persistent failures of one country to enforce its own laws in these areas. If a complaint is upheld by an independent arbitration panel, the offending country could be forced to remedy its failure or be fined up to US$20 million (£13 million). Ultimately, sanctions could be imposed in the form of higher tariffs, although, in the case of Canada, abuses would be dealt with through the federal courts.

In South America, the 1990s have witnessed a dazzling proliferation of new regional trading arrangements. In April 1992 the countries belonging to the *Caribbean Economic Community* (CARICOM) declared their intention to move towards the creation of a common market, including the creation of a common external tariff. In November 1993 the six central American states belonging to the *Central American Common Market* (CACM) signed an agreement providing for the removal of all remaining internal barriers to trade and the adoption of a new, lower common external tariff. In March 1994 *Mexico and Costa Rica* reached an agreement which includes measures to remove nontariff barriers as well as tariffs, provides investors from each country with national treatment, sets rules for intellectual property rights, increases free movement of labour and sets up a disputes panel (see *The Financial Times*, 9 March 1994). This was due to come into effect from 1 January 1995 and was seen as the first step towards Costa Rica joining NAFTA.

In March 1994, Brazil launched an initiative for the creation of a South American Free Trade Area. In May 1994 the Andean Pact countries (Peru, Bolivia, Venezuela, Colombia and Ecuador) reached agreement on the adoption of a four-tier common external tariff to come into force on 1 January 1995. In June 1994 three countries – Colombia, Venezuela and Mexico – signed the so-called *Group of Three Accord* to create a free-trade area over a ten-year period with effect from 1 January 1995. Colombia and Venezuela regarded it as a step towards joining NAFTA. At the same time, the G3 expressed their wish to seek further free-trade agreements with both the CACM and the CARICOM blocs (see *The Financial Times*, 15 June 1994). In August 1995 three-quarters of the countries in the Americas – including Colombia, Mexico and Venezuela, the countries of Central America, Cuba, the Dominican Republic and Haiti and the members of CARICOM – announced their intention to create a new regional economic organisation, the *Association of Caribbean States* (ACS). The plan is to establish a common market of some 204 million people with an annual trade volume of US$180 billion, making it potentially the fourth-largest trading bloc in the world (see *The Financial Times*, 17 August 1995).

However, perhaps the most important development of all was the signing of the *Mercosur Trading Area Agreement* in August 1994 (Mercosur is an acronym for *Mercad Comun del Sur*). This provided for the creation of a customs union made up of Brazil, Argentina, Uruguay and Paraguay with effect from 1 January 1995. It provided for the elimination of tariffs on roughly 90 per cent of all trade between the four (with tariffs on the remaining 10 per cent of trade falling, to reach zero by the year 2000) and a common external tariff covering 80 per cent of products with an average level of 14 per cent, ranging from 0 per cent to 20 per cent (see *The Financial Times*, 25 January 1995). The ultimate target is a common market, including the free movement of labour and capital. Chile and Bolivia both expressed their wish to join Mercosur eventually but as free trade partners (that is, without the CET) so as not to preclude entry to NAFTA. The possibility also exists that Mercosur could sign a free-trade agreement with the *Andean Pact* countries (Peru, Bolivia, Columbia, Ecuador and Venzeuela). A further possibility would be negotiations between Mercosur and NAFTA, creating the possibility of a continent-wide free-trade area. In December 1994, Chile was invited to become a member of NAFTA in what was widely seen as the first step towards the creation of a free-trade zone covering the Americas (see *The Financial Times*, 12 December 1994). The announcement followed an All-Americas Summit in Miami attended by leaders of thirty-four countries, which called for negotiations to be completed by no later than the year 2005 to create a 'free-trade area from Alaska to Cape Horn' by 2006 (see *The Financial Times*, 9 December 1994). However, a potential conflict exists between the desire of the US to extend NAFTA to other Latin American countries and the wish of countries such as Brazil to promote the development of a South American Free Trade Area. By September 1994, an estimated thirty bilateral and multilateral agreements had been entered into by countries in the Latin American region.

The third area of the world in which regional integration has been taking place is *Asia*. Earlier in this chapter, reference was made to *ANZCERTA* (the Australia and New Zealand Closer Economic Relations Agreement) created by Australia and New Zealand out of the former NAFTA set up in 1965. This provided for the elimination of all tariffs by 1 January 1988 and all quantitative restrictions by 1 July 1995. In addition, all direct export subsidies and incentives were to have been ended by 1987. ANZCERTA was modified in 1988 to extend its provisions to services, the harmonisation of quarantine restrictions, business law, technical barriers, customs policies and practices, state government purchasing and export restrictions. On 1 January 1993, the six countries belonging to ASEAN (Singapore, Malaysia, Thailand, Indonesia, the Philippines and Brunei) embarked on a programme for achieving an *ASEAN Free Trade Area* (AFTA) within fifteen years. (Vietnam was admitted as a member of ASEAN in July 1995.) Tariffs on most products were to be progressively reduced on a 'normal track' route to between 0 per cent and 5 per cent. Tariffs on a select group of products were to be eliminated on a 'fast track' route over either a seven-year or a ten-year period. On the other hand, a large number of products were excluded altogether because countries expressed their wish to continue to protect them (see *The Financial Times*, 26 January 1993). In fact, the ASEAN countries only do about 5 per cent of their trade with each other (if entrepot trade is excluded): most of it is with Europe, Japan and the

United States. This has led sceptics to question the degree of urgency with which tariff reductions are likely to be implemented.

A further step towards close integration in the Pacific region was taken with the formation in 1989, on the initiative of Australia and the US, of the *Asia–Pacific Economic Co-operation* forum (APEC). This encompasses fifteen countries: Australia and New Zealand, the six ASEAN countries, the United States and Canada (but not Mexico) plus Japan, South Korea, China, Hong Kong and Taiwan. When it was set up, APEC did not provide for regional trade liberalisation, but only for some limited form of economic co-operation between the countries involved. However, in August 1994, a report by an Eminent Persons Group (EPG) set up by APEC urged member countries to begin progress towards the creation of a free-trade zone by the year 2020. The report was strongly supported by the US, Canada and Australia (and to a lesser extent by Japan) but was strongly opposed by Malaysia. Despite Malaysia's reservations, a summit of APEC leaders, held at Jakarta in November 1994, entered into a commitment to achieve regional free trade by the year 2020 (see *The Financial Times*, 16 November 1994). At a ministerial meeting in Osaka, Japan, in November 1995, agreement was reached on an 'action agenda' for implementing the Jakarta/Bogor Declaration of 1994. One significant aspect of the agreement was that tariff reductions between APEC countries would be extended on a nondiscriminatory basis to nonmember states also. It remains unclear, however, whether countries will be required to dismantle all their tariffs on industrial goods by the deadline of 2020. Uncertainty also exists over the comprehensiveness of the arrangements. In particular, Japan and certain other countries favoured excluding agriculture from the liberalisation process. This, however, was strongly opposed by the United States. The compromise reached at Osaka in November 1995 appears to have involved Japan dropping its insistence on certain sectors such as agriculture being specifically excluded. On the other hand, the adoption of the principle of 'flexibility' seems likely to allow room for some countries to continue their protection of agriculture.

How does the second bout of regionalism differ from the first? One of the key differences is that, unlike the early experiments with regionalism, the current wave has centred on the developed countries. Thus, all the leading trading nations have been active in setting up regional trading blocs of one kind or another. By contrast, during the first wave of regionalism the only part of the developed world where regional trading arrangements had a major effect on world trade was Western Europe; most of the regional trading arrangements were to be found among developing countries. In the second wave of regionalism, developing countries have once again been active in creating free-trade areas/customs unions but the bigger impact on trade has come from trading blocs set up by developed countries.

Secondly, a major role has been played in the latest wave of regionalism by the United States. Thus, in recent years the US has entered into free-trade agreements with Israel, Canada and Mexico, has expressed its wish to extend NAFTA to other South American countries such as Chile and Argentina, and has proposed the creation of an Asian–Pacific trading bloc comprised of the APEC countries. For most of the postwar period, the US espoused nondiscrimination and the merits of a multilateralist approach to trade liberalisation. It tolerated regional trading agreements only so long as these did not threaten progress towards a more open, multilateral trading system. Why the turnaround? The answer lies in the growing sense of frustration felt within the US with the GATT's ability to protect and promote US trading interests. In the early 1980s, the US was anxious to start an eighth round of trade negotiations in order to extend the GATT to new areas of special interest to itself. These were trade in services, intellectual property rights and trade-related investment issues. The US was also keen that the new round should tackle the problem of agricultural protectionism which previous rounds had neglected. Other countries (in particular, in Europe) appeared reluctant to contemplate another GATT round so shortly after the completion of the Tokyo Round. The US saw the pursuit of regional free-trade deals as a means of goading her trading partners into a fresh round of multilateral negotiations. Thus, regionalism was seen as ancillary to multilateralism. The new policy favoured a 'multitrack' approach in which the US would pursue a variety of ways to promote her own interests abroad. The effect of this change in the US stance has been to strengthen significantly the regionalist factor in international trade policy. Bhagwati (1992) expresses this as follows:

> As the key defender of multilateralism through the postwar years, its [the US] decision now to travel the regional route (in the geographical and the preferential senses simultaneously) tilts the balance of forces away at the margin from multilateralism to regionalism.

The third distinguishing feature of the new wave of regionalism is that it is both broader and more intensive than the first. Many more countries and a greater proportion of trade are covered. The number of such arrangements appears to be far greater, and in some parts of the world (such as South America) has made for enormous complexity. One aspect of this has been the emerging phenomenon of so-called 'hub-and-spoke bilateralism' (Baldwin, 1994). This occurs when country A enters into a free-trade agreement with two other countries, B and C, but where there is no free trade agreement between B and C. For example, suppose that, instead of forming NAFTA, the US and Mexico had signed a free-trade agreement but that Canada had preferred not to sign the same agreement with Mexico. Such arrangements necessitate complex rules of origin to prevent large-scale trade deflection as well as having other negative effects on efficiency (see Baldwin, 1994). In addition to the sheer number of agreements which are being concluded, many seek a deeper level of integration than in the past. Thus, they are frequently not restricted to the removal of internal tariffs and/or the establishment of a common external tariff. Internal liberalisation is often extended to cover nontariff barriers and impediments to the free movement of labour and capital, with the aim of creating a common market. Frequently, rules concerned with opening up trade in services and increasing cross-border investment are included. Other issues such as competition policy or antidumping policy might also be incorporated in the agreement. They may even involve the creation of separate dispute-settlement mechanisms, as with NAFTA.

A fourth characteristic of the new regionalism has been its tendency to bring about a tripolarisation of the world trading system. The first regionalism had little or no impact on the geographical structure of world trade. However, there is evidence that the new wave is bringing about a significant reorientation of world trade. It has been argued that three trading blocs are in the process of being established: America, Europe and the Pacific Basin, and that these blocs are shaping the course of world trade (see, for example, Schott, 1991, for an interesting discussion of this subject). Some see in this development a threat to the goal of an open, multilateral world trading order. A particular concern is that these blocs could have a bias towards protectionism which would leave isolated the smaller trading nations which are not members of a bloc. Indeed, this concern has caused many smaller trading nations to seek refuge within one or other of the emerging blocs. Bhagwati (1992) sees in this another undesirable characteristic of the current regionalism. In Europe, a long list of countries keen to join the EU has accumulated. A large number of South American countries are now queuing up to gain admission to NAFTA. Asian concerns about the growing power of the other two blocs has prompted countries to seek closer integration. Thus, much of the regionalism that is taking place appears to be motivated by defensive considerations of this kind rather than by any assessment of the economic desirability or otherwise of such an arrangement.

HAS WORLD TRADE BECOME MORE REGIONALISED?

An issue attracting a growing interest among trade economists is the extent to which trade has become more regionalised. In particular, the question of whether world trade is becoming polarised around the three dominant trading blocs needs to be considered. An answer to this question is provided in part by a useful statistical study of regionalist trends in global trade recently carried out by the GATT Secretariat. This section discusses some of its findings. Anderson and Norheim (1993) explain the methods of measurement used and the major results obtained.

Any attempt to measure whether international trade has become more regionalised comes up against two major problems. The first is how to define geographic regions. For example, should Western Europe be regarded as a region separate from Central and Eastern Europe or should Europe be treated as a single region? Similarly, are Australia and New Zealand part of the same region as Asia or should they be treated separately? Any solution to these problems is to some degree arbitrary. The GATT study uses seven fairly broad regions: Western Europe, Eastern Europe and the former Soviet Union, North America, Latin America, Asia (including Australia and New Zealand), Africa, and the Middle East. The second problem is what method of measuring regionalisation to use. This is much less straightforward than it might seem. The reason is that conventional measures of regional trade dependence are distorted by changes taking place at the same time in a region's share of world trade. Thirdly, how do we interpret any observed tendency for trade to become more geographically biased? We cannot simply conclude that regionalism has proved a stronger force than multilateralism. There is a need to set any increased regional bias alongside changes in the degree of openness of regions. Thus, increased regional bias may be more than offset by an increase in the degree of openness. Table 7.3 sets out the results obtained by Anderson and Norheim (1993) using a variety of different measures of regionalisation.

A simple approach is to take the share of a region's trade which is intra-regional (as opposed to extra-regional). Table 7.3 reveals that, taking the world as a whole, trade was becoming less regionalised from 1928 to 1948 but more regionalised thereafter. Moreover, the average intra-regional trade share was significantly higher by 1990 than at the start of the period, suggesting that, over the period as a whole, trade has become more regionalised. Western Europe had the highest intra-regional share and this increased significantly after 1948. After rising steadily until 1968, the intra-regional share of Eastern Europe fell somewhat. North America had a much lower intra-regional trade share and this increased more slowly than Europe, taking the period as a whole. The share for the Asian region fluctuated much more but increased significantly after 1968. Africa's intra-regional share has fallen steadily as has the share for the Middle East since 1948.

One problem with using the intra-regional trade share is that it is affected by a region's share of global trade. If its share of world trade increases, this imparts an upward bias to its intra-regional trade share without any tendency towards regionalisation taking place. To see this, suppose there are only four countries in the world, A, B, C and D; A and B form one region and C and D the other. Suppose that A accounts for 40 per cent of world trade and B, C and D for 20 per cent each. Each country trades with the other countries in proportion to the other country's share of world trade. The network of trade between the two regions can be illustrated by:

Table 7.3 Measures of the regionalisation of international trade, 1928–90

	1928	1938	1948	1958	1968	1979	1990
A. Intra-regional trade share							
Western Europe	51	49	43	53	63	66	72
Eastern Europe	19	14	47	61	64	54	46
North America	25	23	29	32	37	30	31
Latin America	11	18	20	17	19	20	14
Asia	46	52	39	41	37	41	48
Africa	10	9	8	8	9	6	6
Middle East	5	4	21	12	8	7	6
World total	39	37	33	40	47	46	52
B. The intensity of intra-regional trade index							
Western Europe	1.13	1.14	1.21	1.38	1.51	1.57	1.60
Eastern Europe	4.36	2.61	10.22	7.62	7.30	7.88	10.88
North America	2.59	2.91	2.39	3.07	3.57	3.63	3.50
Latin America	1.37	2.30	1.71	1.95	3.55	3.80	3.53
Asia	2.61	2.83	2.74	3.15	2.84	2.77	2.31
Africa	2.37	1.73	1.27	1.38	1.91	1.24	2.48
Middle East	7.56	3.47	9.55	4.25	3.00	1.17	2.23
World total	1.85	1.92	2.43	2.65	2.81	2.64	2.62
C. The percentage share of GDP traded							
Western Europe	33	24	35	33	34	48	46
Eastern Europe	30[a]	25[a]	25[a]	25[a]	40[a]	40[a]	41
North America	10	8	11	9	10	19	19
Latin America	45[a]	30[a]	30[a]	30	21	27	28
Asia	32	27	25	26	21	27	29
Africa	60[a]	50[a]	50[a]	58	37	56	53
Middle East	60[a]	50[a]	50[a]	46	38	48	49
World total	24	19	22	22	22	35	34
D. The index of propensity to trade intra-regionally							
Western Europe	0.38	0.27	0.90	0.46	0.50	0.75	0.73
Eastern Europe	1.31	0.65	2.56	1.90	2.92	3.15	4.52
North America	0.27	0.22	0.26	0.29	0.34	0.70	0.67
Latin America	0.62	0.69	0.51	0.58	0.76	1.01	0.97
Asia	0.83	0.76	0.67	0.83	0.60	0.76	0.67
Africa	1.42	0.86	0.63	0.63	0.73	0.60	1.21
Middle East	4.53	1.74	4.77	2.47	1.12	0.66	1.19
World total	0.45	0.37	0.54	0.57	0.61	0.91	0.88

Source: Adapted from Anderson and Norheim (1993)

Note: [a] In the absence of reliable estimates, it was necessary to make guesstimates of the trade-to-GDP ratio for these regions in some years.

Region 1

Country A (%)		Country B (%)	
Total exports	40	Total exports	20
To B	13	To A	10
To C	13	To C	5
To D	13	To D	5

Region 2

Country C (%)		Country D (%)	
Total exports	20	Total exports	20
To A	10	To A	10
To B	5	To B	5
To D	5	To C	5

Because the first region includes the largest country, A, its share of world trade is 60 per cent. The share of intra-regional trade in total regional exports is $(13 + 10)/60 = 38.33$ per cent. The second region's share of world trade is 40 per cent and its intra-regional trade share is $(5 + 5)/40 = 25$ per cent. If, on the other hand, country A had the same share of world trade as the other three countries, its intra-regional trade share would have been only 33 per cent.

The solution proposed by Anderson and Norheim (1993) to this problem is to calculate an intensity of intra-regional trade index:

$$I_{ij} = X_{ij}/M_j$$

where X_{ij} is the share of country i's exports going to its partner country j (intra-regional trade share) and M_j is the share of country j in world imports. If X_{ij} equals M_j, the index will have a value of unity. It follows that a value greater than unity would indicate regional bias in trade. In other words, this new index effectively adjusts the intra-regional trade share for a region's share in global trade. As shown in Table 7.3, the intensity of intra-regional trade index for the world as a whole was found to be consistently greater than 1, suggesting geographical bias in trade. Moreover, it rose steadily until 1968. Since then it has fallen somewhat but remains higher than at the commencement of the postwar period. Interestingly, the index for Western Europe was much lower than for other regions but has risen consistently over the time period covered. Eastern Europe had the highest figure, although this was much the same in 1990 as in 1948. North America and Asia both had a higher figure than Western Europe, but the index for Asia was on a downward trend after 1958. In Latin America, trade has become more regionalised. In Africa, a similar trend was apparent after 1948 but there has been little change since 1928. In the Middle East, the trend has been in a reverse direction.

How are we to interpret these results? As we noted above, there is a need to see whether a tendency towards increased regional bias was at the expense of or complementary to increased trade with the rest of the world. Table 7.3 shows that over the period as a whole the share of output (GDP) traded has increased, suggesting that regions have become more open. Taking the world as a whole, the ratio of trade to GDP fell in the interwar period but increased after the Second World War, surpassing the 1928 level. Some decline may have occurred since 1978. This suggests that the increased regionalisation has not in general been at the expense of regions' trade with the rest of the world.

To estimate this, Anderson and Norheim (1993) propose estimating an index of the propensity to trade intra-regionally. This is calculated using the following formula:

$$P_{ij} = T_{ij}/M_j$$
$$= T_i.I_{ij}$$

where T_{ij} is i's exports to j divided by i's GDP, and M_j is country j's share of world trade. This is the same thing as Ti multiplied by the intensity of intra-regional trade index where T_i is the ratio of i's total exports to GDP. In other words, this index measures the ratio of intra-regional exports to GDP divided by the share of the partner country in world trade. The higher the ratio, the greater the propensity to trade intra-regionally. If a country is becoming more open so that its trade to GDP ratio is rising, this will offset any tendency for its intra-regional trade share index to rise. Table 7.3 shows that, for the world as a whole, the propensity to trade intra-regionally has increased despite a fall in the 1930s. Since 1979, the index has fallen slightly in Western Europe and North America. For Asia, it has been highly variable. Therefore, although the growth in the propensity to trade intra-regionally may suggest some tendency to regionalisation of trade, this has been matched by a tendency for regions to become more open.

As Anderson and Norheim (1993) point out, there are great problems in isolating the effects of regional trading arrangements from other influences on trading patterns. We cannot simply conclude that these changes were the result of greater regional integration. To isolate the influence of regional integration from other factors would require a general-equilibrium model of world trade. On the evidence available, however, some conclusions can be drawn. Historically, there has been some tendency towards trade becoming more regionalised but at best it has been a weak one. Moreover, to quite a large extent, it has been offset by a tendency for regions to become more open, partly as a result of global trade liberalisation. However, what we cannot yet say is whether or not the renewed interest in regionalism in recent years is altering the picture. Most of the recent attempts at creating regional trading areas are too much in their infancy to permit meaningful analysis of their effects.

IMPLICATIONS OF THE NEW REGIONALISM

How and why might the new regionalism threaten the ideal of an open, multilateral trading system? What changes to the GATT/WTO rules might be desirable to contain the spread of regionalism? It is clear from the theory of regional integration that there is nothing inherently harmful or damaging about free-trade areas or customs unions. As long as they result in net trade creation, the effect on global economic welfare is positive. The provisions of Article XXIV of the GATT go some way to ensuring that this will be the case. In particular, while not precluding the possibility that a CU/FTA could result in net trade diversion, the requirement that the average level of external tariffs after the formation of the CU/FTA should be no higher than the previous level goes some way to increasing the likelihood that net trade creation will be the outcome. Moreover, the available evidence suggests that, to date, most regional trading blocs formed between developed countries have resulted in net trade creation. Early attempts at regional integration between developing countries were less successful and may have resulted in net trade diversion. Even then, however, the effect on global economic welfare was, at most, marginal.

Supporters of regional integration have argued that regional trading blocs may actually speed up the process of global trade liberalisation. Far from being in opposition to the aim of an open, multilateral trading system, it is argued that they complement it and may even facilitate its realisation. The GATT negotiations, it is alleged, suffer from a number of inherent difficulties which limit both the speed at which the world can move towards freer trade and the scope and depth of trade liberalisation achievable at any one time. There are several reasons for this. Firstly, because GATT is based on the principle of unconditional MFN, it gives rise to the free-rider problem referred to at the beginning of the chapter. Countries may be tempted to hold back from making concessions in the knowledge that any made by other countries will be automatically extended to them. The GATT expects countries to act reciprocally. However, if one country is unwilling to make many concessions, under normal circumstances other countries will be unwilling to do so as well. This gives rise to what Wonnacott and Lutz (1989) have called the 'convoy problem', namely, that the least willing participant dictates the pace of negotiations. One way round this problem is for those countries which wish to move at a more rapid pace towards free trade to negotiate a free-trade area. The effect may even be to galvanise other more reluctant countries to make larger concessions in order to avoid being at a significant preferential disadvantage in the markets of the countries that cut tariffs fastest.

Secondly, it is sometimes argued that negotiations to set up a regional trading bloc take less time because the number of countries involved is fewer and the agenda tends to be less complex. This may be borne out by the time which it took the GATT countries to conclude the Uruguay Round; each successive GATT round has tended to take longer to conclude than its predecessor.

Thirdly, it is argued that GATT negotiations tend to be more limited in scope than regional negotiations. This is because the larger the number of countries involved in negotiations, the narrower the range of issues on which all countries can agree to negotiate. In support of this argument, the success of the EU and more recently NAFTA in extending liberalisation to issues such as services and investment is cited.

Although even the most ardent multilateralist would accept some truth in all these arguments, their importance can be exaggerated. The free-rider problem is a real one whenever a policy of unconditional MFN is adopted. However, it is not clear that, in practice, it has acted as a brake on trade negotiations through the GATT. The experience of many developing countries has been that they lost out by not bargaining in the earlier GATT rounds. Concessions which they received from other GATT countries were generally of less value than those enjoyed by other developed countries. As Bhagwati (1992) has put it, '[Unconditional] MFN does not work in practice as well as it should from the free-riders' perspective.' Moreover, to the extent that it may act as a constraining factor in certain specific areas, it may be possible, as Schott (1989) suggests, to apply a policy of conditional MFN in these cases. Indeed, this was the approach adopted in the negotiations of a code for government procurement and for subsidies in the Tokyo Round.

Concerning the argument that multilateral negotiations tend to be more complex, it is by no means certain that having fewer participants makes agreement any easier. Indeed, if the alternative to the GATT is a series of regional free-trade areas, this may result in even greater complexities, because, when a country participates in more than one agreement, each new agreement affects all the other oustanding agreements and frequently necessitates renegotiation. For example, if the United States and Japan were to negotiate a free-trade agreement, it would affect the concessions which the US has granted Canada and Mexico under NAFTA. Canadian and Mexican exporters would then have to share their preferences in the US market with Japanese exporters. Canada and Mexico could therefore demand some renegotiation of their agreement with the US. This has been referred to as the problem of 'sequencing' (Schott, 1989). In theory, it could be avoided by making each regional agreement 'open-ended' so that, at any time, any country could join the FTA at the appropriate price. In practice, it is unlikely that this would prove acceptable to all countries involved because of the implied uncertainty.

There are four major concerns about the current enthusiasm for regional trading agreements. Firstly, there is a danger that seeking regional trading agreements will divert the energy and resources of governments away from the need to achieve further global trade liberalisation. In this case, regionalism will undermine and not reinforce multilateralism. Thus, in the Uruguay Round negotiations, the preoccupation of the US with the negotiations to establish NAFTA temporarily acted as a distraction. Once NAFTA had been agreed and ratified by US Congress, speedier progress in the GATT negotiations became possible.

Secondly, there is a danger that the proliferation of a large number of regional trading blocs will increase trading tensions between countries. As we have seen, each new agreement entered into by one country with another undermines the value of any preferences offered in previous agreements to other partner countries. In addition, to the extent that regional trading arrangements result in trade diversion, the potential is created to offend trading partners and provoke retaliation. Other technical problems may arise where regional tariff reductions are phased in at different times, inconsistent rulings are made by dispute-settlement procedures set up under different agreements, and where different rules of origin are applied in different trading areas.

Thirdly, to the extent that regionalism polarises world trade into a small number of powerful trading blocs, smaller countries which are excluded are likely to suffer. One of the merits of the unconditional MFN principle is that it protects smaller countries from the big and powerful.

Finally, there is the danger that regionalism might lead to increased protectionism. As trade barriers are reduced internally, higher barriers may be erected against imports from the rest of the world. One reason is that, for an individual country, the costs of imposing restrictions on imports from a supplier in the rest of the world are lowered if that country is part of a regional trading bloc because restrictions need only be imposed on extra-area imports, thus reducing the number of trading partners it risks upsetting. Another reason is that large trading blocs have an incentive to assert monopsonistic power by imposing optimum tariffs in an attempt to shift the terms of trade in their favour. Krugman (1991) provides a model showing that, if the world is divided into a declining number of ever-larger trading blocs, protectionism will increase and global economic welfare will fall. A further reason is the tendency for the internal decision-making process of trading blocs to result in greater protectionism against imports from the rest of the world.

Winters (1994) gives several reasons for how this happens within the EU. Firstly, the European Commission's need to gain the support of individual member states if it is to be effective forces it to 'broker compromises' with national governments. This, he argues, encourages a drift towards generalised protection in EU trade policy. It also creates greater opportunities for Union-wide lobbies (such as farmers, steel producers, and so on) to bring pressure to bear not only on the Commission but on member state governments. Another reason is the so-called 'restaurant bill' problem relevant to the determination of agricultural prices in the EU. If a group of people goes out for a meal together and everyone is required to contribute equally to the cost of the bill, each person will have whatever item on the menu brings them the most satisfaction with little regard for the cost. In the EU, the costs of the CAP are borne collectively by consumers and taxpayers. However, the benefits accrue to producers in the different member states according to how much they produce. This means that, in the annual agricultural price negotiations, each member state government will seek to obtain high prices for those commodities for which they have a high share of production. In other words, the system works to push prices up rather than down. In a similar way, there is a bias towards increased protectionism in the determination of EU industrial policy. The fear of being left on the outside in the event of a protectionist measure being adopted causes member states to press for protection for those products of most concern to them. The result is that even liberal members of the EU who are opposed to protectionist measures may fail to fight vigorously to prevent their adoption. Thirdly, a bias towards protectionism arises from the efforts of the Commission to gain control over trade policy. In order to do so, the Commission is compelled to adopt and to propagate a policy close to that of the most protectionist member state. One example of this concerns EU policy towards imported Japanese cars following the abolition of internal borders. Before 1992, a number of member states applied national restrictions on imports of Japanese cars. With the arrival of the Single Market, it was necessary to replace these with a Union-wide policy. The Commission negotiated a voluntary export restraint agreement with Japan which limits the increase in the number of cars exported by Japan to the entire EU until the end of the century when full liberalisation will be achieved. In order to secure the agreement for national controls to be replaced by Union-wide restrictions, the Commission had to negotiate a level of restraint whch was acceptable to the most protectionist member state (Winters, 1994).

THE REFORM OF GATT RULES

How adequate are existing GATT rules regarding the formation of customs unions/free-trade areas? What changes, if any, are needed to cope with the current wave of regionalism? The need to improve the existing GATT rules as set out in Article XXIV was an issue addressed in the course of the Uruguay Round. Various changes were made and these are set out below. However, before discussing them, it is necessary to identify some of the principal weaknesses with the GATT provisions as they have operated until now:

1 One problem is that the conditions stipulated in Article XXIV for the formation of a customs union/free-trade area are not sufficient to ensure that only unions/areas which are net trade creating are established. As Bhagwati (1992) has explained, it is entirely possible that an arrangement entailing a level of external tariffs which is on average lower than the level in existence before the arrangement was set up could still result in net trade diversion.

2 The method to be used for measuring the incidence of duties before and after the formation of the arrangement is vague. Specifically, there is no indication whether the average level of tariffs should be a weighted or an unweighted mean.

3 Although Article XXIV permits only 100 per cent tariff preferences, the reference to 'substantially all trade' leaves some ambiguity about how this is to be interpreted. Presumably, it allows for the possibility that tariff preferences of less than 100 per cent are acceptable on some component of intra-area trade. But how much trade is 'substantial'?

4 The requirements relating to interim agreements are similarly vague. Article XXIV merely states that these should include a plan and a schedule for the formation of a customs union/free-trade area 'within a reasonable length of time'. But what is reasonable? If an agreement fails to achieve its deadline for removing internal tariffs, there is little to distinguish such an arrangement from a preferential trading arrangement of the kind which Article XXIV is seeking to prevent.

5 Article XXIV says nothing about whether other countries should be allowed to join a customs union/free-trade area or whether the existing members may exclude other countries. As we explain below, there are several reasons for favouring so-called 'open-ended' regional trading arrangements.

6 A major problem has been created by a decision made in 1979 to exempt developing countries from the requirements of Article XXIV. This was part of the Enabling Clause negotiated as part of the Tokyo Round in 1979 and means that developing countries are free to do whatever they like in the area of trading preferences extended towards other developing countries through regional trading agreements. The result has been to reduce substantially the effectiveness of Article XXIV in respect of a significant proportion of world trade.

However, it is not only the GATT rules regulating regional trading arrangements which have proved inadequate; it has also been the failure of the GATT to enforce compliance with these rules. As we explained above, Article XXIV requires any country entering into a CU/FTA to notify the GATT and to provide all the necessary information about the the agreement so that the GATT can ensure that it complies with the other requirements of Article XXIV. If in any respect the agreement fails to comply with these requirements, the GATT may compel the parties concerned to make changes to the agreement to ensure that it does, and the agreement cannot be enforced until these changes have been incorporated. In practice, the GATT has been unwilling to take action in such cases. An important precedent was set when the GATT decided against making a formal ruling on whether the Treaty of Rome establishing the EC was compatible with Article XXIV. The reasons were political. The US supported European integration because it strengthened Western Europe politically and was anxious not to do anything which might cause the EC countries to leave the GATT. Once the EC was allowed to ride roughshod over the GATT, it became difficult to take action against any other subsequent regional trading agreements which were notified. Over the period 1948–90, the GATT received notification of some seventy regional trading arrangements. None of these arrangements was formally declared to be incompatible with Article XXIV yet only four were deemed by consensus to be compatible. As Blackhurst and Henderson (1993) comment: 'under any circumstances, such a record would be a source of concern for a rules-based agreement'. As they explain, the reasons for this situation are threefold. Firstly, countries not participating in a particular arrangement are reluctant to lodge a complaint against it for failing to comply with Article XXIV since the outcome may well be modifications to the arrangement which actually worsen the consequences for the complainant country. Secondly, the reliance of GATT on decision-making by consensus makes it reluctant to force another member to renegotiate an agreement already entered into. Thirdly, undue importance has too often been attached to political considerations, and agreements have been allowed to proceed which might otherwise not do so.

There are a number of ways in which the GATT rules could be altered to limit the harmful effects of regionalism. Bhagwati (1992) has suggested that customs unions/free-trade areas should be required to set the average level of the external tariff following their formation *below* the previous average level so as to reduce the risks of trade diversion. One possibility would be a requirement that the average level of tariffs of the lowest-tariff country before the formation of the CU/FTA should determine the level of the external tariff after. Even this may not be enough to prevent trade diversion, as Bhagwati acknowledges. The growing importance of administered protection in the form of antidumping and countervailing duties and safeguards means that extra-area imports may still be more restricted afterwards even though the level of external tariffs is lower. This makes agreement to contain the potential for these measures to impede trade crucially important for ensuring that regional trading blocs do not lead to trade diversion. McMillan (1993) has proposed rejecting any CU/FTA which results in a lower volume of trade with the rest of the world. This is based on the Kemp–Wan–Vanek model of regional integration which showed that it

278

was possible for any CU/FTA to so structure itself as to make all the member states better off without making the rest of the world worse off (Kemp, 1964; Vanek, 1965). This will be achieved if external tariffs are fixed at the level needed to ensure that the volume of post-integration trade with rest of the world is no lower than before integration. This gets around the problem of what is the 'right' level of external tariffs after integration, but, as Bhagwati (1992) argues, is probably of limited practical usefulness. The effects of different levels of tariffs on intra- and extra-area trade flows is not known in advance and has to be estimated.

Another possibility would be to exclude free-trade areas from the provisions of Article XXIV on the grounds that they are likely to be more damaging than customs unions. Interestingly, in the original US proposals for an International Trade Organisation after the Second World War, only customs unions were to be eligible for exceptional treatment: there was no reference to free-trade areas (Snape, 1993). The reasoning was that the GATT rules relate to 'customs territories' and not to countries. A complete customs union constitutes a customs territory and so needs no exceptional treatment in terms of the MFN rule. It was only subsequently that Article XXIV was extended to cover free-trade areas. As Bhagwati (1992) explains, customs unions with a common external tariff are more likely to result in a downward shift in tariffs. If two countries with very different tariff levels – say, the United States and Argentina – form a free-trade area, the level of external tariffs is left unchanged and there is a great risk of trade diversion. If, however, they form a customs union and adopt a common external tariff, it is more likely that Argentina's tariff will be brought down to the level of that of the United States. Since most tariffs are bound, any rise in the United States' external tariff as a consequence of forming the customs union would allow the rest of the world to demand compensation. In addition, free-trade areas necessitate complex rules of origin because of the different external tariffs among the member states. Frequently, these are used by domestic producers to gain further protection.

Yet another possibility for change would be a requirement for any free-trade area/customs union to adopt an open membership policy. Every regional trading agreement would be required to include an accession clause allowing entry to any country which is able and willing to meet the entry conditions established by the founding members of the bloc. This has several attractions. Firstly, it would deal with some of the problems caused by 'hub-and-spoke' agreements discussed above. Secondly, it would provide what Bhagwati (1992) has called a 'dynamic time-path' whereby regional trading blocs become stepping stones rather than barriers towards the building of a nondiscriminatory, multilateral trading system. As regional trading arrangements are expanded to admit new members, they move closer towards global free trade. Thirdly, it would alleviate some of the anxieties of smaller countries that the spread of regionalism could leave them out in the cold. However, countries forming customs unions/free-trade areas may be reluctant to negotiate agreements to which any other country could later accede without their agreement. Moreover, there are particular problems with customs unions such as the EU, where the accession of a new member affects not only trade but inter-country budgetary transfers and the balance of power in decision-making bodies.

Blackhurst and Henderson (1993) argue that any improvements in the rules contained in Article XXIV are inadequate unless they address the issue of compliance. Their proposals were to step up the *ex post* surveillance process so as to intensify 'peer pressure' on countries to conform to the rules. There should be regular examinations of regional arrangements by a GATT working party, and the results published in a report. Alternatively, they recommend extending the GATT's Trade Policy Review Mechanism (TPRM) to cover regional trading arrangements.

How far have these issues been addressed in the Uruguay Round Final Act? The Understanding on the Interpretation of Article XXIV contains a number of amendments to the Article which go some way towards strengthening the existing rules but not as far as many of the proposals discussed above. They may be summarised as follows:

1 It has been made clear that, henceforth, the calculation of the incidence of tariffs and other measures applied before and after the formation of a customs union should be based on the *weighted* average tariff rates and customs duties and not on the arithmetical average often used by countries in determining the common external tariff. Also, an important clause states that 'for the purpose of overall assessment of the incidence of other regulations of commerce for which quantification and aggregation are difficult, the examination of individual measures, regulations, products covered and trade flows affected may be required'. In other words, when evaluating whether a customs union/free-trade area results in a lower or higher degree of restriction on imports from the rest of the world, account may be taken of measures other than just tariffs.

2 There are stricter rules governing interim agreements. Henceforth, the maximum time period allowed for such agreements other than in exceptional cases, is ten years.

3 There is a reaffirmation and clarification of the requirements set out in Article XXIV with regard to compensation by the members of a customs union/free-trade area of other GATT contracting parties where any bound duty is raised. Negotiations with third countries must take place before the formation of any customs union with a view to achieving 'mutually satisfactory compensation'. Account must be taken of reductions in duties on the same tariff line made by other constituents of the customs union in determining whether the union should offer compensation.

4 There is clarification of the procedures for reviewing customs unions and free-trade areas. Any group of countries forming one must notify the GATT and a working party be set up to examine the notification. The working party must submit a report including recommendations. Interim agreements must include a proposed timetable and list of measures to be completed for the formation of a customs union/free-trade area. Customs unions and constituents of free-trade areas are required to submit periodic reports of their operations to the Council on Trade in Goods.
5 It is made clear that the GATT Dispute Settlement Rules and Procedures are available to countries to deal with any disputes arising from the application of Article XXIV.
6 The General Agreement on Trade in Services (GATS) includes an article on regional integration which is largely modelled on Article XXIV of the GATT.

Clearly, these changes all represent useful improvements to the existing rules and procedures. It remains questionable, however, whether they go far enough in meeting some of the concerns expressed above about the recent regionalist drift. There is an implicit assumption that Article XXIV is basically adequate for ensuring that regionalism does not undermine the multilateralist goal, merely requiring some relatively minor changes. It remains to be seen whether this is the case. It seems more probable that the issue will have to be revisited in subsequent rounds.

CONCLUSION

This chapter has examined one of the most important current developments in international trade policy. In recent decades, regional trading arrange-ments have become a highly important basis for the conduct of trading policy. The GATT rules permit such a departure from the nondiscrimination principle subject to certain conditions. However, the rules contained in Article XXIV were drafted in a different environment when customs unions/free-trade areas were not expected to constitute more than minor exceptions to the general rule. As things have turned out, they have become sufficiently common to threaten the multilateral edifice on which the GATT is based.

A question which must be asked is whether this matters. Economic theory is not very helpful in providing a clear answer. All that can be safely concluded is that customs unions/free-trade areas which are trade diverting are harmful from a global economic point of view. This provides a basis on which to create rules to regulate the formation of customs unions/free-trade areas. However, in practice, the extent to which a particular trading arrangement is likely to be trade diverting cannot be determined with reference to tariffs alone. The ease with which trading blocs can erect higher import barriers through the use of measures such as antidumping and safeguards makes it difficult to quantify *ex ante* the effects of a particular arrangement. It follows that measures to control the growth of 'administered protection' are of crucial importance in an environment in which regional trading blocs are spreading. This is all the more so given the proclivity of such blocs towards protectionism.

On a positive note, regional customs unions/free-trade areas can constitute useful stepping stones towards freer trade. Indeed, this is the reason why they have been tolerated under international trade rules. There need be no conflict between the efforts of countries situated in close geographical proximity to create conditions that favour increased trade with each other and the attempts through the GATT/WTO to promote the same result at a global level. However, to ensure that this is the case, it may be necessary to establish new rules which create conditions favouring what Bhagwati (1992) has called a 'a dynamic time path'. That is to say, there is a need to ensure that customs unions/free-trade areas move in the direction of freer global trade rather than adopting a 'fortress mentality' in relation to the rest of the world. How can this be done? Some of the proposals made by Bhagwati and others and which were discussed towards the end of this chapter provide a solution; for example, rules which force countries to lower their external barriers when they form customs unions or require agreements to be open-ended, allowing other countries to accede at will. The Uruguay Round failed to confront these issues with sufficient boldness. Future rounds will need to do so.

8

THE NEW ISSUES:
SERVICES, TRIPs AND TRIMs

INTRODUCTION

One of the features of the Uruguay Round which distinguished it from previous GATT rounds was the inclusion on the agenda of a number of so-called 'new issues'. Previous GATT rounds were mainly concerned with the liberalisation of trade in goods. Even then, the preoccupation was with lowering tariff barriers on trade in manufactured products mainly between industrialised countries. As we have seen, the earlier rounds failed to make any real progress in opening up trade in agricultural goods. Not until the Tokyo Round was any meaningful attempt made to tackle the problem of nontariff barriers. Even then, it was mainly trade in manufactures exported by the developed countries which was liberalised. Trade in products of interest to developing countries, such as textiles, remained managed.

The Uruguay Round sought to tackle these outstanding or 'old' issues. Initially the view of the developing countries was that not until these remaining problems were resolved should the GATT be extended to any new areas. However, a different view was held by the developed countries, and the United States in particular. The US with the backing of the other advanced industrialised economies was keen to see a number of 'new issues' included on the agenda of the new round. The first of these was trade in *services*. The US indicated that it was unwilling to make any further 'concessions' in relation to manufactured goods unless some attempt was made to improve export opportunities for US service firms. This was a reflection of the growing importance of the service sector within the US economy. At the time, there were no specific provisions within the GATT Agreement relating to services although some of the provisions relating to goods could also be applied to services. Because in most countries the service sector was subject to a high degree of government interference, considerable barriers to trade existed, almost all of the nontariff kind. The US, backed by the other advanced industrialised countries, wanted some initial progress to be made in the course of the Uruguay Round towards lowering these barriers and improving market access as well as establishing new rules and disciplines to govern trade in services.

A further concern of the US was the extent to which US technology was being reproduced or copied by producers in other countries, particularly developing countries, without consent and without due payment of royalties. Whereas the US had laws which protected the owners of so-called intellectual property from its illicit use, this was not the case in all other countries. The US wanted an international agreement to ensure that *intellectual property rights* were respected in all countries. It was largely disillusioned with the attempts to gain voluntary agreement through bodies such as the World Intellectual Property Organisation (WIPO) and favoured incorporating trade-related aspects of intellectual property rights (TRIPs) in the GATT with provision for effective sanctions against those infringing such rights. As with services, this was strongly resisted by the developing countries.

Finally and as a third issue, the US wanted the new round to discuss *trade-related investment measures* (TRIMs) which affect trade. Traditionally, the GATT had been solely concerned with trade and not with investment. However, it was argued that the two could no longer be entirely separated. Globalisation was widely regarded as the main factor contributing to this situation. In particular, policies which governments frequently adopt towards foreign investment have a direct impact on trade. For example, if governments stipulate that foreign companies allowed to invest in their countries must purchase some proportion of their components and parts from local firms rather than import them from abroad, trade is impeded. The US wanted new GATT rules to govern such trade-related investment measures.

This chapter examines each of these 'new' issues. The first half of the chapter discusses both the nature of trade in services and the problems involved in liberalising this trade. The new General Agreement on Trade in Services (GATS), concluded as part of the Uruguay Round, is examined along with future prospects for improved market access in services. The second half of the chapter is concerned with the two other 'new issues', namely, trade-related aspects of intellectual property rights (TRIPs) and trade-related investment measures (TRIMs). In each case, the nature of the issues involved is discussed, followed by a close look at the agreements reached in the Uruguay Round.

TRADE IN SERVICES

The original GATT Treaty contains no specific provisions covering trade in services although the rules applicable to goods may be applied to certain kinds of this trade. Moreover, none of the GATT rounds before the Uruguay Round paid any attention to barriers to trade in services. As a result, this became a neglected area in the process of trade liberalisation, except where countries entered into regional trading agreements which incorporated provisions for services. Partly for this reason, it has become one of the most barrier-ridden areas of trade. Why then the sudden interest in services in the recently concluded Uruguay Round? Undoubtedly, the major reason is the rapid growth of trade in services which has taken place in recent decades and the fact that for certain countries exports of services have become a major source of export earnings.

The growth of trade in services partly mirrors a process which has been taking place domestically within all the advanced industrialised economies. A declining manufacturing sector has gone hand in hand with a growing service sector. Thus, in the UK services now employ 59 per cent of the labour force and account for 51 per cent of GDP, while the comparable figures for the US are 66 per cent and 54 per cent. At the domestic level, several different factors have been at work, causing output of services to expand. As average incomes have risen in the advanced industrialised countries, households have increased their demand for services which improve the quality of their lives and which are associated with the increased leisure time they now enjoy. Many of the consumer-durable goods which consumers bought as they became better off require large services inputs (for example, videocassette recorders, personal computers, and so on), so the demand for these services has grown with consumption. At the same time, the rise of the modern corporation, with its increased sophistication, international scope and complexity, has led to an increased demand for certain kinds of business services. A third factor has been a tendency for firms to hive off to specialist firms services which were previously performed in-house, a process known as 'splintering'. In many cases, this enables firms to obtain better-quality service provision at lower cost.

However, trade in services has also been stimulated by a process of internationalisation which has been taking place in a number of key service sectors. In recent years, trade in services has been growing consistently faster than merchandise trade. Porter (1990) considers there were six factors driving this trend: a tendency towards growing similarity of service needs in different countries; increased mobility of service buyers around the world; increased importance of economies of scale in service provision that favoured supplying global markets; the increased ease with which service personnel can travel to foreign markets to deliver foreign services; technological change making possible greater interaction between service buyers and providers over long distances; and wider differences between countries in the cost, quality and range of services supplied. One result of this is that now, for many advanced industrialised countries and not a few developing countries, earnings from the export of services account for a significant proportion of total export earnings. For example, services account for 39 per cent of export earnings in the US, 34 per cent in the UK, 38 per cent in France, 34 per cent in Switzerland, 38 per cent in Spain and 52 per cent in Singapore. Services also account for a large and growing proportion of the cost of imports of most countries.

What are services and how are they distinguished from goods? Most attempts at defining services have emphasised one or more of the following:

1 goods are tangible while services are intangible;
2 goods are visibile while services are invisible;
3 goods are capable of being stored while services are nonstorable;
4 goods are permanent whereas services are transient.

Objections can be raised to some or all of these characteristics. For example, although services are often invisible, this is not always the case: a haircut is visible if the service is identified by its outcome. Equally, not all goods have permanence: food may be consumed and disappear more quickly than the time taken to perform many services (for example, a live musical concert). Many services are nonstorable and have to be produced and consumed at the same time. This is one reason why trade in services is often lower than trade in goods, but this is not true of all services. A large number of services can now be provided at a distance and communicated electronically (for example, data transmission by fax). Another important group of services is *embodied* in tangible objects (such as a computer program) and are traded in much the same way as goods.

Hill (1977) suggested that the distinction between a good and a service resides in the *effects* of each. He defined a service as 'a change in the condition of a person, or of a good, belonging to an economic unit, brought about by the activity of another economic unit with the former's consent'. Thus, certain services effect changes in the conditions of people, such as education, health or entertainment, while other services effect changes in the conditions of goods, such as transport, warehousing or after-sales services. Some, such as financial services, may affect both persons and goods. By contrast, a good is 'a physical object which is appropriable and therefore transferable between units'. Nicolaides (1989b) questions the emphasis on effect, which pays too much attention to the end result of the activity. The purchase of a good may equally well change the condition of a person, whereas not all services effect any change. He suggests that the emphasis should be placed on services as *processes*. He defines a service as 'an agreement or undertaking by the service-provider to perform now or in the future a series of tasks over a specified period of time towards a particular objective'.

One useful distinction is between those services which require close physical proximity of user and provider and those which do not. The former are often referred to as *nontraded* or *factor services*. Where services have to be produced and consumed at the same time, a number of consequences follow. Either the service-provider must move where to the service-demander is located or the service-demander must move to the service-provider. Thus, Stern and Hoekman (1987) draw a distinction between *demander-located services* and *provider-located services*. Demander- or user-located services require the service-provider either to set up a branch in the foreign market or to move temporarily to the foreign market to perform the service. Examples of the former are services such as accounting, advertising, banking, consultancy and distribution. An example of a temporary movement of the service-provider is engineering services. Thus, demander- or user-located services necessitate either foreign direct investment by service-providers and/or labour migration, in the form of a temporary or permanent movement of service personnel. Provider-located services require the users to move to the country where the service they require is provided. Examples include tourism, education, health, and airport services.

Services which do not require user and provider to be in close physical proximity are variously known as 'separated' (Sampson and Snape, 1985), 'disembodied' or 'long-distance' services (Bhagwati 1984). The service may be thought of as having been separated from its original production, or disembodied, and embodied instead in goods for sale separately. Examples of separated services are books, scientific documents, legal documents, computer software, films and records. Trade in these kinds of service is very much like trade in goods; indeed such trade is often classified as merchandise rather than services. This begs the question: what distinguishes such services from goods? To varying degrees, all goods are embodiments of factor services. The answer is the proportion of the value of the traded substance which can be attributed to value added by a service as opposed to a manufacturing activity. Where a very high proportion of the value added is accounted for by a service activity, it should be regarded as a service rather than a good. However, any attempt to distinguish between trade in separated services and goods will necessarily always be arbitrary and indeed may serve little purpose. A further category of separated services is messages which are communicated through modern telecommunication services. These require no embodiment of the service in a good, although as Grubel (1987) points out, all such messages are recordable and measurable and are therefore similar in kind to separated services such as books or floppy discs.

The issue of how services are defined has assumed some importance in international trade policy in recent years. Developing countries who were less keen on the inclusion of services in the Uruguay Round negotiations tended to argue for a narrow definition while developed countries favoured a broad definition. It is clear that trade in certain factor or nonseparated services would involve the GATT in investment matters rather than in the trade issues with which the GATT has in the past been primarily concerned. Liberalising trade in these services requires countries reducing their restrictions on factor movements. A key issue is the right of establishment, that is to say, the right of a foreign service-provider to set up a branch in another country and for service personnel to enter and stay in the foreign country to provide the service. Developing countries argued that this was not an issue with which the GATT should be concerned. If these issues were to be the subject of negotiations between countries, any agreement reached should be distinct from any other GATT-based agreement. The implication was that negotiations should be confined to separated or long-distance services and that only trade in such services constituted 'pure' service trade. In the case of trade in services, however, and to a much greater extent than trade in goods, the traditional distinction between trade and investment breaks down. In the end, the argument was won by the 'broad definition' school and trade in services was defined to include all aspects. In fact, as Bhagwati (1987) argues, to exclude services which require significant factor movements would rule out an important class of services of which certain developing countries could become leading exporters.

One of the problems encountered in the negotiations to liberalise trade in services has been the inadequacy of much of the available data as a measure of the true extent of the trade. Conventionally, statistical data on trade in services is derived from the 'invisibles' component of the current account of a country's balance of payments. Countries which belong to the IMF are required to collect and report these amounts according to carefully defined guidelines laid down by the IMF. The results are published in the *IMF Balance of Payments Yearbook*. Invisibles have three main elements: a country's net earnings or payments arising from the export and import of services; net investment income on property held abroad; and transfers. The first component measures the value of exports of certain kinds, including shipping, other transportation, passenger services, travel, other private services and other government services. Other private services include the income of temporary workers, income from royalties and other intellectual property, and residual services. The latter covers a vast range including the fastest-growing services such as insurance, banking, telecommunications, construction, software and data-processing. Transfers include the transfers of migrant workers, workers' remittances and other official transfers.

However, as the GATT Secretariat concluded in a major study of trends in services trade, official statistics can only provide approximate estimates of the true extent of such trade and almost certainly understate its true extent (GATT, 1989). Firstly, a large but unknown proportion of trade in services goes unrecorded. Unlike trade in goods, trade in services cannot be recorded at the border or customs post but has to depend on the reported earnings less payments of service firms and other relevant data. One aspect of this which may be particularly important is the element of services trade which is intra-firm or in-house. Secondly, some trade in separated services is subsumed under the heading of trade in goods, where services are embodied in goods. Thirdly, the statistics may fail to record trade in certain kinds of nonseparated services. As explained above, trade in demander-located services involves a movement of capital and/or labour to a foreign country. Capital flows are recorded elsewhere in the balance of payments. However, it is not the factor flow as such which constitutes trade but the earnings of factors which are derived from providing a service in the foreign country. The item 'net investment income from property held abroad' will include some of these earnings, although this will also include the earnings of nonservice firms. Generally speaking, it includes only those earnings which are repatriated to the home country and so excludes earnings reinvested abroad. Migrant transfers and workers' remittances may also record some of the earnings derived by labour from service activities abroad. Finally, while tourism is recorded under invisibles, trade in some demander-located services (such as medicine and education) may not be.

Liberalising trade in services

For a variety of reasons, trade in services is subject to more government-imposed distortion than trade in goods. This makes the welfare gain from liberalising trade in services potentially very great. However, the barriers impeding such trade are generally very different from those affecting goods. Merchandise trade is largely impeded by tariffs or other kinds of border control. The degree of restriction is generally not too difficult to calculate and thus to quantify. Border restrictions may also constitute a barrier for traded or separated services since this kind of trade is no different to goods trade. However, for nontraded services, border measures are less important than other types of restriction. Since these kinds of services require the movement of factors, controls on factor movements act as the main impediment to trade. In particular, restrictions on the right of establishment may effectively deny access to the market of the importing country for foreign service providers. Even if the importing country does allow foreign service firms the right of establishment, it may still discriminate against them in other ways by denying them the same rights as national firms. The impact of restrictions of these kinds are much more difficult to measure. This makes negotiations more complex because it is not possible for countries to calculate the benefit or loss from any particular concession.

Trade barriers in the service sector mainly result from the desire of governments to exercise a high degree of regulatory control over service provision. Thus, government regulation is far more widespread in the service than the goods sector. This may be due to certain characteristics of service provision which result in the market failing to allocate resources in an efficient manner. On the other hand, it may equally well occur for protectionist reasons as when a service sector is deemed to be of sufficient national importance to justify government intervention. Nicolaides (1989b) suggests two reasons why government regulation of service provision can be justified on efficiency grounds; firstly, the fact that the information available to buyers is often imperfect or incomplete. There seem to be two aspects to this: because of the intangible nature of services and the fact that a service may only be purchased at the same time as it is provided, buyers cannot assess the quality of a service in advance of consumption; at the same time, there is a problem of asymmetric information between service-providers and buyers. The service-provider has more information about the service than the buyer. This seems to be particularly true of professional services like accountancy, medicine and law. As a result, government regulation is needed to protect the consumer from low-quality services. Regulation is also needed to deal with the 'adverse selection' problem whereby high-quality services suffer because buyers are not able to distinguish between providers of differing competence. Secondly, services sometimes suffer from a problem of 'systemic failure'. This can be seen in the banking sector where the failure of one bank may have adverse effects on the entire banking system if the confidence of depositors is undermined. Regulation is needed to prevent unsound or imprudent banks inflicting damage on competent ones.

Where, because of market imperfections, governments regulate any economic activity, a barrier to trade is necessarily created, particularly where rules differ between countries. On grounds of economic efficiency such regulation is desirable and it should not be the aim of trade policy to eliminate the restriction. Rather, the major concern must be to ensure that the policy in question is efficient in the sense that it deals with the specific market imperfection at which it is aimed and with minimal adverse side-effects. The problem with many forms of regulation in the service sector is that they give rise to a number of undesirable distortions. This is the case whenever regulation discriminates against a particular country. The discrimination may be intentional or incidental. For example, if government-imposed rules for a particular service sector are more lenient in one country than another, service firms in the stricter country may be at a competitive disadvantage when selling services to a country with more lenient requirements. Potential may also exist for competition to be distorted whenever regulatory policies leave a large measure of discretion to regulatory authorities in applying the rules to different firms. Nicolaides (1989b) argues that this is more likely to be the case where a country depends on self-regulation of a particular service activity as opposed to relying on government-imposed rules. For example, regulation of financial services in the UK largely relied on self-regulation until the passing of the 1986 Financial Services Act which provided for more formal supervision.

What is not clear, however, is whether the end result of all service-sector regulation is increased efficiency. Very often, efficiency arguments are mixed in with protectionist motives. In this case, mutual gains may be achieved by a reciprocal lowering of barriers in the same way as for goods. However, the method of bringing this about must necessarily be different for services compared with goods. Because of the complex and diverse forms in which trade in services is restricted, it is more difficult for countries to reach agreements in which each country offers reciprocal concessions. As stated above, quantifying the effects of lowering any particular barrier in services is problematic. Very often, there is more than one barrier impeding access. However, as Nicolaides (1989b) shows, many barriers arise as a result of legitimate regulatory intervention by governments necessary to correct a particular form of market failure. The solution is not to remove the restriction but to ensure that the particular form of regulatory measure does not create undesirable trade distortions. A further consideration is that, whenever regulatory policies differ between countries, trade barriers inevitably emerge in order to prevent the effectiveness of policy in the more strictly regulated country being undermined by the less strictly regulated one. For example, in the banking sector, one country may impose stricter capital and liquidity requirements than another. To ensure that foreign banks do not undermine the effectiveness of these measures, restrictions may have to be placed on their freedom to set up branches in a country with stricter requirements. These considerations may favour a dual approach; on the one hand, there may be particular service sectors where countries choose to negotiate a reciprocal lowering of existing barriers to ensure improved market access; on the other hand, a rules-based approach is also necessary in which countries agree to adhere by certain international principles designed to ensure fairness and efficiency in the global allocation of resources.

GATT rules applying to trade in goods are based on the principle of unconditional most-favoured-nation (MFN) treatment which each contracting party is required to extend to every other. A key issue in both academic debate and, above all, in the actual services negotiations within the GATT has been whether this principle should be applied to trade in services. This would mean that each country undertook to treat both the traded services and the service-providers of other countries equally and not to discriminate against those coming from one particular country. Grey (1990) has urged caution in seeking to apply this principle to trade in services in the same way as to trade in goods. To begin with, as we have seen in earlier chapters, there have been so many exceptions to the unconditional MFN rule as applied to goods that we must doubt whether it can practically be applied to services. He concludes:

> With regard to the concept of *unconditional MFN treatment*, there would appear to be little scope for the application of such a clause, given the emerging concern for a measure of *reciprocity*, particularly as regards services delivered by establishments.

On the other hand, he adds: 'It would be a serious mistake, though, to set this key policy concept aside.' Reciprocity makes nondiscriminatory treatment conditional upon the other country treating the traded services or service-providers of the country imposing the restrictions in an equivalent way: 'I will treat your service firms in the same way as you treat mine.'

It is worth pointing out that the principle has a precedent within the GATT. It was adopted as the basis for the GATT Codes on Subsidies and Countervailing Duties and Government Procurement in the Tokyo Round. A country is required to extend the benefits contained in the two codes only to those countries adhering to the Agreement and can withdraw benefits from any country which ceases to do so. It has come to be adopted as a key principle by a number of countries and regions with respect to their service sectors. For example, the European Community had an important clause in its 1989 Second Banking Directive which threatened to withdraw certain benefits from foreign banks operating in the Single Market (for example, suspension or delays in authorisation) and coming from a country which denied national treatment to EC banks.

Reciprocity is also widely practised in the civil aviation industry. For example, one country may reduce or withdraw landing rights from the carrier of another country which is deemed to be discriminating against the airline of the former in its route allocations. This was illustrated by the recent conflict between the US and Japan which began when Japan refused to allow United Airlines to extend its New York–Tokyo flights to Sydney (so-called 'beyond rights') which, the US alleged, violated the 1952 bilateral aviation agreement between the two countries. The US responded with threats to withdraw equivalent rights from Japanese airlines. Since countries with a fairly open policy towards their service industries (such as the US) are unlikely to be willing to grant guarantees of access to foreign service firms without a reciprocity proviso, unconditional MFN may be difficult to apply to services.

A second principle in any rules-based approach to the liberalisation of services trade is the *principle of national treatment*; that is, treating foreign service-providers in the same way as national firms. It therefore addresses a different aspect of nondiscrimination. It has been suggested that this is preferable to a stipulation that countries treat all foreign service firms equally (see Nicolaides, 1989b) in view of the difficulties of applying unconditional MFN in a world where regulatory systems differ so much. The principle allows each country to continue to operate whatever regulatory system it deems appropriate, subject only to the requirement that national and foreign firms are treated alike. The principle already has an international track record. For example, it is written into the Chicago Convention of 1944 which established the International Civil Aviation Organisation (ICAO) to regulate the industry. Countries are to afford national treatment to foreign airlines with respect to the use of airports and other facilities, although it does not cover route-sharing. The principle of national treatment is also established by the OECD in its Decision on National Treatment (OECD, 1978) which requires OECD countries to treat multinational companies equally with nationally owned companies once they have been established. This applies to service industries as well as manufacturing but does not specifically cover rights of establishment. The GATT itself under Article III also requires signatories to provide national treatment to products imported from other member states 'with regard to matters affecting the internal taxation and regulation of trade in goods'. Since this applies to goods, it cannot be applied to nontraded services although it could be applied to separated services. In many service industries, however, it seems unlikely that all countries would be prepared to agree to this principle. For example, many countries are not prepared to allow foreign airlines equal rights with domestic carriers to operate domestic routes. The same is true of shipping, where many countries restrict shipping within their own territorial waters to vessels owned by domestic shipping companies.

Regional liberalisation of trade in services

Liberalisation of trade in services has taken place at both the regional and the multilateral level. Let us begin with regional trading agreements. Services trade has been included in a number of the regional trading arrangements discussed in Chapter 7. The EU's Single Market programme and the agreement setting up the European Economic Area (EEA) provided for a fully liberalised market in services. In fact, the original Treaty of Rome contained articles which provided for the free movement of persons, services and capital as well as of goods. These included the 'right of establishment' and the 'freedom to supply services' set out in Article 59. This stated that 'restrictions on the free supply of services within the Community shall be progressively abolished in the course of the transitional period'. Article 67 also provides for the abolition of all restrictions on the movement of capital 'belonging to persons resident in member states and any discriminatory treatment based on nationality or place of residence or the place in which such capital is invested'. However, it said nothing about how these objectives were to be achieved. In practice, little progress was made in the area of services in the first decades of the Community.

The EC's White Paper on the Internal Market published in 1985 (the Cockfield Report) included legislative proposals for achieving a European common market for services. The measures were intended to cover both traditional services, such as transport, banking and insurance, and new service areas, such as information marketing and audiovisual services. The approach adopted was a dual one. Firstly, member states were required to apply the principle of mutual recognition of each other's national laws and regulations. Secondly, some element of rule harmonisation was attempted. However, harmonisation was confined to agreeing certain minimal requirements acceptable to all member states for individual service industries. Provided that these requirements were met, member states agreed to extend mutual recognition to service-providers of other member states. The approach can be illustrated by the example of financial services. In December 1989, the EC passed the Second Banking Directive which paved the way for a single market in banking services. Henceforth, banks would be issued with a single banking licence enabling them to operate in any part of the EC market, provided that they satisfied the provisions relating to minimum capital and solvency. It meant that any bank operating outside its own home country would have to meet the same standards as other banks. The licence covered a wide range of activities including deposit-taking and lending, money transmission, securities trading and providing financial advice. It meant that no member state could any longer deny right of access to a bank from another member state which held the single banking licence. A member state operating stricter regulatory requirements for its own domestic banks could not require a bank based in another member state to adhere to its own restrictions. On the other hand, all registered banks would have to meet the agreed minimum requirements with regard to capital and solvency.

An Investment Services Directive similarly prepared the way for investment firms to do business anywhere in the Single Market. It was modelled on the Second Banking Directive. The legal framework for a single insurance market was also agreed in time for the 1 January 1993 deadline. The approach was much the same as for other financial services; namely, mutual recognition by national regulatory authorities and freedom for companies to operate on the basis of a single insurance licence. One controversial aspect of the EC approach to liberalising the market for financial services was the policy adopted towards providers of financial services from third countries. The Second Banking Directive contained a controversial reciprocity provision whereby the EC is empowered to take retaliatory measures against any other country which denies national treatment to EC banks. However, before such measures can be taken, the Commission is required to draw up proposals for the Council to negotiate 'comparable access'. Retaliation could take the form of suspension of or delays in requests for authorisation. It should be pointed out that this was a considerably watered-down version of the reciprocity provision contained in the original draft under which a foreign bank could be refused a banking licence if EC banks were denied national treatment and competitive opportunities in foreign markets.

A key service sector which was left out of the original EC proposals for a single market but which subsequently has become the subject of an EC Single Market initiative is telecommunications. A distinctive feature of liberalisation of this sector has been the need to achieve harmonisation of technical standards. The attempts by the EC to liberalise this market sector has involved action at several different levels. Firstly, in November 1988 the EC agreed a controversial directive which guaranteed broadcasters the right to transmit TV channels anywhere in Europe, provided that they contained a majority of EC programmes and achieved minimum quality and morality standards. Subsequently, this involved the EC in a lengthy controversy with the US in the Uruguay Round negotiations over films. Secondly, in 1988, relying on Article 90 of the Treaty of Rome which allows the EC to take action against public monopolies failing to comply with the EC's competition rules, the EC issued a directive to liberalise the market for terminal equipment. Trade in this equipment had long been restricted by national monopolies, discriminatory public procurement policies and problems of different technical standards. Thirdly, in December 1989 the EC agreed a further package of measures to open up the EC market for advanced telecommunication services such as electronic mail and access to databases. As part of the same package, basic data services were subject to liberalisation with effect from the beginning of 1993. Traditionally, these services have been monopolised by the various national post, telegraph and telephone authorities (PTTs), with no outside competition. A related harmonisation directive sought to define the technical and legal standards under which service-providers could gain access to networks. Recently, the EU has announced its intention to introduce further measures with a view to achieving full liberalisation of all telecommunication services (including international and domestic telephone calls) by 1 January 1998.

The EC White Paper *Completing the Internal Market* named transport as another key service sector where liberalisation was essential. Article 7 of the Treaty of Rome made a clear provision for the setting up of a Common Transport Policy based on 'no discrimination on grounds of nationality'. A key issue was the failure of member states to allow the practice of 'cabotage' – allowing road haulage carriers of other member states to operate transport services within their own state. A European Court of Justice ruling in 1985 required the member states to make urgent progress towards ending this practice. There was strong resistance from certain countries (notably France and Germany) who were afraid that their own more highly regulated and costly markets would be vulnerable to competition from cheaper, more efficient hauliers in other member states. France felt especially vulnerable because of her large and centrally located domestic market. Nevertheless, in December 1989, agreement was reached on a temporary and partial liberalisation of the transport market. This was achieved by giving each member state an initial quota of cabotage permits valid for a specified period of time (up to two months) for distribution to individual companies which allowed hauliers to do business across the Community. At the same time, hauliers practising cabotage would be required to observe certain minimum requirements to ensure public safety and environmental considerations. This experimental phase lasted until the end of 1992 at which point it was replaced by a plan for total deregulation by the end of 1998. Thus, opening up the market for road transport has required specific measures to abolish discriminatory laws, and action to achieve some elements of harmonisation in the areas of safety and environmental controls.

Attempts to liberalise the market for air transport in the EC have proved more difficult. This market remains highly regulated, most air travel being subject to bilateral agreements between governments providing for route-sharing, capacity controls, revenue-sharing, the fixing of fares, and arrangements for landing slots and other ground facilities. An important aspect of these arrangements was to prevent any airline offering air services outside its home country. For example, Aer Lingus could not offer a service between Paris and Rome. In 1988, the EC introduced an initial set of liberalisation measures. These allowed airlines limited 'fifth freedom' advantages – they could operate services between any two countries other than their own home country provided that they used regional and not main airports. The second aviation package introduced further liberalisation by making possible 'fifth freedom' services from main airports.

The Canadian–US Free Trade Agreement (CUSFTA) included a chapter on services (Chapter XIV) which was widely regarded as being of fairly minimal significance. It established the principle of national treatment and granted the right of establishment to service-providers in each member state. However, this was qualified by two considerations. Firstly, these principles were only applicable to new measures introduced by either country. Existing regulatory measures were 'grandfathered', which means that they were introduced before the signing of the agreement and therefore not subject to the terms of the agreement. Secondly, the agreement did not apply to all services, only to those specifically listed in the Annex to the Chapter; these were financial services, tourism, architecture, computer services and telecommunications network-based enhanced services. A significant omission was transport service. CUSFTA also included a 'right of temporary entry' clause for professional workers (Chapter XV). The North American Free Trade Area (NAFTA) essentially built on CUSFTA. All services are subject to obligations for national treatment and nondiscrimination unless specifically excluded or unless there are special derogations for specific policy measures listed in country annexes.

Finally, the Australia–New Zealand Agreement on Closer Economic Relations (ANZCERTA) also contains provisions for services, including a guarantee of national treatment for all service-providers, except where a particular service is specifically excluded from the agreement, and also the right of establishment.

The Uruguay Round negotiations

The original proposal to include services in the Uruguay Round negotiations came from the United States, supported by Canada, Japan and the European Community. According to McCulloch (1993), there were three groups within the US pressing for services to be included: US-based companies in the financial services sector (most notably American Express) keen to secure increased access to markets abroad; US public officals and business people concerned about the US trade deficit in manufactures and arguing that US comparative advantage was shifting towards services; and trade policy experts wishing to see trade liberalisation extended to services. Initially, the proposal was strongly opposed by a number of developing countries led by India and Brazil (the so-called Group of Ten). Their opposition was based on a number of considerations. Firstly, a fear that free trade in services would result in a number of their service sectors (such as banking) falling under foreign control. Secondly, the argument that many service sectors were already covered by other international agreements (shipping by the UNCTAD Liner Conference, aviation by IATA, for example). Thirdly, the fear that they would get caught in a damaging trade-off between services and manufactures, with developed countries making the lowering of any trade barriers on goods conditional upon a liberalisation package which included services. These countries argued that further progress was still necessary to bring down trade barriers affecting goods before services could be included. One aspect of this was a proposal from the developed countries to offer 'roll-backs' of voluntary export restraints and 'standstills' on new protection of goods of interest to developing countries as concessions. Developing countries argued that these should not be concessions but merely an acceptance of existing obligations and should not be linked to the issue of liberalisation of services trade, which was a new issue.

Because of the opposition expressed by the Group of Ten to the inclusion of services, the 1982 GATT ministerial meeting was only able to agree on the need to exchange information on services. Subsequently, only seventeen countries submitted reports to the GATT Secretariat. In June 1985, Brazil argued that the issue of services should be kept separate from any negotiations concerned with goods, a 'dual-track' or 'twin-track' approach. In this way, developing countries' fears of a trade-off between goods and services along the lines explained above could be assuaged. When the Uruguay Round was launched at Punta del Este in September 1986, it was this approach which was adopted. A special Group of Negotiations on Services (GNS) was established, although it would report to the Trade Negotiations Committee (TNC). It was stated that the aim of the negotiations was

to establish a multilateral framework of principles and rules for trade in services, including possible disciplines for individual sectors, with a view to expansion of such trade under conditions of transparency and progressive liberalisation and as a means of promoting economic growth of all trading partners and the development of developing countries.

(GATT, 1986)

The text also stated that

Such framework shall respect the policy objectives of national laws and regulations applying to services and shall take into account the work of relevant international organisations.

(Ibid.)

The statement that the aim of any agreement should be the promotion of economic growth and development was included at the insistence of the developing countries. But the Declaration left unclear the precise status of the negotiations over services: was the intended result to add to the GATT a services agreement or to create an entirely separate agreement governing services?

In January 1987, an initial negotiating agenda for the GNS was agreed. This contained five headings. Firstly, the need to establish a precise definition of the term 'trade in services' and to address the problem of the low quality of statistical information about services trade. Countries were not agreed on what should be counted as trade in services. At the same time, it was argued by some countries that the lack of an adequate database was a barrier to concluding negotiations on services since the impact of any concessions could not be determined. Secondly, the need to establish 'broad concepts on which principles and rules for trade in services, including possible disciplines for individual sectors might be based'. A key issue here was the applicability of GATT rules for goods to trade in services. Thirdly, what should be the coverage of any agreement? Should any sectors be excluded? If the aim was to be the maximum possible participation of countries, there would have to be provision for countries excluding sensitive sectors. Fourthly, the relationship between any such agreement and the various other international agreements which exist for specific service sectors should be looked at, for example, the Chicago Convention regulating air transport or the UN Liner Code governing international shipping. Finally, there was the need to identify the various types of barriers to trade in services on which progress could be made in achieving liberalisation.

Subsequently, various countries submitted papers. A significant difference was apparent between the proposals put forward by the United States and the European Community. The US paper proposed 'a general framework of principles which would ensure unimpeded cross-border trade and movement of service-providers' (Nicolaides, 1989b). There were five main elements contained in the proposals: transparency, nondiscrimination, national treatment, market access, and disciplines on state-sanctioned monopoly providers of services. The kind of most-favoured-nation treatment proposed, however, was conditional MFN, that is, the benefits of the agreement would only be extended to other countries signing the agreement. The agreement should cover all cross-border movement of services and the establishment of foreign subsidiaries.

The EC proposals differed markedly in their approach from those of the US. The former were as described by *The Financial Times* (18 December 1987) in a leader article as 'low-key and workmanlike, concentrating on the need to establish procedures through which barriers to international trade in services can be negotiated away'. A key proposal was for the creation of a regulatory committee to which countries would notify any barriers perceived to be impeding market access. The task would then be to secure the modification or elimination of the barrier through negotiation. Principles such as the right to national treatment or nondiscrimination were seen by the EC as ultimate objectives rather than starting points. They would become binding commitments only when applied on a sector-specific level. However, the absence of any binding commitment to nondiscrimination would make any agreement unattractive to smaller countries. The *FT* leader concluded: 'the framework agreement on services has to be more than a declaration of principle without procedures, on the lines of the US proposal, and more than procedures without principles, as is implicit in the low-keyed EC approach'.

The viewpoint of the developing countries was best illustrated by a paper submitted by Argentina. While accepting the desirability of an agreement on services, it argued that the aim of such an agreement should be to promote the growth and development of the developing countries. This meant that, where necessary, developing countries should be allowed to restrict trade in services.

In December 1988, at the Mid-term Review meeting of the Uruguay Round, it was agreed that the second half of the Round should be concerned with five 'signposts':

1 The GNS was to agree a draft framework agreement for trade in services by the end of 1989.
2 The GATT Secretariat was to prepare a list of service sectors which might be covered by the agreement.
3 The participants were to submit their own list of service sectors in which they have an interest.
4 The GNS was to examine next the implications of applying particular trade concepts, principles and rules to specific service sectors.
5 Specific concepts and principles identified included: the need for transparency in service laws and regulations; the achievement of progressive liberalisation of trade in services; the application of 'national treatment' requirements; the application of most-favoured-nation/

nondiscrimination provision; expectation of market access for service suppliers; facilitation of the expansion of the services sector of developing countries and their increased participation in world trade; safeguards and exceptions; and recognition of the right of governments to regulate the service sector (consistent with commitments made under the multilateral framework) (see GATT, 1988).

In December 1989, the Group of Negotiations on Services (GNS) reached a draft agreement on a framework for trade in services. The agreement stipulated certain principles which were to apply to all services included in the agreement. These principles include: nondiscrimination (for every country subscribing to the agreement); transparency (openness about rules, regulations and procedures affecting services trade); national treatment; and progressive lowering of remaining barriers (but with special flexibility for developing countries). All types of service trade would be covered but countries should be allowed to put 'reservations' on any particular sector which they want to exclude. Subsequently, this latter loophole became the subject of considerable contention as the United States made clear its wish for the exclusion of certain key sectors (namely, shipping, aviation and banking). This then paved the way for other countries to request similar exceptions. Other rules covered safeguards and exceptions, state aids, regional trading blocs, methods of bargaining and disputes settlement.

Paradoxically, the major obstacle to securing agreement on the draft was disagreement between the western industrialised nations. Developing countries largely accepted the timetable and content of the proposals. A number of factors accounted for the change in their stance. Firstly, the proposed agreement contained special provisions to enable them to liberalise their service markets more slowly. Secondly, developing countries became increasingly aware that inefficient service industries acted as a drag on their domestic economies, reducing the competitiveness of their exports of goods *and* services, and hence rate of economic growth and development. Liberalising access to their domestic markets could therefore be beneficial. Thirdly, this realisation had led many developing countries, impressed by the relative success of the South-East Asian industrialising countries and under pressure from western international lending institutions (such as the IMF and World Bank), to adopt policies of privatisation, deregulation and trade liberalisation. A multilateral agreement on services was seen as a means of 'locking-in' domestic policy changes and resisting domestic pressures from adversely affected interest groups (Hoekman, 1993).

The main disagreement between the developed countries centred on the sectors which were to be excluded from the framework provisions. A particular problem was the reluctance of the United States to include three key service sectors in the agreement: telecommunications, civil aviation and shipping. With regard to telecommunications, it argued that the US market was already more open than those of other countries, in contrast to Europe. If the US agreed to nondiscrimination, it would be unable to apply pressure on European countries to open up their markets to US companies. Similarly, the US claimed to operate a relatively liberal policy towards shipping and was reluctant to surrender a bargaining counter which could be used to force other countries similarly to open up their shipping trade to US shipping companies. Civil aviation was widely regarded as being one service sector where the MFN principle would be difficult to apply without renegotiating the complex network of bilateral agreements signed between countries under the Chicago Convention. Nevertheless, in opposition to the US, other countries did favour some application of the MFN principle to aviation; for example, ending discrimination in areas other than landing rights, for example ancillary services such as ground handling and computer reservations. The European Community demanded similar special treatment for broadcasting. It insisted on the right to continue to limit the amount of television viewing time accounted for by non-European programmes. The solution to the problem was to deal with these particular sectors in special annexes to the framework agreement. In addition to transport services, financial services and telecommunications were the subject of specially negotiated annexes. In the case of financial services, a key issue was to agree rules for the prudential supervision of financial institutions needed to safeguard investors.

The Draft Final Act presented by Arthur Dunkel, the GATT Director-General, in December 1992, in an attempt to force negotiators to conclude the Uruguay Round within the agreed time period, contained three elements. Firstly, a framework General Agreement on Trade in Services (GATS) which set out various principles or rules which should govern trade in services. These included national treatment, transparency and most-favoured-nation (MFN) treatment. Secondly, four annexes which contained separate provisions for financial services, telecommunications, civil aviation and movement of labour. Thirdly, there were country schedules in which individual countries made specific market-opening commitments in the sectors listed in their schedules. Although most countries made service offers, these did not add up to very much. Hence the threat by the US to withdraw key service sectors – namely, maritime transport, civil aviation, financial services and telecommunications – from the agreement unless other countries made better offers to open up their services markets. It was not permissible for any country permanently to exclude any sector from the agreement but temporary exemptions of up to ten years were allowed, subject to a review after five years. The EC also made similar threats to exclude specific sectors unless the US improved its market-opening offer in banking. In the last months of the negotiations, the US also indicated that it wanted more in the way of concessions from Europe in the audiovisual sector. When, finally, negotiations were concluded in December 1993, differences between the US and Europe over financial services, audiovisuals and shipping remained unresolved. Instead, it was agreed to negotiate separate deals for these sectors plus telecommunications at a later date. Air transport was left out of the agreement altogether.

The General Agreement on Trade in Services (GATS)

The GATS is divided into three parts.

Parts I and II: general obligations and disciplines

The list of obligations and disciplines set out in Parts I and II applies to any measures taken by member states which affect trade in services (except services supplied in the exercise of governmental authority). Trade in services is defined to cover all modes of supply: cross-border transactions (which do not require the movement of providers or consumers); services which require the movement of consumers to the country where the service is being provided; services which require the commercial presence of the service-provider in the territory of another member state; and services which require the temporary movement of natural persons (service-suppliers or persons employed by a service-supplier).

The major obligation contained in this part of the agreement is the unconditional *most-favoured-nation* rule set out in Article II. This is defined as 'treatment no less favourable than that it accords to like services and service suppliers of any other country'. However, member states may request *temporary* exemption of a particular sector from the nondiscrimination provisions of Article II. Such exemptions should not exceed a period of ten years and would be reviewed after five years.

Other general obligations include:

1 *Transparency* (Article III): requiring each country to 'publish promptly and, except in emergency situations, at the latest by the time of their entry into force, all relevant measures of general application, which pertain to or affect the operation of this Agreement'. In addition, member states are required to establish within two years 'enquiry points' which can provide upon request information to other countries regarding measures in force.

2 *Economic integration* (Article V): allowing countries to enter into regional agreements involving liberalisation of services trade. The conditions are that any such agreement should have 'substantial coverage' (in terms of sectors, volume of trade affected and modes of supply) and should provide for 'the absence or elimination of

substantially all discrimination ... between or among the parties'. However, developing countries would be allowed greater flexibility with regard to these conditions to take account of their level of development. The same requirements for notification of such agreements to the Council for Trade in Services are stipulated as for all regional trading arrangements including provisions for periodic review.

3 *Domestic regulation* (Article VI): recognising a country's right to regulate but requiring that 'all measures of general application affecting trade in services are administered in a reasonable, objective and impartial manner' in sectors where countries have made specific commitments. It states that 'measures relating to qualification requirements and procedures, technical standards and licensing requirements' should not 'constitute unnecessary barriers to trade in services' and provides for the future establishment and development by the Council of Trade in Services of disciplines necessary to ensure that these requirements are met.

4 *Recognition* (Article VII): providing for member states mutually to recognise through harmonisation or otherwise 'the education or experience obtained, requirements met, or licences or certifications granted in a particular country'.

5 *Monopolies and exclusive service suppliers* (Article VIII): requiring countries to ensure that monopoly service-suppliers do not act in a discriminatory manner inconsistent with Article II and with specific commitments, and do not abuse their monopoly power when providing a service to another country.

6 *Business practices* (Article IX): containing a recognition that 'certain business practices of service suppliers' can restrict competition and, if necessary, that countries should seek to eliminate such practices.

7 *Emergency safeguards* (Article X): simply stating that 'there shall be multilateral negotiations on the question of emergency safeguards based on the principle of nondiscrimination' within three years of the agreement entering into force.

8 *Payments and transfers* (Article XI): stating that a country 'shall not apply restrictions on international transfers and payments for current transactions relating to its specific commitments'.

9 *Balance of payments safeguards* (Article XII): allowing countries to apply restrictions to trade in services in the event of a serious balance of payments crisis, provided that the measures do not exceed those needed to deal with the crisis and provided that they do not discriminate among members. The measures must also be temporary and be phased out progressively as the situation allows.

10 *Exceptions* (Article XIV): these are to include any measures necessary to protect public morals, maintain public order, protect public health, prevent fraud, protect individual privacy and ensure public safety.

11 *Subsidies* (Article XV): recognising that subsidies may distort trade in services and providing for future negotiation of the 'necessary multilateral disciplines'.

Parts III and IV: specific commitments

A list of specific commitments which countries have agreed to apply only to those service sectors and sub-sectors listed in their schedules is contained in Part III.

1 *Article XVI* sets out a country's obligations in respect of *market access*. It lists measures which a country may not adopt in sectors where market access commitments are undertaken. These include: limits on the number of service suppliers; on the total value of service transactions; on the number of service operations; on the number of natural persons to be employed necessary for the supply of a particular service; measures which force a service-supplier to supply a service through a particular legal means; and limits on the percentage share of a foreign investment which may be accounted for by foreign shareholders.

2 *Article XVII* requires countries to guarantee *national treatment* for foreign service-suppliers in those sectors listed in their schedules. This is defined as 'treatment no less favourable than that it accords to its own like services and service-suppliers'. However, this need not mean identical treatment to that which it accords to domestic service-suppliers as, in some cases, this could mean less favourable treatment for foreign service-suppliers.

3 *Article XIX* requires all members of the GATS to enter into successive rounds of negotiations no later than five years after the agreement comes into force to achieve a 'progressively higher level of liberalisation'. However, it specifically recognises that greater flexibility should be allowed for developing countries in the opening up of their service sectors in accordance with their 'development situation'.

4 *Article XX* of Part IV makes it clear that schedules of specific commitments must specify '(a) terms, limitations and conditions of market access; (b) conditions and qualifications of national treatment; (c) undertakings relating to additional commitments; (d) where appropriate the time-frame for implementation of such commitments; (e) date of entry into force of such commmitments'.

Annexes

Attached to the framework agreement are a number of annexes for sectors which are to be subject to special provisions. Firstly, there is an annex of exemptions from Article II, the MFN requirement. Secondly, there is an annex on movement of natural persons supplying services or employed by a service supplier. Thirdly, there are sector-specific annexes for financial services, telecommunications, air transport services, basic telecommunications and maritime transport services.

* * * *

This three-tiered structure for the GATS conforms with what was proposed by leading experts on the subject in the early stages of the negotiations (see Jackson, 1988). It would not have been possible to gain the assent of many countries to a set of general obligations to be applied to all service activities in an indefinite and unclear way. This would have been equivalent to asking countries to sign a blank cheque since the information did not exist for determining the precise effect of each obligation on all service activities. For example, few countries would have been prepared to agree to the principle of national treatment being applied to all service sectors. The preferred approach was therefore to experiment with these rules in a small number of service sectors initially and, in the light of that experience, seek to apply similar rules to other sectors as and when countries were ready to do so. Furthermore, it is clear that many of the rules which are desirable for most trade in services may not be workable in particular service sectors. Hence, these sectors had to be treated separately.

There seems to be widespread agreement that the section of the agreement setting out general obligations leans in the direction of the 'soft' approach favoured in the negotiations by the EC and many developing countries and contrasts with the 'hard' approach of the US (Hoekman, 1993). The most important general binding obligation contained in the first part of the agreement is that of nondiscrimination or most-favoured-nation treatment. It should be pointed out that this is an obligation to extend unconditional MFN to other members. On the other hand, countries are allowed temporary exemptions from Article II for sectors listed in the annexes. It was always recognised that there would have to be some exceptions for specific sectors. However, concern has been expressed about the extent to which countries have used this clause to exempt important sectors from the MFN requirement. It remains to be seen whether these exemptions will undermine the application of the MFN principle.

Other principles such as national treatment and market access are given only a sector-specific application. That is to say, they only apply to those sectors which countries specifically list in their schedules. Moreover, if countries list specific measures in their schedules, these principles may not even apply to the latter. Hoekman (1993) makes the point that this 'positive list' approach whereby countries must list the sectors to which these obligations apply – as opposed to the 'negative list' approach of applying the obligations to all sectors except those listed – was a concession to the developing countries.

Clearly, the impact of the agreement will depend on the number of specific commitments or sectoral offers that countries make, their sectoral coverage and the extent of liberalisation which these entail. Using data compiled by the World Bank and OECD, Hoekman (1993) found initial offers made by both industrialised and developing countries to be wide-ranging in their sectoral coverage. By early 1993, the EU and the US had made offers covering respectively two-thirds and one-half of the GNS list of service sectors. The average unweighted coverage ratio of initial offers of industrialised countries exceeded 75 per cent. For developing countries, the weighted average coverage ratio was estimated at 31 per cent. In many cases, however, offers made merely entailed a commitment to maintain the status quo which, although important, does not result in any actual liberalisation of trade. This makes it difficult to gauge the likely impact of sectoral offers on world trade. Nevertheless, aside from the specific sector commitments made by countries, the rules and disciplines set out in the GATS will boost trade in services. As Hoekman points out, to the extent that service suppliers are faced with discriminatory treatment at the present time, the application of the MFN principle should itself result in improved market access. Also, the establishment of the contact/enquiry point system can be expected to improve export opportunities. Governments may also find that the existence of the GATS makes it easier to implement domestic policies of deregulation in their service industries and to resist attempts by domestic suppliers and other interest groups to restrict market access.

One disappointing outcome of the services negotiations was the failure of countries to reach agreement on four sectors: basic telecommunications, maritime transport, financial services and movement of labour. Instead, negotiations on these sectors were to continue within a five-year period following the conclusion of the Round. Negotiations on the opening up of the basic telecommunications sector (mostly voice telephone networks) floundered on the unwillingness of countries to allow state-owned monopolies to be subject to competition from foreign companies. Increasing privatisation and/or deregulation in many countries, however, has meant that more countries are willing to agree to liberalisation. The unwillingness of the US to make more than a few concessions on ocean shipping prevented progress in this sector. Likewise, liberalisation in the financial services sector was held up by US was unwillingness to provide nondiscriminatory access for financial services from other countries unless these countries (in particular Japan and certain other Asian and Latin American countries) made more substantial market-opening offers. Finally, on people moving temporarily abroad to provide services (labour movement), developed countries were not prepared to go as far as most developing countries (India and the Philippines in particular) were seeking.

In a recent and more critical assessment of the GATS, Hoekman (1995) has questioned both the degree of liberalisation which it has achieved and the mechanisms which it establishes as a basis for future rounds of negotiations. Although the sectoral coverage of specific commitments by member states is high, many of these commitments are inadequate because they relate only to certain aspects of the Agreement. The willingness of a country to enter a particular sector on its schedule says nothing about the degree of liberalisation which this will entail. In most cases, commitments involve little more than a binding of the status quo; that is to say, countries agree not to introduce measures which violate the principles of national treatment or market access set out in the GATS. Far from implying any element of liberalisation, it may mean that because exceptions can be entered, certain policies violating the principle of the GATS are effectively reinforced. Moreover, it does not preclude the possibility that a country might introduce other measures which are not covered by the GATS market-access article and therefore not prohibited. Furthermore, measures showing the proportion of sectors which countries have entered in their schedules says nothing about the relative importance of these sectors in their trade or GDP. Hoekman (1995) has sought to get round some of these problems by calculating sectoral coverage taking into account the degree of restrictiveness implied and the relative importance of a sector in a country's GDP and in global GDP. One significant result is that the proportion of sectors in which commitments implied no restrictions at all on either market access or national treatment had a weighted coverage ratio of only 28 per cent for higher income countries and only 6.4 per cent for other GATS members. With regard to the specific commitments actually made by countries, Hoekman (1995) comments: 'it appears that virtually all commitments are of a standstill nature, i.e. consist of a binding of (or part of) the status quo', indicating that this was the perception of the negotiators themselves.

Hoekman expresses additional concerns about the structure established by the GATS as a basis for progressive liberalisation in the future. He identifies four particular structural weaknesses of the GATS. Firstly, it does not do enough to further the goal of transparency: it does not provide for countries supplying any information about restrictions and discrimination in those sectors in which they have chosen to make no commitments. Yet, because of the preferred positive-list approach, only sectors in which countries have chosen to make commitments are covered. Without information of this kind, future negotiations are necessarily made more difficult.

Secondly, GATS adopts a largely sector-specific approach in the sense that most of the commitments which member states enter into depend on the sectors which they select to include on the GATS' positive list. A sectoral approach means that future negotiations will tend to be driven by the special concerns and interests of service-providers in each service industry. Also, with the positive-list approach preferred by the GATS negotiators, it becomes easier for individual sectors to argue against their inclusion. A negative-list approach would have been better because the onus would be upon individual sectors to justify why they should be excluded.

Thirdly, the specific commitments entered into by member states are scheduled according to the mode of service supply: cross-border, consumption abroad, commercial presence (FDI) or temporary entry of natural persons. Hoekman sees this as creating the potential for further distortions if countries make greater commitments under a particular mode of supply. For example, a country may make its least restrictive commitments under the commercial presence mode of supply in order to encourage direct investment by foreign service-providers in their country. Indeed, this appears to have been the approach adopted by developing countries in the services negotiations.

Finally, there are problems in the rather limited number of generic rules contained within the GATS. Since there is no general requirement that the status quo in relation to matters such as national treatment and market access be bound, a possible incentive exists for countries to adopt policies that are in principle prohibited, with a view to negotiating these away in the future.

The GATS thus contains the potential for increasing restrictions on trade in services. Despite these criticisms, Hoekman (1995) concludes that these 'architectural shortcomings' are not too difficult to put right in the future although this will be necessary if the GATS is to bring further liberalisation of services trade in the future.

An addendum

At the time this book was being completed, agreement was reached on a package of measures for liberalising financial services after several months of tense negotiations. This was an interim pact intended to run up to the end of 1997 but which excluded the United States, the first time ever that a global trading agreement has been reached without the participation of the US. When the deadline was reached for the negotiations at the end of June 1995, the US indicated that it could not grant access to its financial services market on a nondiscriminatory (MFN) basis because of the inadequacy of the liberalisation proposals made by other countries (chiefly, Asian) participating in the negotiations. Particular US concerns were reported to have been the refusal of certain emerging economies to enshrine in the WTO agreement existing foreign ownership levels and operating freedoms (de Jonquires and Williams, 1995). In effect, the US made clear that, while foreign companies already operating in the US would not be denied continuing access and would be assured equal treatment with domestic firms, new entrants would receive no such assurances. Instead, the US promised to treat these countries as well and no better than US companies are treated in the foreign market. It was her clear intention to use the promise of MFN treatment to prise further concessions out of countries whose markets were important to the US. Developing countries, on the other hand, indicated that they could move no faster than domestic opposition would allow. There were also concerns that too rapid an opening-up of their financial markets could precipitate a Mexican-type financial crisis.

The US position was not shared by the EU. Writing in *The Financial Times*, the EU's prime negotiator, Sir Leon Brittan, urged the US to reach agreement, on the grounds that the package offered substantial benefits. At the same time, little could be gained from efforts to gain bilateral leverage since most of the countries at which US threats were aimed were unlikely to seek access to the markets of developed countries. Even if such an approach could work, it would do so too slowly and serve to undermine the search for multilateral solutions to trading problems in other areas (Brittan, 1995).

In the face of US intransigence, the EU successfully pressed for a postponement of the negotiating deadline. At the same time, it managed to persuade other WTO members to stand by their existing commitments, even given the reluctance of the US to come on board. The solution achieved was an interim agreement running for two and a half years to the end of 1997. Coverage was reported to amount to as much as 90 per cent of world financial services, including banking, securities markets and insurance equivalent to about 5 per cent of world output. In fact, most of the concessions made by countries amount merely to guarantees of existing market access rather than leading to genuine market-opening measures (*The Financial Times*, 27 July 1995). The most important offers came from the Asian countries, including commitments by Japan and South Korea to improve foreign access to their insurance and securities markets and by Thailand to raise its offers on banking licences.

Although disappointing in its failure significantly to open up market access in financial services and to incorporate the US fully, the agreement is the first of its kind. Moreover, it includes several emerging nations which in the past have opposed liberalisation, as well as bigger zones such as the EU and Japan. It therefore constitutes an important basis for future liberalisation. It remains to be seen what outcome will follow the next set of sectoral negotiations covering telecommunications.

TRADE-RELATED INTELLECTUAL PROPERTY RIGHTS (TRIPS)

The second of the 'new issues' placed on the agenda of the Uruguay Round comprised trade-related aspects of intellectual property rights, or TRIPs for short. As with services, it was introduced at the bequest of the advanced industrialised nations and the United States in particular. Their concern was with the alleged 'theft' through so-called piracy, counterfeiting and imitation of knowledge created by companies in the western industrialised countries. They wanted an international agreement to protect intellectual property rights as a quid pro quo for further lowering trade barriers against goods coming from developing countries. This was one aspect of the Uruguay Round which was concerned essentially with increasing rather than reducing protection. Although agreement was eventually reached, the issue generated some of the greatest heat of any item on the agenda of the Round. The developed countries saw the matter as one of natural rights, specifically the right to protection against a practice which they viewed as tantamount to theft. The copying or imitating of someone else's ideas without the agreement of the proprietor of the knowledge and without compensation was viewed as being an infringement of the rights of the inventor, author or creator. Developing countries viewed the matter in an entirely different manner. They saw any attempt to enforce protection of intellectual property rights as an attempt by western companies to exploit monopoly power and extract increased economic rents at the expense of relatively poor consumers in developing countries. To a greater extent than almost any other issue in the Round, intellectual property rights became a confrontation between developed and developing countries.

What are intellectual property rights? Maskus (1991) has defined intellectual property as 'an asset created by the discovery of new information with commercial or artistic usefulness'. By its very nature, knowledge assumes many of the features of a public good. Once produced, it is difficult to restrict the benefits which the knowledge generates to those prepared to pay for it. This reduces the market value of the knowledge since no buyer will pay a high price for knowledge which can be obtained more cheaply or freely by some other means. The true social value of the knowledge in question thus exceeds its private value. Put differently, the creator of the knowledge fails to appropriate the true return on his/her investment. Hence, society will tend to underinvest in creating new knowledge, increasingly so the greater are the difficulties of achieving full appropriability.

In most western industrialised countries, this has led to the passing of laws which give some protection to innovators. Hence, the notion of an intellectual property right. It should be emphasised that protection is usually confined to the physical expression of a new idea whether in the form of a product, the process of producing a product, book, musical recording, and so on, rather than the idea itself. Stern (1987) defines intellectual property rights as 'a state-granted power to secure the aid of the state, for a limited number of years, to prevent unauthorised persons from commercially exploiting a new idea, which the person owns'.

Patents

Intellectual property rights come in a number of different forms. Patent law grants protection to the innovator of a new industrial product or process of manufacture. Usually, a patent grants the holder a temporary monopoly in the country in which it is registered. Practice varies between countries but in the UK and most of Europe the normal duration of a patent is twenty years from the date the patent is filed. In the US, patents are normally granted for seventeen years from the date the grant is issued. Since it usually takes two to three years to grant a patent, the period is more or less equivalent to that in Europe. National patent laws also differ in the products which are eligible for such protection. For example, pharmaceuticals are not patentable in all countries. Patents for the same product or process can be registered in more than one country. Patents may also be sold or licensed to another producer in return for payment of royalties, giving the owner of the patent a share in future profits. In some countries, the patent owner may be required by law to license any other company wishing to use its patent, provided that it pays a reasonable royalty. Differences in national patent laws give rise to barriers to trade as goods coming from a country in which a patent is not registered or allowed cannot be allowed entry to the country in which it is. Alternatively, a different company may hold the same patent in different countries. A further possibility is that the owner of a patent may have licensed a company in another country to produce the product or use the process but the agreement precludes selling the product in the licensor's domestic market. In the European Union, the Treaty of Rome allows member states to restrict imports of goods from other member states in order to protect industrial and commercial property. However, restrictions on parallel importing are not permissible. Therefore, if a licensor has licensed another company to produce the product or use the process in some other member state in return for royalties, it is not permissible for the licensor's home country to restrict the importation of the good from the licensee's home country. The fact that differences in patent law in different member states give rise to barriers to the free movement of goods clearly conflicts with the EU's objective of a single market. Hence, the Union has proposed creating a Union framework for patents.

Copyright

Copyright law protects the representation of ideas in the form of books, musical recordings, computer software, paintings, and so on. Generally, copyright protection runs for the author's life plus fifty years or, where there is no author, fifty years from the date of publication. Differences nevertheless exist between countries over the products which should be covered by copyright law. For example, in the recent past, there has been much dispute about whether the law should be applied to computer software. Enforcement practice may also differ between countries. Products which breach copyright law may be allowed to circulate more freely in some countries than in others because the former lack the means with which to outlaw illegal products.

Trade marks

In most countries trade marks are protected from unauthorised use. A company must register its trade mark in each country in which it intends to make sales; but, again, countries disagree on how widely to define a trade mark. Should it be confined to the company logo on the product or should it embrace the distinctive physical appearance of the product? American law is much tougher in this respect than UK law. Should it be applied to exclude goods which are different but which use the same mark? Much depends on the objectives which trade mark law seeks to attain. The primary objective may be to protect the buyer from confusion over the true source of the good. Alternatively, trade mark law may be seeking to protect the owners from competition from goods which undermine the value of the trade marks in which they have invested money.

Trade secrets

In some countries trade secrets are recognised and given legal protection. A trade secret is any information belonging to a company which it does not wish to be made known to any other company. In some countries, any good which has been manufactured and sold using illegally obtained trade secrets may be prevented from entering that country's market.

Intellectual property rights and the GATT

One of the main reasons that countries such as the United States insisted on intellectual property rights being included on the agenda of the Uruguay Round was the rapid growth in recent years in intellectual property trade and the growing importance of high-technology products in world trade. According to Maskus (1991), the value of US trade in a selected sample of goods embodying large components of intellectual property rose by 76 per cent between 1983 and 1987 compared with 44 per cent for overall US merchandise trade. Maskus further demonstrates that the US possesses a strong revealed comparative advantage in most but not all goods included in the sample. These include industries such as pharmaceuticals, polymerisation products, data-processing machines, measuring and con-trolling instruments, printed matter, and recorded discs and tapes. This makes it important for the US to secure greater international protection for its own producers in these industries. However, the need to secure greater protection against infringements of trade marks also applies in industries such as travel goods, watches, toys and sporting goods in which the US has a strong revealed comparative disadvantage. From the point of view of the United States, this has seemed all the more important given the reality of a widening trade deficit and growing domestic pressure to raise trade barriers against imports from newly industrialising countries.

Trade in intellectual property is not simply through goods and services. It also takes place through companies selling ideas to other countries by means of licensing agreements and through foreign direct investment. Figures quoted by Maskus (1991) show that the United States is overwhelmingly the main supplier of technological ideas to the rest of the world. In 1985, the US enjoyed a net balance on trade in technology (defined as net receipts of royalties and licence fees for the use of technological information) of US$8.5 billion. The only other major net exporter was the UK, with a surplus of US$0.2 billion. All other countries were net importers of technology although the trend in Japan's balance was towards becoming a net exporter. However, since a great deal of trade in intellectual property rights is known to take place within rather than between firms, measures of direct trade in intellectual property fail to capture its true dimensions.

In the early stages of the Uruguay Round negotiations, it was argued, not least by the developing countries which stood to lose most from the inclusion of intellectual property rights in any GATT package, that these were already adequately covered by other bodies. Most important in this regard was the work of the World Intellectual Property Organisation (WIPO), an agency of the United Nations. Its concern has been to encourage and assist in the adoption of international conventions which set out minimum levels of intellectual property protection. Subsumed within WIPO are various international agreements or treaties, such as the Paris Convention of 1883 which sets out minimum standards for national legislation, the Berne Convention for the Protection of Literary and Artistic Works, the Universal Copyright Convention of 1952 and the Patent Co-operation Treaty of 1970. In some cases, such as patents, signatories to these agreements remain free to determine their own levels of IP protection. However, minimum requirements for such legislation are stipulated, including in most cases the principle of national treatment. If WIPO were successful in establishing a set of rules and minimum levels of intellectual property protection in all countries of the world, the issue of intellectual property rights might not have assumed such importance in GATT negotiations. However, WIPO's influence is far from being universal: a large number of countries remain outside the various international agreements. In particular, until now many developing countries have not recognised the concept of intellectual property rights. In so far as it has been possible to secure the agreement of a large number of countries to minimum levels of IP protection, the standards applied have usually been regarded by some developed countries as too low. Furthermore, WIPO lacked any mechanism for forcing countries to adhere to agreed rules.

This raised the question whether GATT could be any more successful. Given the fundamentally different philosophical positions of developed and developing countries with regard to the necessity to protect intellectual property, it might be argued that any attempt to secure agreement on a set of rules and disciplines would be doomed to failure. As with WIPO, whatever agreement was reached would be at such a low minimum level as to be of little value. From the point of view of the developed countries, however, negotiation through the GATT created opportunities for trade-offs. On the other hand, given that any extension of protection would benefit developed countries at the expense of developing countries, it was unlikely that the latter would give their consent without a quid pro quo. Multilateral trade negotiations offered an opportunity for precisely such a trade-off. If developed countries were willing to make concessions of benefit to developing countries which compensated them for the losses implied by an extension of IP protection, it might be possible to make more rapid progress than would be possible through a body such as WIPO. For example, if developed countries were willing to make substantial concessions to developing countries in the areas of agriculture and textiles, developing countries might be willing to agree to a deal being reached on increased IP protection. Stern (1987) even argued that the lack of intellectual property laws in developing countries could be viewed as a tax on the returns from intellectual property and therefore equivalent in kind to a tariff. Although it might be difficult to measure precisely the size of this tax, he argued that it might not be too difficult to negotiate broadly equivalent concessions in the form of tariffs or tariff-equivalents.

In fact, such a trade-off was effectively offered by the United States in a different form following the passage through Congress of the famous Section 301 legislation and its use against a number of developing countries. Section 301 of the 1974 US Trade and Tariff Act and its subsequent amendments in the 1988 Omnibus Trade and Competitiveness Act (so-called Super 301) provides for retaliatory action against countries which, among other things, deny adequate and effective protection of intellectual property rights. It is the task of the United States Trade Representative (USTR) to prioritise foreign countries deemed to be denying US firms adequate IP protection and which fail to enter into negotiations to provide it. If these countries fail to take the necessary measures within a stipulated period of time, the USTR is authorised to introduce retaliatory measures. One of the first countries to face retaliatory measures under the Super 301 provisions was Brazil which in 1988 was accused of failing to provide patent protection for US pharmaceutical products. After the two countries had failed to resolve the dispute through agreement, a discriminatory 100 per cent *ad valorem* tariff was imposed on certain Brazilian imports. These tariffs were lifted in 1990 after the Brazilian government promised to introduce new legislation on patents and trade marks. India was also included on the list of countries deemed to be denying US pharmaceuticals adequate patent protection. In April 1992, after India failed to agree new measures, the US withdrew tariff preferences on Indian pharmaceutical exports. Mrs Carla Hills, the USTR, described the measure as 'a rifle shot absolutely focused on the entities that are benefiting from the theft of our patents' (*The Financial Times*, 30 April 1992). Thailand and Taiwan were also named as 'violating' US intellectual property rights and were threatened with retaliation. Faced with such threats, most of these countries succumbed and introduced the degree of IP protection demanded by the US. In April 1994, China became the latest developing country to be considered for Super 301 treatment, for alleged piracy of computer software and music recordings. In February 1995, the US announced a list of Chinese imports worth US$1 billion which would be subject to punitive sanctions if no agreement could be reached within twenty days. As it turned out, agreement was reached at the last minute; China agreed to a tougher enforcement policy on IPRs and improved market access for US exporters of legitimate software and audiovisual products.

Through the Super 301 provisions, the US threatened any country that did not offer adequate and effective IP protection with denial of market access. The implication was that, if developing countries were not prepared to negotiate a TRIPs agreement through the GATT, they would face withdrawal of previous concessions under Super 301 to force an agreement on a bilateral basis. Subramanian (1990) called this 'status quo reciprocity' since the US was offering the guarantee of (or, in the case of countries already facing retaliation, a return to) the status quo as the concession in return for a multilateral agreement on IP protection. Super 301 worked like a big stick wielded at the developing countries to force them to negotiate. Subramanian described it as 'the conspicuously invisible ghost in this tale of doubt, lurking on the margins of the multilateral arena, but like Hamlet's father's ghost, defining and determining the outcome'.

The case for extending IP protection through the GATT was presented by the developed countries. Firstly, it was argued that the owners of intellectual property were entitled as of right to protection from copying or imitation. The use of the word 'right' has been challenged on the grounds that intellectual property rights are not 'rights' in the same sense as basic human rights (Deardorff, 1990b). Even if they are so regarded, it is not clear that the role of the GATT is to protect human rights. Deardorff argues that the western conception of intellectual property rights is largely cultural-specific and is not shared by nonwestern countries. Even in western countries, these

315

rights have to be defined and a time period stipulated for the duration of any protection which is agreed. The case for extending IP protection internationally is better made on the basis of the economic benefits and costs of doing so. On the other hand, a distinction must be drawn between copyright and trade mark protection and other forms such as patent protection. Breach of copyright or fraudulent use of another company's trade mark may be deemed as morally offensive as ordinary theft. Patent protection is less obviously a matter of basic rights.

Secondly, the developed countries argued that absence of IP protection imposed a considerable cost on their economies: estimates put the loss to industries in the EC, Japan and the US at US$43–61 billion (see *The Financial Times*, 3 April 1990). Foreign infringement of developed-country intellectual property rights reduces the price which an inventor can charge for his product or process or the price which he can charge another producer under a licensing agreement for use of the new technology. Consequently, the economic rent received by the inventor is reduced. On the other hand, consumers in developing countries where IP protection is nonexistent gain from lower prices. In this respect, the issue is mainly a distributional one.

The question needs to be posed as to whether *global* economic welfare is increased or lowered by extending IP protection. As Deardorff (1990) has convincingly argued, even if it can be demonstrated that domestic IP protection is necessary so as to ensure an optimal quantity of invented goods, it does not follow that it is efficient to extend such protection to the rest of the world. The costs from doing so may outweigh the benefits. Indeed, Deardorff argues that they will do so if IP protection is extended beyond a certain level. The benefits from extending protection arise from the increased level of invention which results due to innovators enjoying higher returns on their inventions. In welfare terms, this gain is measured by the increased profit in the markets where IP goods now enjoy extended protection. The costs arise because foreign consumers must now pay more for goods which were previously available in unprotected markets. This will be measured by the loss of consumer surplus less the increased monopoly profits of producers to give the so-called deadweight loss. Now, Deardorff argues, the greater the area over which IP protection is extended, the smaller the marginal benefit and the greater the marginal costs. Where the protected market for new inventions is already very large and the unprotected market quite small, it is unlikely that increased protection will result in many new inventions. Hence, the marginal benefit from extended protection will decline. On the other hand, as IP protection is extended, the global deadweight loss rises. Deardorff concludes: 'all of this suggests that there will be an optimal geographical extent of patent protection that need not be the whole world'. He favours the exemption of developing countries from patent protection (although not trade mark or copyright protection) on both efficiency and equity grounds. On efficiency grounds, the combined market of the developed countries should be sufficient to ensure an excess of marginal benefits of extended IP protection over marginal costs. On equity grounds, extending IP protection to poor countries transfers wealth from poor to rich countries, which runs counter to the goal of achieving a more equal global distribution of income. Newly industrialising countries should however be encouraged to adopt greater IP protection.

Maskus (1991) has a model of the static welfare effects of extending IP protection internationally to simulate various possible cases using available data about the effects of IP infringements on US companies. He found that 'in most cases static global welfare would suffer from the extension of IP protection by information-importing countries'. The crucial question is whether these *static* costs will be more than offset by the the the *dynamic* gains which might result from greater innovative activity. The main benefits of any such induced innovation will, however, accrue primarily to the developed countries where the majority of new products and processes are discovered and, to a limited extent, middle-income and rapidly industrialising developing countries. The least developed countries would gain little. However, it is not clear to what exent patent protection does stimulate innovation. The available empirical evidence suggests that patent protection may be important in a few sectors (notably, chemicals and pharmaceuticals) where fixed R&D costs are high and imitation relatively easy. In other sectors, however, it has been found to be of less value than such factors as the degree of competition, the rate of market growth and level of factor costs.

Developed countries are also inclined to argue that extended IP protection would increase technology transfer and foreign direct investment (FDI) to developing countries. For example, in the computer software industry it is frequently argued that lack of adequate protection has stopped software firms investing in or supplying certain countries with the latest products. In industries embodying new technologies, western companies may be less inclined to enter into licensing agreements with developing countries in which there is inadequate or ineffective IP protection. The pharmaceuticals industry is another example where the lack of patent protection may have been a factor deterring FDI in some developing countries. On the other hand, cases can be cited where low levels of IP protection have proved highly successful in promoting the development of local industries by preventing markets being monopolised by foreign companies. Indeed, until recently, by confining protection only to works manufactured in the United States, the US used her own copyright laws in this way. Decisions about whether to invest in a particular country take into account a variety of criteria. IP rights might be one consideration and in a few cases could be overriding. In general, however, they are not the decisive determinant. The UNCTC (1990) has concluded that 'while a causal link may exist between intellectual property protection, on the one hand, and foreign investment and technology flows, on the other, this link may not be automatic and can only be confirmed through experience and empirical evidence'.

Intellectual property rights and the Uruguay Round

Subramanian (1990) saw the pressure for greater IP protection in the industrialised countries as coming from three main interest groups. Firstly, the high-technology industries (for example, pharmaceuticals/chemicals and information technology) were anxious to secure greater protection of their technology through extension and improvement of patent and copyright laws, protection of trade secrets, increased protection of industrial design, and so on. Second were producers of luxury consumer goods, anxious to secure protection from trade in counterfeit goods through the extension of trade mark law. Thirdly, the entertainment industries, which were concerned about breach of copyright in respect of musical recordings, motion pictures, and so on. Two separate issues were involved: (a) and improvement in standards of protection was the primary concern of the high-technology industries; and (b) improved enforcement procedures mattered more to the luxury goods and entertainment industries.

The 1986 Punta del Este Ministerial Declaration which launched the Uruguay Round listed 'trade-related aspects of intellectual property rights, including trade in counterfeit goods' as an item to be included on the agenda of the Round. It stated:

> In order to reduce the distortions and impediments to international trade, and taking into account the need to promote effective and adequate protection of intellectual property rights, and to ensure that measures and procedures to enforce intellectual property rights do not themselves become barriers to legitimate trade, the negotiations shall aim to clarify GATT provisions and elaborate as appropriate new rules and disciplines. Negotiations shall aim to develop a multilateral framework of principles, rules and disciplines dealing with inter-national trade in counterfeit goods, taking into account work already undertaken in the GATT.
>
> These negotiations shall be without prejudice to other complemen-tary initiatives that may be taken in the World Intellectual Property Organisation and elsewhere to deal with these matters.
>
> (Quoted in Finger and Olechowski, 1987)

The statement reflects the consensus which was achieved on the necessity for a framework of rules dealing with trade in counterfeit goods. However, different views remained over the extension of other forms of IP protection. The reference to WIPO reflected the views of developing countries which

318

continued to regard it, rather than the GATT, as the appropriate forum for matters relating to intellectual property rights.

When GATT negotiators met in Montreal in December 1988 for the Mid-term Review of the Uruguay Round, TRIPs was one of the three main areas where agreement proved too difficult, forcing adjournment of the talks until April 1989. After intensive discussions, agreement was reached on the following agenda for future negotiations:

Without prejudice to future decisions on the institutional aspects of any resultant agreement, negotiations are to cover the applicability of basic principles of the GATT and other relevant international agreements; adequate standards and principles concerning the availability, scope and use of trade-related intellectual property rights; the provision of effective and appropriate means for the enforcement of such rights; multilateral dispute settlement; and transitional arrangements aiming at the fullest participation in the results of the negotiations. The negotiations will also comprise principles, rules and disciplines dealing with international trade in counterfeit goods.

Consideration will also be given to concerns raised by participants relating to the underlying public policy objectives of their national systems for the protection of intellectual property, including developmental and technological objectives.

(GATT 1988)

With reference to this aspect of the Mid-term Agreement, *The Financial Times* (10 April 1989) commented:

the mid-term review has broken, at least temporarily, the vicious circle of wrangling between developing and industrial countries over whether the ultimate responsibility for trade-related rules should lie with the GATT or the World Intellectual Property Organisation which the US regards as ineffectual. Work can now begin on organising new rules for protecting intellectual property, leaving the decision over who should apply them till later.

Major obstacles in the negotiations were differences between the industrial countries over patent law. The United States wanted its own *first-to-invent* system for awarding patents and its more lengthy enforcement procedure to form the basis of any agreement. By contrast, most other countries operated a *first-to-file* system. Under the US system, any foreigner applying for a patent in the US is required to ship laboratory notes to the US because the invention of a product or process is only deemed to have taken place once the notes have been landed and legally authenticated. Further costly delays can result if another party is also seeking the same patent since it is necessary to prove which was the first inventor. It was argued that the US system encouraged infringers of patents to mount spurious defences in order to keep a contested patent in the courts for as long as possible (often many years) in an effort to force the patent holder to capitulate under the weight of massive costs. At worst, the infringer would end up paying royalties on sales, as he would otherwise have to do in any case.

The agreement which emerged after lengthy negotiations went most of the way towards meeting the demands of the developed countries. The agreement is in seven parts. *Part 1* sets out *general provisions and basic principles*. These make it clear that it is a requirement that signatories pass the necessary national laws so as to bring into effect the provisions of the agreement. In doing so, these laws must be in conformity with the requirements of *national treatment* (Article 3) and *most-favoured-nation treatment* (Article 4). The principle of national treatment requires each country to accord to the nationals of other countries 'treatment no less favourable than that it accords to its own nationals with regard to the protection of intellectual property'. The principle of most-favoured-nation treatment requires that 'any advantage, favour, privilege or immunity granted by a Member to the nationals of any other country shall be accorded immediately and unconditionally to the nationals of all other Members'. There are, however, provisions for exemptions from both requirements. For example, with regard to MFN treatment, there are grandfather rights for agreements entered into before the Uruguay Round was completed.

Part 2 is concerned with *standards concerning the availability, scope and use of intellectual property rights*. In this section, it is made clear that the agreement covers seven categories of intellectual property:

1 *Copyright* is protected for at least fifty years (as required under the Berne Convention) and includes computer programs and data compilation. Authors of computer programs and cinematographic works largely have exclusive rental rights, and so do performers and producers of sound recordings and broadcasts.
2 *Trade marks* (defined as 'any sign or any combination of signs, capable of distinguishing the goods or services of one undertaking from those of another') are protected for at least seven years.
3 *Geographical indications* are defined as 'indicators which identify a good as originating in the territory of a Member, or a region or locality in that region, where a given quality, reputation or other characteristic of the good is essentially attributable to its geographic origin'. This is important for wine growers who need to prevent fraudulent attribution of geographical origin.
4 *Industrial designs* are protected for at least ten years.
5 *Patents* covering new products or processes enjoy protection from the filing date for a period of twenty years, regardless of the place of invention, the field of technology and whether products are imported or locally produced. The most important permitted exclusions were so-

called 'patents on life', defined as 'plants and animals other than micro-organisms and essentially biological processes for the production of plants or animals, other than nonbiological and microbiological processes'. These provisions created considerable controversy in the negotiations. The United States wanted greater international patent protection for life forms but was bitterly opposed by other groups who regarded such patents as unethical. It remains unclear how far this exclusion will succeed in preventing patents on life forms being taken out and enforced. However, there is a stipulation that these specific provisions should be reviewed four years after the agreement comes into force. Strict limits are also placed on compulsory licensing of patented products by governments. Governments may only license production of a patented good without the patent holder's consent if the patent holder refuses use of the patent on 'reasonable commercial terms and conditions' and subject to the patent holder being paid 'adequate remuneration' (Article 31).

6 *Lay-out designs (topographies) of integrated circuits* are protected for ten years. Both the US and Japan have specific laws covering this area while the UK uses its copyright laws for this purpose.

7 *Protection of undisclosed information*: for the first time ever, trade secrets are protected from unauthorised disclosure.

Part 3 deals with the issue of *enforcement* of intellectual property rights, requiring countries to put in place effective procedures to deal with infringements.

Part 4 deals with the *acquisition and maintenance of intellectual property rights*, that is, the registration of rights, and so on.

Part 5 deals with *dispute prevention and settlement*, including a requirement that national laws and regulations governing the protection of IP rights satisfy the usual GATT requirement for *transparency* (Article 63). There is a provision for the notification of all such laws and regulations and their review by a newly established *Council for Trade-related Aspects of Intellectual Property Rights*. It also makes clear that disputes concerning IP rights will be subject to the integrated dispute-settlement machinery of the new World Trade Organisation (WTO). The significance of this is the scope that it creates for 'cross sanctions' (that is, retaliation on goods trade for breaches of the intellectual property agreement). On the other hand, countries are required to abide by the disputes procedures of the WTO and this should limit attempts by countries to settle disputes unilaterally. For example, the measures taken by the United States under the Super 301 provisions against countries deemed to be infringing US IP rights would presumably be illegal.

Part 6 deals with the *transitional arrangements*. Whereas developed countries are required to apply the provisions of the agreement within a year, developing countries (and economies in transition from central planning to market-based) are allowed a transitional period of five years (Article 65). Least developed countries are not required to apply the provisions (except the National Treatment and MFN provisions) for eleven years (Article 66). Moreover, where a developing country has to apply protection to an area of technology not currently subject to IP protection, it can delay applying *patent* protection for another five years over and above the five-year transitional period. This is of particular significance for pharmaceutical companies in developed and developing countries since many developing countries have not in the past extended IP protection to drug companies in the developed countries. Clearly, any drug coming on the market in the next ten years will not be affected by the provisions. However, developing countries are required to permit the filing of patents for pharmaceuticals and agricultural chemical products from the time of the agreement and to treat them in ten years' time as if legislation had been in effect from the point when they came on the market (Article 70:8). Most drugs require at least ten years' safety testing before they can be marketed so these provisions ensure that products invented now will receive protection. If they are marketed earlier, the patent holder would be given exclusive marketing rights in the interim (Article 70:9). In fact, US pharmaceutical companies had fought a hard and unsuccessful battle to secure 'pipeline' protection for drugs already invented but not yet on the market. This would have involved retroactive recognition of patents and, not surpisingly, was rejected by most other countries. Pipeline protection of this kind has been an aspect of some of the new IP laws introduced by developing countries (such as China) in recent years under threat of US retaliation under the Super 301 provisions.

Finally, *Part 7* of the agreement sets out the *institutional provisions*, including the creation of a new Council for Trade-related Aspects of Intellectual Property Rights to supervise the agreement.

The IP agreement is widely regarded as a triumph for the United States in its attempt to gain extended international IP protection. The US has secured an agreement which should ensure that nearly all forms of intellectual property rights are guaranteed protection in all countries which are WTO members. The fact that the agreement is now firmly embedded within the WTO means that any breaches of the agreement will be subject to the new integrated disputes mechanism with its provisions for automatic adoption of panel reports and cross-retaliation where reports are not implemented. Although the US expressed dissatisfaction with some aspects of the agreement, it was widely agreed that it had secured a better deal than it might once have hoped for. In particular, it had gained the agreement of the developing countries to incorporating IP rights into the GATT and its successor, the WTO.

At the commencement of the Round, the developing countries had been strongly opposed to any such agreement. What changed their minds? Largely, fear of the alternative. The US had made it abundantly clear that it intended to make increased use of the Super 301 provisions against any developing country which failed to provide US companies with adequate and effective IP protection. Indeed, during the course of the negotiations, a number of developing countries had introduced IP legislation for fear of US retaliation. Having done so, little was to be lost by giving their assent to an international agreement. Moreover, if by so doing unilateralist measures by the US could be averted, so much the better. It remains to be seen whether this will indeed be the case. Moreover, the agreement provides for a lengthy transitional period for the least developed countries and a shorter transitional period for other developing countries. However, there can be no doubt that the main beneficiaries of the agreement are the advanced industrialised countries. For developing countries, the cost of agreeing to such a deal will depend upon the offsetting benefits contained within the wider package, especially the provisions for increased access for developing- country exports to the markets of the developed countries.

TRADE-RELATED INVESTMENT MEASURES (TRIMs)

The third of the new issues covered by the Uruguay Round was that of trade-related investment measures (TRIMs). The issue has become an important one in recent decades with the growth of foreign direct investment (FDI) and the increased importance of multinational corporations in the world economy. For a variety of reasons, governments intervene both to influence the flow of foreign capital into their economies and in order to control the activities of multinational corporations operating inside their economies. Such intervention may have effects on the level of the host country's imports or on its exports or on both. In brief, such measures can be trade distorting. Certain developed countries, most notably the United States, have taken the view that these considerations necessitate such measures being treated as 'trade related' and therefore a matter for the GATT (and its successor, the WTO). This is despite the fact that investment issues have traditionally been kept separate from trade issues, with the GATT confining itself to issues which are overtly trade matters.

Interventions by governments in an effort both to influence the flow of inward investment to their country and to control foreign companies which operate within their borders may take many different forms, some of which have a direct effect on trade and which are therefore obviously trade distorting and others which have only a minimal and largely indirect effect on trade or in some cases no effect at all. Firstly, there are the various kinds of investment incentives which governments may offer foreign companies in an effort to attract investment into the country. These include different forms of tax relief and exemptions, accelerated depreciation, import duty exemptions, subsidies, investment grants, priority access to credit, tariff protection and other forms of financial inducement or protection. It is possible to distinguish between those measures which seek to lower the costs of inputs or factors (for example, investment grants) and those which seek to raise the value of the final commodity or output (for example, tariffs or export subsidies). Secondly, there is another set of measures which are more concerned with maximising the performance of foreign producers once they have set up in the host country. The claim for these measures is that they seek to ensure that a greater proportion of the benefit from the investment accrues to the host country. Although these include a wide range of different measures, two of the most frequently cited examples of performance requirements are local-content rules and export-performance criteria. Local-content rules prescribe minimum percentages of inputs which must be locally sourced. The main reason for their use is to ensure that foreign companies buy more of their inputs locally, thereby boosting domestic production of components and parts and ensuring that less of the benefit from the foreign investment 'leaks' abroad. In particular, they are often used to ensure that inward investment by foreign companies does not take the form of a so-called 'screwdriver' operation, in which the foreign affiliate is little more than an assembly plant putting together goods largely manufactured elsewhere, thus bringing little technological gain to the host country. Local-content rules are also commonly used as rules of origin in regional or preferential trading blocs to ensure that only those products which have been substantially produced inside the bloc qualify for tariff-free access. Local-content rules clearly give rise to a trade distortion, having much the same impact as a quantitative restriction on imports. Host countries' export-performance criteria stipulate that a foreign investor must export a certain proportion of its output or achieve a certain level of exports. Such measures seek to ensure that the foreign investor makes a positive contribution to the host country's balance of payments. Similar in kind are trade-balancing requirements which link the imports of inputs to some specified performance in the export of the final product. All such measures have clear trade-distorting effects. However, not all investment measures adopted by governments have such an obvious effect on trade.

Greenaway (1991) identifies three distinct motives for governments to use such measures. The first is the 'resource allocation target', or the desire to influence the global allocation of resources by shifting foreign investment in its favour. As we have seen, governments give incentives to foreign firms in an effort to attract footloose foreign capital to the host country so as to boost local output and employment, improve the balance of payments and bring about technology transfer. The second is the 'insurance target', or the efforts of host country governments to ensure that as much as possible of the benefits generated by foreign investment accrue to the local economy rather than leaking out abroad in repatriated profits, higher imports, increased service payments or migrant transfers. Many of the performance measures discussed above are clearly intended for this purpose. The third effect is what Greenaway calls the 'rent shifting target': where foreign direct investment is attracted to a country either by the lure of generous investment incentives or the guarantee of a protected domestic market, the foreign producers will receive rents, the distribution of which, as between the foreign company and the local economy, the government of the host country may wish to alter. This it can do when it begins to bargain with the foreign company over the conditions governing its establishment of an affiliate in the host country. This may seem contradictory since what the host country government concedes with one hand it seeks to reclaim with the other. In reality, as Greenaway argues, the opaqueness of these arrangements may suit the host country government in much the same way as do negotiations over voluntary export restraints. For the foreign company, too, the arrangements enable it to give the appearance of conceding something when in fact it is not doing so at all. Greenaway sees in this last motive a strong argument for not treating TRIMs as border measures worthy of regulation under the GATT. TRIMs such as local-content rules or export-performance requirements are measures designed to influence the terms on which a foreign company is allowed to invest. As such, they are not weapons of trade policy.

Nevertheless, it is the case that some TRIMs do have trade-distorting effects. With the increased importance of FDI, it is therefore inevitable that some countries will insist on TRIMs being discussed within the GATT/WTO. However, given the fact that the primary impact of most TRIMs is not on trade, there is a need to distinguish between those which are obviously trade distorting, such as local-content rules and export requirements, and those which have largely incidental and not very important effects on trade, such as requirements regarding local equity participation or technology transfer. However, that still leaves a problem of how to determine the impact of a particular trade measure. Ideally, any rules introduced for TRIMs should be concerned with the *effects* of the measure (that is, its impact on trade flows) and not the *measure itself*. Yet TRIMs often operate alongside other measures and it is frequently not possible to isolate the impact of the TRIM in question from that of other measures. It is easier to estimate the impact of all investment measures taken together than do so for any particular measure in isolation. As Guisinger (1987) argues, investment incentives and tariffs can be treated as equivalent to a cash grant payable to an investor in the first year of his operations. This may make possible some quantification of the impact of such measures and the calculation of their tariff equivalent. On the other hand, it seems unlikely that in the future countries would agree on the inclusion of all investment measures in this way.

The TRIMs Agreement

The wish to include TRIMs on the agenda of the Uruguay Round was first raised by the United States as early as 1982. An influential side-issue was an attempt by the US to challenge, through the GATT, aspects of Canada's foreign investment policy which the US regarded as trade distorting. Specifically, the US objected to the use of local purchasing and manufacturing requirements under Canada's Foreign Investment Review Act (FIRA) of 1973 as trade distorting and inconsistent with the national treatment standard and other GATT provisions. The US also challenged the export requirements under the law which amounted to unwarranted interference in trade, had implications for dumping abroad and 'nullified and impaired' previous trade commitments. The GATT panel set up to investigate the complaint found that the provisions designed to increase local content constituted discrimination in favour of domestic products and as such violated GATT national treatment standards under Article III. However, the export requirements were found to be consistent with Canada's GATT obligations. The FIRA panel case illustrated that certain GATT provisions, namely, those requiring national treatment, could be used against certain kinds of TRIMs. On the other hand, it was made clear that the GATT rules did not cover any aspect of the right of a country to regulate the entry or expansion of foreign direct investments but only questions affecting a country's obligations under the GATT.

The 1986 Ministerial Declaration launching the Uruguay Round included TRIMs and set the aims of the negotiations to be 'an examination of the operation of the GATT articles related to the trade restrictive and distorting effects of investment measures', followed by the elaboration 'as appropriate' of 'further provisions that may be necessary to avoid such adverse effects on trade'. Thus, the focus of the negotiations was to be the adverse trade effect of investment measures and not the legitimacy of the measures *per se*. A distinction can be drawn between the stance of developed and developing countries. The developed countries generally favoured a dual-track approach, distinguishing trade-distorting TRIMs (such as local-content requirements, export-performance measures and trade-balancing measures) from investment measures which are not inherently trade distorting. With the single exception of the EC, developed countries favoured the prohibition or phasing out of all trade-distorting TRIMs. (The EC maintained that existing GATT rules were adequate for dealing with these measures.) With regard to TRIMs that were not inherently trade distorting, they favoured some mechanism for notifying such measures and for ensuring that complaints about such measures could be dealt with on a case-by-case basis through an agreed dispute-settlement procedure. The developed countries agreed that developing countries should be subject to some form of differential and more favourable treatment. Developing countries held strongly to the view that TRIMs are investment and not trade measures. If these were to be brought within GATT rules and discipline, the focus should therefore be on the effects of such measures and not on the measures themselves. To a large extent, however, existing GATT rules and disciplines were considered to be adequate. If new rules were to be introduced covering TRIMs, developing countries argued for special account to be taken of their developmental needs.

What did the Uruguay Round achieve in respect of TRIMs? The Agreement on Trade-related Investment Measures only covers investment measures related to trade in *goods*. Services-investment measures are covered by the GATS and are therefore subject to national offers. (As was explained above, pp. 302–5, the GATS operates on the basis that countries make specific commitments in respect of national treatment and market access. Therefore, liberalisation of TRIMs affecting service-providers depends on the willingness of countries to include specific sectors and measures in their schedules.) The TRIMs Agreement contains a statement recognising the principle that certain investment measures *can* cause trade-restrictive and trade-distorting effects. However, it goes little further than to reaffirm the existing GATT rules. Thus, member states must not apply any TRIMs which are inconsistent with GATT obligations regarding (a) national treatment (Article III of the GATT); or (b) the general elimination of quantitative restrictions (Article XI). An annex to the Agreement provides an illustrative list of measures which are inconsistent with these provisions. TRIMs inconsistent with these obligations include local-content and trade-balancing requirements. Developing countries are allowed temporary exemptions from these provisions on balance of payments grounds. The Agreement requires member states to notify the WTO of all nonconforming TRIMs and to eliminate them within two years for developed countries, five years for developing countries and seven years for least developed countries. Other parts of the Agreement reaffirm the commitment to transparency; establish a Committee on TRIMs to monitor and implement the Agreement; and affirm that GATT dispute-settlement provisions shall also apply to disputes relating to the TRIMs Agreement. Finally, the Agreement commits the member states to review the Agreement no later than five years following the establishment of the WTO, with consideration being given to whether the Agreement should be complemented with provisions on investment and competition policy.

This last aspect of the Agreement was arguably the most important, as in other respects the Agreement does little more than reaffirm provisions contained within the GATT concerning certain types of TRIMs which most obviously distort trade. These provisions have always been available for countries to use if they so wished. In practice, countries have rarely sought to do so and it is by no means clear that they will be more likely to do so as a result of repeating the existing rules. On the other hand, this may well have been the most that was achievable for the time being. A sufficiently large number of countries (mainly developing countries plus some industrialised countries) were clearly unprepared for an agreement which would prohibit outright a large number of trade-distorting TRIMs. On the other hand, the new Agreement does create a mechanism for the notification of TRIMs inconsistent with the GATT and brings the settlement of disputes involving such measures within the ambit of the new WTO dispute-settlement machinery. There is also a clear timetable for the elimination of these measures, albeit with some exceptions. The fact that further negotiations must take place by the year 2000 means that the Agreement must be seen as merely a first step in the extension of trading rules to investment policies. Nevertheless, the Agreement is narrow in its application. Certain types of TRIMs which may equally well distort trade are not covered. TRIMs affecting service-providers are subject to an arguably less exacting set of arrangements. It is therefore unlikely that it will satisfy for long the wishes of those developed countries which have pushed for the inclusion of TRIMs in GATT negotiations.

CONCLUSION

This chapter has examined the three major 'new issues' which entered the latest round of multilateral trade negotiations. The inclusion of each of these areas enormously complicated the negotiations and contributed in no small measure to the failure to conclude the Round by the original deadline. Negotiations concerned with matters such as services, TRIPs and TRIMs are necessarily more complex because the factors impeding free trade are both more varied and less readily quantifiable. TRIPs differ somewhat from services and TRIMs because TRIPs involve extending rather than reducing protection. Although the gains to developed countries from improved IP protection are not easy to determine, the winners and losers from such an agreement are more readily identifiable. In the case of services and TRIMs, however, the impact of any 'concession' made is not easy to know. This makes it difficult for countries to judge the appropriate offers to make in return for the benefits requested of other countries. Moreover, the barriers impeding trade are not primarily border measures of the kind that countries are more used to discussing in GATT fora. Rather, they arise from government intervention which is often motivated by a variety of considerations in which trade restriction need not be the sole or even primary intent.

Nevertheless, the extension of international trade policy into these areas is inevitable. The massive growth in the volume of world trade in services and the significance of earnings from the export of services for a number of major developed countries has meant that meaningful progress in the liberalisation of world trade could not be brought about without including these sectors. In a similar manner, the growth of FDI and the increasing globalisation of production has meant that trade and investment issues can no longer be easily separated. The growth of trade in high-technology products has also brought to the forefront the issue of IP protection. The increasing number of trade disputes arising from issues relating to alleged 'theft' of intellectual property or the failure of countries to enforce IP laws was undermining the GATT, while the failure of the GATT to address these issues was causing many countries to seek solutions through unilateral retaliation rather than reliance on multilateral mechanisms.

Thus, the agenda of international trade policy has changed irreversibly. The next century is likely to see further changes in the range of issues discussed at multilateral trade gatherings. Some of the issues which are likely to dominate the future agenda are discussed in the next chapter. Such change is inevitable as the relative importance of different forms of trade alters and as new types of trade emerge that are not covered by rules developed in a previous era. It is also the case that, as traditional barriers to trade are lowered, the importance of other forms of interference with trade become more apparent.

The Uruguay Round has made important progress in bringing three issues of crucial importance to world trade at the present time within the framework of the rules-based system set up after the Second World War. At the commencement of the Uruguay Round, it was uncertain whether it would even be possible to discuss these matters. In particular, developed and developing countries appeared at loggerheads regarding the appropriateness of addressing these issues when, in the opinion of developing countries, so many old issues remained unresolved. The realisation that offsetting gains might be obtainable from a willingness to make concessions in these areas prompted a sufficiently large number of developing countries to change their minds. Even then, given the different initial positions of the main negotiators, it is remarkable that any agreement emerged on such contentious matters.

On reflection, these agreements leave a lot to be desired. This is especially true of the GATS, as was explained above. The degree of liberalisation is minimal and there are doubts about the framework established as a mechanism for bringing about further liberalisation in the future. Nevertheless, perhaps too much should not be expected at the first attempt. Many of the shortcomings of the agreements should be possible to address. A start has been made in subjecting an important, new and highly complex sector of trade to rules of a similar kind to those applying to other forms of trade. There is plenty of scope for refining these rules in the future and for persuading countries to see the value of making more specific commitments in this sector, not only as a means of extracting concessions from other trading partners but also as a means of improving the efficiency of their economies and thereby enhancing their own economic welfare.

329

9

THE EMERGING AGENDA

INTRODUCTION

With the Uruguay Round now complete, attention has necessarily switched to the future. Two questions in particular need to be addressed. Firstly, what are likely to be the effects of the Uruguay Round as and when it is fully implemented? Secondly, what issues will dominate the agenda of multi-lateral trade negotiations as the world enters the twenty-first century? This chapter modestly seeks to examine both these issues.

In answer to the first of these questions, an attempt is made to appraise the results of the Uruguay Round viewed as a package. Reference is made to the various quantitative estimates available of the likely welfare gain to the world as a whole from the full implementation of the Agreement. Consideration is also given to the distribution of this gain as between developed, developing and least developed countries. Any appraisal of the Round must also take into account nonquantifiable gains such as those which result from improvements in the mechanisms for rule enforcement and dispute settlement. In this respect, an especially significant result has been the setting up of a new World Trade Organisation (WTO) with responsibility for all the agreements reached in the course of the Round and for ensuring that these agreements are fully implemented and rules enforced. We therefore include a brief discussion of the future role of the WTO.

In tackling the second question, the chapter seeks to identify several key issues which are likely to occupy a prominent place on the future agenda of multilateral trade negotiations. Clearly, there will be a need to return to certain issues on which the Uruguay Round made only limited progress. There seems to be widespread agreement that an area in which much greater progress towards liberalisation has still to take place is that of *services*. The tentative first steps which were taken in the course of the Round need to be built upon. Those countries which reap substantial export earnings from services will wish to see more progress made in increasing access to the markets of trading partners. The rapid growth of world trade in

330

services also means that the importance of services in world trade is certain to grow. Likewise, the agreement achieved on *agriculture* is widely regarded as disappointing in the extent to which it brings agricultural trade under the same discipline as trade in other products. Agricultural exporting countries, in particular, will wish for much more rapid progress in this area in the future.

In addition, at least four other new issues are likely to preoccupy negotiators in the future. The first of these is the issue of *environmental standards*. Not only do environmental issues constitute a potential threat to the process of trade liberalisation as countries use environmental concerns as a pretext for imposing import restrictions; but also the application of different environmental standards in different countries is leading those with tougher regulations to accuse trading partners with laxer regimes of 'eco-dumping'. This raises the question of whether international trading rules should establish minimal environmental standards and, if necessary, allow importing countries to impose restrictions on countries which fail to adhere to those standards. Failure to reach agreement on these matters at a multilateral level may lead to a proliferation of restrictions and put in jeopardy the gains from the Uruguay Round.

The second new issue concerns *labour standards*. In recent years, there has been a growing demand from developed countries for rules to allow protection against so-called 'social dumping' by developing countries with inadequate labour standards. The strongest criticism has been made against countries which use child or prison labour, tolerate inhuman working conditions and deny workers the rights to form trade unions and to strike. In the immediate prelude to signing the Uruguay Round Final Act in April 1994, both the United States and France threatened to delay ratification unless it was agreed that future negotiations would address this issue.

Thirdly, the issue of *competition policy* looks likely to find a place on the agenda of the next round of trade negotiations. There is now widespread agreement that differences between countries in the degree to which anticompetitive practices are tolerated within their domestic markets has implications for trade. For example, restrictive agreements or close-knit relationships between manufacturers and distributors may make it difficult for foreign suppliers to penetrate the market of the importing country. US exporters have often complained that the Japanese system of *keiretsu* (which links together Japanese companies in large conglomerate groups) impedes access to the Japanese market. Although unfair trading laws do exist in Japan, the United States has argued that these laws are only weakly enforced. Highly cartelised domestic markets may also be a factor that gives rise to dumping. As we saw in Chapter 4, if competition in the domestic market of the exporting country is restricted, it is probable that goods will be exported abroad at a lower price than the price charged domestically. There also exists a possible overlap between trade policies designed to combat 'unfair' trading, such as antidumping policy, and the attempts of national competition laws to outlaw similarly anticompetitive practices. If the primary concern about dumping is with its anticompetitive effects, there may be value in an approach which links antidumping with competition policy.

Finally, the growing overlap between trade and foreign direct investment means that the issue of *investment flows* is likely to enter the trade policy agenda in the next century. It will not be possible readily to separate the two issues as has been the case in the past: investment flows have not been considered to be a GATT issue. The question of formulating rules governing foreign investment practices and the policies which host countries apply to foreign companies was considered to be a matter for bodies such as the OECD. Such an approach is unlikely to be acceptable to the advanced industrialised countries in the future. As we saw in Chapter 8, the link between trade and investment matters is especially apparent in the area of services where a prerequisite of trade is often the movement of both capital and personnel to the foreign market. Increasingly, the same is true of much trade in goods. Barriers to investment create barriers to trade. Improved market access often requires a relaxation of regulatory measures that prevent or restrict foreign firms setting up in the foreign market.

ASSESSING THE EFFECTS OF THE URUGUAY ROUND

In earlier chapters the main agreements reached in the Uruguay Round have been set out and discussed. The question which concerns us here is the likely global impact of the entire package as and when it is implemented. It should be borne in mind that most of the measures agreed are subject to a staging requirement which means that it will be up to ten years before most of the package takes full effect. The primary focus of concern is the probable impact of the Round on the level and rate of growth of world trade, income and output growth. A number of attempts have been made using computable general equilibrium (CGE) models of the world economy to quantify the likely effects of the Round. The value of CGE models is that they link together all the industries in an input–output framework, taking into account both the direct and indirect effects of changes in the prices of the products of one sector on all other sectors. Clearly, this is the only way in which any meaningful estimates of the effects of the Round can be made.

Nevertheless, simulations of this kind are not without their difficulties. It is useful to begin by setting out some of the main drawbacks. Firstly, many of the effects of the Round are very difficult, if not impossible, to quantify. Whereas economists can make reasonably intelligent guesses as to the effects of a given level of tariff reduction, nontariff barriers create bigger problems because of the need to calculate the tariff equivalent. The beneficial effects on trade of improved trading rules and a more effective mechanism for settling disputes are clearly impossible to measure. Here, the main benefit is likely to come from higher levels of investment and hence output and growth due to enhanced investor confidence.

Secondly, even when the effects of liberalisation are readily quantifiable, many models confine their estimates to the once-and-for-all static gains from trade liberalisation. Yet there are now grounds for supposing that these effects are quantitatively less important than the longer-run dynamic gains which trade liberalisation leads to. Thus, there are likely to be positive effects on factors such as a country's rate of technological change, the degree of competition, the scope for more fully exploiting available economies of scale, and the improvement in macroeconomic prospects from being able to expand the level of aggregate demand faster without running into inflationary bottlenecks.

Recently, the work of Baldwin (1989), building on the 'endogenous growth' model proposed by Romer (1986), has drawn attention to the medium-term effects on economic growth of trade liberalisation which create even larger potential gains than those measured in a conventional model. First applying it in a study of the effects on the EU of the 1992 Single Market, Baldwin estimated larger potential gains from the Single Market because integration was assumed to lead to a *permanently* higher rate of economic growth, not just a once-and-for-all rise in output. Specifically, the increase in the level of output brought about by the more conventional effects of removing trade barriers increased the level of savings and investment on the assumption that the ratio of savings/investment to national income is constant. Higher investment increases the stock of physical capital, which leads to a further rise in output and to more savings and investment, in multiplier fashion. In other words, trade liberalisation sets in motion a virtuous circle which results in a permanently higher growth rate.

Thirdly, many models make conventional assumptions about market structure, returns to scale and factor mobility. However, modern international trade theory strongly suggests that the introduction of nonstandard assumptions has a significant effect on the size of the gain from liberalisation. Specifically, the existence of imperfect competition, the presence of economies of scale internal to the firm and the existence of external economies (the spillover effects which a higher level of industrial output has on the costs of all of the firms making up the industry) create the potential for welfare gains over and above the conventional gains from improved resource allocation. This is because the presence of these factors means that lower trade barriers are more likely to lead to increased intra-industry as opposed to inter-industry trade. The welfare gains from intra-industry trade are now generally recognised as being greater than those from inter-industry trade. (See Gimwade, 1989, on intra-industry trade.)

One of the earliest attempts to estimate the probable effects of a successful completion of the Uruguay Round was a joint study by the World Bank and OECD (Goldin *et al.*, 1993). This predicted that the successful completion of the Uruguay Round would add US$213 billion annually to world income by the year 2002 (at 1992 prices) or the equivalent of roughly 1 per cent of the gross world product. The bulk of the gain (roughly US$190 billion) was found to come from the liberalisation of agricultural trade (the study assumed this would result in a 30 per cent cut in tariffs and subsidies) with the rest of the gain (US$23 billion) coming from reductions in tariffs on industrial products. One reason for this is the much higher level of 'tariff equivalents' which exist for agricultural goods than for manufactures. Applying the same tariff reductions to these amounts necessarily yields a much greater potential gain from liberalisation in agricultural than in industrial goods. Roughly US$120 billion would go to the OECD countries and US$70 billion to the developing countries. Not surpisingly, countries with high levels of agricultural protection (especially those of the EU, Japan and the EFTA countries) would enjoy the biggest gains. However, because agricultural trade liberalisation was expected to raise world agricultural prices, developing countries who were net importers of food would lose, particularly those of Sub-Saharan Africa.

However, the study suffers from several weaknesses. To begin with, it takes into account only some of the agreed measures of liberalisation: for example, no account is taken of possible gains from liberalising trade in services. Secondly, as the authors acknowledge, the model used was originally designed for estimating the effects of liberalising agricultural trade and so has only a limited application to other sectors. Thirdly, the model estimates only conventional, static welfare gains and omits the nontraditional, dynamic gains discussed above. Finally, the World Bank/OECD study was completed before the Round was finalised and so could not provide a perfect analogue of the measures eventually adopted.

The study by Nguyen *et al.* (1991, 1993) also predated the the conclusion of the Round although subsequently the authors reworked their results in the light of the agreement reached. Their original study put the gains at US$262.5 billion, but this is now recognised as a substantial overestimate. The reasons given were that the final agreement fell short of the expectations embodied in the Dunkel Draft Final Act on which the original study was based. The reworked version of their estimates put the gain at just under US$70 billion or roughly 0.4 per cent of world gross product. As in the World Bank/OECD study, the bulk of these gains come from agricultural trade liberalisation (US$36.9 billion), with liberalisation in textiles accounting for a substantial amount of the remainder (US$10.1 billion). Because the distortionary effects of these measures are most serious for the developed countries, it is these which enjoy the largest gains. Developing countries still gain, but this comes more from a strengthening of GATT rules and disciplines.

Another study of the likely effects of the Round published before the Round was completed was by the GATT Secretariat (GATT, 1993b). Using as its basis the offers in place in November 1993, the GATT Secretariat predicted that the Round would add US$745 billion to world trade (an increase of roughly 12 per cent) by the year 2002 (at 1992 prices) and provide a net gain to world income of US$230 billion. The estimated welfare gain was thus close to that of other equivalent studies. Subsequently, using a new economic model which takes into account possible dynamic gains, the Secretariat upgraded its estimate to over US$500 billion. Even the new model fails to incorporate all the likely beneficial effects of increased trade on factors such as the rates of capital investment, economic growth and technological change, so the estimate probably constitutes the minimum.

A more satisfying result is obtained by François et al. (1994) since they use a model which incorporates many of the nontraditional, dynamic effects now considered to be of critical importance including imperfect competition and scale economies. Moreover, one version of the model incorporates the medium-term dynamic effects of trade liberalisation which Baldwin (1989) has suggested may be important. Furthermore, the analysis is based on the final offers which countries made and is therefore as close as possible to a simulation of the actual outcome. Their results predict an increase in the volume of world trade of between 8.6 per cent (using a constant-returns-to-scale, perfect-competition model) and 23.5 per cent (using an increasing-returns-to-scale, imperfect-competition model). The difference between the two estimates is largely accounted for by the incorporation of monopolistic competition in the latter, which gives rise to increased intra-industry trade. In terms of income effects, the estimated gain for the world is put at between US$109 billion, using static specifications (the basic, static, constant returns-to-scale model), and US$510 billion, using dynamic specifications (which incorporate scale economies, imperfect competition and dynamic investment-income linkages) by the year 2005 (in 1990 dollars). The second of these figures is estimated at 1.36 per cent of world GDP. The static welfare gains are in line with other studies but the total gains are considerably higher when nontraditional, dynamic gains are included. In particular, the scope which trade liberalisation creates for intra-industry trade in a monopolistically competitive model has a major impact. Clearly, a sizeable part of the gain from the Round is to be found in the scope which it creates for increased intra-industry trade.

Unlike some of the previous models, this one finds that the most important source of overall gain follows from the elimination of quotas on industrial products, namely, the MFA quotas for textiles and quotas on Japanese cars in the EU market. These account for US$324 billion out of the the total gain of US$510 billion. The second-largest source of gain comes from reducing industrial tariffs if scale and specialisation economies are included. Agricultural liberalisation gives a further gain of US$53 billion.

While a large proportion of these gains accrue to the developed countries, as in previous studies, the dynamic specification shows sizeable gains being reaped by developing countries. A static specification shows these countries losing because the loss of MFA quota rents more than offsets any gain from increased market access for textile exports.

It must be emphasised that even the latter study provides only a minimum estimate of the likely gains, on the assumption that the Agreement is fully implemented. This is because it can only take into account the quantifiable effects of some of the liberalisation measures. For this reason, many of the effects of the GATS Agreement covering trade in services are not included. Likewise, beneficial effects on trade from a strengthening of trade rules, enforcement procedures and disputes settlement are omitted. Nevertheless, what can be stated with a reasonable degree of certainty is that the total effect of the Round should, within ten years of the date of implementation, boost world income by an amount equivalent to at least 1 per cent and more probably closer to 1.4 per cent relative to what it would otherwise be. Whether this will happen will, however, depend on a large number of factors. How and when the package is implemented is clearly important. Some aspects of the Agreement (such as the provisions for phasing out MFAs) leave uncertainties in this respect. Much, too, will depend on the impact of the newly created WTO in bringing stricter adherence to trade rules and more effective settlement of trade disputes. Another key issue could be the extent to which countries – the advanced industrialised countries in particular – are able to undermine the benefits of the agreement by the use of measures such as antidumping. As we observed in Chapter 4, the new Antidumping Code is disappointing in several respects and may fail to curb the tendency, apparent before the Round, for countries (particularly the advanced industrialised countries) to use antidumping as a convenient form of protectionism.

THE WORLD TRADE ORGANISATION (WTO)

One of the most important results of the Uruguay Round was the agreement to set up a new World Trade Organisation (WTO) as the replacement for the GATT. This creates for the first time an international organisation with a permanent existence to be responsible for trading relationships between countries, analagous to the International Monetary Fund (IMF) and World Bank (IBRD) on the monetary front and with power to force member states to adhere to the rules. The GATT was not an organisation, but rather a treaty which countries signed. When they did so, they became 'contracting parties' but not 'members' as such. Moreover, the GATT never had a permanent existence but only ever a provisional application. There was a widely held view that these peculiar features of the GATT reduced its effectiveness as the basis for a rules-based system of world trade. Therefore, one of the issues addressed in the Round was how, if at all, the GATT structure could be strengthened and whether this should entail changing its constitutional structure. Out of these discussions emerged a blueprint for a WTO.

In fact, the idea of having an international organisation for trade analagous to the IMF on the monetary front was not new. After the Second World War when the GATT came into being, it was the intention of the allied powers to create an International Trading Organisation (ITO) along similar lines. A charter was drafted by the US on which agreement was reached at Havana in 1948 (the Havana Charter). Intertwined with the negotiations to set up an ITO were parallel negotiations for drafting a GATT which would set out certain obligations (primarily on tariffs) for countries signing the Agreement, including the obligation to enter into multilateral negotiations to reduce tariffs. The intention was that, if and when the ITO was set up, the GATT would be subsumed within the ITO. As it turned out, the ITO never came into being because US Congress was unwilling to approve the Havana Charter. However, when the GATT negotiations were completed in October 1947, the Havana Charter had not been submitted to Congress for approval. Yet, in order to carry out multilateral tariff negotiations under the 1945 US tariff-cutting authority before it expired in mid-1948, it was considered preferable to press ahead with applying the GATT rather than to await the ratification of the Charter. For this reason, the GATT was adopted by a Protocol of Provisional Application whereby the Treaty was to be provisionally applied by the countries signing it. This has remained the case ever since.

One aspect concerns the obligations of contracting parties under the Protocol. Under the Protocol, countries were only required to apply Part II of the GATT, which contains most of the substantial obligations, to the fullest extent consistent with their existing legislation. This meant that, where a conflict occurred, a country could invoke so-called 'grandfather rights' which exempted it from applying the relevant provisions. In other words, countries need not apply all the measures contained in Part II of the Treaty. Although many of these grandfather rights have since been extinguished, they can be and still are used by countries to gain exemption from certain provisions of the GATT. For example, the United States was able to claim certain exemptions from the GATT provisions for agricultural goods by invoking grandfather rights.

A further aspect has been the difficulty of amending the GATT to include new obligations as the need for new rules arose. This required the agreement of two-thirds of the contracting parties and could in any case only be binding on those countries which accepted it. The solution to this problem adopted by the contracting parties was to develop various 'side agreements' or 'codes'. For example, when the need to negotiate new disciplines to regulate the use of nontariff barriers emerged in the course of the Tokyo Round, this was the approach adopted. However, a drawback is that the application of these agreements was necessarily limited to the countries prepared to sign the new Code. Thus a situation could arise where countries could be omitted from certain features of the GATT so long as they adhere to the obligations contained in the main Agreement. In other words, they could choose which aspects of the GATT they wished to be committed to. Given the need to be constantly developing and modifying GATT rules to take account of the changing nature of trade policy, this constituted a major drawback.

A further problem arising from the peculiar status of the GATT concerned rule application and dispute settlement. Because the GATT is a treaty and not an organisation, it must operate on the principle of consensus. Rather than impose decisions of the contracting parties on a recalcitrant country, the approach has been to secure its agreement to a remedy of the particular violation or failure to comply. The procedure which is set out in Articles XXII and XXIII of the GATT is as follows. Any country which considers another contracting party to have acted in a way which 'nullifies or impairs' any benefit accruing to it under the GATT may make a complaint to the GATT. Countries must first seek to resolve their dispute by bilateral consultation and negotiation. However, if this is unsuccessful, the matter may be taken to the GATT. In this case, the procedure is to set up a panel of experts to investigate the complaint and make recommendations to the contracting parties (that is, the GATT Council). For the recommendations of the panel to become effective, they must be adopted by the Council. However, because GATT works on the basis of consensus, the losing contracting party can always block acceptance. In practice, most panel reports are adopted by the contracting parties despite this problem. However, there is a further problem of noncompliance: many reports that are approved are not subsequently complied with. GATT rules do allow contracting parties to suspend GATT obligations from other parties in serious cases of this kind. However, in practice, this has rarely been done. These weaknesses of the GATT have undoubtedly contributed to the growing tendency for countries (especially the largest trading nations) to resolve disputes outside the GATT. For example, Section 301 and Super 301 of US trade law provide for bilateral retaliation against countries which discriminate against or treat US exports unfairly.

Most of these problems flow from the fact that the GATT is only a treaty, and are not helped by the fact that the Treaty is ambiguous in terms of the powers which it bestows on the contracting parties jointly to enforce decisions of the parties. Because the WTO is an organisation, it overcomes many of these problems although it remains to be seen how this will work in practice. The provisions for the creation of the WTO are set out in Part II of the Uruguay Round Final Act (GATT, 1994a). Article 1 of the Agreement Establishing the Multilateral Trade Organisation states that the new organisation is 'to provide the common institutional framework for the conduct of trade relations among its Members' to encompass all the agreements and associated legal instruments contained within the Final Act. These agreements are fivefold:

1 the Agreements on Trade in Goods. This includes the so-called 'GATT 1994', the Uruguay Round Protocol GATT 1994, plus the various agreements covering agriculture, textiles and clothing, trade-related investment measures, subsidies and countervailing measures, safeguards, and so on. GATT 1994 consists of the provisions contained in GATT 1947 'as rectified, amended or otherwise modified', subsequently, the provisions of the legal instruments that have entered into force under GATT 1947 (for example, protocols of accession, special waivers and other decisions of the contracting parties) and the various Under-standings on Interpretation negotiated as part of the Uruguay Round. This is referred to as GATT 1994. The Uruguay Round Protocol GATT 1994 contains the results of the market-access negotiations for reducing or eliminating tariffs and nontariff barriers as recorded in the national schedules of concessions and annexed to the Protocol;
2 the Agreement on Trade in Services (GATS);
3 the Agreement on Trade-related Aspects of Intellectual Property Rights including trade in counterfeit goods (TRIPs);
4 the Understanding on Rules and Procedures Governing the Settlement of Disputes;
5 the Trade Policy Review Mechanism

Any country joining the WTO agrees to adhere to all and not just some of these agreements. This represents a major difference from the GATT, although this does not apply to the so-called 'plurilateral agreements' except for those countries which have accepted them. The plurilateral agreements are the trade in civil aircraft agreement, the government procurement agreement, the international dairy agreement, and the arrangement regarding bovine meat. The option is open for a country not to join the WTO if it does not wish to be be bound by all the agreements which come under the WTO umbrella. A country which is a signatory of GATT 1947 and which chooses not to join the WTO would remain a contracting party of GATT 1947. This is because, according to the Agreement Establishing the WTO (Article II: 4), GATT 1994 is legally distinct from GATT 1947. Such a country will therefore enjoy the protection of GATT 1947 without the need to acccept all the obligations of being a member of the WTO. However, it appears to be equally possible for a country that joins the WTO not to remain a contracting party of GATT 1947. Indeed, the US has already indicated its intention of exercising this option. This could mean that a country which rejects WTO membership may cease to enjoy protection from trade measures imposed by the US which breach obligations under GATT 1994. For example, if the US were to double import duties on a product coming from a country outside the WTO, the latter country would cease to enjoy the right to complain and seek a settlement through the GATT now that the US is no longer a signatory of GATT 1947. There exists therefore a strong incentive for countries to join the WTO and thereby accept parts of the package which it might otherwise prefer to opt out of. To that extent, the WTO amounts to a significant extension of GATT rules and disciplines (Hindley, 1994).

A further significant change concerns the area of dispute settlement. The WTO has the task of administering the Uruguay Round document, Understanding on Rules and Procedures Governing the Settlement of Disputes. Article IX makes clear that the WTO 'shall continue the practice of desision-making by consensus followed under the GATT 1947'. However, the Understanding sets out a new procedure for the adoption of panel reports where countries fail to reach a consensus. Paragraph 16 states that:

> Within sixty days of the issuance of a panel report to the Members, the report shall be adopted at a DSB (Dispute Settlements Body) meeting unless one of the parties to the dispute formally notified the DSB of its decision to appeal or the DSB decides by consensus not to adopt the report.

> (GATT, 1994)

Where there is no appeal, a consensus is therefore now required for a panel report *not* to be adopted. If one of the parties appeals, the DSB cannot consider the panel report until after the appeal has been completed. A new Appellate Body is established for this purpose and must reach a decision within sixty days. However, its report has to be adopted by the DSB unless there exists a consensus *not* to do so. These procedures should make it more difficult for losing parties to block the acceptance of a panel report.

Other rules set out much stricter procedures for resolving disputes, including strict time limits on the period for bilateral consultations before requesting a disputes panel and an automatic right to a panel unless the WTO Council votes against. Strict time limits are now set for all stages of the settlement process. Where a complaint is upheld, the offending country has up to twenty days in which to agree a remedy. Failure to do so allows the complaining party to suspend 'concessions or other obligations under the covered agreements'. It should first seek to do so with respect to the same sector as that in which the violation, nullification or impairment occurred. However, if the party concerned considers that not practicable or effective, it may suspend concessions or other obligations in other sectors of the same agreement or even under another covered agreement. Thus, if the impairment took the form of an infringement of rights under the intellectual property rights agreement, the offended country could retaliate by withdrawing concessions or other obligations on trade in goods. This possibility of cross-retaliation should make countries more willing to comply with WTO rulings. These changes mean a more effective system for enforcing trade rules with a shift in emphasis away from reliance on negotiation and consensus and towards dependence on fixed rules, more carefully prescribed procedures and stricter timetables.

It remains to be seen how well the WTO will live up to the high hopes which have been placed in it. An early challenge to its authority came in March 1994 with a decision by the United States to revise its Super 301 trade law which had been allowed to lapse in 1990. In October 1994, however, the US announced its intention not to draw up a list of trading practices which unreasonably and unfairly discriminated against American exporters and effectively dropped its attempt to revive Super 301. Further concern was raised by the decision of the US Congress to set up a panel of US judges to review dispute-settlement decisions involving the US. If the panel considers that any three decisions within the next five years have been 'unjust', Congress will review US membership of the WTO with a view to possible withdrawal. Much depends on the interpretation of 'unjust'. Does this mean decisions contrary to WTO procedures or those which conflict with US economic interests? If the latter, the authority of the new disputes panel might very soon be undermined (de Jonquires, 1995).

Clearly, the success or otherwise of the WTO hinges on the effectiveness of the new dispute-settlement machinery. The manner in which it handles some of the first cases on which it is required to make a ruling will be crucial. If these decisions are widely seen to be the result of fair and impartial procedures, and rulings are respected by member states, the WTO will succeed in establishing its authority. If, alternatively, decisions are subject to frequent challenges from member states and rulings are systematically disregarded, it will fail the make the hoped-for impact (de Jonquires, 1995). Then the danger is that member states may revert to bilateralist and unilateralist solutions to trading problems. Regional rivalries over the appointment of the first person to head the WTO provided a less than auspicious start.

TRADE POLICY AND THE ENVIRONMENT

There can be no doubt that the first contender for a place on the agenda for future trade negotiations will be the issue of trade policy and the environment. At the signing of the Uruguay Round agreement at Marrakesh in April 1994, it was agreed to set up a Committee on Trade and the Environment to study and report to the WTO within two years on a range of relevant issues. Among them are the impact on market access of environmental measures, and whether trade rules need to be modified to accommodate multilateral environmental agreements which contain trade provisions (see *The Financial Times*, 23 March 1994). In recent years, environmental issues have assumed an increased importance in trade policy partly as a result of two events. The first was a dispute between the United States and Mexico over an embargo imposed by the US on imports of Mexican tuna on the grounds that tuna fish were caught in ways which also killed dolphins. A court case in the US had ruled that, in conformity with the Marine Mammal Protection Act (MMPA), tuna were not to be imported from any country whose fishermen destroyed more than 1.25 times as many dolphins as the American fishing fleet did in the eastern Pacific in the same year.

Following a complaint by Mexico, a GATT panel investigated the dispute; it reported in late 1991, concluding that the US was in violation of its GATT obligations. The panel's case rested on three arguments. Firstly, under Article III of the GATT, imported products must be treated as favourably as national ones, and the way the product is produced is not a good enough reason to discriminate against it. Secondly, although Article XX(V) of the GATT allows countries to restrict imports so as to protect animal health or natural resources, this did not justify the tuna embargo as the US sought to argue, because any harm occurring took place outside US jurisdiction. Thirdly, it was not legitimate for a country to restrict trade on one product in order to enforce preservation policies relating to another unrelated product. There were further problems arising from the standard for dolphin kills laid down by the US, which was deemed to have been retroactive and variable: Mexican fisherman could not possibly know in advance what 1.25 times the American kill would be. Although the panel report was never adopted by the GATT Council, it attracted considerable opposition from environmental groups in the US, and others who saw the report as a challenge to US sovereignty. Several years later, the EU brought a further complaint to the GATT objecting to a second embargo imposed under the MMPA on all countries that import and process tuna from Mexico or any other offending country. This secondary embargo stated that, not only must a country trading with the US kill fewer dolphins, it must also adopt fishing methods which conform with those used by US fishing fleets. In May 1994, the second panel report ruled against the US, using somewhat different reasoning. It argued that countries *may* use trade measures to protect 'the global commons' or environmental resources outside their own jurisdiction. However, the measures must be carefully designed so as to protect the resources in question and, even then, are only permissible if no other more GATT-consistent measures are available. The US embargo failed to meet these requirements.

The second event which served to focus attention on the links between environmental issues and trade policy was the formation of NAFTA. Concern about so-called 'eco-dumping' loomed large in the debate within the US which preceded the signing of the Agreement. Opponents of NAFTA exploited US concerns about Mexico's lower environmental standards in an effort to prevent NAFTA being ratified. In an effort to address these concerns and gain acceptance for the NAFTA agreement, President Clinton negotiated a special side-agreement providing for environmental protection. This committed the three countries – the US, Canada and Mexico – not to lower environmental standards but to adopt measures to raise existing levels. In addition, a special border environment institution was to be created to co-ordinate action on water and solid waste pollution in the region along the US–Mexican frontier. The inclusion of special provisions within a trading agreement for tackling problems arising from differences in environmental standards and preventing eco-dumping was novel. Moreover, it drew attention to the link between environmental and trade policy. One result was that environmental groups began pressing for new rules to be introduced to the GATT that would address environmental concerns.

Esty (1994) sees the environmentalist challenge to free trade as based on four propositions. Firstly, there is the argument that trade liberalisation by promoting economic growth damages the environment through unsustainable consumption of natural resources and waste production. The argument is subject to several objections. To begin with, trade liberalisation can equally well assist the achievement of environmental objectives. By promoting a more efficient use of resources, it conserves scarce resources and relieves the problem of unsustainable resource consumption. Nor is economic growth itself detrimental to the environment. In most developing countries, poverty is the cause of environmental degradation. Low incomes are associated with overpopulation and subsistence farming, both of which are linked with damage to the environment. Higher incomes should lead to less damage to the environment and greater expenditure on ensuring proper use of the environment. Likewise, protectionism can equally well result in environmental damage. For example, protectionist agricultural policies in developed countries frequently result in more land-intensive farming methods, in water and soil pollution through increased use of chemicals in the form of artificial fertilisers and pesticides, and in soil erosion through the cultivation of marginal land. Protectionism is as likely to bring environmental damage as free trade. A related issue concerns the increase in transportation activity resulting from more trade. Environmentalists argue that this is associated with more damage to the environment from factors such as increased oil spillages at sea and greater air pollution from the engines of aircraft. On the other hand, examples may equally well be found where trade liberalisation reduces the risk of environmental damage from transport activity. For example, lower import barriers on processed commodities may result in more raw materials being processed by the countries in which they are extracted so reducing the bulkiness of goods shipped (Anderson, 1995).

Secondly, environmentalists complain that trade rules and agreements result in environmental regulations being undermined unless specific clauses are included to permit restrictions to be imposed. The problem stems from the existence of different environmental standards in different countries. These in turn reflect different needs and preferences, with some countries attaching greater priority to protecting the environment. On the one hand, there is a need to defend a country's legitimate rights to enforce within its own territory the specific regulations its people want. On the other hand, the wish to protect the regulatory regime of a country must not become a cover for essentially protectionist measures. Harmonisation of standards removes the problem but denies countries the right to choose the degree of regulation (if any at all) they consider appropriate. The alternative is to allow trade restrictions to be imposed to ensure that production in countries with lower environmental standards does not undermine standards in countries with tougher regimes. On the other hand, Bhagwati (1995) has argued that cross-country intra-industry differences in environmental standards reflect a legitimate diversity of preferences. Poorer countries may attach a lesser importance to controlling pollution than do richer countries. Why should richer countries be allowed to impose trade restrictions on poorer countries simply because pollution taxes are lower in the latter?

Thirdly, many environmentalists regard trade policy as an essential instrument for enforcing international environmental agreements. Unlike the two previous arguments which were essentially defensive, Esty (1994) sees this argument as representing part of the environmentalists' 'offensive agenda'. This is a proposition to use trade policy as a weapon to achieve internationally agreed environmental objectives. Examples of international agreements containing trade provisions include the Montreal Protocol on Substances that Deplete the Ozone Layer (1989), which provides for discrimination against imports from nonsignatories, and the Convention on International Trade in Endangered Species of Wild Fauna and Flora (CITES) (1975) which, in 1989, resulted in a trade ban on products from endangered African elephants. The argument rests on the premise that many environmental problems are global in nature such that the actions of one country have spillover effects on other countries. In addition, there is the need to prevent countries from 'free-riding', enjoying the benefits from the restrictions agreed by countries signing the agreement but not themselves participating in restraint by signing or implementing it.

Fourthly, the second part of the environmentalists' offensive agenda is the concern about eco-dumping. Countries with low environmental standards can sell their products at lower cost than can producers in countries with higher standards. They thereby put pressure on countries with tough environmental standards to reduce the rigour of their regulatory regime. The fear is that, through a flight of capital and labour to countries with lower standards, there will occur a competitive lowering of standards, triggering a 'race to the bottom'. This is another aspect of the 'spillover' problem whereby the pollution taxes chosen by one country impose costs on other countries. Anderson (1995) perceives that, from the late 1960s onwards, environmentalists became increasingly aware that one way in which pollution-intensive industries could be persuaded to accept tougher standards was by granting them in return protection against imports from lower-standard developing countries. In other words, trade restrictions became a convenient device for buying-off producer opposition to higher standards in the advanced industrialised countries. In addition, environmentalists pointed to what they perceived to be the greater ease with which firms could in the modern context relocate production in lower-standard or 'pollution-haven' countries.

Most trade economists would accept that the last two arguments reflect genuine concerns. However, as Anderson (1995) convincingly argues, there are grave dangers in using trade policy for these purposes. To begin with, there are often alternative, more efficient methods for achieving the same objectives. Secondly, there is a risk that trade policy will be captured by producer interest groups for protectionist purposes, using environmental arguments as the pretext. Thirdly, the use of trade policy for such ends threatens to increase the number of trade disputes arising between countries. If these cannot be resolved in mutually agreed ways, there is a danger that confidence in a rules-based system of international trade will be undermined. Furthermore, because environmental standards are typically lower in developing countries, it pits rich against poor countries and North against South. There are normative issues involved which concern the right of richer, developed countries to demand that poorer countries incur the expense of applying similar environmental standards. There are even more complex issues concerning the extent to which scarce resources or endangered species existing within the territory of a particular country or region represent 'global commons', as environmentalists maintain.

Similar conclusions were reached by the World Bank in 1992 following a major study of the effects of trade policy on the environment (World Bank, 1992). It largely rejected the use of trade measures as a device for achieving environmental objectives except in certain narrowly defined circumstances. Where action is needed to achieve such objectives, it concluded that other, more efficient methods exist. An important conclusion was that the cost advantage enjoyed by producers in countries with laxer environmental standards is generally exaggerated. This is because the costs of meeting environmental standards, even in countries with strict rules, was low in relation to total costs. For example, in the United States, where standards are generally high, the costs of pollution abatement and control were found to account for an average of only 0.54 per cent of a company's overall costs. Partly for these reasons, the World Bank rejected the view that laxer environmental standards contribute to a migration of pollution-intensive industries to these countries. The available empirical evidence fails to provide strong support for linking the growth of pollution-intensive industries with laxer controls in developing countries. Although there has been a rapid growth of these industries in developing countries, this is a reflection of industrialisation rather than of any tendency for producers to migrate to countries with laxer standards. Legal liability and reputation in the company's home market also act to deter producers from shifting production to such countries merely to reduce environmental costs. The region which was found to have the fastest growth of so-called 'dirty industries' was Eastern Europe, but this was the result of consumer choice being politically suppressed.

The General Agreement contains no explicit reference to environmental issues. However, there are provisions contained within Article XX which allow exceptions to the general principles of the GATT in certain specific situations including environmental regulations. Article XX(b) permits measures 'necessary to protect human, animal or plant life or health'. The key word is 'necessary'. This has been interpreted in GATT cases to mean 'least GATT-inconsistent'. Thus, in 1987, a GATT panel ruled that a cigarette import ban by Thailand which was not accompanied by equivalent production limits on the state cigarette monopoly was not justifiable. Environmental groups have complained that this interpretation of a 'necessary' measure is too narrow because, in most cases, it is not too difficult to find a less 'GATT-inconsistent' measure. Article XX(g) allows countries to adopt or enforce measures 'relating to the conservation of exhaustible natural resources', provided that such measures are intended to reinforce restrictions on domestic production or consumption. In 1987 the United States lodged a complaint against a Canadian restriction on the export of unprocessed salmon and herring, justifed by the Canadians as a conservation measure. A complaints panel found that the measures were unacceptable because Canada had placed no equivalent limits on domestic consumption of these products and, therefore, the restriction could not be regarded as being primarily aimed at making domestic regulations effective. The requirement that the measure should merely 'relate' to the conservation of natural resources has been interpreted by GATT panels to mean 'primarily aimed' at addressing conservation goals. This allows for the possibility of 'mixed motives' so long as the primary aim is environmental.

A criticism of Article XX concerns its limited scope. Its coverage is limited to exhaustible natural resources and so excludes the atmosphere, the oceans, the ozone layer and other elements of the 'global commons'. Moreover, it cannot be applied to environmentally harmful measures pursued outside the jurisdiction of the nation imposing the measures. This was the ruling of the GATT panel which, in 1991, reported on the Mexican complaint against the US law which banned imports of tuna caught in nets that can also kill dolphins. Environmental groups have argued that measures pursued by certain countries which harm the environment have global or transboundary spillover effects. It is therefore inappropriate to confine Article XX to measures which are pursued only within the country imposing the measure. A more substantial criticism concerns the fact that Article XX cannot be applied to the matter of *how* a product is produced, only to *what* is produced. The GATT rules do not permit discrimination against a 'like product' produced in another country even if the method of production is different. The logic behind this is the need to ensure that trade takes place on the basis of a country's comparative advantage; this would be undermined if trade measures could discriminate against products made by different (cheaper or more efficient) methods. However, several critics see this as untenable in an ecologically interdependent world (Esty, 1994). How a product is produced, the argument goes, is often what matters, not just for the country producing the product but for the world as a whole which is thereby affected.

Little attempt was made in the Uruguay Round to tackle environmental issues as these were not part of the agenda when the Round was launched in 1986. However, the Final Act did contain a number of relevant provisions. The Preamble to the Agreement Establishing the World Trade Organisation (WTO) declared an objective of the new organisation to be:

> expanding the production and trade in goods and services, while allowing for the optimal use of the world's resources in accordance with the objective of sustainable development, seeking both to protect and preserve the environment and enhance the means for doing so in a manner consistent with their respective needs and concerns at different levels of economic development.
>
> (GATT, 1994)

Apart from this, there were a number of aspects of the Final Act which included environmental provisions. The Agreement on Technical Barriers to Trade (TBT) and the Agreement on Sanitary and Phytosanitary Measures (SPS) build on the Tokyo Round Technical Barriers Code and cover measures taken by governments to protect human, animal and plant life, or health and the environment. The agreements recognise the rights of governments to take such measures but establish certain rules designed to protect against their misuse. However, the most significant result to emerge from the Round as far as environmental issues are concerned was the decision to set up a Committee on Trade and Environment with a wide-ranging brief to investigate and report back (within two years) to the WTO on matters pertaining to both trade and the environment. The issues to be explored by the Committee include the impact on market access of environmental measures, and whether trade rules need to be modified to accommodate multilateral environmental agreements with trade provisions. The Committee will consider some of the most controversial issues, such as processing and production methods (PPMs) – should trade rules be revised to allow discrimination between identical products produced in different ways? – and eco-dumping (see *The Financial Times*, 23 March 1994).

TRADE POLICY AND LABOUR STANDARDS

Closely entwined with the issue of the environment and trade policy is that of labour standards. Concern among certain developed countries about 'social dumping' surfaced in the last stages of the Uruguay Round and in the run-up to the signing of the final agreement at Marrakesh in April 1994. Specifically, the United States threatened not to sign the Final Act unless the issue of workers' rights was put on the agenda of the soon-to-be-formed World Trade Organisation. The US had made previous but unsuccessful attempts to get workers' rights included on the agenda of the Uruguay Round. This pressure from the developed countries to bring labour standards within the ambit of the GATT and the future WTO was strongly resisted by the developing countries. The latter regarded the move as an attempt by the developed countries to introduce protectionism under the cloak of a professed concern over human rights. The outcome of this last-minute rift between signatories of the Final Act was a compromise whereby reference to labour standards was omitted from the formal documents of the Uruguay Round. However, along with other issues, there was an agreement that it could be examined by the WTO after it was set up. Subsequently, France has been in the forefront of developed countries arguing for workers' rights to be on the agenda of the WTO.

Traditionally, the issue of labour standards has been viewed as a matter for the International Labour Organisation (ILO) rather than being a GATT issue. The ILO has sought to set universal standards for the labour sector through its International Labour Code. This is enshrined in two major instruments: the International Labour Conventions and International Labour Recommendations. The former require ratification by member states and become embodied in national laws. The latter are standards which are intended as a guide to action. Existing ILO Conventions cover workers' rights, such as the right to form and join trade unions, freedom from forced labour and from discrimination, equal remuneration for work of equal value, the abolition of child labour, minimum standards of health and safety, employment policy and the fixing of minimum wages. However, the approach of the ILO is a voluntary one. Developing countries have often been criticised for slowness in ratifying conventions, particularly those relating to employment and working conditions. Developed countries have also expressed concern about the effectiveness with which ratified standards are implemented in developing countries. On the other hand, developing countries have frequently questioned the relevance of some of the provisions to their own situation. It is often argued that a developing country seeking to industrialise must necessarily attach less importance to achieving certain labour standards since its most immediate need is to overcome poverty. This might be the case when it comes to the task of implementing standards relating to hours of work, minimum wages, child and female labour, night work and social security. Furthermore, developing countries often cannot afford the administrative machinery required to ensure effective enforcement of national labour laws.

Dissatisfaction with the essentially voluntary approach of the ILO to ensuring 'fair trade' has led to growing demands from organised labour in developed countries for a 'social clause' to be introduced to the GATT. As with environmental standards, the issue has assumed a new importance with the gradual decline of traditional trade barriers and the increased ease with which multinational companies can switch investment abroad (Anderson, 1995). Lower trade barriers mean that a requirement to raise labour standards in any one country has a relatively much greater effect on the cost competitiveness of producers in that country to the extent that similar standards are not adopted in other countries. The greater freedom with which multinational companies can switch production (especially labour-intensive, final-assembly stages) may mean that lower labour standards in developing countries have a significant effect on the level of investment, output and employment in developed countries. The rapid growth of the newly industrialising countries of South-East Asia and Latin America has meant more intense competition for the developed countries. This has coincided with a decline in manufacturing industry in many of the developed regions of the world. Rightly or wrongly, lower labour standards in NICs are perceived as giving these countries an 'unfair' competitive advantage.

For these reasons, social clauses have recently been inserted into a number of trading agreements. In 1984, the US Generalized System of Preferences (GSP) was modified to allow preferences to be withdrawn from any beneficiary country which fails to enforce certain minimum workers' rights. These include the right of association, the right to organise and bargain collectively, prohibition of forced labour, a minimum age of employment, and minimum conditions of work including acceptable wages and hours of work. A precedent was also created by the inclusion within NAFTA of a side-agreement on labour standards parallel to that covering environmental standards. In the months immediately preceding the vote by the Congress and Senate on the NAFTA, Ross Perot and other opponents of NAFTA made great play with what was termed 'the giant sucking sound', namely, the danger that US jobs would be 'sucked away' to locations south of the US–Mexican border by the attractions of lower wages and poorer labour standards. The side-agreement on labour standards requires each country to promote freedom of association, the right to strike and to bargain collectively, a ban on forced labour, restrictions on child labour, equal pay for men and women, compensation for work accidents and the protection of migrant workers. Each country is required over a period of time to take action to improve working conditions and living standards, with annual reviews to monitor progress. The agreement also contains a special disputes procedure to be used where central or local governments in all three countries fail to enforce labour laws already in place. If a complaint about nonenforcement cannot be satisfied by consultation, an arbitration panel of experts may be set up on the vote of two out of the three NAFTA signatories. The panel will make a ruling and, if no action plan is then agreed to remedy the situation, can fine the offending government up to US$20 million. If a member state defies a panel ruling or refuses to pay the fine, the complainant country may impose trade sanctions by suspending benefits in proportion to the amount of the fine. In the case of Canada, however, it was agreed that compliance would be enforced through the federal courts (see *The Financial Times*, 14–15 August 1993).

In a similar fashion, the Treaty on European Union (the Maastricht Treaty), signed by the EC members in February 1992, included a Protocol on Social Policy as an annex. This commits eleven of the twelve member states (the UK would not agree to sign) to applying 'co-operation procedure' in a number of fields relating to employment policy. The EU's co-operation procedure involves two readings by the European Parliament and a decision by qualified majority vote, or unanimous voting in certain cases, in the Council of Ministers. It seeks to achieve a degree of harmonisation between member states in the area of social and employment policy. It covers health and safety at work, working conditions, information and consultation of workers, equality at work between men and women, and the integration of persons excluded from the labour market. Unanimous voting is required for issues such as social security and social protection of workers, the protection of workers made redundant, representation of the interests of workers and employers, and the promotion of employment and job creation.

Early proposals for including labour standards in international trading rules favoured inserting a 'social clause' in Article XIX of the GATT. This would allow countries to impose import restrictions on goods from an exporting country which failed to observe certain of the labour conventions contained within the ILO. More recently and with the creation of the WTO, there have been proposals from international trade union leaders to make membership of the WTO conditional upon ratification of certain of the ILO labour conventions, including those relating to forced labour, freedom of association, discrimination and child labour. Failure to enforce these standards properly could eventually lead to sanctions, imposed in the form of punitive tariffs (Goodhart, 1994). Supporters of these proposals argue that, without minimum labour standards being incorporated into trade policy rules, international competition will lead to a gradual downward harmonisation of standards, the 'race to the bottom'.

However, developing countries have so far strongly resisted any attempt to impose minimum labour standards, seeing this as 'a convenient cover for trade protectionism' (as the Malaysian trade minister was quoted as saying – *The Financial Times*, 14 April 1994). Developing countries have argued that different labour standards, like differences in wage-rates, are a legitimate source of comparative advantage reflecting real differences in resource endowments and societal preferences. Furthermore, many have argued that any attempt to force up labour standards in countries dominated by reliance on self-employment and large numbers of small, family-based enterprises confronts grave difficulties (OECD, 1995).

There is a need to distinguish between arguments primarily concerned with creating a 'level playing field' and those whose main concern is humanitarian, that is, outlawing such practices as slavery, child labour and suppression of the rights of free speech and assembly. Even if arguments about the need to establish similar working conditions in different countries are less convincing, the moral case for action to enforce basic human rights in countries where these are not upheld is overwhelming. It is, however, necessary to ask whether trade policy is the best means for bringing this about. The danger is that any attempt to use trade policy for this purpose will result in misuse. The problem is that trade policy is not formulated in a vacuum but evolves through a political process which creates many opportunities for well-organised sectional interests to capture it for their own purposes. In an ideal world, governments could be relied upon not to use human rights as a pretext for protectionism. In reality, governments are often influenced by whichever interest group is able to exert the greatest lobbying power. One of the aims in the creation of the GATT was to establish certain international rules which governments could use as a basis for resisting domestic protectionist interests. It follows that any weakening of those rules would create opportunities for sectional interests to obtain a trade policy which benefits them. In this case the losers would be consumers in the developed countries and the developing countries whose exports were restricted. Yet, as a recent OECD study has argued, the best way to raise labour standards in developing countries is to bring about increased prosperity in these countries (OECD, 1995). This will not be possible if developed countries raise barriers against products coming from developing countries.

Nevertheless, it seems unlikely that these arguments will be sufficient to convince either producers or organised labour in developed countries, who fear competition from countries lacking minimum labour standards. It may, therefore, be in the best interests of developing countries to make a positive response to the demands of the developed world. If a multilateral agreement cannot be reached on the issue of labour standards, developed countries will seek unilateral solutions. One way forward might be for developing countries to agree to a programme for raising labour standards and improving their enforcement mechanisms in return for offers of improved market access for their products in developed countries (Anderson, 1995). If it were agreed that this would not entail harmonisation of labour standards between developing and developed countries (which makes neither economic nor moral sense), the outcome need not be wholly unwelcome to developing countries. Concomitant with this might be a recognition that the surest way of bringing about improved labour standards in developing countries is increased prosperity, which presupposes increased and not reduced trade. Such an agreement could also include a restraint on developed countries from using trade restrictions unnecessarily for social objectives.

TRADE POLICY AND COMPETITION POLICY

Another key issue on the new agenda for trade policy will concern whether trade policy should be extended to cover competition policy. Should trade rules be extended to cover anticompetitive practices such as cartels, informal price agreements, the abuse of monopoly power, and so on? In the past, these have been areas of national rather than international concern. Many countries have their own antitrust laws or competition policy although they differ considerably. Traditionally, the main concern of the GATT has been with achieving improved market access through reductions in trade barriers and the abolition of discrimination arising from either border measures or other 'domestic' policies. Competition policies have only ever been deemed to be a GATT concern if they result in discrimination between national and foreign products. It is of course true that the GATT's objective of freer trade and the domestic policy objective of fostering more competitive markets are closely linked. Trade liberalisation is an effective way of injecting more competition into previously protected domestic markets. Thus, whether or not this is explicitly stated, an implicit aim of GATT has been the promotion of competition. The issue under consideration is whether the rules of GATT's successor, the WTO, should be enlarged to give more explicit recognition to this linkage.

One of the aspects of this linkage which has attracted a great deal of interest in recent years concerns the subject of antidumping policy. A particular form of dumping which has attracted much interest in economics textbooks but which is not widely considered to be important in practice has been that of predatory pricing. As we saw in Chapter 4, the necessary conditions for this to constitute a rational strategy even for a dominant producer are rarely present. Nevertheless, there can be no denying that if and when predatory pricing is used by a dominant producer to drive out rivals in a foreign market it constitutes a form of anticompetitive behaviour which should be prosecuted. Where this is taking place within the domestic market, it is generally covered by national competition laws. However, where it affects trade it becomes an issue for the antidumping authorities of the importing country. But if all countries were to adopt similar laws for dealing with this practice, there would be no need for an antidumping policy. It could be argued that this would be a preferable situation, given the risks that antidumping policy creates of being used for essentially protectionist purposes.

However, in law, dumping is not confined to cases of below-cost pricing. Any situation where an exporter is charging a price abroad which is lower than the price charged at home may lead to antidumping measures being imposed. One of the main arguments of proponents of antidumping policy is that dumping is an expression of the absence of normal competitive conditions in the domestic market of the foreign producer. A foreign producer can only charge a lower price abroad than at home if it enjoys market dominance at home and if import barriers are sufficiently high to prevent the good from being profitably exported back to the foreign country. This allegation has often been made by antidumping authorities in the EU and the US against exports coming from Japan and other South-East Asian economies. Attention is drawn to both 'hidden barriers', which make it difficult for western exporters to penetrate the domestic markets of these countries, and the absence of strict competition laws to ensure that normal competitive conditions prevail in the home market. Thus, the argument goes, antidumping policy is a way of compelling the exporting country to open up its domestic market. In particular, countries applying antidumping measures often regard them as a device to compel the exporting country to lower import barriers and provide improved market access. However, antidumping policy is not the most efficient way of achieving this objective. It relies upon the exporting firms which are subject to the antidumping duties putting pressure on their own governments. In any case, in the investigation of dumping in the importing country, little account is usually taken of whether dumping is the result of import barriers or restricted competition in the foreign market. Furthermore, the use of antidumping policy for this purpose creates the risk that the policy will be hijacked by protectionist interests in the importing country, with consequent damage to consumers and other producers there. A preferable way of tackling the problem would be through a policy of trade liberalisation which deals directly with the source of the problem, and the establishment of a proper and workable competition policy in the foreign country as part of an agreed set of international competition rules.

A further aspect of the linkage between trade policy and competition policy is concerned with the effects on market access of the absence of national competition laws and/or the failure to enforce them. As we have seen, market access has traditionally been the primary concern of the

GATT. Yet market access can be restricted if the government of the foreign country tolerates uncompetitive practices by domestic producers. In recent years, this issue has been at the heart of accusations by western exporters that Japan competes 'unfairly' by failing to enforce proper competitive conditions within its domestic market. The target has been the Japanese system of *keiretsu* which links together different companies in corporate groups or families. They usually include provisions for mutual protection, entail some element of joint ownership and frequently lead to close alliances. It is argued that, because *keiretsus* occupy such a dominant position in the Japanese economy, normal competitive conditions do not exist within its markets. Specifically, it has been argued that *keiretsus* result in anticompetitive behaviour and entry-deterring practices. The latter is a particular concern of western companies seeking to penetrate the Japanese market. It is argued that Japanese manufacturers and component suppliers are typically linked together in a long-term relationship which makes entry by new firms extremely difficult. In a similar manner, *keiretsus* which link together manufacturers with distributors are often seen as creating a barrier for western companies. The complex system of cross-shareholdings which bind together the members of the *keiretsu* family are also considered to constitute a seemingly impervious wall against foreign takeovers.

The *keiretsu* system has been a major issue in the ongoing dispute between the US and Japan over trade matters. The US has long regarded *keiretsus* as one of the primary barriers accounting for Japan's low level of manufacturing imports relative to domestic consumption and her large and persistent trade surplus. Thus, it was one of the issues raised by the US in the Structural Impediments Initiative (SII) talks between the two countries which were launched in 1990. The issue of anticompetitive practices has continued to occupy an important place on the agenda of the more recent 'framework talks' which in 1993 replaced the SII. Although Japan does have competition laws, a constant allegation is that they are poorly enforced. Regardless of the validity or otherwise of these arguments as applied to Japan, it is clearly the case that the absence of properly enforced competition laws can impede market access. As other trade barriers are lowered, it therefore looks certain that pressure will increase for competition policy to be brought within the WTO.

There are various possibilities. One radical suggestion has been that a special International Competition Policy Office (ICPO) should be set up within the WTO to investigate and prohibit cross-border cartels (which are often deliberately ignored by national competition authorities) and to make recommendations to member states to deal with abuses by cartels and multinational companies (Scherer, 1994). An alternative proposal is for a competition policy code within the WTO to commit members to enforce antitrust laws in a nondiscriminatory way with access to the new WTO dispute-settlements system when countries breach the code (Graham, 1994).

The idea that international trading rules should control anticompetitive behaviour which affects trade is not new. The Havana Charter of 1948, which provided for the ill-fated International Trade Organisation stated as one of its goals the prevention of business practices which interfere with competition, limit market access or promote monopoly control of markets. Although the GATT contains no clause outlawing anticompetitive practices pursued by private companies, since its only concern is with government practices, there are certain provisions of the GATT which can be applied to competition policy-related disputes, as Hoekman and Mavroidis (1994a) have demonstrated. However, these are confined to cases where anti-competitive business practices are supported by the government of a contracting party and where this disturbs competitive conditions established by the GATT regime. Support may take the form of passive tolerance (for example, by excluding the offending firm from competition laws or by not enforcing those laws) as well as more active forms of involvement (such as explicitly exempting firms from antitrust laws). In these cases, a contracting party could argue that a GATT obligation has been violated or could bring a nonviolation complaint arguing that a measure which is not GATT-inconsistent has none the less resulted in 'nullification or impairment' of an existing tariff concession (under Article XXIII). Cases of governments passively supporting anticompetitive practices (with which the US has sometimes charged the Japanese government) can only be challenged by bringing a nonviolation complaint. Even then, it would be necessary to argue that nonenforcement of competition laws, for example, amounted in effect to a subsidy to the domestic industry. Thus, there is some rather limited scope within the GATT as it stands for addressing competition policy-related issues.

However, there are no provisions for dealing with anticompetitive practices which impede market access but which are not supported actively or passively by governments. Moreover, existing GATT rules suffer from failure to address the issue of competition policy *per se*. Yet, as we have seen, differences in national competition laws may distort trade. However, Hoekman and Mavroidis (1994a) question the desirability of introducing competition policy to the agenda of any future round of multilateral trade negotiations. One reason is scepticism about the prospects for securing multilateral agreement on common competition policies. This has only ever been achieved at a bilateral or regional level as in the EC/European Economic Area and then as part of a far-reaching programme of trade liberalisation measures covering goods, services and factors of production. Another reason is concern that 'the process is captured by specific industry or government interests' and/or that 'governments more interested in regulating than freeing international trade/competition [may] seek to attain their objectives in a less than transparent manner' (Hoekman and Mavroidis, 1994a). Thirdly, they question whether the traditional 'public choice rationales' which underlie GATT-style negotiations could apply to co-operation on competition policy. This is because the degree of market-access restriction is rarely sufficient for the potential gains from removing these barriers to offset the losses to both importers and exporters from the removal of competition policy exemptions. There is therefore a practical problem in establishing a sufficiently large group of potential winners to offset the political power of the losers in order to allow liberalisation to take place. Their conclusion is that it would be better to concentrate future negotiations on further liberalisation of markets before pursuing harmonis-ation of competition policies. At best, some progress might be possible in agreeing to extend the new WTO dispute-settlement mechanism to competition policy-related concerns.

In the absence of agreement to harmonise competition policies, it may prove difficult to bring antidumping policy within the framework of competition law enforcement in the manner favoured by some trade economists and discussed above. In a different paper, Hoekman and Mavroidis (1994b) suggest an alternative approach which makes antidump-ing investigations a joint responsibility of the competition authorities in both the exporting and the importing country and the antidumping authorities. Following a complaint of dumping, the competition authorities in *both* countries would seek to determine whether the domestic markets of both countries are contestable. If the competition authorities in the exporting country find that the exporting firm has violated competition laws, the normal remedies would be applied. If the importing country's competition authorities found the domestic market not to be contestable, this would suggest that dumping, if it occurred, would not be harmful. Alternatively, because competition laws are not the same in all countries, it is possible that the authorities in the exporting country might reveal the existence of barriers which do not violate national laws. In this case, the importing country would be allowed to start an antidumping action. Yet a third possibility is that the authorities in the importing country might disagree with the findings of the antitrust investigation in the exporting country. In this case, they could either invoke WTO dispute-settlement mechanisms or initiate antidumping action. In other words, antidumping actions would be conditional upon a prior demonstration that the market of the exporting country is incontestable while that of the importing country is contestable *and* that the matter cannot be resolved through the application of competition laws. Hoekman and Mavroidis (1994b) see in their proposal the merit that it avoids the need to secure harmonisation of competition laws, which may prove difficult to achieve in practice at the multilateral level (although more success might be possible bilaterally or regionally). At the same time, competition policy considerations are brought into the unfair-trading realm in a way which meets some of the criticisms of antidumping policy as it is currently applied.

INTERNATIONAL INVESTMENT FLOWS

Finally, laws on investment flows are likely to constitute another item on the agenda of any future round of multilateral trade negotiations. As we discussed in Chapter 8, investment issues entered multilateral trade negotiations for the first time in the course of the Uruguay Round. The focus was primarily on investment policies which distort or restrict trade. However, a new item on the future agenda of the WTO will almost certainly be the creation of a framework for global investment flows. Traditionally, this has not been regarded as a province of the GATT or the WTO. Rather, the task of agreeing rules for the regulation of foreign direct investment (FDI) has fallen to the Organisation for Economic Co-operation and Development (OECD). A Code of Liberalisation of Capital Movements was agreed between the OECD members in 1961 designed to bring about a dismantling of existing barriers to capital movements between these countries. This was followed in 1976 by the Declaration on International Investment and Multinational Enterprises which contained a set of guidelines for multinational companies covering matters such as information disclosure, competition, financing, employment and industrial relations, and science and technology. For example, the guidelines required multinationals to refrain from transfer price manipulation although the obligation was couched in somewhat vague terms. However, compliance was purely voluntary. In addition, the code set out a number of general principles. Perhaps most important of all was a commitment by the signatories to ensure national treatment, that is, to treat national and foreign firms equally. There was also a commitment to bring about more co-operation between OECD member states in the area of investment incentives.

Recently, some major capital exporters have been seeking to bring about a strengthening of the OECD code. Negotiations are due to commence in May 1996 on the creation of a new set of international rules governing foreign direct investment. The rules will seek to ensure the right of companies to establish operations abroad and to protect them from restrictions on their right to withdraw capital as well as from the threat of expropriation of assets. In addition, it is intended that the rules will go much further in ensuring equality of treatment of foreign firms with local firms. However, the problem with any such agreement is that it would initially be restricted to the western industrialised economies. Although it could later be extended to the developing countries, the latter have hitherto strongly resisted interference by developed countries in their investment policies. Moreover, developing countries are unlikely to be willing to sign an agreement the negotiation of which they were never a party to. An alternative view is that the desire of these countries to attract foreign capital may make them more willing than in the past to embrace strong investment rules.

The fact that any OECD code excludes developing countries is one reason why some of the industrialised countries have favoured seeking an agreement under the auspices of the WTO. There is also a conviction that agreement could be easier to reach, even among the industrialised countries, if negotiations took place through the WTO. Negotiating investment rules within the context of multilateral trade negotiations may allow for trade-offs that can help overcome the reluctance of countries to make concessions on sensitive issues. The European Union Trade Commissioner, Sir Leon Brittan, has indicated his preference for the WTO as the appropriate forum, in part because of the legal difficulty which the EU faces in negotiating as an entity rather than as separate member states in the OECD as opposed to the WTO. A further advantage of incorporating investment rules in the WTO is that noncompliance could presumably be dealt with under the WTO's new dispute-settlement mechanisms, thereby giving greater force to any code agreed.

This begs the question whether rules governing foreign direct investment should legitimately be regarded as a WTO issue. The case for extending WTO rules to direct investment lies in the increasing difficulty of separating trade from investment matters. The rapid growth of direct investment abroad has brought about globalisation of production. Increasingly, products are manufactured on a worldwide basis. This has taken the form of splitting up the production process and relocating different stages of production in different countries. One result has been a rapid growth of trade in intermediate goods, often between different affiliates or subsidiaries of the same multinational company (so-called intra-firm trade). As was shown in Chapter 8, the linkage between trade and investment is especially apparent in the service sector, where the delivery of certain sorts of services presupposes both direct investment abroad and the temporary or permanent movement of personnel to the foreign country. For major capital exporters such as the US, the global operations of domestic companies often far exceed their purely US operations. In these circumstances, access to foreign markets is not just a matter of lower trade barriers but also of the right of establishment and the elimination or reduction of discrimination by host countries against foreign companies. For example, much of the dispute between the US and Japan has been concerned not just with the barriers which it is claimed Japan applies to manufacturing imports. A major concern for US negotiators has been barriers which discriminate against US companies wishing to establish subsidiaries in Japan.

Whatever the merits, or otherwise, of separating investment from trade issues, it looks certain that investment policies will occupy a place on the agenda of international trade negotiations in coming decades. These are likely to take the form of efforts to apply the principle of national treatment to direct investment. This is not just a matter of gaining some broad adherence to the general principle of national treatment. Rather, the need is to give some concrete substance to the principle in complex and potentially controversial areas. Countries differ greatly in the rules which are applied to company acquisitions or takeovers. Some countries are anxious to retain the right to discriminate against foreign companies where national security is threatened. A key issue in past negotiations affecting the US has been whether any agreed rules should have the same force when applied at state as at federal level. Countries are likely to face strong domestic resistance to changing these policies in the face of external pressure. Clearly, they will demand a long list of exemptions covering particular practices and sectors. It follows that any agreement reached will, initially, not be comprehensive. The wider the scope of the agreement sought, the more difficult it will be to negotiate and speedily achieve an outcome.

CONCLUSION

This chapter began with a summary of the results of the Uruguay Round. It was seen that the results of most studies of the Round show the potential for a considerable increase in global economic welfare if and when its results are fully implemented. The chapter continued with an examination of what many regard as the most important achievement of the Round, namely, the creation of a new permanent World Trade Organisation. We saw that the creation of the WTO represents a significant change in the institutional framework governing international trade policy, giving both permanence to world trading rules, which was not possible under the GATT, and setting in place new and stricter procedures for ensuring adherence to those rules. It remains to be seen how well these rules will work. At the time of writing, the WTO is facing a number of challenges. The authority with which it is able to deal with breaches of the rules will be crucial for establishing its credibility. Arguably, any improvement in the application and enforcement of world trading rules counts for as much as scheduled commitments entered into by countries offering improved market access to trading partners.

The rest of the chapter sought to identify some of the issues which are likely to dominate the agenda of world trade negotiations in the next few decades. Clearly, there remain a number of areas which the Uruguay Round left incomplete and which therefore will return to the agenda of the next round of negotiations. The agricultural package was disappointing in respect of the depth of liberalisation agreed, but was better than no agreement at all. Likewise, the General Agreement on Services (GATS) was widely regarded as little more than a start in the process of extending multilateral rules and disciplines to trade in services. The level of commitments fell a long way short of what many had hoped for. Negotiations in several key sectors (namely, financial services, telecommunications, maritime transport, movement of workers) were not complete in time for the conclusion of the Round and have been carried over. Subsequently, agreement was reached in July 1995 on a package of measures for opening up trade in financial services. Although this was achieved without the agreement of the United States, it does provide for a substantial increase in world trade in an important group of service activities. It remains to be seen how willing countries will be to make significant concessions in the other sectors where negotiations have still to be concluded.

In addition to these ongoing items, this chapter has examined several other issues which look certain to appear on the agenda of the next round. Two related issues concern the questions of environmental and labour standards. In part, these arise from concerns in the developed countries about 'eco-dumping' and 'social dumping'. The rapid growth of the newly industrialising countries combined with the gradual lowering of formal trade barriers has brought these issues to the fore. It has been argued here that any attempt to modify WTO rules to allow the developed countries greater freedom in putting up trade barriers to combat these problems risks playing into the hands of protectionists. On the other hand, it is clear that developed countries are determined to press these matters. The two other factors which are likely to enter the agenda of multilateral trade negotiations as we approach the new century are competition policy and international investment flows. The inclusion of these topics will bring the WTO into new and largely uncharted territory. Hitherto, neither has been considered a GATT concern. This approach can no longer be sustained. Strong and probably irresistible pressures will build up for new rules to cover these matters.

The question may well be asked whether, with the disappearance of the GATT, there will be another 'round' of multilateral negotiations of the kind which has occurred in the past. It seems quite probable that multilateral trade negotiations will in future be conducted in a different way. The vast range of issues which are now covered by trade negotiations, their increasing complexity and the ever-increasing number of countries participating may mean that the Uruguay Round was the last of its kind. Peter Sutherland, the former GATT Director-General, has suggested that future negotiations might take place within the framework of newly created biennial Ministerial Conferences, giving a degree of permanence to the process of negotiation. (The regulations setting up the WTO provide for a Ministerial Conference of WTO members every two years.) There may, however, still be a need for a formal round of negotiations with an agreed agenda. What is clear is that, in some shape or form, multilateral negotiations to bring about freer trade and to establish clear rules to govern the trade policies of countries will continue. However, as we discussed in Chapter 5, these look set to take place alongside a growing trend towards regional trade liberalisation. It is conceivable that the attraction of negotiating regional free trade will prove stronger than the multilateralist alternative. If so, the WTO could find itself engaged in an increasingly intense struggle for authority with ever more powerful regional trading blocs. This may yet prove to be the most important issue in the opening decades of the new century.

BIBLIOGRAPHY

Anderson, Kym (1993), *Economic Growth, Environmental Issues and Trade*, CEPR Discussion Paper No. 830, London: Centre for Economic Policy Research (CEPR)
—— (1995), *The Entwining of Trade Policy with Environmental and Labour Standards*, CEPR Discussion Paper No. 1158, London: Centre for Economic Policy Research
—— and Blackhurst, Richard (eds) (1992), *The Greening of World Trade Issues*, Hemel Hempstead, Herts.: Harvester Wheatsheaf
—— and —— (eds) (1993), *Regional Integration and the Global Trading System*, Hemel Hempstead, Herts.: Harvester Wheatsheaf
—— and Norheim, Hege (1993), History, geography and regional economic integration. In Anderson and Blackhurst (eds) (1993)
—— and Tyers, Rodney (1986), International effects of domestic agricultural policies. In Snape (ed.) (1986)
—— and —— (1991), *Global Effects of Liberalizing Trade in Farm Products*, Thames Essays No. 55, London: Trade Policy Research Centre/Harvester Wheatsheaf
Areeda, P. and Turner, D. (1975) Predatory pricing and related practices under section 2 of the Sherman Act. *Harvard Law Review*, Vol. 88, pp. 697–733
Arndt, R.W. (1968), On discriminatory v. nonpreferential tariff policies. *Economic Journal*, Vol. 78, pp. 971–9
Balassa, Bela (1974), Trade-creation and trade-diversion in the European Common Market. *Manchester School*, No. 2
—— and Michalopoulos, Costas (1985), *Liberalising World Trade*, World Bank Discussion Paper, Washington, D.C.: World Bank
Baldwin, Richard (1994), *Towards an Integrated Europe*, London: Centre for Economic Policy Research (CEPR)
—— and Kreuger A.(eds) (1984), *The Structure and Evolution of Recent U.S. Trade Policy*, Chicago, Ill.: University of Chicago Press, National Bureau of Economic Research
Baldwin, Robert E. (1989), The growth effects of 1992. *Economic Policy*, No. 9
—— (1993), Adapting the GATT to a more regionalised world: a political economy perspective. In Anderson and Blackhurst (eds) (1993)
—— and Murray, Tracy (1977), MFN tariff reductions and developing country trade benefits under the GSP. *Economic Journal*, Vol. 87
—— and Steagall, Jeffrey W. (1994), *An Analysis of US International Trade Commission Decisions in Antidumping, Countervailing Duty and Safeguard Cases*, Discussion Paper No. 990, London: Centre for Economic Policy Research
Banks G. and Tumlir, J. (1986), *Economic Policy and the Adjustment Problem*, Thames Essay No. 45, London: Trade Policy Research Centre

BIBLIOGRAPHY

Batchelor, Roy and Minford, Patrick (1977), Import-controls and devaluation as medium-term policies. In Corbet *et al.* (1977)

Beath, John (1991), Innovation, intellectual property rights and the Uruguay Round. *World Economy*, Vol. 13, No. 3

Bellis, J.-F. (1990), The EC antidumping system. In Jackson and Vermulst (eds) (1990)

Bernhardt, D. (1984), Dumping, adjustment costs and uncertainty. *Journal of Economic Dynamics and Control*, Vol. 8, pp. 349–70

Bhagwati, Jagdish (1984), Splintering and disembodiment of services and developing nations. *World Economy*, Vol. 7, pp. 133–43

—— (1987), Services. In Finger and Olechowski (eds) (1987)

—— (1988), *Protectionism*, Cambridge, Mass., and London: MIT Press

—— (1991), *The World Trading System at Risk*, Hemel Hempstead, Herts.: Harvester Wheatsheaf

—— (1992), Regionalism versus multilateralism. *World Economy*, Vol. 15, No. 5

—— (1995), *Free Trade, 'Fairness' and the New Protectionism: Reflections on the agenda for the World Trade Organisation*, IEA Occasional Paper 96, London: Institute of Economic Affairs (IEA)/Wincott Foundation

Blackhurst, Richard and Henderson, David (1993), Regional integration agreements, world integration and the GATT. In Anderson and Blackhurst (eds) (1993)

Bleaney, M.F. and Greenaway, David (1993), *Long Run Trends in the Relative Price of Primary Commodities and in the Terms of Trade of Developing Countries*, Oxford: Oxford Economic Papers

Boonekamp, Clemens F.J. (1987), Voluntary export restraints. *Finance and Development*, December; reprinted in King (1990)

Bourgeois, J. and Messerlin, P. (1993), Competition and the Antidumping regulations. Paris: Institut d'Etudes Politiques de Paris, mimeo

Brander, James A. (1986), Rationales for strategic trade and industrial policy. In Krugman (1986)

—— and Spencer, Barbara (1981), Tariffs and the extraction of foreign monopoly rents under potential entry. *Canadian Journal of Economics*, Vol. 14, pp. 371–89

—— and —— (1984), Tariff protection and imperfect competition. In Kierzkowski (1984)

—— and —— (1985), Export subsidies and market share rivalry. *Journal of International Economics*, Vol. 18, pp. 83–100

Brittan, Leon (1995), Why apathy must not prevail. *The Financial Times*, 19 June

Broadman, Harry G. (1994), GATS: the Uruguay Round accord on international trade and investment in services. *World Economy*, Vol. 17, No. 3

Cable, V. (1981), *Protectionism and Industrial Decline*, London: Overseas Development Institute/Hodder & Stoughton

—— (1987), Textiles and clothing. In Finger and Olechowski (eds) (1987)

Cline, William R. (1987), *The Future of World Trade in Textiles and Apparel*, Washington, D.C.: Institute for International Economics

—— (1995), Evaluating the Uruguay Round. *World Economy*, Vol. 18, No. 1

Collyns, Charles and Dunaway, Steve (1987), *The Costs of Trade Restraints*, IMF Staff Papers, Washington, D.C.: International Monetary Fund

Commission of the European Community (1989), *Sixth Annual Report from the Commission to the European Parliament on the Community's AntiDumping and AntiSubsidy Activities*, Brussels: European Commission

—— (1991), *Development and Future of the CAP* (MacSharry Report), Bulletin Supplement 5/91, Brussels: European Commission

—— (1994), EC agricultural policy. *European Economy*, No. 4

Cooper, C.A. and Massell, B.F. (1965), A new look at customs union theory. *Economic Journal*, Vol. 75, pp. 742–7

Corbet, Hugh, Corden, W.M., Hindley, Brian, Batchelor, Roy and Minford, Patrick (1977), *On How to Cope with Britain's Trade Position*, Thames Essays, No. 8, London: Trade Policy Research Centre

Corden, W.M. (1966), The structure of a tariff system and the effective rate of protection. *Journal of Political Economy*, Vol. 74, pp. 221–37

—— (1971), *The Theory of Protection*, Oxford: Oxford University Press

—— (1972), Economies of scale and customs union theory. *Journal of Political Economy*, Vol. 80, pp. 465–75

—— (1974), *Trade Policy and Economic Welfare*, Oxford: Clarendon Press

—— (1985), *Protection, Growth and Trade: Essays in international economics*, Oxford: Basil Blackwell

Cournot, Augustin (1838), *Recherches sur les principes mathématiques de la théorie des richesses*, Paris: Hachette

Davies, S.W. and McGuiness, A.J. (1982), Dumping at less than marginal cost. *Journal of International Economics*, Vol. 12, pp. 169–82

Deardorff, Alan V. (1990a), Economic perspective on antidumping law. In Jackson and Vermulst (eds) (1990)

—— (1990b), Should patent protection be extended to all developing countries? *World Economy*, Vol. 13, No. 4

de Clercq, Willy (1988), Fair practice, not protectionism. *The Financial Times*, 21 November

de Jonquires, Guy (1995), Early test for the WTO. FT Exporter 2, *The Financial Times*, 31 January

—— and Williams, F. (1995), Trade winds blow through talks. *The Financial Times*, 26 June

de Melo, Jaime, Hamilton, Carl B. and Winters, Alan L. (1990), *Voluntary Export Restraints: A case study on effects in exporting countries*, Seminar Paper No. 464, Stockholm: Institute for International Economic Studies, University of Stockholm

de la Torre, Augusto and Kelly, Margaret, R. (1992), *Regional Trade Arrangements*, IMF Occasional Paper 93, Washington, D.C.: International Monetary Fund

Destler, I.M. (1992), *American Trade Politics*, 2nd edn, Washington, D.C.: Institute for International Economics, and New York: 20th Century Fund

Devault, J. (1990), The administration of US antidumping duties: some empirical observations. *World Economy*, Vol. 13, No. 1, pp. 75–88

Dupuit, Jules (1844), On the measurement of the utility of public works, *Annales Ponts et Chaussees*, Vol. 8

Easterbrook, F. (1981), Predatory strategies and counterstrategies. *University of Chicago Law Review*, Vol. 263

—— (1984), The limits of antitrust. *Texas Law Review*, Vol. 1

Erzan, R. and Holmes, P. (1990), Phasing out the Multi-fibre Arrangement. *World Economy*, Vol. 13, No. 2, pp. 191–211

Erzan, Refik, Goto, Junichi and Holmes, Paula (1989), *Effects of the MFA on Developing Countries' Trade*, Seminar Paper No. 449, Institute for International Economic Studies, University of Stockholm

Esty, Daniel C. (1994), *Greening the GATT: Trade, Environment, and the Future*, Washington, D.C.: Institute for International Economics

Ethier, Wilfred J. (1982), Dumping. *Journal of Political Economy*, Vol. 90, No. 31, pp. 487–506

Feenstra, R.C. (1984), Voluntary export restraints in US autos, 1980–81: quality, employment and welfare effects. In Baldwin and Kreuger (eds) (1984)

BIBLIOGRAPHY

Finger, J. Michael and Olechowski, Andrzej (eds) (1987), *The Uruguay Round: A handbook for the multilateral trade negotiations*, Washington, D.C.: World Bank

Fitchett, Delbert (1987), Agriculture. In Finger and Olechowski (eds) (1987)

Ford, R. and Suyker, W. (1989), *Industrial Subsidies in the OECD Economies*, OECD Working Paper No. 74, Paris: OECD

François, Joseph F., McDonald, Bradley and Nordstrom, Hakan (1995), *The Uruguay Round: A Global Equilibrium Assessment*, Discussion Paper No. 1067, London: Centre for Economic Policy Research

Frey, Bruno (1984), *International Political Economics*, Oxford: Martin Robertson

—— (1985), The political economy of protection. In Greenaway (ed.) (1985)

—— and Schneider, Friedrich (1982), *International Political Economy: An emerging field*, Seminar Paper No. 227, Stockholm: Institute for International Economic Studies, University of Stockholm

General Agreement on Tariffs and Trade (GATT) (1969), *Basic Instruments and Selected Documents*, Vol. IV: *Text of the General Agreement 1969*, Geneva

—— (1979a), *The Tokyo Round of Multilateral Trade Negotiations: Report by the Director-General*, Geneva

—— (1979b), *Agreement on the Implementation of Article VI of the General Agreement on Tariffs and Trade* (The GATT Antidumping Code), Geneva

—— (1985), *Trade Policies for a Better Future: Proposals for Action* (The Leutwiler Report), Geneva

—— (1986), *GATT Focus: The Punta del Este Ministerial Declaration, 1986.* Reprinted in Finger and Olechowski (eds) (1987)

—— (1988), *GATT Activities 1988*, Geneva

—— (1990), *International Trade 88–89*, Geneva

—— (1993a), *International Trade 91–92*: Statistics, Geneva

—— (1993b), *An Analysis of the Proposed Uruguay Round Agreement with Particular Emphasis on Aspects of Interest to Developing Countries*, Geneva

—— (1994a), *Multilateral Trade Negotiations/The Uruguay Round: Trade Negotiations Committee, Final Act embodying the results of the Uruguay Round of multilateral trade negotiations*, Geneva

—— (1994b), *Agreement on the Implementation of Article VI of GATT 1994* (The New Antidumping Code). In GATT (1994a)

Goldin, Ian, Knudsen, Odin and van der Mensbbrugghe, Dominique (1993), *Trade Liberalisation: Global economic implications*, Paris: OECD, and Washington, D.C.: World Bank

Goodhart, David (1994), A bid to push the world to rights. *The Financial Times*, 5 April

Graham, E. (1994), Competition policy and the new trade agenda. In Graham and Richardson (eds) (1994)

—— and Richardson, D. (eds) (1994), *Global Competition Policies*, London: Institute for International Economies, Longmans

Greenaway, David (1982), Identifying the gains from pure intra-industry exchange. *Journal of Economic Studies* Vol. 9, No. 3

—— (1983), *International Trade Policy*, London: Macmillan

—— (1984), Multilateral Trade Policy in the 1980s. *Lloyds Bank Review*, January

—— (1988a), Estimating the welfare effects of voluntary export restraints and tariffs: an application to nonleather footwear in the UK. *Applied Economics*, Vol. 18, pp. 1065–83

—— (1991), Trade related investment measures: political economy aspects and issues for GATT. *World Economy*, Vol. 13, No. 3

—— (1993), Trade and foreign direct investment. *European Economy*, No. 52, ECSC–EEC–EAEC, Brussels/Luxembourg

—— (ed.) (1985), *Current Issues in International Trade, Theory and Policy*, London: Macmillan

—— (ed.) (1988b), *Economic Development and International Trade*, London: Macmillan

Greenaway, David and Hindley, Brian (1986), *What Britain Pays for Voluntary Export Restraints*, London: Trade Policy Research Centre

Greenaway, David and Milner, Chris (1986), *The Economics of Intra-Industry Trade*, Oxford: Basil Blackwell

—— and —— (1993), *Trade and Industrial Policy in Developing Countries*, London: Macmillan

Greenaway, David and Nam, C. (1988), Industrialisation and macroeconomic performance in developing countries under alternative trade strategies. *Kyklos*, Vol. 41, pp. 419–36

Grey, Rodney de C. (1986), Contingent protection, managed trade and the decline of the trade relations system. In Snape (ed.) (1986)

—— (1990), *Concepts of Trade Diplomacy and Trade in Services*, Thames Essays, No. 56, London: Harvester Wheatsheaf/Trade Policy Research Centre

Grimwade, Nigel (1989), *International Trade: New patterns of trade, production and investment*, London: Routledge

—— (1991), Antidumping policy and the consumer. *Consumer Policy Review*, Vol. 1, No. 3

Grossman G.M. (1986), Strategic export promotion: a critique. In Krugman (1986)

Grubel, H.G. (1987), Traded services are embodied in materials or people. *World Economy*, September

Guisinger, Stephen (1987), Investment related to trade. In Finger and Olechowski (eds) (1987)

Haaland, Jan I. and Tollefsen, Truis Cook (1994), *The Uruguay Round and Trade in Manufactures and Services: General equilibrium simulations of production, trade and welfare effects of liberalization*, Discussion Paper No. 1008, London: Centre for Economic Policy Research

Haberger, Arnold C. (1963), The measurement of waste. *American Economic Review, Papers and Proceedings*, May

Hamilton, Carl (1983), *Voluntary Export Restraints, Trade Diversion and Retaliation*, Seminar Paper No. 253, Stockholm: Institute for International Economic Studies, University of Stockholm

—— (1984a), *Voluntary Export Restraints: ASEAN systems for allocation of export licences*, Seminar Paper No. 275, Stockholm: Institute for International Economic Studies, University of Stockholm

—— (1984b), *Voluntary Export Restraints in Asia: Tariff equivalents, rents and trade barrier formation*, Seminar Paper No. 276, Stockholm: Institute for International Economic Studies, University of Stockholm

—— (1984c), *Economic Aspects of 'Voluntary' Export Restraints*, Seminar Paper No. 290, Stockholm: Institute for International Economic Studies, University of Stockholm

—— (1984d), *The Upgrading Effect of Voluntary Export Restraints*, Seminar Paper No. 291, Stockholm: Institute for International Economic Studies, University of Stockholm

—— (1985a), Voluntary export restraints and trade-diversion. *Journal of Common Market Studies*, Vol. xxiii, No. 4, pp. 346–55

—— (1985b), Economic aspects of voluntary export restraints. In Greenaway (ed.) (1985)

BIBLIOGRAPHY

Hamilton, Colleen and Whalley, John (1995), Evaluating the impact of the Uruguay Round results on developing countries. *World Economy*, Vol. 18, No. 1

Helpman, E. and Razin, A. (eds) (1991), *International Trade and Trade Policy*, Cambridge, Mass.: MIT Press

Hertel, Thomas W. (1989), PSEs and the mix of measures to support farm incomes. *World Economy*, Vol. 12, No. 1

Hill, T.P. (1977), On goods and services. *Review of Income and Wealth*, Series 23, No. 4

Hindley, Brian (1987), Different and more favourable treatment – and graduation. In Finger and Olechowski (eds) (1987)

—— (1989a), The design of Fortress Europe. *The Financial Times*, 6 January

—— (1989b), The economics of dumping and antidumping action: is there a baby in the bathwater? Paper presented to a Workshop on Policy Implications of Antidumping Measures, organised by the European Institute for Advanced Studies in Management (EIASM), Brussels, October

—— (1994), *Two Cheers for the Uruguay Round: Trade policy review 1994*, London: Trade Policy Unit of the Centre for Policy Studies

Hine, Robert C. (1992), Regionalism and the integration of the world economy. *Journal of Common Market Studies*, Vol. xxx, No. 2

Hoda, A. (1994), Trade liberalisation: results of the Uruguay Round. Paper presented at the OECD Workshop on the *New World Trading System*, Paris, 25–6 April

Hoekman, Bernard M. (1993), *Developing Countries and the Uruguay Round Negotiations on Services*, Discussion Paper No. 822, London: Centre for Economic Policy Research

—— (1995), *Tentative First Steps: An assessment of the Uruguay Round agreement on services*, Discussion Paper No. 1150, London: Centre for Economic Policy Research

—— and Mavroidis, Petros C. (1994a), *Competition, Competition Policy and the GATT*, CEPR Discussion Paper No. 876, London: Centre for Economic Policy Research; reprinted in *World Economy*, Vol. 17, No. 2

—— and —— (1994b) *Antitrust-based Remedies and Dumping in International Trade*, CEPR Discussion Paper No. 1010, London: Centre for Economic Policy Research

Hudec, Robert E. (1987), *Developing Countries in the Legal System*, Thames Essays, No. 50, London: Trade Policy Research Centre

Ingco, Merlinda (1995a), Agricultural liberalisation in the Uruguay Round. *Finance and Development*, Vol. 32, No. 3

—— (1995b), *Agricultural Liberalisation in the Uruguay Round: One step forwards, one step back?* World Bank Working Paper, Washington, D.C.: World Bank

Ingersent, K.A., Rayner, A.J. and Hine, R.C. (1995), Ex post evaluation of the Uruguay Round agricultural agreement. *World Economy*, Vol. 18, No. 5

International Monetary Fund (IMF) (1988), *The CAP and the EEC*, Occasional Paper No. 62, Washington, D.C.: IMF

Iqubal, Z. (1974), The Generalised System of Preferences and the comparative advantage of less developed countries in manufactures. Washington, D.C.: International Monetary Fund, mimeo

Jackson, J. (1988), The constitutional structure for international cooperation in trade in services and the Uruguay Round of GATT. In Stern (1988)

—— (1992), *The World Trading System*, Cambridge, Mass. and London: MIT Press

Jackson, John H. (1990), *Restructuring the GATT System*, Chatham House Papers, London: Royal Institute of International Affairs/Pinter Publishers

—— (1993), Regional trade blocs and the GATT. *World Economy*, Vol. 16, No. 2

367

—— and Vermulst, Edwin A. (eds) (1990), *Antidumping Law and Practice: A comparative study*, Hemel Hempstead, Herts.: Harvester Wheatsheaf

Jacquemine, Alexis and Sapir, Andre (1988), European integration or world integration? *Weltwirtschaftliches Archiv*, B124, Heft 1

Johnson, H.G. (1953), Optimum tariffs and retaliation. *Review of Economic Studies*, Vol. 22, pp. 153–68

—— (1965), An economic theory of protectionism, tariff bargaining, and the formation of customs unions. *Journal of Political Economy*, Vol. 73, pp. 256–83

Joskow, P. and Klevorick, A. (1979), A framework for analysing predatory pricing policy. *Yale Law Journal*, Vol. 89, pp. 213–70

Josling, T.E. (1973), *Agriculutural Protection: Domestic policy and international trade*, Rome: Food and Agricultural Organisation

—— (1975), *Agricultural Protection and Stabilisation Policies: A framework of measurement in the context of agricultural adjustment*, Rome: Food and Agicultural Organisation

—— (1993), Agricultural issues in transatlantic trade relations. Paper presented at the Conference on Transatlantic Trade after the Uruguay Round, organised by the Centre for Research on Economic Development and International Trade (CREDIT), University of Nottingham, April

Karsenty, Guy and Laird, Sam (1986), *The Generalised System of Preferences: A quantitative assessment of the direct trade effects and of policy options*, UNCTAD Discussion Paper 18, Geneva

Kelly, William B. Jr (ed.) (1963), *Studies in United States Commercial Policy*, Chapel Hill, N.C.: University of North Carolina Press

Kemp, M.C. (1964), *The Pure Theory of International Trade*, Englewood Cliffs, N.J.: Prentice-Hall

—— (1969), *A Contribution to General Equilibrium Theory of Preferential Trading*, Amsterdam: North-Holland

—— and Wan, H. Jnr (1976), An elementary proposition concerning the formation of customs unions. *Journal of International Economics*, Vol. 6, pp. 95–8

Kierzkowski, Henryk (ed.) (1984), *Monopolistic Competition and International Trade*, Oxford: Clarendon Press

King, Philip (1990), *International Economics and International Economic Policy: A reader*, New York: McGraw-Hill

Kostecki, Michel (1987), Export-restraint arrangements and trade liberalization. *World Economy*, Vol. 10, No. 4, pp. 425–54

Kreinin, Morchedai (1979), *Effect of European Integration on Trade Flows in Manufactures*, Seminar Paper No. 125, Stockholm: Institute for International Economic Studies, Stockholm University

Krueger, Anne O. (1990), Import-substitution versus export promotion. In King (1990)

Krugman, Paul (1986), *Strategic Trade Policy and the New International Economics*, Cambridge, Mass., and London: MIT Press

—— (1989), Rethinking international trade. *Business Economist*, Spring

—— (1990), Is free trade passé? In King (1990)

—— (1991), Is bilateralism bad? In Helpman and Razin (eds) (1991)

Laird, Samuel and Finger, J. Michael (1986), Protection in developed and developing countries. Paper presented at the Conference on the Role and Interests of the Developing Countries in the Multilateral Trade Negotiations, Bangkok, Thailand, 30 October–1 November

Laird, Samuel and Sapir, Andre (1987), Tariff preferences. In Finger and Olechowski (eds) (1987)

BIBLIOGRAPHY

Laird, Samuel and Yeats, Alexander (1990), Trends in nontariff barriers of developed countries, 1966–1986. *Weltwirtschaftliches Archiv*, Band 126, Heft 2, pp. 299–325

Langhammer, Rolf J. (1983), *Ten Years of the EEC's Generalised System of Preferences for Developing Countries: Success or failure?* Kiel Working Paper No. 183, September

—— (1992), The developing countries and regionalism. *Journal of Common Market Studies*, Vol. xxx, No. 2

—— and Sapir, Andre (1987), *Economic Impact of Generalised Tariff Preferences*, Thames Essays, No. 49, London: Trade Policy Research Centre

Lavergne, R.P. (1983), *The Political Economy of US Tariffs: An empirical analysis*, Toronto: Academic Press

Leibenstein, H. (1966), Allocative efficiency versus 'X-efficiency'. *American Economic Review*, Vol. 56, pp. 392–415

Lipsey, R.G. (1957), The theory of customs unions: trade-diversion and welfare. *Economica*, Vol. 24, pp. 40–6

Loo, T. and Tower, E. (1988), *Agricultural Protectionism and Less Developed Countries*, Canberra: Centre for International Economics

MacBean, A.I. and Nguyen, T. (1988), Export instability and growth performance. In Greenaway (ed.) (1988b)

Marques-Mendes, A.J. (1986), The contribution of the European Community to economic growth. *Journal of Common Market Studies*, Vol. xxiv, No. 4

Marshall, Alfred (1920), *Principles of Economics*, London: Macmillan

Maskus, Keith (1991), Normative concerns in the international protection of intellectual property rights. *World Economy*, Vol. 13, No. 3

—— (1993), Trade-related intellectual property rights. *European Economy*, No. 52, ECSC–EEC–EAEC, Brussels/Luxembourg

Mayes, David G. (1978), The effects of economic integration on trade. *Journal of Common Market Studies*, Vol. xvii, No. 1

McCulloch, Rachel (1993), Services and the Uruguay Round. *World Economy*, Vol. 13, No. 3

McDonald, Bradley (1991), Agricultural negotiations in the Uruguay Round. *World Economy*, Vol. 13, No. 3

McGhee, John (1958), Predatory price cutting: the Standard Oil (NJ) Case. *Journal of Law and Economics*, Vol. 1, pp. 137–69

—— (1980), Predatory pricing revisited. *Journal of Law and Economics*, Vol. 289

McMillan, John (1993), Does regional integration foster open trade? Economic theory and GATT's Article XXIV. In Anderson and Blackhurst (eds) (1993)

Meade, J.E. (1956), *The Theory of Customs Unions*, Amsterdam: North-Holland

Messerlin, Patrick (1987), Nonborder measures to assist industry. In Finger and Olechowski (eds) (1987)

—— (1989), The EC's antidumping regulations: a first economic appraisal, 1980–85. *Weltwirtschaftliches Archiv*, Vol. 125, pp. 563–87

—— (1991a), Antidumping regulations or pro-cartel law? The EC chemical cases. *World Economy*, Vol. 13, No. 4

—— (1991b), The Uruguay Round negotiations on antidumping enforcement. In Tharakan (ed.) (1991)

—— (1993), Services. *European Economy*, No. 52, ECSC–EEC–EAEC, Brussels/Luxembourg

—— and Reed, Geoffrey (1995), Antidumping policies in the United States and the European Community. *Economic Journal*, Vol. 105, pp. 1565–75

Meyer, F.V. (1978), *International Trade Policy*, London: Croom Helm

Miner, William M. and Hathaway, Dale E.(eds) (1988), *World Agricultural Trade:*

Building a Consensus, Institute for Research on Public Policy/Institute for International Economics, Nova Scotia

Morkre, M.E. and Kelly, K.H. (1994), *Effects of Unfair Imports on Domestic Industries: US antidumping and countervailing duty cases, 1980–1988*, Washington, D.C.: Bureau of Economics, Federal Commission

Mundell, R.A. (1964), Tariff preferences and the terms of trade. *Manchester School of Economic and Social Studies*, Vol. 32, pp. 1–13

National Consumer Council (NCC) (1990a), *Consumer Electronics and the EC's Antidumping Policy*, by Nigel Grimwade, Working Paper 1, London: International Trade and the Consumer

—— (1990b), *Textiles and Clothing*, by Judith Eversley, Working Paper 2, London: International Trade and the Consumer

—— (1990c), *Cars: The cost of trade restrictions to consumers*, by Garel Rhys and John Bridge, Working Paper 4, London: International Trade and the Consumer

—— (1991), *Intellectual Property: The consumer view of patents, copyright, trade marks and allied rights*, by Diana Whitworth, Working Paper 6, London: International Trade and the Consumer

—— (1993), *International Trade: The consumer agenda*, London: NCC

Nguyen, T., Perroni, C. and Wigle, R. (1991), The value of a Uruguay Round success. *World Economy*, Vol. 14, pp. 359–74

——, —— and —— (1993), An evaluation of the Draft Final Act of the Uruguay Round. *Economic Journal*, November

——, —— and —— (1995), A Uruguay Round success? *World Economy*, Vol. 18, No. 1

Nicolaides, P. (1989a), *The Hydra of Safeguards: An intractable problem for the Uruguay Round*, Royal Institute of International Affairs Discussion Paper 21, London: Chatham House

—— (1989b), *Liberalizing Service Trade: Strategies for success*, Chatham House Papers, London: Royal Institute of International Affairs/Routledge

Ohyama, M. (1972), Trade and welfare in general equilibrium. *Keio Economic Studies*, Vol. 9, pp. 37–73

Olechowski, Andrzej (1987), Nontariff barriers to trade. In Finger and Olechowski (eds) (1987)

Organisation for Economic Cooperation and Development (OECD) (1978), *National Treatment and Foreign-controlled Enterprises Established in OECD Countries*, Paris: OECD

—— (1984), *International Investment and Multinational Enterprises: The 1984 review of the 1976 Declarations and Decisions*, Paris: OECD

—— (1987a), *National Policies and Agricultural Trade*, Paris: OECD

—— (1987b), *The Costs of Restricting Imports: The automobile industry*, Paris: OECD

—— (1990), *Reforming Agricultural Policies. Quantitative restrictions on production: Direct income support*, Paris: OECD

—— (1991), *Agricultural Policies, Markets and Trade: Monitoring outlook 1991*, Paris: OECD

Overseas Development Institute (ODI) (1995), *Developing Countries and the WTO*, Briefing Paper 3, London: ODI

Owen, N. (1983), *Economies of Scale, Competitiveness and Trade Patterns within the European Community*, Oxford: Oxford University Press

Oxley, Alan (1990), *The Challenge of Free Trade*, Hemel Hempstead, Herts.: Harvester Wheatsheaf

Page, Sheila (1981), The revival of protectionism and the consequences for Europe. *Journal of Common Market Studies*, pp. 17–40

—— and Davenport, Michael (1994), *World Trade Reform: Do developing countries gain or lose?* ODI Special Report, London: ODI

Palmeter, N. David (1991), The rhetoric and reality of the United States antidumping law. *World Economy*, Vol. 14, No. 1

Porter, Michael E. (1990), *The Competitive Advantage of Nations*, London: Macmillan

Prebisch, R (1950), *The Economic Development of Latin America and its Principal Problems*, New York: United Nations

Robertson, David (1992), *GATT Rules on Emergency Protection*, Thames Essays, No. 57, London: Trade Policy Research Centre and Hemel Hempstead, Herts.: Harvester Wheatsheaf

Robson, Peter (1987), *The Economics of International Integration*, 3rd edn, London: Allen & Unwin

Rodrick, Dani (1994), *Developing Countries after the Uruguay Round*, Discussion Paper No. 1084, London: Centre for Economic Policy and Research

Romer, P. (1986), Increasing returns and long-run growth. *Journal of Political Economy*, Vol. 94, pp. 1002–37

Ryan, Cillian (1993), Trade liberalisation and financial services. *World Economy*, Vol. 13, No. 3

Salvatore, Dominic (1989), A model of dumping and protectionism in the United States. *Weltwirtschaftliches Arhiv*, pp. 763–81

Sampson, G. and Snape, R. (1985), Identifying the issues in trade in services. *World Economy*, Vol. 8, pp. 171–81

Sapir, Andre (1985), North–South issues in trade in services. *World Economy*, Vol. 8

—— and Lundberg, Lars (1984), The US Generalised System of Preference and its impact. In Baldwin and Kreuger (eds) (1984)

Sapsford, D. (1985), The statistical debate on the net barter terms of trade: a comment and some additional information. *Economic Journal*, Vol. 95, pp. 781–8

Scherer, F. (1994), *Competition Policies for an Integrated World Economy*, Washington, D.C.: Brookings Institution

Schott, Jeffrey J. (1991), Trading blocs and the world trading system. *World Economy*, Vol. 14, No. 1

—— (1994), *The Uruguay Round: An assessment*, Washington, D.C.: Institute for International Economics

—— (ed.) (1989), *Free Trade Areas and U.S. Trade Policy*, Washington, D.C.: Institute for International Economics

Silberston, Z.A. (1989), *The Future of the Multi-fibre Arrangement: Implications for the UK economy*, London: HMSO

Singer, H.V. (1950), The distribution of gains between borrowing and investing countries. *American Economic Review*, Vol. 40, pp. 473–85

Smith, Murray (1993), The North American Free Trade Agreement: global impacts. In Anderson and Blackhurst (eds) (1993)

Snape, Richard (1993), History and economics of GATT's Article XXIV. In Anderson and Blackhurst (eds) (1993)

—— (ed.) (1986), *Issues in World Trade Policy: GATT at the crossroads*, London: Macmillan

Spraos, J. (1980), The statistical debate on the net barter terms of trade. *Economic Journal*, Vol. 90, pp. 107–28

Stegemann, Klaus (1989), EC antidumping policy: are price undertakings a legal substitute for illegal price fixing? Paper presented at the Workshop on Policy Implications of Antidumping Measures, organised by the European Institute for Advanced Studies in Management, Brussels, October

Stern, R. (1987), Intellectual property. In Finger and Olechowski (eds) (1987)

BIBLIOGRAPHY

—— (1988), *The Multilateral Trading System*, Hemel Hempstead, Herts.: Harvester Wheatsheaf

—— and Hoekman, B. (1987), Negotiations on services. *World Economy*, Vol. 10, No. 1

Subramanian, Arvind (1990), TRIPs and the paradigm of the GATT: a tropical, temperate view. *World Economy*, Vol. 13, No. 4

Swinbank, Alan (1994), EU agricultural trade relations with its neighbours. Paper presented to Conference on the EU's Relations with its Neighbours, organised by the Centre for Research in Economic Development and International Trade (CREDIT), University of Nottingham, April

Tangermann, Stefan, Josling, T.E. and Pearson, Scott (1987), Multilateral negotiations on farm support levels. *World Economy*, Vol. 10, No. 3, pp. 265–81

Tharakan, P.K.M. (1993), Contingent protection: the US and the EC antidumping actions. Paper presented to the Conference on Transatlantic Trade after the Uruguay Round, organised by the Centre for Economic Research in Economic Development and International Trade (CREDIT), Nottingham, April

—— (1995), Political economy and contingent protection. *Economic Journal*, Vol. 105, pp. 1550–64

—— (ed.) (1991), *Policy Implications of Antidumping Measures*, Amsterdam: North-Holland

Trela, Irene and Whalley, John (1989), *Unravelling the Threads of the MFA*, Seminar Paper No. 448, Stockholm: Institute for International Economic Studies, Stockholm University

Tyson, Laura d'Andrea (1992), *Who's Bashing Whom? Trade conflict in high technology industries*, Washington, D.C.: Institute for International Economics

United Nations Centre on Transnational Corporations (UNCTC) (1990), *New Issues in the Uruguay Round of Multilateral Trade Negotiations*, UNCTC Current Studies, Series A, No. 19, New York: United Nations

Vanek, J. (1965), *General Equilibrium of International Discrimination*, Cambridge, Mass.: Harvard University Press

Viner, Jacob (1923), *Dumping: A problem in international trade*, Chicago, Ill.: Chicago University Press

—— (1950), *The Customs Union Issue*, Carnegie Endowment for International Peace

Walter, Ingo (1972), Nontariff protection among industrial countries: some preliminary evidence. *Economia Internazionale*, Vol. 25, pp. 335–54

Whalley, John (1992), CUSTA and NAFTA: can WHFTA be far behind? *Journal of Common Market Studies*, Vol. xxx, No. 2

Winters, L. Alan (1994), *The EC and World Protectionism: Dimensions of the political economy*, Discussion Paper No. 897, London: Centre for Economic Policy Research

Wolf, Martin (1986), The MFA: an obstacle to development. Paper presented at the Kiel Conference on Free Trade in the World Economy, June

—— (1989a), Why voluntary export restraints? An historical analysis. *World Economy*, Vol. 12, September

—— (1989b), *How to Cut the Textile Knot: Alternative paths to liberalisation of the MFA*. Seminar Paper No. 453, Stockholm: Institute for International Economic Studies, Stockholm University

Wonnacott, P. and Lutz, Mark (1989), Is there a case for free trade areas? In Schott (ed.) (1989)

Wonnacott, R.J. and Wonnacott, P. (1981), Is unilateral tariff reduction preferable to a customs union? The curious case of the missing foreign tariffs – or beware of the large country assumption. *American Economic Review*, Vol. 71, pp. 704–14

World Bank (1986), *The World Development Report 1986*, Washington, D.C.: World Bank

—— (1987), *The World Development Report 1987*, Washington, D.C.: World Bank, and Oxford: Oxford University Press

—— (1990), *Report on Adjustment Lending II*, Washington, D.C.: World Bank

—— (1992), *The World Development Report 1992*, Washington, D.C.: World Bank

World Trade Organisation (WTO) (1995), Special Report: the WTO and the Developing Countries. *Focus*, No. 1, January–February

Yamey, B. (1972), Predatory price cutting: notes and comments. *Journal of Law and Economics*, Vol. 129

Yeats, Alexander J. (1979), *Trade Barriers Facing Developing Countries*, London: Macmillan

—— (1987), The escalation of trade barriers. In Finger and Olechowski (eds) (1987)

Yoffie, David B. (1991), *Global Semiconductor Industry 1987*, Harvard Business School Cases 9–388–052, Cambridge, Mass.: Harvard Business School

INDEX